# Lecture Notes in Computer Science 4347

*Commenced Publication in 1973*
Founding and Former Series Editors:
Gerhard Goos, Juris Hartmanis, and Jan van Leeuwen

T0223355

Javier Lopez (Ed.)

# Critical Information Infrastructures Security

First International Workshop, CRITIS 2006
Samos, Greece, August 31 - September 1, 2006
Revised Papers

 Springer

Volume Editor

Javier Lopez
University of Malaga
Computer Science Department
E.T.S.I. Informatica
Campus Teatinos, 29071 Malaga, Spain
E-mail: jlm@lcc.uma.es

Library of Congress Control Number: 2006938669

CR Subject Classification (1998): C.2, D.4.6, E.3, K.6.5, K.4.1, K.4.4, J.1

LNCS Sublibrary: SL 5 – Computer Communication Networks and
Telecommunications

ISSN        0302-9743
ISBN-10     3-540-69083-2 Springer Berlin Heidelberg New York
ISBN-13     978-3-540-69083-2 Springer Berlin Heidelberg New York

Springer is a part of Springer Science+Business Media

springer.com

© Springer-Verlag Berlin Heidelberg 2006
Printed in Germany

Typesetting: Camera-ready by author, data conversion by Scientific Publishing Services, Chennai, India
Printed on acid-free paper      SPIN: 11962977      06/3142      5 4 3 2 1 0

# Preface

Key sectors of modern economies depend highly on ICT. The information flowing through the resulting technological super-infrastructure as well as the information being processed by the complex computing systems that underpin it becomes crucial because its disruption, disturbance or loss can lead to high financial, material and, sometimes, human loss. As a consequence, the security and dependability of this infrastructure become critical and its protection a major objective for governments, companies and the research community.

CRITIS has been born as an event that aims to bring together researchers and professionals from universities, private companies and public administrations interested or involved in all security-related heterogeneous aspects of critical information infrastructures.

This volume contains the proceedings of the 1st International Workshop on Critical Information Infrastructure Security (CRITIS 2006), that was held between August 31 and September 1, 2006 on Samos, Greece, and was hosted by the University of the Aegean, Department of Information and Communication Systems Engineering, Laboratory of Information and Communication Systems Security (Info-Sec-Lab).

In response to the CRITIS 2006 call for papers, 57 papers were submitted. Each paper was reviewed by three members of the Program Committee, on the basis of significance, novelty, technical quality and relevance to critical infrastructures. At the end of the reviewing process, only 22 papers were selected for presentation, resulting in an acceptance rate of 38%. Revisions were not checked and the authors bear full responsibility for the content of their papers.

Additionally, CRITIS 2006 was fortunate to have Andrea Servida, Deputy Head of Unit of the European Commission (Information and Society and Media Directorate General) as invited speaker, giving the talk "Security and Resilience in Information Society: The European Approach." I thank him very much for his contribution.

Other persons deserve many thanks for their support and contribution to the success of the conference. Sokratis Katsikas and Reinhard Posch were General Co-chairs, and Stefanos Gritzalis, a driving force of the event, was Organization Chair. I sincerely thank them for their total support and encouragement, and for their contribution to all organizational issues. My special thanks to Rodrigo Roman for preparation and maintenance of the Workshop Web site, and to Costas Lambrinoudakis, George Kambourakis, Dimitris Geneiatakis, Giorgos Karopoulos and Irene Gonidelli for their help in the organizational tasks. Without the hard work of these colleagues and the rest of the local organization team, this conference would not have been possible. Finally, I would like to thank all the authors who submitted papers and the participants from all over the world who chose to honor us with their attendance.

August 2006

Javier Lopez

Program Chair

# CRITIS 2006
# 1st International Workshop on
# Critical Information Infrastructures Security

Samos, Greece
August 31 – September 1, 2006

*Organized by*
Department of Information and Communication Systems Engineering,
Laboratory of Information and Communication Systems Security (Info-Sec-Lab)
University of the Aegean
Greece

## General Co-chairs

Sokratis Katsikas     University of the Aegean, Greece
Reinhard Posch     Technical University of Graz, Austria

## Organization Chair

Stefanos Gritzalis     University of Aegean, Greece

## Program Chair

Javier Lopez     University of Malaga, Spain

## Program Committee

Marc Dacier     Institut Eurécom, France
George Davida     University of Wisconsin-Milwaukee, USA
Ed Dawson     QUT, Australia
Yvo Desmedt     University College London, UK
Myriam Dunn     ETH Zurich, Switzerland
Claudia Eckert     Fraunhofer-SIT, Germany
Steven Furnell     University of Plymouth, UK
Urs Gattiker     CyTRAP-RiskIT, Switzerland
Adrian Gheorghe     ETH Zurich, Switzerland
Eric Goetz     Dartmouth College, US
Juan M. Gonzalez-Nieto     QUT, Australia
John Griffin     IBM T.J. Watson Research Center, USA
Stefanos Gritzalis     University of the Aegean, Greece
Dieter Gollmann     TU Hamburg, Germany
Bernhard M. Hämmerli     HTA Lucerne, Switzerland

| | |
|---|---|
| Tom Karygiannis | NIST, USA |
| Håkan Kvarnström | TeliaSonera, Sweden |
| Diego Lopez | RedIRIS, Spain |
| Eric Luiijf | TNO, Netherlands |
| Masahiro Mambo | University of Tsukuba, Japan |
| Fabio Martinelli | CNR, Italy |
| Catherine Meadows | Naval Research Lab., USA |
| Simin Nadjm-Tehrani | Linköping University, Sweden |
| Peter Neumann | SRI, USA |
| Eiji Okamoto | University of Tsukuba, Japan |
| Andrew Powell | NISCC, UK |
| Kai Rannenberg | Goethe University Frankfurt, Germany |
| Michel Riguidel | ENST, France |
| Rodrigo Roman | University of Malaga, Spain |
| Roberto Setola | Univ. Campus Bio-Medico di Roma, Italy |
| Stefaan Seys | Katholieke Universiteit Leuven, Belgium |
| Sujeet Shenoi | University of Tulsa, USA |
| Stephen D. Wolthusen | Royal Holloway, UK |
| Moti Yung | Columbia University, USA |
| Yuliang Zheng | University of North Carolina, USA |
| Jianying Zhou | Institute for Infocomm Research, Singapore |

## External Reviewers

Efthimia Aivaloglou, Elisavet Constantinou, Alessandro Falleni, Lothar Fritsch, Matt Henricksen, Michaela Iorga, Spyros Kokolakis, George Mohay, Maria Papadaki, Heiko Rossnagel, Dries Schellekens, Falk Wagner.

# Table of Contents

# CRUTIAL: The Blueprint of a Reference Critical Information Infrastructure Architecture*

Paulo Veríssimo, Nuno Ferreira Neves, and Miguel Correia

University of Lisboa, Faculty of Sciences
Bloco C6, Campo Grande, 1749-016 Lisboa - Portugal
{pjv,nuno,mpc}@di.fc.ul.pt
http://www.navigators.di.fc.ul.pt

**Abstract.** In the past few decades, critical infrastructures have become largely computerised and interconnected all over the world. This generated the problem of achieving resilience of critical information infrastructures against computer-borne attacks and severe faults. Governments and industry have been pushing an immense research effort in information and systems security, but we believe the complexity of the problem prevents it from being solved using classical security methods.

The paper focuses on the computer systems behind electrical utility infrastructures. It proposes the blueprint of a distributed systems architecture that we believe may come to be useful as a reference for modern critical information infrastructures in general. The architecture is instantiated with a set of classes of techniques and algorithms, based on paradigms providing resilience to faults and attacks in an automatic way.

## 1 Introduction

The largely computerised nature of critical infrastructures on the one hand, and the pervasive interconnection of systems all over the world, on the other hand, have generated one of the most fascinating current problems of computer science and control engineering: *how to achieve resilience of critical information infrastructures.*

This problem is concerned with ensuring acceptable levels of service and, in last resort, the integrity of systems themselves, when faced with threats of several kinds. In this paper we are concerned with threats against computers and control computers, not the physical infrastructures themselves. These threats range from accidental events like natural faults or wrong manoeuvres [15, 23], to attacks by hackers or terrorists [5, 12, 14, 17, 28]. The problem affects systems with great socio-economic value, such as utility systems like electrical, gas or water, or telecommunication systems and computer networks like the Internet. In consequence, the high degree of interconnection is causing great concern, given

---

* This work was mainly supported by the EC, through project IST-4-027513-STP (CRUTIAL), and also by the FCT, through LASIGE and projects POSI/EIA/61643/2004 (AJECT) and POSI/EIA/60334/2004 (RITAS).

the level of exposure of very high value systems and components to attacks that can be perpetrated in an anonymous and remote way.

Although there is an increase in the concern for using security best practices in these systems [2, 4], we believe that the problem is not completely understood, and can not be solved with classical methods. Its complexity is mainly due to *the hybrid composition of those infrastructures*:

- The operational network, called generically SCADA (Supervisory Control and Data Acquisition)[1], composed of the computer systems that yield the operational ability to supervise, acquire data from, and control the physical processes. In fact, to the global computer system, SCADA computer systems (e.g., controllers) "are" the controlled processes (e.g., power generators), since by acting on the former, for example, through a network message, one changes the state of the latter.
- The corporate intranet, where usual departmental services (e.g., web, email, databases) and clients reside, and also the engineering and technical staff, who access the SCADA part through ad-hoc interconnections[2].
- The Internet, through which intranet users get to other intranets and/or the outside world, but to which, and often unwittingly, the SCADA network is sometimes connected to.

Besides the complexity due to this hybrid composition, this mixture has given an unexpected *inter-disciplinary nature* to the problem: SCADA systems are real-time systems, with some reliability and fault tolerance concerns, but they were classically not designed to be widely distributed or remotely accessed, let alone open to other more asynchronous and less trusted subsystems. Likewise, they were not designed with security in mind. In consequence, in scientific terms, our problem can be formulated as follows:

- The computer-related operation of a critical utility infrastructure is a distributed systems problem including interconnected SCADA/embedded networks, corporate intranets, and Internet/PSTN[3] access subsystems.
- This distributed systems problem is hard, since it simultaneously includes facets of real-time, fault tolerance, and security.

In this paper, we focus on the computer systems behind electrical utility infrastructures as an example, and we propose: (1) *the blueprint of a distributed systems architecture* that we believe may come to be useful as a reference for modern critical information infrastructures; (2) *a set of classes of techniques and algorithms* based on paradigms providing resilience to faults and attacks

---

[1] Or PCS (Process Control System).

[2] In some companies there is a (healthy) reluctance against interconnecting SCADA networks and the corporate network or the Internet. However, in practice this interconnection is a reality in many companies all over the world. We believe this is indeed the situation in most companies and this is the case we are interested in this paper.

[3] Public Switched Telephone Network.

in an automatic way. This work is ongoing and is done in the context of the recently started CRUTIAL European project, CRitical UTility InfrastructurAL resilience [6], details of which are given in the end.

As a final note, whilst it is usual to use the designation "critical information infrastructures" to denote the computer related part of the physical critical infrastructures, we do not make a differentiation of the two in this paper.

## 2    Rationale for the Model and Architecture

Before we proceed, let us bring some further insight on the problem of critical infrastructures:

- Critical Information Infrastructures (CII) feature a lot of legacy subsystems and non-computer-standard components (controllers, sensors, actuators, etc.).
- Conventional security and protection techniques, when directly applied to CII controlling devices, sometimes stand in the way of their effective operation.

These two facts will not change, at least for a long time, so they should be considered as additional research challenges. Despite security and dependability concerns with those individual components being a necessity, we believe that the crucial problem is with the forest, not the trees. That is, the problem of critical information infrastructure insecurity is mostly created by the informatics nature of many current infrastructures, and by the generic and non-structured network interconnection of CIIs, which bring several facets of exposure, from internal unprotected wireline or wireless links, to interconnections of SCADA and corporate intranets to the Internet and PSTN. This situation is conspicuous in several of the attacks reported against CIIs. For instance, the attack of the Slammer worm against the Davis-Besse nuclear power plant (US) was due both to this combination of a computerised CII with non-structured network interconnections and lack of protection [8]. Although the network was protected by a firewall, the worm entered through a contractor's computer connected to the CII using a telephone line.

The problems that may result from this exposure to computer-borne threats range from wrong manoeuvering to malicious actions coming from terminals located outside, somewhere in the Internet. The potential targets of these actions are computer control units, embedded components and systems, that is, devices connected to operational hardware (e.g., water pumps and filters, electrical power generators and power protections, dam gates, etc.) or to telecom hardware (core routers, base stations, etc.). The failure perspectives go from unavailability of services supposed to operate 24×7, to physical damage to infrastructures. In the electrical power provision these situations have already been witnessed [6]: among the blackouts that occurred in several countries during the summer of 2003, the analysis report [7] of the North American one highlighted the failure of various information systems as having thwarted the utility workers' ability to contain the blackout before it cascaded out of control, leading to an escalating failure.

Whilst it seems non-controversial that such a status quo brings a certain level of threat, we know of no work that has tried to equate the problem by defining a reference model of a *critical information infrastructure distributed systems architecture*, providing the necessary global resilience against abnormal situations.

We believe that evaluation work based on such a model will let us learn about activity patterns of interdependencies, which will reveal the potential for far more damaging fault/failure scenarios than those that have been anticipated up to now. Moreover, such a model will be highly constructive, for it will form a structured framework for: conceiving the right balance between prevention and removal of vulnerabilities and attacks, and tolerance of remaining potential intrusions and designed-in faults.

What can be done at architectural level to achieve resilient operation? Note that the crux of the problem lies with the fact that access to operational networks, such as remote SCADA manoeuvering, ended up entangled with access to corporate intranets and to public Internet, without there being computational and resilience models that *represent* this situation, unlike what exists in simpler, more homogeneous settings, e.g. classical web-based server infrastructures on Internet. Our point is that interference and threats start at the level of the macroscopic information flows between these subsystems, and can in consequence be stopped there. This should not prevent the study of techniques at the controller level, but in this paper we will not focus on this latter issue.

Now, given the simultaneous need for real-time, security and fault tolerance, this problem is hard vis-a-vis existing paradigms. For example, many classical distributed systems paradigms handle each of those facets separately, and just solve part of the problem. A unifying approach has gained impressive momentum currently: *intrusion tolerance* [27]. In short, instead of trying to prevent every single intrusion or fault, they are allowed, but tolerated: systems remain to some extent faulty and/or vulnerable, attacks on components can happen and some will be successful, but the system has the means to trigger automatic mechanisms that prevent faults or intrusions from generating a system failure.

Our approach is thus equated along the following propositions:

**Proposition 1.** Classical security and/or safety techniques alone will not solve the problem: they are largely based on prevention, intrusion detection and ad-hoc recovery or ultimately disconnection.

There is a recent and positive trend to make SCADA systems and CIIs at large more secure [2, 4, 12, 20, 21]. However, classic engineering remedies place real-time and embedded (RTE) systems at most at the current level of commercial systems' security and dependability, which is known to be insufficient [5, 9, 22]: systems constantly suffer attacks, intrusions, some of them massive (worms); most defences are dedicated to generic non-targeted attacks; attacks degrade business but only do virtual damage, unlike RTE systems where there is a risk of great social impact and even physical damage. On the other hand, some current IT security techniques can negatively affect RTE system operation, w.r.t.

availability and timeliness. For example, if security is based on disconnection, significant performance degradation, or even defensive restrictions can prevent the actuation or monitoring of the infrastructure.

**Proposition 2.** Any solution, to be effective, has to involve automatic control of macroscopic command and information flows, occurring essentially between the physical or virtual LANs[4] composing the critical information infrastructure architecture, with the purpose of securing appropriate system-level properties.

We believe that a key to the solution lies with controlling the command and information flow at macroscopic level (organisation-level). We are talking about an architectural model, a set of architectural devices, and key algorithms, capable of achieving the above-mentioned control of the command and information flow. The devices and algorithms should be capable of securing a set of system-level properties characterising whatever is meant by correct and resilient behaviour.

**Proposition 3.** We lack a reference architecture of "modern critical information infrastructure" considering different interconnection realms and different kinds of risk, throughout the physical and the information subsystems of a CII.

We must consider the physical or virtual LANs composing the operational SCADA/embedded networks, the corporate intranets, and the Internet/PSTN access networks, as different first order citizens of the architecture. Likewise, the notion that risk factors may vary and be difficult to perceive accurately, brings the need to reconcile uncertainty with predictability in architecture and algorithmics.

## 3   CRUTIAL Architecture

The CRUTIAL architecture encompasses:

- Architectural configurations featuring trusted components in key places, which a priori induce prevention of some faults, and of certain attack and vulnerability combinations.
- Middleware devices that achieve runtime automatic tolerance of remaining faults and intrusions, supplying trusted services out of non-trustworthy components.
- Trustworthiness monitoring mechanisms detecting situations not predicted and/or beyond assumptions made, and adaptation mechanisms to survive those situations.
- Organisation-level security policies and access control models capable of securing information flows with different criticality within/in/out of a CII.

---

[4] Local Area Networks.

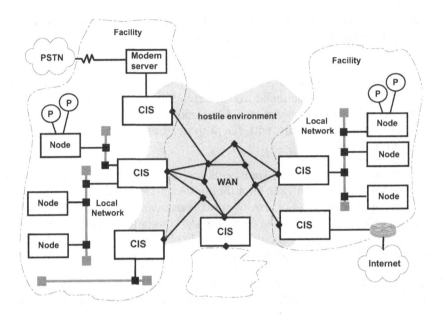

**Fig. 1.** CRUTIAL overall architecture (WAN of LANs connected by CIS, $P$ processes live in the several nodes)

We build on results from the MAFTIA project[5] in this field [26], but extend them significantly to attend the specific challenges of the critical information infrastructure problem, for example, timeliness, global access control, and above all non-stop operation and resilience.

Given the severity of threats expected, some key components are built using architectural hybridisation methods in order to achieve *trusted-trustworthy* operation [26]: an architectural paradigm whereby components prevent the occurrence of some failure modes *by construction*, so that their resistance to faults and hackers can justifiably be trusted. In other words, some special-purpose components are constructed in such a way that we can argue that they are always secure, so that they can provide a small set of services useful to support intrusion tolerance in the rest of the system.

Intrusion tolerance mechanisms are selectively used in the CRUTIAL architecture, to build layers of progressively more trusted components and middleware subsystems, from baseline untrusted components (nodes, networks) [26]. This leads to an automation of the process of building trust: for example, at lower layers, basic intrusion tolerance mechanisms are used to construct a trustworthy communication subsystem, which can then be trusted by upper layers to securely communicate amongst participants without bothering about network intrusion threats.

One of the innovative aspects of this work, further to intrusion tolerance, is the resilience aspect, approached through two paradigms: *proactive-resilience* to

---

[5] Malicious-and Accidental-Fault Tolerance for Internet Applications. The web site of the project is at www.maftia.org

achieve exhaustion-safety [18], to ensure perpetual, non-stop operation despite the continuous production of faults and intrusions; and *trustworthiness monitoring* to perform surveillance of the coverage stability of the system, that is, of whether it is still performing inside the assumed fault envelope or beyond assumptions made [3]. In the latter case, dependable adaptation mechanisms are triggered.

Finally, the desired control of the information flows is partly performed through protection mechanisms using an adaptation of *organisation-based access control* models [10] for implementing global-level security policies.

The mechanisms and algorithms in place achieve system-level properties of the following classes: trustworthiness or resistance to faults and intrusions (i.e., security and dependability); timeliness, in the sense of meeting timing constraints raised by real world control and supervision; coverage stability, to ensure that variation or degradation of assumptions remains within a bounded envelope; dependable adaptability, to achieve predictability in uncertain conditions; resilience, read as correctness and continuity of service even beyond assumptions made.

### 3.1   Main Architectural Options

We view the system as a WAN-of-LANs, as introduced in [24]. There is a global interconnection network, the WAN, that switches packets through generic devices that we call *facility gateways*, which are the representative gateways of each LAN (the overall picture is shown in Figure 1). The WAN is a logical entity operated by the CII operator companies, which may or may not use parts of public network as physical support. A LAN is a logical unit that may or may not have physical reality (e.g., LAN segments vs. VLANs[6]). More than one LAN can be connected by the same facility gateway. All traffic originates from and goes to a LAN. As example LANs, the reader can envision: the administrative clients and the servers LANs; the operational (SCADA) clients and servers LANs; the engineering clients and servers LANs; the PSTN modem access LANs; the Internet and extranet access LANs, etc.

The facility gateways of a CRUTIAL critical information infrastructure are more than mere TCP/IP routers. Collectively they act as a set of servers providing distributed services relevant to solving our problem: *achieving control of the command and information flow, and securing a set of necessary system-level properties.* CRUTIAL facility gateways are called *CRUTIAL Information Switches (CIS)*, which in a simplistic way could be seen as sophisticated circuit or application level firewalls combined with equally sophisticated intrusion detectors, connected by distributed protocols.

This set of servers must be intrusion-tolerant (i.e., must tolerate intrusions), prevent resource exhaustion providing perpetual operation, and be resilient against assumption coverage uncertainty, providing survivability. The services implemented on the servers must also secure the desired properties of flow control, in the presence of malicious traffic and commands, and in consequence be themselves intrusion-tolerant.

---

[6] Virtual LANs.

An assumed number of components of a CIS can be corrupted. Therefore, a CIS is a logical entity that has to be implemented as a set of replicated physical units (CIS replicas) according to fault and intrusion tolerance needs. Likewise, CIS are interconnected with intrusion-tolerant protocols, in order to cooperate to implement the desired services.

## 3.2   CRUTIAL Nodes

The structure of some of the CII nodes, which we call *CRUTIAL nodes*, can follow the node structuring principles for intrusion-tolerant systems explained in [26]:

- The notion of *trusted* – versus untrusted – *hardware*. For example, most of the hardware of a CIS is considered to be untrusted, with small parts of it being considered trusted-trustworthy.
- The notion of *trusted support software*, trusted to execute a few critical functions correctly, the rest being subjected to malicious faults.
- The notion of *run-time environment*, offering trusted and untrusted software and operating system services in a homogeneous way.
- The notion of *trusted distributed components*, for example software functions implemented by collections of interacting CIS middleware.

In the context of this paper, we consider only one instantiation of CRUTIAL nodes, the CRUTIAL Information Switch (CIS) nodes. However, other specific nodes, for example, controllers needing to meet high trustworthiness standards, may be also built to a similar structure. A snapshot of the CRUTIAL node is depicted in three dimensions in Figure 2, where we can perceive the above-mentioned node structuring principles.

Firstly, there is the *hardware* dimension, which includes the node and networking devices that make up the physical distributed system. We assume that

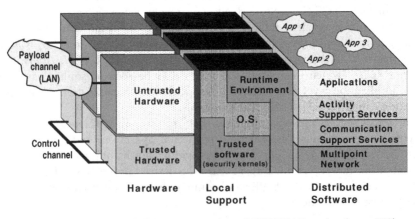

**Fig. 2.** Architecture and interconnection of CRUTIAL nodes (e.g., CIS)

most of a node's operations run on untrusted hardware, e.g., the usual machinery of a computer, connected through the normal networking infrastructure, which we call the *payload channel*. However, some nodes– CIS, for example– may have pieces of hardware that are trusted, for example, that by construction intruders do not have direct access to the inside of those components. The type of trusted hardware featured in CIS is an *appliance board with processor*, which may or not have an *adapter to a control channel* (an alternative trusted network), as depicted in Figure 2. This appliance is plugged to the CIS's main hardware.

Secondly, services based on the trusted hardware are accessed through the *local support* services. The rationale behind our trusted components is the following: whilst we let a local node be compromised, we make sure that the trusted component operation is not undermined (crash failure assumption).

Thirdly, there is the *distributed software* provided by CRUTIAL: middleware layers on top of which distributed applications run, even in the presence of malicious faults (far right in Figure 2). In the context of this paper, we will discuss the layers of *middleware* running inside a CIS.


## 4   CRUTIAL Middleware

We now observe the part of the system made of the WAN and all the CIS (facility gateways) that interconnect all the internal LANs of the critical information infrastructure to the WAN (recall Figure 1).

We model this setting as a distributed system with $N$ nodes (CIS). We use the weakest fault and synchrony models that allow to carry out the application tasks. So, we use the asynchronous/arbitrary model, which does not make any assumptions about either time needed to make operations and faults/intrusions that can occur, as a starting point, and strengthen it as needed. For example, by resorting to hybrid models using wormholes [25], and assuming some form of partial synchrony.

We assume that the environment formed by the WAN and all the CIS is hostile (not trusted), and can thus be subjected to malicious (or arbitrary, or Byzantine[7]) faults. On the other hand, LANs trust the services provided by the CIS, but are not necessarily trusted by the latter. That is, as we will see below, LANs have different degrees of trustworthiness, which the CIS distributed protocols have to take into account. CIS securely switch information flows as a service to edge LANs as clients.

We assume that faults (accidental, attacks, intrusions) continuously occur during the life-time of the system, and that a maximum number of $f$ malicious (or arbitrary) faults can occur within a given interval. We assume that services running in the nodes (CIS) cooperate through distributed protocols in such an

---

[7] Arbitrary faults, which include attacks and intrusions, are usually called "Byzantine faults" after the seminal paper that explained the problem in terms of "Byzantine generals" [11]. Byzantine fault tolerance and intrusion tolerance usually mean the same in the literature.

environment. In consequence, these nodes have to be replicated for fault/intrusion tolerance.

Some of the services running in CIS may require some degree of timeliness, given that SCADA implies synchrony, and this is a hard problem with malicious faults, so we plan to do research in this issue. We also take into account that these systems should operate non-stop, a hard problem with resource exhaustion (the continued production of faults during the life-time of a perpetual execution system leads to the inevitable exhaustion of the quorum of nodes needed for correct operation [18]).

## 4.1 LAN-Level Services

A LAN is the top-level unit of the granularity of access control, regardless of possible finer controls. It is also and correspondingly, a unit of trust or mistrust thereof. In fact, we are not concerned with what happens inside a LAN, except that we may attribute it a different levels of trust. For instance, if the LAN is a SCADA network, the level of trust is high, but if it is the access to the Internet then the level of trust is low.

Traffic (packets) originating from a LAN receive a label that reflects this level of trust, and contains access control information, amongst other useful things.

The trustworthiness of a label (that is, the degree in which it can or not be tampered with) can vary, depending on the criticality of the service. In the context of this paper, and without loss of generality, we assume it is an authenticated proof of a capacity.

## 4.2 WAN-Level Services

The collection of CIS implements a set of core services, aiming at achieving the objectives we placed as desirable for a reference model of *critical information infrastructure distributed systems architecture*:

- Intrusion-tolerant information and command dissemination between CIS units, with authentication and cryptographic protection (broadcast, multicast, unicast).
- Pattern-sensitive information and command traffic analysis (behaviour and/ or knowledge-based intrusion detection) with intrusion-tolerant synchronisation and coordination between local Intrusion Detection Systems (IDSs).
- CIS egress/ingress access control based on LAN packet labels and/or additional mechanisms, implementing an instance of the global security policy.

The CIS middleware layers implement functionality at different levels of abstraction, as represented in Figure 3. As mentioned earlier, a middleware layer may overcome (through intrusion tolerance) the fault severity of lower layers and provide certain functions in a trustworthy way.

The lowest layer is the *Multipoint Network* module (MN), created over the physical infrastructure. Its main properties are the provision of multipoint addressing, secure channels (IPsec, SSL, etc.), and management communications,

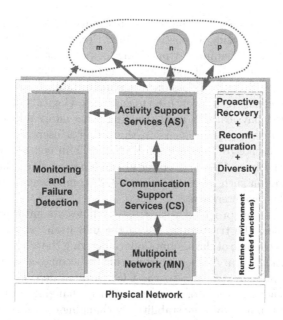

**Fig. 3.** CIS middleware

hiding the specificities of the underlying network. The *Communication Support Services* module (CS) implements basic cryptographic primitives, Byzantine agreement, consensus, group communication and other core services. The CS module depends on the MN module to access the network. The *Activity Support Services* module (AS) implements building blocks that assist participant activity, such as replication management (e.g., state machine, voting), IDS and firewall support functions, access control. It depends on the services provided by the CS module.

The block on the left of the figure generically implements Monitoring and Failure Detection. Failure detection assesses the connectivity and correctness of remote nodes, and the liveness of local processes. Trustworthiness monitoring and dependable adaptation mechanisms also reside in this module, and have interactions with all the modules on the right. Both the AS and CS modules depend on this information.

The block to the right represents the support services. These include the usual operating system's services, but also the trusted services supplied in support to the algorithms in the various modules: proactive recovery, reconfiguration, and diversity management.

## 5   CRUTIAL Information Switches (CIS)

Let us briefly discuss how CIS are made trusted-trustworthy components. CIS are built with a combination of untrusted and trusted hardware of varying degrees, depending on the needs and criticality of the traffic (sink or source) and the services they support. CIS individual resilience is enhanced by proactive resilience mechanisms, using a construct called Proactive Resilience Wormhole, described elsewhere [19], aiming at providing for perpetual execution of a given set of CIS, despite continued intrusion and/or failure of an assumed simultaneous maximum number of CIS at an assumed maximum rate.

These notions can be recursively used to construct a logical CIS which is in fact a set of replicated physical CIS units, running some internal intrusion-tolerant protocols so that the whole appears to the protocol users as a single logical entity sinking/sourcing to/from a given LAN, but is in fact resilient to attacks on the CIS themselves. This is a powerful combination since the resilience of protocols running on such intrusion-tolerant CIS components is commensurate to arbitrary-failure counterparts.

CIS are in addition provided with trustworthiness monitoring subsystems, aiming at assessing the trustworthiness of the CIS itself: as a function of the evolution of the coverage of the assumptions underlying the whole FIT (fault and intrusion tolerant) design. As such, trustworthiness becomes a dynamic property, which provides further resilience to the CIS, through dependable adaptation: automatically reacting to environment uncertainty (changing fault and/or attack levels) and maintaining coverage stability, by changing operation parameters or modes automatically. Finally, for very high levels of resilience, CIS construction and or reconfiguration in the course of proactive recovery may be based on diversity techniques (ex. n-version programming, obfuscation, etc.) [13].

The desired properties of the (logical) CIS have to be assured using proper methodologies. At a first stage, we plan to test CIS using attack injection techniques [16], in which attacks are generated and performed automatically with the purpose of finding vulnerabilities. However, ultimately CIS will have to pass a certification process based on the Common Criteria [1].

## 6   Conclusion

The paper presents a blueprint of a distributed systems architecture for resilient critical information infrastructures, with respect to both accidental faults and malicious attacks and intrusions. The rationale for this work was based on three fundamental propositions: classical security and/or safety techniques alone will not be enough to solve the problem; any effective solution has to involve automatic control of macroscopic command and information flows between the LANs composing the CII; and, the unifying paradigm should be a reference architecture of "resilient critical information infrastructures" performing the integration of the different realms of a CII system.

The proposed solution encompasses a range of mechanisms of incremental effectiveness, to address from the lower to the highest criticality operations in a CII. Architectural configurations with trusted components in key places induce prevention of some attacks. Middleware software attains automatic tolerance of the remaining faults and intrusions. Trustworthiness enforcing and monitoring mechanisms allow unforeseen adaptation to extremely critical, not predicted situations, beyond the initial assumptions made.

Functionally, the information flow is controlled by basic mechanisms of the firewall and intrusion detection type, complemented and parameterised by organisation-level security policies and access control models, capable of securing information flows with different criticality within a CII and in/out of it.

**Acknowledgements.** CRUTIAL is a project of the IST programme of the European Commission. Several institutions participate to the project: CESI RICERCA (Italy), FCUL (Portugal), CNR-ISTI (Italy), LAAS-CNRS (France), K.U.Leuven-ELECTA (Belgium), CNIT (Italy). Details about the project can be found in the CRUTIAL portal: http://crutial.cesiricerca.it/.

# References

1. ISO/IEC Standard 15408, Evaluation Criteria for IT Security, parts 1 to 3, 1999.
2. President's Critical Infrastructure Protection Board and Office of Energy Assurance U.S. Department of Energy. *21 Steps to Improve Cyber Security of SCADA Networks.* U.S. Department of Energy, 2002.
3. A. Bondavalli, S. Chiaradonna, D. Cotroneo, and L. Romano. Effective fault treatment for improving the dependability of COTS and legacy-based applications. *IEEE Transactions on Parallel and Distributed Systems*, 1(4):223–237, 2004.
4. E. Byres, J. Karsch, and J. Carter. NISCC good practice guide on firewall deployment for SCADA and process control networks. Technical report, NISCC, February 2005. Revision 1.4.
5. J. Cieslewicz. Attacks and accidents: Policy to protect the power grid's critical computing and communication needs. Senior interdisciplinary honors thesis in international security studies, Stanford University, May 2004.
6. G. Dondossola, G. Deconinck, F. Di Giandomenico, S. Donatelli, M. Kaaniche, and P. Veríssimo. Critical utiliy infrastructural resilience. In *International Workshop on Complex Network and Infrastructure Protection*, March 2006.
7. US-Canada Power System Outage Task Force. *Interim Report: Causes of the August 14th Blackout in the United States and Canada.* November 2003.
8. D. Geer. Security of critical control systems sparks concern. *IEEE Computer*, pages 20–23, January 2006.
9. L. A. Gordon, M. P. Loeb, W. Lucyshyn, and R. Richardson. 2006 CSI/FBI computer crime and security survey. Computer Security Institute, 2006.
10. A. A. El Kalam, R. Elbaida, P. Balbiani, S. Benferhat, F. Cuppens, Y. Deswarte, A. MiFge, C. Saurel, and G. Trouessin. Organization-based access control. In *IEEE 4th International Workshop on Policies for Distributed Systems and Networks*, pages 277–288, June 2003.
11. L. Lamport, R. Shostak, and M. Pease. The Byzantine generals problem. *ACM Transactions on Programming Languages and Systems*, 4(3):382–401, July 1982.
12. H. Li, G. W. Rosenwald, J. Jung, and C. Liu. Strategic power infrastructure defense. *Proceedings of the IEEE*, 93(5):918–933, May 2005.
13. B. Littlewood and L. Strigini. Redundancy and diversity in security. In P. Samarati, P. Rian, D. Gollmann, and R. Molva, editors, *Computer Security – ESORICS 2004, 9th European Symposium on Research Computer Security*, LNCS 3193, pages 423–438. Springer, 2004.
14. H. Luiijf and M. Klaver. The current state of threats. In *e-Security in Europe: Todays Status and The Next Step*, October 2004.

15. V. Madani and D. Novosel. Getting a grip on the grid. *IEEE Spectrum*, 42(12):42–47, December 2005.
16. N. F. Neves, J. Antunes, M. Correia, P. Verfssimo, and R. Neves. Using attack injection to discover new vulnerabilities. In *Proceedings of the International Conference on Dependable Systems and Networks*, June 2006.
17. J. Pollet. Developing a solid SCADA security strategy. In *Proceedings of the ISA/IEEE Sensors for Industry Conference*, pages 148–156, November 2002.
18. P. Sousa, N. F. Neves, and P. Verissimo. How resilient are distributed *f* fault/intrusion-tolerant systems? In *Proceedings of the IEEE International Conference on Dependable Systems and Networks*, June 2005.
19. P. Sousa, N. F. Neves, and P. Veríssimo. Resilient state machine replication. In *Proceedings of the 11th Pacific Rim International Symposium on Dependable Computing*, pages 305–309, December 2005.
20. J. Stamp, J. Dillinger, W. Young, and J. DePoy. Common vulnerabilities in critical infrastructure control systems. Technical report, Sandia National Laboratories, May 2003.
21. K. Stouffer, J. Falco, and K. Kent. Guide to supervisory control and data acquisition (SCADA) and industrial control systems security. Recommendations of the National Institute of Standards and Technology. Special Publication 800-82, NIST, September 2006. Initial Public Draft.
22. D. Turner, S. Entwisle, O. Friedrichs, D. Ahmad, J. Blackbird, M. Fossi, D. Hanson, S. Gordon, D. Cole, D. Cowlings, D. Morss, B. Bradley, P. Szor, E. Chien, J. Ward, J. Gough, and J. Talbot. Symantec Internet security threat report. Trends for January 05–June 05. Symantec, Volume VIII, September 2005.
23. M. van Eeten, E. Roe, P. Schulman, and M. de Bruijne. The enemy within: System complexity and organizational surprises. In M. Dunn and V. Mauer, editors, *International CIIP Handbook 2006*, volume II, pages 89–110. Center for Security Studies, ETH Zurich, 2006.
24. P. Veríssimo. Lessons learned with NavTech: a framework for reliable large-scale applications. DI/FCUL TR 02-17, Department of Informatics, University of Lisbon, December 2002.
25. P. Veríssimo. Travelling through wormholes: a new look at distributed systems models. *SIGACTN: SIGACT News (ACM Special Interest Group on Automata and Computability Theory)*, 37(1):66–81, 2006.
26. P. Veríssimo, N. F. Neves, C. Cachin, J. Poritz, D. Powell, Y. Deswarte, R. Stroud, and I. Welch. Intrusion-tolerant middleware: The road to automatic security. *IEEE Security & Privacy*, 4(4):54–62, Jul./Aug. 2006.
27. P. Veríssimo, N. F. Neves, and M. Correia. Intrusion-tolerant architectures: Concepts and design. In R. Lemos, C. Gacek, and A. Romanovsky, editors, *Architecting Dependable Systems*, volume 2677, pages 3–36. 2003.
28. C. Wilson. Terrorist capabilities for cyber-attack. In M. Dunn and V. Mauer, editors, *International CIIP Handbook 2006*, volume II, pages 69–88. Center for Security Studies, ETH Zurich, 2006.

# Experiment Based Validation of CIIP

Per Mellstrand and Rune Gustavsson

Blekinge Institute of Technology
per.mellstrand@bth.se, rune.gustavsson@bth.se

**Abstract.** The connection between critical infrastructure Protection (CIP) and critical information infrastructures protection (CIIP) is a major research area. We describe our view of how a combined experimental approach can be used to build targeted resilient software required for critical infrastructure.

**Keywords:** Critical Infrastructures, Resilient Software, Vulnerability Assessment.

## 1 Protection of Critical Information Infrastructures

Critical Infrastructure Protection (CIP and Critical Information Infrastructure Protection (CIIP) are in focus of ongoing R&D efforts worldwide. Among the most important critical infrastructures we find energy system in most listings and investigations. Critical Information Infrastructures is a rather late focus area of R&D. From one point of view this is very natural since critical infrastructures are often connected with, or are embedding of, information infrastructures. In fact, much of the critically (vulnerability) is due to the dependencies between those infrastructures. However, at this point there is no consensus what a CIIP would be. There are several EU project aiming at increasing our understanding in the subject areas in order to identify suitable direction of future R&D [1][2].

In this paper we advocate an experiment-based approach towards identifying and pursuing a principled research agenda towards CIIP. The following Figure 1 illustrates our experimental set up as well as our approach.

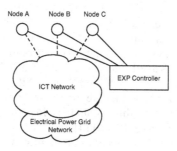

**Fig. 1.** Experimental Environment with nodes. The network contains both physical and simulated parts.

J. Lopez (Ed.): CRITIS 2006, LNCS 4347, pp. 15 – 29, 2006.

Firstly, we believe that it is advantageous to study embedded CII in a CI rather than an isolated CII focus. That kind of investigation might be purposeful when we have a better understanding of the underpinnings of CII. Secondly we will use the figure to pinpoint the goals and contributions of the paper.

## 1.1 The Anatomy of Critical Information Infrastructures

The purpose of an embedded CII is to drive the corresponding CI in a proper way. In this metaphor the role of information is comparable to that of energy in many CIs. In fact many of our CI are derived and created from the industrial revolution during the last couple of centuries. Understanding of the concept of energy came rather late in that revolution (mid 1850´s) and after the invention and use of energy-based artifacts such as the steam engine. But an understanding of energy allowed us to transform energy in suitable forms and transport it to the point of use as well a enabling new kinds of energybased products and services (Radio, telecommunications and TV). In a sense the industrial revolution led to and was dependant on a proper understanding of energy. That understanding was indeed an emergent property and enabler of the industrial revolution. In fact, the energy metaphor of information was also a basic underpinning of the ongoing efforts on GRID computing [3]. Our point of view is, however, that the energy metaphor of information is oversold and does not guide us in understanding the role of information in the ongoing building up of an information society [4].

Given the embedding of a CII in a CI (energy system) of Figure 1 we can identify the following types of information:

- $I_1$ Control information interpreted by users. Information from the ICT networks supporting monitoring and user driven system actions of the CI and CII.
- $I_2$ Intra system information exchange: Information between the two critical infrastructures CI and CII.
- $I_3$ Information enabling processes: Typical information (code) that enable proper running of software of the systems.

Furthermore, we note that the greatest causes of system complexity and vulnerabilities are in the different interfaces between system components and that the glue of critical systems, of both kinds, is software. Or, to quote from [13]: "This leaves SCADA/EMS as the vulnerability of greatest concern. Unfortunately, SCADA/EMS components – computers, networks, and software – will remain complex and unreliable for a long time because securing an information system is well known to be problematic. Thus far, it has been impossible to build software that is guaranteed to be bug-free. These software flaws leads to networks becoming disconnected, data being lost, and computers being disabled. As long as software is flawed, there will be faults in industrial control systems such as SCADA and EMS". A recent report on infrastructure interdependencies where fault reports from 12 years were analyzed concluded that software faults, including malicious logic and authorization violation, constitues for more than 65% of all faults [14].

From the information security research community we have the following CIA-model of information protection:

- Confidentiality - Information should not leak to unauthorized agents.
- Integrity - The information should not improperly be changed.
- Availability - The information should be available to the intended user in the right format and in the right time.

The CIA model is declarative, i.e., there are no or few guidelines on how to engineer information systems that ensure CIA protection. From a system engineering point of view we most thus derive operationalisations of the CIA declaratives [8,9]. In effect, we aim at to ensure a proper behaviour of our system(s) in Figure 1. To that end we introduce the following equation:

Behaviour = Representation + Interpretation (1)

The information types mentioned earlier ($I_1$, $I_2$, and $I_3$) gives different operational semantics to equation (1). For information type $I_1$, the intended reading is that the information $I_1$, should be represented in such a way that the intended user could make the right intepretations (given the right skill, knowledge, and tools) in order to behave as intended (take the appropriate actions). Classical information security efforts enforce CIA protection by typically have encrypted representation and access control (the C and I parts). The availability part is often left to the system designer to ensure. We will not, in this paper, further address $I_1$ protection as such but note that from a system behaviour point of view (Figure 1) proper $I_1$ protection presuppose that we have proper protection of information types $I_2$ and $I_3$ in place.

For information type $I_2$ the intended reading of equation (1) is that the representation of data (format) should be a format that could correctly be interpreted by the receiving module in order to create the proper behaviour. This kind of machine-readable formats and behaviour semantics are in focus of contemporary R&D on semantic web and (to a lesser degree) in web services [8,11]. However, there is at this point little done in principles of $I_2$ centric information protection. We will to some extent focus on those issues in the experiment set up of Figure 1, (Figure 4).

The main focus, however, of our current R&D on behaviour protection is related to information of type $I_3$. The intended semantics of equation (1) in this case is correct execution of programs (code) in context dependant run-time environments [5,7,12].

## 1.2 Our View of Critical Information Infrastructure Protection (CIIP)

From the analysis of the previous section we have identified three different types of information that requires quite different approaches and mechanisms to ensure proper protection. Our operationalisations of the CIA model as a set of behaviour criteria allows us to develop a principled engineering approach towards CIIP as ensured behaviours. Before we go into details we remark that the CII and the corresponding CI are embedded in physical infrastructures (Computer systems and networks). Protection of those physical infrastructures are parts of CIP (computer security and network security) and hence properly addressed in that setting. However, specifically CIA problems with information of type $I_3$ will, and do, cause direct problems for the behaviour of the physical infrastructure. Furthermore, network security typically try to protect information ($I_1$ and $I_2$) in transit from a CIA point of view. The different information types thus exemplify different critical dependencies between CI and CII. Our behaviour approach also allows us to handle system breakdowns in a principled way [8,9]. In fact we have devised hardening schemas to protect run-time environments as well as methods supporting self-healing and self-configuration [9,12]. We have adopted a service-oriented system view towards CIP and CIIP. We configure our system as a bundle of services to meet functional and non-functional criteria. In the configuration we take into account dependability criteria and related requirements on instrumentation to support relevant inspection and control of behaviours [8].

## 2 Next Generation Infrastructures and Information Infrastructures

One of the key properties that make the next generation critical infrastructure ICT systems so attractive is the greatly increased use of open protocols and inexpensive ICT components (COTS). By using these technologies it is possible to build cost-effective networked systems with good performance and a high degree of vendor independence. For some critical infrastructures, such as the electrical powergrid, there are also new re quirements such as the greatly increased use of distributed generation (DES and RES) that require far more flexible ICT systems (SCADA) than what is used today. For these and other reasons, it is highly likely that we in the near future will see an increased use of ICT systems to control different aspects of real-world non-ICT critical infrastructures.

Because of the complex nature of critical infrastructure there are typically several different situations where ICT systems could be used to control aspects of the actual infrastructure. These situations range from making highly critical decisions (such as load shedding to avoid break-downs) to more mundane day-to-day operations (supply demand matching and charging). Thus, it is likely that there will be several different ICT networks that affect a specific critical infrastructure, and that there will be different requirements for the different types of networks and information types (Section 1). Some of these networks might be so sensitive that only special-purpose hardware, software and protocols will be used, but there is a large call for more typical, cost-effective, ICT components (e.g. COTS) in connection with critical infrastructure systems as well. This is also the case for safety-critical control. In practice this means TCP/IP based communication networks where nodes from different vendors that run different software will be interconnected and the function of these networks will have a large impact on the function of the actual critical infrastructure.

### 2.1 Critical Infrastructures and Critical Information Infrastructures

This use of open heterogeneous ICT networks to control actual, physical, critical infrastructure is not only of interest to the infrastructure community; since these networks are in fact pseudo-open intranets where "normal quality"-software control the function of critical infrastructures, this is in our opinion clearly an interesting question for the security and dependability communities.

There are several important questions for the CIP/CIIP communities to address, which roughly can be divided in two main categories;

1.  To which degree can heterogeneous networks are permitted to control critical infrastructures (a techno-political discussion), and
2.  In which ways can we improve the security/dependability/resilience mechanisms to allow normal software to be used in a more dependable fashion and hence extend the usable scope for open heterogeneous systems.

These questions are linked together in the sense that if there are no domain-specific ways to make normal ICT systems more dependable, there is an evident limit on the degree of control we can allow such systems to have on a critical infrastructure.

There are many different approaches aimed at making "normal quality" software more dependable; in other work we have argued for methods that harden the execution environment for a single node in a domain-specific way, as well as for the need of increased use of experimental environments to permit more realistic experimentation. We will describe these aspects in more detail in the next section 3.

To meet the requirements for implementation and maintenance of dependable infrastructure we argue for a two-dimensional combined structured approach aiming at domain-specific hardened systems. Firstly, to extend the use of execution analysis methods normally used only for hardening also to inject faults into the executing program, and secondly, the use of an experimental environment that enables a varying degree of actual and simulated components. By integrating the experimental environment with hardening/fault injection tools we can perform and monitor a chain of fault injection-hardening pairs to find weaknesses and gain knowledge of how to build environments that can handle these in run-time with increasing degree of robustness and resilience. Experiments can be performed with a varying degree of real components in realistic as well as non-realistic (such as fault-provoking) environments. This chain of information retrieval and hardening in the context of an experimental environment is illustrated in Figure 1.

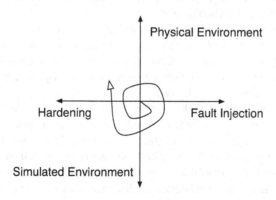

**Fig. 2.** Combining an experimental environment with a dynamic tool permits a two-dimensional experimental approach

## 3   A Combined Approach for Informed Dynamic Dependability

To build secure critical information systems we must have ways to ensure dependable execution of the software involved in, i.e. the $I_3$ aspect of, these systems (section 1). Generic approaches, such as static analysis, formal validation, and re-implementation of certain well-known problematic interfaces are all good in this sense, but for critical infrastructure systems we strongly believe such approaches alone are not sufficient. Only very small parts of a software system can realistically be validated in a formal way leaving the majority without protection, and even if skilled human auditors and sophisticated automated tools perform static analysis of a program there can be a number of complex run-time enabled situations that could not be taken into account. Then there must be ways to handle these situations so that the real-world critical system controlled is not harmfully affected. In our approach, a fundamental assumption that we make about normal software engineering methods is that *these systems will never be completely free from errors* and that there are severe consequences if these software fail.

We believe one of the key ways to increase the dependability in these systems is by using methods that target the software execution and in run-time prevent vulnerabilities (defects) to be exploited. Such methods should be able to detect and respond to unwanted execution, preferably in an unknown program, to make sure the larger system can survive an attack. We use the term dynamic method to refer to a method that can protect an executing program in run-time from a pre-determined class of potential exploits. The programs that are protected in this fashion will be resilient to the given class of exploits, typically without any need for recompilation or other modification. [12]

To create this protection we must firstly have *echanisms* that allow us to in runtime determine safe from unsafe execution, and secondly *knowledge* about what actually onstitutes safe and unsafe execution in the specific domain. From a practical standpoint, the mechanisms should also provide means to alter execution, such as to terminate a program in the simplest case, should unsafe execution be detected. To increase the protection of a specific system beyond the level of what good generic methods can do, we must have knowledge of the specific system and what constitutes safe and unsafe execution for this particular system.

We must have information about a particular system and its domain that we can use to build knowledge model of what execution that is safe and what is unsafe. This knowledge will typically include aspects of how the system is used and what are the consequences should the system fail (i.e. non-technical aspects), but also concrete practical information about how the system executes.

When we have established both *mechanisms* that we can use to build *methods* as well as *knowledge* about what constitutes safe and what constitutes unsafe execution for a given domain, we can create informed dynamic protection for the given system. In this article we present our views of how we can use a combined approach of dynamic methods to protect as well as gain information about executing systems, when the systems execute in an experimental environment that can create both realistic as well as synthetic environments. [5,6,7]

### 3.1  Mechanisms for Hardening and Fault Injection

One of our key-concepts in our work is what we call "environment hardening" that closely relates to the terms "resilient software" and "fault tolerant software". The main idea is that by taking advantage of existing separation of software execution in layers, it is possible to modify the lower layers, such as libraries, in a domain-specific way that enables construction of targeted software execution environments. Thus we can create environments that give non-cooperating software certain properties, such as a higher degree of resilience to certain exploitable attacks. [12]

There is much related work in this field, most often targeted towards specific vulnerabilities and a more generic domain (i.e. how can we make format-string vulnerabilities non-exploitable in Linux, technically in GNU libc, by using a modified library implementation). In our opinion this type of work is very useful for creating solid implementations of standardized interfaces. For targeted systems, such as embedded ICT systems, these methods alone are not enough; to allow safe execution in a targeted system, such as critical infrastructure ICT, we should be able to make decisions based on specific knowledge of the particular system properties as well as specific information about the execution state. This allows for a flexible handling of less critical systems, and also a more targeted hardening of more critical systems since run-time aspects, such as privileges, but also program state such as function parameters and return values, can be considered when making a decision in run-time.

To provide this type of protection dynamic methods have mechanisms for analyzing an executing program at run-time to determine if the program is executing in a safe or nsafe way. In some cases, the behaviour of such methods is already configurable and can be made domain-specific given a correct configuration for the particular domain at hand. Other methods are less configurable and requires a larger degree of adaptation for use in informed domain-specific systems. Both types, however, can be seen as one analysis step (i.e. determining whether the execution is safe according to some criteria) and a separate action step (which actions will be taken depending on the result of the analysis).

In most cases, the purpose of this approach is to protect the program should potentially unwanted execution be detected. However, if we separate the analysis

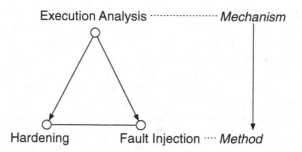

**Fig. 3.** Both hardening and fault injection can be built as different methods using the same basic mechanism

*Mechanism* from the action *method* we can use a different action which rather than protect the program could inject a fault or behaviour in some other unexpected/unwanted way.

Fault injection is in this case a method performed as the result of the mechanism analysis which means that if the mechanism can use domain-specific knowledge the fault injecting method can benefit from this. This is in some contrast to typical fault injection that mimics common error situations (out of disk space, communication errors, ...), as it is possible to use the analysis mechanism to find either a typical or atypical situation and then either protect or provoke (such as injecting a fault) the executing program. [10]

## 3.2  The Plibc Policy Execution System

The plibc system is a policy execution engine, i.e. a system that allows the execution of a program to be controlled by a local policy, that operates entirely in user-land. [12] It can be loaded into a non-cooperating program where it will intercept certain function calls. To use the plibc system one first writes a textual policy file where triggers and actions are expressed in a simple scripting language. This file is compiled to a binary policy file which is read and enforced by the plibc system inside the non-cooperating program in run-time. This layout enables a fast operation of the system and the typical overhead when used for hardening a system is only a few per cent in worst-case scenarios. An example of a plibc policy that denies the standard-compliant but often exploited "%n" directive is shown below;

```
deny printf if param-match 1 "%n"
deny printf if param-match 1 "%hn"
```

For our initial experimentation with the injection-hardening aspect presented in this article we have extended the plibc system to also do fault injection in parallel with hardening. In this case the modification from a pure hardening method is comparably simple, as the separation between methods/actions (such as deny in the case above) and the mechanism analysis (does parameter one match "%n") is quite strong.

## 3.3  Experimental Environments

When experimenting with how a program or system behaves in run-time (dynamic properties) as opposed to how it is syntactically constructed (static properties) the program must of course actually execute. For some trivial programs this is as easy as executing the program on the developers' computer and see how it behaves. For many systems, such as ICT systems for critical infrastructure, the situation is not in all cases as easy. These systems are designed to function in network constellations with other software and possibly even with special hardware systems.

To test networked systems in a realistic setting they must either execute in a real environment where all the surrounding nodes are present, or in an environment where the executing program can behave as if this was the case - an experimental environment. Also it not always beneficial to execute a system in an entirely realistic environment. For example, we might want to experiment with how a system behaves in stressed situations when the surrounding environment does not fully function, in extreme load or when there are local software problems such as out-of-memory situations. We can create such an environment for each situation we want to experiment with, but this will be time-consuming and difficult.

When more complex experimentation is needed we argue that instead of building these experimental environment manually there is a significant gain in using an experimental environment or a framework that provides assistance in creating experimental environments. This is particularly true when creating environment where some parts should be simulated or targeted to generate a sub-optimal / provoking environment. The main advantage of using an experimental environment in this case is evident if these is support to script/modify component behaviour in a structured way. In summary we need controlled environment to enable controlled execution testing and assessment.

Our EXP system is a framework for building experimental environments particularly targeted for open heterogeneous TCP/IP based networks. [7] While a complete description of the EXP system is outside the scope for this article, we provide a short summary which we hope is useful for understanding our reasoning and arguments for a combined approach for assessing dynamic dependability. The EXP system consists of a number of generic services which can be combined with experiment-specific services and configuration to build an experimental environment. All services are configured through a central generic configuration service which provides means to associate certain nodes in a network with a class and then provide configuration based on class and inherited properties. This is also combined with the embedded scripting language Lua which enables generation of dynamic configuration content. The most central services in the Exp framework are;

- Network - Exp contains pre-configured networks both for flat LAN style, physical WAN, and WAN by means of VLANs
- Restoration - pc computer nodes can automatically be saved restored to a specific state depending on the role they have
- Configuration - generic as well as experiment-specific services can be configured from a single service, including the use of role-based configuration and scriptgenerated data
- Drone nodes - Some nodes typically those that perform simpler tasks can be built to execute in RAM-based images based on the role a particular node has

The EXP system permits construction of fairly complex experiment networks without requiring the experiment to be built from scratch, and thanks to the scriptable configuration engine, many aspects of the experiment service configuration can be easily scripted.

## 4  Initial Experimentation

To test an implementation with our combined approach, we designed an experiment system with the purpose of testing a small networked system in stressed situations, in

fact for understanding CIIP with information of type in section 1. We used the existing EXP system to build the environment, and used a modified version of the plibc
hardening tool to also allow domain-specific injection of faults. This setup enabled us
to create combined hardening/fault policies that was injected into a pseudo-
cooperating mode on the network (i.e. there was a helper program on the node, but the
program which was subject to the policy was not modified). The EXP controller sent
execution policies to the node, and the node responded with a log of the actual execution. The flow of information is illustrated in Figure 4.

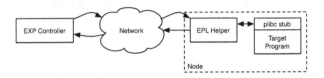

**Fig. 4.** Combining an experimental environment with a dynamic tool permits a two-
dimensional experimental approach

We used the program `fetch` from the standard FreeBSD distribution which is a
program that downloads files given an URL. The fetch program uses the OpenSSL
library to access URLs using the encrypted https shema, and this was one of the components we wanted to stress.

### 4.1 Execution

The first experiment was with a low-probability fault in the C library memory alloca-
tion.This mimics the situation when a node is running out of memory, either because
there is a real low-memory condition or, for example, because of a ulimit memory
restriction. This situation can be described in plibc as;

```
allow malloc if prob 0.999
trace malloc "i"
return malloc 0
```

Using these settings the `malloc` function will function normally in 99.9% of all
invocations, but on a random 0.1% the plibc library will trace the invocation chain
and make the function return NULL. These are fairly generic rules to determine the
resilience of the program against simple memory faults.

The fetch program was executed 1000 times, each time in a clean environment,
and the results from the execution (logs, and core dumps) was analysed. Out of
1000 invocations 177 (17.7%) resulted in core dumps, 1 (0.1%) in a the program
hanging and the remaining 822 (82.2%) in that the program terminated without
a crash.

### 4.2 Analysis

Analysing the core dump files we identified 9 functions where the program had
crashed and one for the hang (See Appendix A for details on logs and crashes).

Combining these with the trace produced by plibc we identified where the memory was allocated for each respective crash. Combining these two sources of information we can easily determine if a crash is local (i.e. the same function, or a function close seen from am invocation perspective, allocated the memory and crashed) or if there was a propagation of the error.

In our test the fetch program crashed 26 times in the C library memory copying function memcpy. Using the plibc trace we identified that in 24 of these 26 cases the memory was allocated by the function EVP_MD_CTX_copy_ex (in OpenSSL) which was also the function that invoked memcpy and cased the crash. The remaining two invocations to malloc were done in functions that directly called EVP_MD_CTX_copy_ex and the problem was with an in-parameter. This is a typical local vulnerability in the OpenSSL library, and one we believe could have been caught using good static methods as well.

As an example of a non-local error discovered in this initial experimentation we discovered a crash in the function BN_num_bits (OpenSSL Big Number Math Library). The fault in that execution, however, was in BN_new invoked by X509_NAME_set The interesting aspect of this fault is that the BN_new handles the fault (by returning NULL) but this is not handled correctly by the invoking function. Comparing the plibc trace with the crash core dump, we see that there is 18+5 = 23 function invocations between the fault and the crash. From this data we cannot determine if any additional functions had used the value and that had already returned.

The first common function between the fault location and the crash is ssl3_connect which is a 300-line function that handles the over-all SSL version 3 procedure. Analysing the source code of OpenSSL reveals that these 23 functions that the fault propagated through are implemented in 16 different source code files. In this case a static tool might have had some success analysing the original error, but we believe it would be difficult to detect the consequences in the 23 different functions.

The third case, the hang, was caused by a the fetch program building an incorrect HTTP query when a particular allocation failed. This caused the server to wait for a complete query and the program hung.

### 4.3 Feedback

At this point we draw two conclusions from the experiment. Firstly, that the OpenSSL library *cannot* handle out-of-memory situations in a satisfactory way. If we were to protect the fetch program immediately, we would have to compensate for this in some way. A fast way would be a matching plibc rule;

```
on return deny malloc if return-value 0
```

which would case plibc to terminate the program as soon as a out-of-memory situation is reported by malloc. The second conclusion is that since the OpenSSL library uses a wrapped memory allocator (CRYPTO_malloc) this would be a good place to check for out-of-memory conditions. Also, we see that there are small number of functions (such as `EVP_MD_CTX_copy_ex`) in OpenSSL that handle memory allocations in a sloppy way. These functions, once identified, could be *fixed to remove many of the vulnerabilities* we see. This is the most important feedback for the next cycle of analysis.

### 4.4 Next Cycle

Given the feedback from the more generic cycle we can move to more domain-specific injections (See Figure 2) to tailor focused experiments. For example, the error where fetch hung because of an incorrect query being generated may be of interest in a critical infrastructure. Can we assert that this error will nor propagate to the server? For the fetch program the most likely candidates for this type of errors are string formatting functions, which we can provoke further to identify these situations. The next step is to increase both the stress and move to a domain closer to our target environment as shown in Figure 2 on page 5.

## 5  Conclusions

Understanding the basic principles of assuring Critical Infrastructure Protection is a big challenge of societal importance. We propose in this paper a structured approach to that end. As a first step we investigate the anatomy of CIIP as such and propose a classification of three kinds of information depending on its role in Critical Information Infrastructures. Basically we identify human readable information ($I_1$), information between system components ($I_2$) and information (code, $I_3$) that supports computations in both CI and CII.

We argue that CIIP, when I is of type $I_3$, is a stepping stone towards general CIIP. To that end we propose in this paper a structured experimental approach to validate and ensure CIIP for this information. We have some very promising results already of which some are reported in this paper. Very briefly summarized, we combine hardening / fault tolerance mechanisms with internal fault injection in a controlled environment to experiment with run-time dependability. This allows us to experiment with non-cooperating software and assert correct function in different execution situations as well as extract internal execution state useful for other protection mechanisms.

Furthermore, we are presently extended our experimental settings to also take into account CIIP on a system level (that is, $I_2$) [8]. To ensure a full-fledged CIIP we of course also have to focus on related $I_1$ issues. However, this is out of scope in our present R&D efforts.

## References

[1] EC Critical Information Infrastructure Research Co-ordinatiion (CI2RCO): www.ci2rco.org
[2] EC sixth framework program "A coordination Action on ICT vulnerabilities of power systems and the relevant defence methodologies", ("GRID")

[3] Global Grid Forum: www.gridforum.org/

[4] Europe's Information Society: europa.eu.int/information_society/text_en.htm

[5] Mellstrand, P., Gustavsson, R., "Dynamic Protection of Software Execution Environment" Proceedings of the 2ndInternational Conference on Critical Infrastructures, 2004

[6] Mellstrand, P., Gustavsson, R.,"Preventing Buffer Overflows by Dynamic Environ- ment Hardening", Proceedings of the 3rd International Conference on Critical Infrastructures, 2006

[7] Mellstrand, P., Gustavsson, R., "An Experiment Driven Approach Towards Dependable and Sustainable Future Energy Systems", Proceedings of the 3rd International Conference on Critical Infrastructures, 2006

[8] Gustavsson, R. (2006). Ensuring dependability in service oriented computing. In Proceedings of The 2006 International Conference on Security & Management (SAM'06) at The 2006 World Congress in Computer Science, Computer Engineering, and Applied Computing, Las Vegas, 2006.

[9] Gustavsson, R and Mellstrand, P. (2006). Ensuring Quality of Service in Service Oriented Critical Infrastructures. In Proceedings of International Workshop on Complex Network and Infrastructure Protection, CNIP 2006, March 28 - 29, 2006. Invited paper to journal

[10] Hsueh, T. Tsai and R. Iyer. Fault injection techniques and tools. IEEE Computer, p 75-82, April 1997.

[11] Antoniou, G., and van Harmelen, F. (2004). A Semantic Web Primer. The MIT Press, Cooperative Information Systems series

[12] Mellstrand, P. (2005) Protecting Software Execution by Dynamic Environment Hardening. BTH licentiate dissertation series no. 2005:12.

[13] Lewis, T. (2006) Critical Infrastructures Protection in Homeland Security. Defending a Networked Nation. Wiley-Interscience, ISBN-13: 978-0-471-78628-3

[14] Rahman, H. A., Beznosov K., Marti, J. R. "Source of Failures and Their Impacts on Critical Infrastructures as Identified from 12 Years Public Failure Reports", Proceedings of the 3rd International Conference on Critical Infrastructures, 2006

## Appendix A: Traces and Technical References

For our initial experimentation we used the fetch utility included in FreeBSD 6.1-STABLE on the i386 platform. This program is dynamically linked to the system-provided libopenssl.so.4 and libcrypto.so.4 libraries. The OpenSSL version these were built from is included in the FreeBSD distribution and is, as far as we can see, 0.9.7e.

## Functions in Which Fetch Crashed/Hung

During the exeution of the experiment, fetch crashed in the following functions (with number of times in paranteses); BN_copy (3), BN_num_bits (1), DH_OpenSSL (2), MD5_Init (15), OPENSSL_cleanse (2), SHA1_Init (101), SSL_CTX_ctrl (23), asn1_ex_c2i (4), memcpy (26) and hung in read (1).

For the memcpy crashes, the memory was allocated from EVP_MD_CTX_copy_ex (24), tls1_clear(1) and ssl3_get_finished(1)

For the BN_num_bits crash faults had been injected in ERR_load_ERR_strings (1), lh_insert (3), BN_new (1). We have analysed the former injections and believe that these had nothing to do with the crash. The complete trace given by plibc for the BN_new fault is;

```
malloc(20)
traceback for malloc:
0x281dd7cc, 0x281dc705, 0x281c9776, 0x281c98a2,
0x281ce9c3, 0x281cf06b, 0x281cfb60, 0x281cf402,
0x281cf60b, 0x281cfa3f, 0x281cfea3, 0x281c73a9,
0x281c227a, 0x281c0b0d, 0x281bfb73, 0x2816fa55,
0x2816ff1e, 0x281102df, 0x280fe0a9, 0x2810ba49,
0x280fb313, 0x2810ba66, 0x280ea25f, 0x280e6a9a,
0x280e7f9b, 0x280eb05c, 0x8049dec, 0x804b33c,
0x804925a
```

Looking up these addresses in the symbol table gives;

```
0x281dd7cc <CRYPTO_malloc+64>
0x281dc705 <BN_new+37>
0x281c9776 <X509_NAME_set+522>
0x281c98a2 <X509_NAME_set+822>
0x281ce9c3 <asn1_ex_c2i+311>
0x281cf06b <asn1_ex_c2i+2015>
0x281cfb60 <ASN1_item_ex_d2i+1184>
0x281cf402 <asn1_ex_c2i+2934>
0x281cf60b <asn1_ex_c2i+3455>
0x281cfa3f <ASN1_item_ex_d2i+895>
0x281cfea3 <ASN1_item_d2i+63>
0x281c73a9 <d2i_RSAPublicKey+37>
0x281c227a <d2i_PublicKey+246>
0x281c0b0d <X509_PUBKEY_get+89>
0x281bfb73 <X509_get_pubkey+51>
0x2816fa55 <X509_get_pubkey_parameters+77>
0x2816ff1e <X509_verify_cert+1006>
0x281102df <ssl_verify_cert_chain+267>
0x280fe0a9 <ssl3_connect+4793>
0x2810ba49 <SSL_connect+37>
0x280fb313 <ssl23_connect+1895>
0x2810ba66 <SSL_connect+66>
0x280ea25f <_fetch_ssl+119>
0x280e6a9a <_http_request+1766>
0x280e7f9b <fetchXGetHTTP+47>
0x280eb05c <fetchXGet+184>
0x8049dec <_init+4076>
0x804b33c <_init+9532>
0x804925a <_init+1114>
```

In this trace we cannot see main as the symbol table for the fetch binary is stripped. The core dump file reveals a trace as follows;

```
0x281dc5ac <BN_num_bits>
0x281cccff <BN_mod_exp_mont>
0x281aee01 <RSA_PKCS1_SSLeay>
0x281add60 <RSA_public_decrypt>
0x281ad53b <RSA_verify>
0x280fed78 <ssl3_connect>
0x2810ba49 <SSL_connect>
0x280fb313 <ssl23_connect>
0x2810ba66 <SSL_connect>
0x280ea25f <_fetch_ssl>
0x280e6a9a <_http_request>
0x280e7f9b <fetchXGetHTTP>
0x280eb05c <fetchXGet>
```

# Security Requirements Model for Grid Data Management Systems*

Syed Naqvi[1,2], Philippe Massonet[1], and Alvaro Arenas[2]

[1] Centre of Excellence in Information and Communication Technologies (CETIC), Belgium
{syed.naqvi,philippe.massonet}@cetic.be
[2] CCLRC Rutherford Appleton Laboratory, United Kingdom
{s.naqvi,a.e.arenas}@rl.ac.uk

**Abstract.** In this paper, we present our ongoing work of a policy-driven approach to security requirements of grid data management systems (GDMS). We analyse the security functionalities of existing GDMS to determine their shortcomings that should be addressed in our work. We identify a comprehensive set of security requirements for GDMS followed by the presentation of our proposed Security Requirements Model. Derivation of security policies from security requirements and their consequent refinement is also presented in this paper. Our approach of addressing modelling issues by providing requirements for expressing security related quality of service is the key step to turn storage systems into knowledge representation systems.

**Keywords:** Grid security, requirements analysis, distributed data management.

## 1 Introduction

Grids enable access to, and the sharing of, geographically distributed heterogeneous resources such as computation, data and information sources, sensors and instruments, for solving large-scale or complex problems. One of the key Grid applications is the use of grids in emergency response. In this kind of applications, Grids become a critical information infrastructure providing essential information to emergency departments in order to minimise adverse impacts of potential tragedies. For instance, Grids may be useful in preventing floods, which can be achieved by integrating data from various sources - networks of sensors in a river basin, weather prediction centres, historical flood datasets, topography, population and land use data - for processing in sophisticated numerical flood models. The massive data sets that would need to be accessed and processed would require huge network facilities, data storage, and processing power to deliver accurate predictions. This paper focuses on one element of such critical infrastructure: Grid data management systems (GDMS).

We have carried out a formal analysis of security requirements for semantic grid services to explore how these requirements can be expressed as metadata associated to these services. It also explores issues of negotiation of the QoS parameters in order

---

* This research work is supported by the European Network of Excellence **CoreGRID** (project reference number 004265). The CoreGRID webpage is located at www.coregrid.net.

J. Lopez (Ed.): CRITIS 2006, LNCS 4347, pp. 30–41, 2006.

to reach Service Level Agreements (SLA). This work is being used to gridify the *FileStamp* distributed file system which is currently using the peer-to-peer technology for the exchange of data resources across the distributed sites. In this paper, we present a case study of *FileStamp* to explain security requirements model for GDMS.

This paper is organized in the following manner: an overview of the security functionalities of existing GDMS is given in section 2. *FileStamp* distributed file system is presented in section 3. Section 4 illustrates our proposed security requirements model. Our approach vis-à-vis the related work is discussed in section 5. Finally some conclusions are drawn in section 6 along with the outline of our future directions.

# 2 Overview of Security Functionalities in GDMS

Grid data management systems [1] offer a common view of storage resources distributed over several administrative domains. The storage resources may be not only disks, but also higher-level abstractions such as files, or even file systems or databases.

In this section, an overview of the security functionalities of various existing GDMS is presented:

## 2.1 ARMADA

Using the Armada framework [2], grid applications access remote data sets by sending data requests through a graph of distributed application objects. The graph is called an *armada* and the objects are called *ships*.

Armada provides authentication and authorization services through a security manager known as the *harbor master*. Before installing an untrusted ship on a harbor, the harbour master authenticates the client wishing to install the ship and authorizes use of the host resources based on the identity of the client and on the security policies set by the host.

The harbor master uses authentication mechanisms, provided by the host machine, to identify clients that wish to install ships on the harbor. The host provides mechanisms that implement security policies set by the host administrator. The options for implementing authentication include using SSH or using Kerberos authentication service.

The most common approaches used to protect system resources from untrusted code are hardware protection (e.g., running the untrusted code in a separate Unix process), software fault isolation (SFI) [3], verification of assembly code [4-5], and use of a type-safe language (e.g., Java or Modula3 [6]). Hardware protection requires untrusted code to run in a separate address space from the harbor. While this clearly protects the harbor from the client code, the overhead of communicating through normal IPC system calls is quite high. Both SFI and verification of assembly code offer promising solutions, but they typically target a limited set of machines, making them non-portable. Type-safe languages provide portability and memory protection for untrusted code: two important features for heterogeneous grid environments.

## 2.2 GridNFS

GridNFS [7] is a middleware solution that extends distributed file system technology and flexible identity management techniques to meet the needs of grid-based virtual organizations. The foundation for data sharing in GridNFS is NFS version 4 [8], the IETF standard for distributed file systems that is designed for security, extensibility, and high performance.

The challenges of authentication and authorization in GridNFS are met with X.509 credentials, which can bridge NFSv4 and the Globus Security Infrastructure, allowing GSI identity to be used in access control lists on files exported by GridNF servers.

The addition of data servers to the NFSv4 protocol does not require extra security mechanisms. The client uses the security protocol negotiated with a state server for all nodes. Servers communicate over RPCSEC_GSS, the secure RPC mandated for NFSv4. A failed state server can recover its runtime state by retrieving each part of the state from the data servers and the failure of a data server is not critical to system operation.

## 2.3  GFARM

The Gfarm file system [9] is a parallel file system, provided as a Grid service for peta-scale data-intensive computing on clusters of thousands of nodes. To execute user applications or access Gfarm files on the Grid, a user must be authenticated by the Gfarm system, or the Grid, basically by using the Grid Security Infrastructure [10] for mutual authentication and single sign-on. However, the problem here is that the Gfarm system may require thousands of authentications and authorizations from amongst thousands of parallel user processes, the Gfarm metadata servers, and the Gfarm file system daemons, thus incurring substantial execution overhead. To suppress this overhead, the Gfarm system provides several lightweight authentication methods when full Grid authentication is not required, such as within a trusted cluster.

## 2.4  GVFS

Grid Virtual File System (GVFS) [11] is a virtualized distributed file system for providing high-performance data access in grid environments and seamless integration with unmodified applications.

GVFS utilizes user level proxies to dynamically map between short-lived user identities allocated by middleware on behalf of a user. The data transfer in GVFS is on demand and transparent to the user. GVFS employs client-side proxy managed disk cache through user-level proxies that can be customized on a per-user or per-application basis. For instance, cache size and write policy can be optimized according to the knowledge of a Grid application. A more concrete example is enabling file-based disk caching by meta-data handling and application-tailored knowledge to support heterogeneous disk caching. The proxy cache can be deployed in systems which do not have native kernel support for disk caching, e.g. Linux. Because the proxy behaves both as a server (receiving RPC calls) and a client (issuing RPC calls), it is possible to establish a virtual file system by forwarding along a chain of multiple proxies. Thus in addition to the server-side proxy (responsible for authenticating requests and mapping identities), another proxy can be started at the client-side to establish and manage disk caches. Furthermore, a series of proxies, with independent caches of different sizes, can be cascaded between client and server, supporting scalability to a multi-level cache hierarchy.

The GVFS literature does not provide details about the security functionalities. It only mentions the use of Secure Shell - Data access is forwarded by GVFS proxies via SSH tunnels.

## 3   *FileStamp*: A Distributed File System

In this section, we present a case study of *FileStamp* – an existing distributed file system. *FileStamp* is basically a peer-to-peer file sharing system which is in the process of gridification at present.

The exponential growth in the scale of distributed data management systems and corresponding increase in the amount of data being handled by these systems require efficient management of files by maintaining consistency, ensuring security, fault tolerance and good performance in terms of availability and security. Read only systems such as CFS [12] are much easier to design as the time interval between meta-data updates is expected to be relatively high. This allows the extensive use of caching, since cached data is either seldom invalidated or kept until its expiry. Security in a read-only system is also quite simple to implement. Digitally signing a single root block with the administrator's private key and using one-way has functions allow clients to verify the integrity and authenticity of all file system data. Finally, consistency is hardly a problem as only a single user, the administrator, can modify the file system.

Multi-writer file systems face a number of operational issues not found in the read only systems. These issues include maintaining consistency between replicas, enforcing access control, guaranteeing that update requests are authenticated and correctly processed, and dealing with conflicting updates.

*FileStamp* is a distributed file system. It is developed to find a solution to the problems encountered in multi-writer file systems. It is a highly scalable, completely decentralized multi-writer peer-to-peer file system. The current version of the *FileStamp* is based on Pastis [13] architecture. It aims at making use of the aggregate storage capacity of hundreds of thousands of PCs connected to the Internet by means of a completely decentralized network. Replication allows persistent storage in spite of a highly transient node population, while cryptographic techniques ensure the authenticity and integrity of file system data.

Routing and data storage are handled by the Pastry [14] routing protocol and the PAST [15] distributed hash table (DHT). The good locality properties of Pastry/PAST allow Pastis to minimize network access latencies, thus achieving a good level of performance when using a relaxed consistency model. In Pastis, for a file system update to be valid, the user must provide a certificate signed by the file owner which proves that he has write access to that file.

Pastis security features require considerably enhancement for the successful gridification of the *FileStamp*. These include the use of standard credentials for authentication (such as X.509 certificate); authorization scheme for policy the management and enforcement (such as CAS: Community Authorization Service [16]); encrypted movement of data between remote sites; and some dependable fault tolerance mechanism. These requirements are elaborated in [17]. However, to understand the proposed fault-tolerance mechanism, consider a grid storage system shown in figure 1a. Data elements A and B are distributed over several resources. $A_1$ and $A_2$ are the subparts of A; $B_1$ and $B_2$ are the subparts of B. Figure 1b depicts a failure situation where a node is broken down. The resource broker will start searching resources that match the storage requirements and preferences of the stakeholders of the data elements. This is a critical phase as security negotiations and the matching of security parameters have to be resolved besides seeking the storage capacities and other performance parameters. The security assurances should be met before moving the dataset to a new node. Figure 1c shows that the resource broker didn't find a node that can host both $A_1$ and $B_2$ simultaneously (as was the case before the failure occurred) and hence it found two different nodes – one for $A_1$ and the other for $B_2$ – to maintain the same security level of these elements.

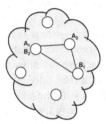 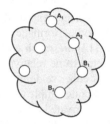

**Fig. 1a.** Distributed data elements

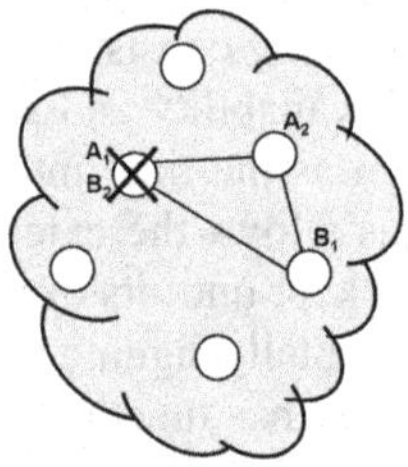

**Fig. 1b.** 1 storage site is broken down

**Fig. 1c.** Redistribution of data-set

## 4 Security Requirements Model

This section presents a concise security requirements model of distributed file systems. This model is built by using KAOS [18] requirements engineering tool Objectiver [19]. This model is although not comprehensive yet it is used to illustrate the various components of the security requirements model.

### 4.1 Problem Statement

We consider a simple problem statement so that more attention could be given to elaborate the various components of the security requirements model rather than indulging into the complexities of the model itself.

The problem addressed in this section is to assure fault tolerant and secure management of a distributed file system (*FileStamp*). Fault tolerance is attained by keeping an adequate number of replicas at different nodes; whereas the secure management is based on the encrypted transfer of files between the nodes. The various parameters involved in attaining in these two broad requirements are illustrated in this section.

### 4.2 Goal Model

Figure 2 depicts the overall goal model of the security requirements of a distributed file system. It illustrates that the main goal of the system is to assure that the files are

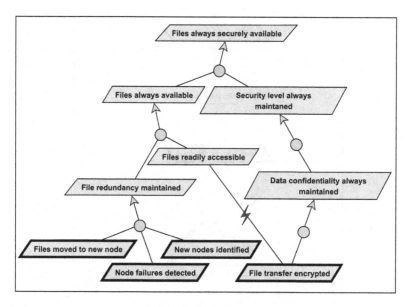

**Fig. 2.** Goal Model

always secure and available. This overall goal is refined with the sub-goals of availability and security. These sub-goals are further refined to describe the set of auxiliary sub-goals needed to elaborate the upper level goals. Finally a set of requirements is associated with each refined sub-goal to demonstrate the prerequisite of attainment of these goals. In figure 1, the goals and sub-goals are represented by thin-lined parallelograms whereas the requirements of the refined goals are represented by the thick-lined parallelograms. A goal model also includes the constraints of attaining certain goals. For example, in figure 1, the goal *files readily accessible* is constrained by the data confidentiality requirement of *encrypted file transfer*.

### 4.3 Responsibility Model

By definition, the responsibility model is derived from the goal model. A responsibility model contains all the responsibility diagrams. A responsibility diagram describes for each agent, the requirements and expectations that it is responsible for, or that have been assigned to it.

Figure 3 contains the responsibility diagrams of the problem statement considered in this section. It assigns the responsibility of the requirement *encrypted file transfer* to the *data manager*. Likewise, the responsibility of the requirement *node failures detected* is assigned to the *data monitor* that monitors the object *node* and employs the *monitor* and *notify* operations to keep an eye on the performance.

### 4.4 Object Model

The object model is used to define and document the concepts of the application domain that are relevant with respect to the known requirements and to provide static

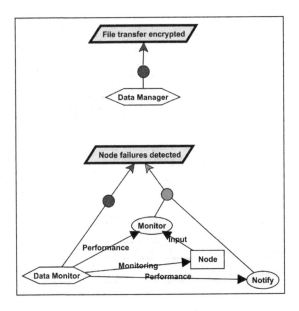

**Fig. 3.** Responsibility Model

constraints on the operational systems that will satisfy the requirements. The object model consists of objects pertaining to the stakeholders' domain and objects introduced to express requirements or constraints on the operational system. There are three types of entities that can be found in the object model: entities (independent passive objects); agents (independent active objects); and associations (dependent passive objects).

In figure 3, *node* is an object that is used as an input to the *monitor* operation. The *monitor* operation satisfies the requirement of node failure detection.

The object model is compliant with UML class diagrams as the entities correspond to UML classes; associations correspond to UML binary association links or n-array association classes. Inheritance is available to all types of objects including associations. Objects can be qualified with attributes.

### 4.5  Operation Model

The operation model describes all the behaviours that *agents* need to fulfil their requirements. Behaviours are expressed in terms of operations performed by agents.

Figure 4 shows the operation model of the problem statement considered in this section. The file transfer requirement (with or without encryption) requires an operation *move files*. Likewise the requirement of identifying new nodes requires an operation of *find available nodes*. Another example is the use of *monitor* and *notify* operations for the requirement of the detection of node failures.

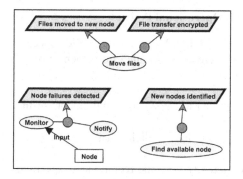

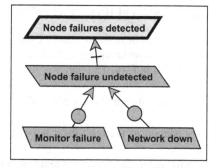

**Fig. 4.** Operation Model          **Fig. 5.** Obstacles Model

### 4.6  Dealing with Obstacles

Obstacles are the situations where a goal, a requirement or an expectation is violated. In such situation, the obstacle is said to *obstruct* the goal, requirement or expectation. Dealing with obstacles allows analysts to identify and address exceptional circumstances.

Figure 5 depicts the obstacles model of the problem statement considered in this section. It shows that undetected node failures are the obstacles for the requirement of node failure detection.

## 5  Discussions

We have considered the *FileStamp* as a case study to interrelate security requirements and security policies for grid data management system. It is a part of our ongoing work of a policy-driven approach to security requirements. The implementation of this approach in the real systems requires formal derivation of security policies from the requirements model we have presented in the preceding section. These crude policies need to undergo refinement process so that operational policies can be obtained. These operational policies can be directly implemented to a system – GDMS in the context of our current work.

### 5.1  Derivation of Security Policies from Security Requirements

Security policies define the types of security measures that are used and what scope those measures have but not how those measures are designed or implemented. System security policies are derived from security requirements that specify the risks and threats that must be countered. These policies are system-specific and reflect the threat environment and the security problems assumed by system designers.

We need to derive implementable policy from the high level requirements model. This policy is then refined into operational policy. At the operational stage, it is ready to be implemented in the real systems.

## 5.2   Refinement of High-Level Policies into Operational Policies

Policy refinement is the process of transforming a high-level, abstract policy specification into a low-level, concrete one. The objectives of a policy refinement process are identified in [20]. They are:

- Determination of the resources that are needed to satisfy the requirements of the policy.
- Translation of the high-level policies into operational policies that the system can enforce.
- Verification that the lower level policies actually meet the requirements specified by the high-level policy.

The first of these objectives involves mapping abstract entities defined as part of a high-level policy to concrete objects/devices that make up the underlying system. The second specifies the need to ensure that any policies derived by the refinement process be in terms of operations that are supported by the underlying system. The final objective requires that there be a process for incrementally decomposing abstract requirements into successively more concrete ones, ensuring that at each stage the decomposition is correct and consistent.

For the refinement of higher level policies into operational policies, we need a formal representation for objects, their behaviour and organisation; a technique for refining high-level goals into more concrete ones; and finally a means of inferring the combination of operations that will achieve the concrete goals. We intend to use the formalism presented in [21] to model the behaviour and organisation of the objects, together with the goal elaboration technique presented in [22] to refine high-level goals into concrete ones. However, the refined goals cannot be directly used in policies without first identifying the operations that will achieve them.

## 5.3   Related Work

Some techniques have been defined with the objective of taking security into account at requirement engineering. A main inspiration in our work is [23], which further extend KAOS for the specification and analysis of security requirements. The extended framework addresses malicious obstacles (called anti-goals) set up by attackers to threaten security goals. Threat trees are built systematically through anti-goal refinement until leaf nodes are derived that are either software vulnerabilities observable by the attacker or anti-requirements implementable by this attacker. Then, new security requirements are obtained as countermeasures. Massacci proposes in [24] extensions to the Tropos methodology –an agent-oriented software engineering methodology for modelling and analysis trust and security requirements. Central to their work is that is the assumption that in modelling security and trust it is necessary to distinguish between the actors that manipulate resources, accomplish goals or execute tasks, and actors that own the resource or the goals. They first develop a trust model, determining the trust relationship between actors, and then a functional model, where it is analysed the actual delegations against the trust model, checking whether an actor that offer a service is authorised to have it.

A first attempt to derive policies from high-level goals is presented by Bandara et al in [25]. Their main objective is to refine high-level policies -represented as a goal-into low-level operations that will allow a given system to achieve the desired goal. Their approach combines the KAOS requirement-engineering methodology, the Event Calculus, and abductive reasoning techniques. We have been inspired by their work, but taking an alternative approach. We use security requirements to derive the high-level policies, which can then be further refined using their approach. Close to Bandera's work is the work of Rubio-Loyola [26], which refines policies by applying requirement engineering and model checking techniques. His approach allows one to find system executions aimed at fulfilling low-level goals that logically entail high-level administrative guidelines. From system executions, policy information is abstracted and eventually encoded into a set of refined policies specified in Ponder. Above approaches have been applied to the networking management domain. Our interest is in applying them to the Grid area.

## 6  Conclusions

In this paper we have presented our work on modelling of security requirements of grid data management systems (GDMS). This work addresses issues related to storage management policies by modelling security requirements at the application level, and the requirements on mechanisms for using storage semantic web services. We have illustrated our proposed model with the help of a case study of the gridification of an existing distributed file system – *FileStamp*.

Our approach is a pioneer work towards the gridification of a grid data management system as most of the gridification efforts are limited to the fabric layer and the applications layer. Our long term objective is to transform storage systems into knowledge representation systems with suitable security features.

Our immediate future directions are the further elaboration and refinement of our model in the KAOS. Then we shall work on the derivation of security policy from the comprehensive and refined requirements model and eventually the refinement of the high level policy into operational policy for its implementation on a real grid data management system. We shall employ the Service Level Security Agreements to settle the conflicts.

## References

1. Grid File System Working Group (GFS-WG) Information Document, *A Survey of the Major Grid File Systems*, Global Grid Forum (GGF) Eleventh Meeting (GGF11), Honolulu, Hawaii, USA, June 6-10, 2004
2. Oldfield, R., Kotz, D., Armada: A Parallel File System for Computational Grids, Proceedings of the First IEEE/ACM International Symposium on Cluster Computing and the Grid 2001 (CCGRID2001), 15-18 May 2001, pp 194-201

3.  Wahbe R., Lucco S., Anderson T. E., and Graham S. L., *Efficient Software-based Fault Isolation*, Proceedings of the Fourteenth ACM Symposium on Operating Systems Principles, Ashville, NC, 1993. ACM Press. pp 203-216,
4.  Morrisett G., Walker D., Crary K., and Glew N., *From System F to Typed Assembly Language*, Proceedings of the Twenty-Fifth ACM Symposium on Principles of Programming Languages, San Diego, CA, Jan. 1998
5.  G Necula., *Proof-Crrying Code*, Proceedings of the Twenty-Fourth ACM Symposium on Principles of Programming Languages, pages 106-119, Paris, France, 1997.
6.  Nelson G., *System Programming in Modula-3*. Prentice Hall, 1991
7.  Honeyman P., Adamson W. A., McKee S., *GridNFS: Global Storage for Global Collaborations*, CITI Technical Report 05-3, 17 May 2005
8.  S. Shepler, B. Callaghan, D. Robinson, R. Thurlow, C. Beame, M. Eisler, and D. Noveck, *Network File System (NFS) version 4 Protocol, RFC 3530*, 2003.
9.  Tatebe O., Soda N., Morita Y., Matsuoka S., Sekiguchi S., *Gfarm v2: A Grid file system that supports high-performance distributed and parallel data computing*, Proceedings of the 2004 Computing in High Energy and Nuclear Physics (CHEP04), Interlaken, Switzerland, September 2004.
10. Foster I., Kesselman C., Tsudik G., Tuecke S., *A Security Architecture for Computational Grids*, ACM Conference Proceedings 1998, ISBN 1-58113-007-4, pp 83-92
11. The Grid Virtual File System (GCFS) Project of University of Florida – http://www.acis.ufl.edu/~ming/gvfs/
12. Dabek F., Kaashoek M., Karger D., Morris R., and Stoica I., *Wide-Area Cooperative Storage with CFS*, In the proceedings of 18th ACM Symposium on Operating Systems Principles (SOSP'01), chateau Lake Louise, Banff, Canada, October 2001
13. INRIA Project PASTIS http://regal.lip6.fr/projects/pastis/pastis_fr.html
14. Rowstron A. and Druschel P., *Pastry: Scalable, Distributed Object Location and Routing for Large-Scale Peer-to-Peer Systems*, Proceedings of the IFIP/ACM International Conference on Distributed Systems Platforms (Middleware), 2001, pp 329-350
15. Druschel P., and Rowstron A., *Past: Persistent and Anonymous Storage in a Peer-to-Peer Networking Environment*, Proceedings of the 8th IEEE Workshop on Hot Topics in Operating Systems (HotOS-VIII)? 2001), pp. 65-70
16. Foster I., Kesselman C., Pearlman L., Tuecke S., and Welch V., *The Community Authorization Service: Status and Future*, In Proceedings of Computing in High Energy Physics 03 (CHEP '03), 2003
17. Naqvi S., Massonet P., Arenas A., Security Requirements Analysis for FileStamp Distributed File System, CoreGRID Technical Report # TR-0038, 2006
18. KAOS Project: www2.info.ucl.ac.be/research/projects/AVL/ReqEng.html
19. Objectiver: The Requirements Engineering Tool – www.objectiver.com
20. Moffett J. and Sloman M., *Policy Hierarchies for Distributed Systems Management*, IEEE JSAC, vol. 11, pp. 1404-14, 1993.
21. Bandara A., Lupu E., and Russo A., *Using Event Calculus to Formalise Policy Specification and Analysis*, Proceedings of the 4th IEEE Workshop on Policies for Networks and Distributed Systems (Policy 2003), Lake Como, Italy, 2003.
22. Darimont R. and Lamsweerde A., *Formal Refinement Patterns for Goal-Driven Requirements Elaboration*, Proceedings of the *4th ACM Symposium on the Foundations of Software Engineering (FSE4)*, pp. 179-190, 1996.
23. Lamsweerde A., *Elaborating Security Requirements by Construction of Intentional Anti-Models*, Proceedings if ICSE 04, 26th International Conference on Software Engineering, ACM-IEEE, 148-157, 2004.

24. Giorgini P., Massacci F., Mylopoulos F., Zannone N., *Requirements Engineering Meets Trust Management: Model, Methodology and Reasoning*, In Proceedings of the Second International Conference on Trust Management. Lecture Notes in Computer Science, vol. 2995, 2004.
25. Bandara A., Lupu E., Moffett J., Russo A., *A Goal Based Approach to Policy Refinement*, Fifth IEEE International Workshop on Policies for Distributed Systems and Networks, 2004
26. Rubio-Loyola J., Serrat J., Charalambides M., Flegkas P., Pavlou G., Lafuente A., *Using Linear Temporal Model Checking for Goal-oriented Policy Refinement Frameworks*. Sixth IEEE International Workshop on Policies for Distributed Systems and Networks, 2005

# Assessing the Risk of an Information Infrastructure Through Security Dependencies

F. Baiardi[1], S. Suin[1], C. Telmon[1], and M. Pioli[2]

[1] Dipartimento di Informatica, Università di Pisa
[2] Enel Distribuzione, ENEL
{f.baiardi,stefano}@unipi.it

**Abstract.** We outline a framework for the risk assessment of information infrastructures that generalizes the notion of dependency with respect to security attributes such as confidentiality, integrity or availability. Dependencies are used to model an infrastructure at distinct abstraction levels, to discover attack strategies and to define risk mitigation plans. A plan is formulated in terms of set of countermeasures because single countermeasures may be ineffective due to alternative threat attack strategies. We do not detail the assessment steps and focus on the integration of their results to define risk mitigation plans. Lastly, we discuss the development of programming tools to support the assessment.

**Keywords:** risk assessment, mitigation plan, countermeasure, vulnerability, ranking.

## 1 Introduction

The output of a risk assessment of an ICT, or information, infrastructure [1,3,5,6] is a risk mitigation plan that defines the countermeasures to be applied to reduce the risk at an acceptable level for the owner. Risk is formally defined as the product of the probability of a successful attack and of the corresponding impact, the damage due to the attack. If vulnerabilities are known, then each vulnerability V may be paired with the risk it introduces because of the attacks it enables. The return of the investment to remove V [8] is the difference between this risk and the investment. The problem posed by this approach is that the probabilities it requires can be determined only if historical data about the infrastructure are available. For most information infrastructures this is seldom the case. Furthermore, to mitigate risk, several countermeasures have to be applied simultaneously because of alternative attack strategies that compose simple attacks into mo! re com plex ones [2,11,15,16]. Hence, the return of removing a single vulnerability cannot be easily estimated and approximated strategies are adopted. These strategies rank vulnerabilities to define a optimal order to remove them, i.e. to apply the corresponding attack countermeasures [3,13].

We present an approximated risk assessment strategy for an information infrastructure that defines cost effective risk mitigation plans by composing set of countermeasures rather than single ones. The framework models an infrastructure as a set of interdependent components, each defining a set of operations

J. Lopez (Ed.): CRITIS 2006, LNCS 4347, pp. 42–54, 2006.

working on an internal state and that are invoked by some users. Three attributes for each component are introduced, namely confidentiality, integrity and availability. Each may be controlled by invoking some component operations. The relations among components are described by security dependencies [3,10,9]. A security dependency involves some source components, a destination one and a security attribute for each component. The meaning is that the control of the attributes of the source components implies that of the attribute of the destination one. The infrastructure is modeled as a labeled hypergraph with a node for each component and a hyperarc for each dependency. The number of hyperarcs and of nodes depends upon the abstraction level of the model. Security dependencies are inspired to cascade failures and domino effect models [3,13]. Several approaches and tools have exploited this notion, sometimes without introducing it in an explicit way. An excellent survey of approaches and tools is [9]. To the best of our knowledge, our approach is the one that exploits this notion at distinct abstraction levels, according to the detail level of the assessment.

Sect.2 of the paper defines the modeling of the infrastructure, of attacks and threats. Sect.3 introduces the notion of minimal set of countermeasures. Sect. 4 defines the ranking of countermeasures and the deduction of mitigation plans. Sect.5 and 6 discuss, respectively, the notion of risk and the development of programming tool to assist the assessment. Important analyses such as the vulnerability or the impact ones will not be described, as their methodologies are fully orthogonal to our framework that aims to integrate their results to define a cost effective risk mitigation plan.

## 2  Modeling Infrastructures, Attacks and Threats

This section describes the modeling of entities of interest.

### 2.1  Component Dependencies and Infrastructure Hypergraph

The framework models the infrastructure as a set of interdependent components, each consisting of some internal state and of the operations it implements. Three security attributes of a component are considered:

1. confidentiality. Its control implies the ability of reading the component state;
2. integrity. Its control implies the ability of updating the state;
3. availability. Its control implies the ability of managing the component, i.e. of determining the users that can invoke its operations.

The framework does not describe the state or the operations and represents user rights as a set of pairs ⟨*component, attribute*⟩, where attribute ∈ {$c, i, a$}. A user controls an attribute because of either the component operations it can invoke or dependencies from other components. Each security dependency, or simply dependency, is characterized by the source components from where it originates, by a destination one and by a security attribute for each component. Distinct dependencies correspond to alternative ways of controlling an attribute.

A first example of dependency is the one between a password and the resources it controls. Anyone that controls the password confidentiality, i.e. can read it, can access the resources that the password protects. If just one password is introduced, the control of its confidentiality implies that of several components. If, instead, several passwords exist, then each one enables a limited control and the confidentiality of several ones has to be controlled to control several components. A second example concerns a web server connected to a network through components that route and deliver requests to the server. Anyone that controls the availability of the components fully controls the server availability. Consider now a firewall that protects a computer network. The control of the availability of the communication infrastructure between the network and the outside world depends upon the integrity of the firewall rules.

The infrastructure hypergraph IH is a labeled directed hypergraph that represents components and dependencies. IH includes a node n(C) for each component C and one hyperarc from $\{n(C1),...,n(Ck)\}$ to n(C) for each dependency from $\{C1,...,Ck\}$ to C. As shown in Fig. 1, there is one label for each tail of the hyperarc and one for the head, to denote, respectively, the attributes to be controlled and the controlled one.

Starting from the set S of the rights of a user U and the dependencies in IH, we determine all the attributes U controls by computing TC(S, IH), the transitive closure of S, according to paths of IH. At first, we consider an element $\langle C, w \rangle$ of S and mark any tail leaving from n(C) and labeled by w. After examining all the elements in S, we consider a hyperarc h such that all its tails have been marked. Assume the head of h is labeled by g and the destination node is n(D). We mark n(D) and any tail leaving from it that is labeled by g. Furthermore, if g = a, U manages the component D. Hence, we also mark any tail leaving from n(D) because U can assign to itself any rights on D and so it can control any attribute of D. The procedure is iterated till no node can be marked. The components corresponding to the marked nodes, together with the labels of the hyperarcs used to reach each node, define the rights in the transitive clos! ure of S. We detail in the following why we assume a user grants rights only to herself. As an

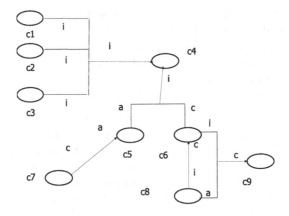

**Fig. 1.** An Infrastructure Hypergraph

example, in the hypergraph in Fig.1, a user that controls the confidentiality of c7 and the integrity of c8 controls the availability of c5, the confidentiality of c6 and the integrity of c4.

## 2.2   Modeling Threats and Attacks

This section describes the modelling of threats and of elementary attacks. We will consider only intelligent threats, each with a predefined set of goals.

To handle uniformly insiders and external threats, we model each threat as a further user that initially owns some rights on some components. Hence, a user U is anyone interested in attacking the infrastructure and it is paired with information about goals, resources it can accesses and initial rights. SGoal(U) is the set of the goals of U. Each goal $g$ is a set of rights and U **achieves** $g$ when and if it owns any right in $g$. R(U) describes the resources U can exploit in its attacks. Elements of R(U) are tuples of elements, each describing a distinct resource such as computational resources, know how, knowledge about the infrastructure and so on. We do not detail alternative definitions of R(U) because we are only interested in a partial order for each resource. These orders supports the definition of a partial order ◁ among the tuples of R(U) based upon a pair wise comparison of the tuples. The last information paired with U is Init(U), the rights of U before executing any attack.

Consider, as an example, a web server that receives its data from a database system. This infrastructure may be modeled as two components, the web server and the database. The integrity of web server data depends upon the integrity of those in the database. Here, three classes of users may be introduced that initially have, respectively, some rights on the web server, on the database or no rights at all. The first two classes model users that can access or update information in the components, the last one users that cannot access any information. The goal of users that aim to deface the web server is to control the server integrity. Instead, that users interested in manipulating the data is to control the database integrity. Because of dependencies, any user that controls the database integrity also controls that of the web server.

We describe now the modeling of elementary attacks that are composed into attack strategies against the infrastructure [12,16,18,19,20,21]. Even if the definition of elementary attack depends upon the component abstraction level, we define an attack A to be elementary if it consists of a sequence of predefined actions against one infrastructure component denoted by T(A). These actions may be successful if the components are affected by all the vulnerabilities in the set V(A). Distinct sets of vulnerabilities correspond to distinct attacks that may exploit the same mechanism, i.e. a buffer or a stack overflow. pre(A), the **precondition** of A is the set of rights a user U needs to execute A. If A is successful, U achieves any right in post(A), the postcondition or the **effect** of A. pre(A) and post(A) are disjoint. Owning the rights in pre(A) is a necessary, but not sufficient, condition to execute A, because this also requires that U can access R(A), the res! ources to implement A. This is possible if R(A)◁ R(U). If A is successful, U owns any right in TC(U(BA)∪ post(A), IH), the transitive closure of the union of the rights U(BA),that U owns before A, with those acquired because of the success of A. IH is the infrastructure hypergraph.

The last information paired with A is comp(A), a relative evaluation of the complexity of A. The lowest complexity corresponds to an attack that can be implemented by a programming tool, because any user can execute it. At the opposite extreme we have attacks that cannot be implemented by a tool and require a deep technical know how and detailed knowledge on the infrastructure. The number of discrete intervals within the range is a function of the accuracy of the assessment.

## 2.3   Infrastructure Evolutions

A user U can achieve a goal $g$ by composing elementary attacks into strategies. Since U continues to execute elementary attacks till achieving $g$, we can characterize the state of the infrastructure in terms of the users that are considered and of the transitive closure of each user rights in the considered state. A state transition is fired by a successful elementary attack. Hence, an infrastructure state S is modeled as a tuple. $\langle \langle U1, S1 \rangle, ..., \langle Un, Sn \rangle \rangle$ where U1, .., Un are the users and Si is the set of rights of Ui. Since ER(Ui,S), the rights of Ui in the state S, results from a transitive closure, ER(Ui,S)= TC(ER(Ui,S), IH) holds for $1 \leq i \leq n$ in any state S. An attack A is feasible for Ui in a state S if pre(A) $\subseteq$ ER(Ui, S) and R(A)◁ R(Ui).

At first, we consider attack strategies of a single user and then generalize to a set of users. An **evolution due to Ui** is a non empty sequence of infrastructure states St1, ..., Stfin where:

1. St1 is the initial infrastructure state,
2. in any intermediate state Stj the attack Aj is feasible for Ui,
3. after the execution of Aj in Stj, Ui owns the transitive closure of rights in the union of post(A) and of ER(Ui,Stj),
4. in the final state Stfin, and only in this state, Ui achieves $g$, a goal in SGoal(Ui),
5. by executing any Aj, Ui achieves at least one right $er$ such that:
   (a) Ui does not own $er$ in the state Stj before executing Aj,
   (b) $er$ belongs either to $g$ or to the preconditions of an attack executed after Aj.

The last condition implies that Ui executes any evolution attack to own a right that either belongs to $g$ or to the precondition of one of the following attacks. We assume that Ui has to execute at least one attack to achieve any goal. The number of attacks bounds the length of evolutions because a user never needs to repeat an attack. .

Each evolution due to Ui describes a strategy of Ui to compose elementary attacks to achieve the corresponding goal. Hence, if there is not an evolution where Ui achieves a goal $g$, then no sequence of attacks enables Ui to achieve $g$. If all the evolutions due to Ui are known, we can represent the corresponding infrastructure states and state transitions as a finite state automaton. The automaton has a single initial state, the initial infrastructure state, and a final state for each goal in SGoal(Ui) that Ui can achieve. The attack graph of Ui represents states and transitions of the automaton as graph nodes and arcs. An attack path starts in the **initial node** of the graph, corresponding to the initial state of the automaton, and ends in a **success node**, a state where Ui achieves one of its goals. Distinct goals correspond to distinct success states. Each arc is paired with an attack [18,1,8]. Assume, as an example, that Ui that can a! chieve one of its goals by an attack A, but to execute A Ui requires some privileged account on a computer node. Hence, at first, Ui should control the confidentiality of a password of an account and then increase its level of privilege through a second attack, before executing A. Besides the initial states and the final one, the automaton has at least two further states where Ui controls, respectively, the confidentiality of a password of a non privileged account and a privileged account.

Two distinct evolutions are **equivalent** if they enable a user to achieve the same goal and they correspond to distinct paths of the attack graph leading to the same final node. Two evolutions are **disjoint** if they exploit distinct elementary attacks. Consider, as an example, a processing node N and the set S of nodes of the infrastructure that N trusts. A user that controls any node in S, controls N as well. If the goal of Ui is the control of N, all the evolutions that result in the control of distinct nodes in S are equivalent because they enable Ui to achieve its goal. The evolutions are disjoint because their elementary attacks have distinct targets. Consider now the evolutions resulting in the control of the same node in S. If they compose in a different way the same elementary attacks, then they are equivalent but not disjoint.

When considering evolutions due to a set of users, three cases are of interest:

- **concurrent** evolution: each user autonomously achieves one of its goals because any user will grant only to itself a right on a component it manages. Since this evolution results from the interleaving of one evolution for each user, the assessment can consider any user in isolation,
- **collusion** evolution: two users, U1 and U2, cooperate because U1 grants to U2 at least one right on a component U1 manages,
- **competition**: U1 revokes at least one right of U2 to stop an attack. This models either a denial of service attack or an action against an attacker.

Both concurrent and collusion evolutions are monotonic because a user never loses a right[9]. A worst case for collusion evolutions can be deduced by introducing virtual users, each owning the rights of the users that cooperate. Even if the framework can describe any evolution, this work is focused on concurrent evolutions. Since concurrent evolutions can be described through automata as well, we can build both an automaton and a graph that describe any sequence of attacks of any user against the infrastructure.

The notion of evolution is an important difference between our framework and those focused on reliability because it models intelligent attack strategies against the infrastructure and it is strongly related to both attack trees [7] and goal oriented planning [17]. In planning terminology, an infrastructure state corresponds to the current state of the world, while attacks are the operators that update this state till a goal is achieved. Hence, the computation of evolution can exploit most planning algorithms and the corresponding heuristics. Monotonic evolutions simplify the planning because a user never loses a right. However, while planning algorithms are usually focused on one optimum or optimal plan, we are interested in discovering all the evolutions.

## 3   Countermeasures

After defining the enabling set of an evolution and attack countermeasures, we introduce minimal sets of countermeasures, the building blocks of a risk mitigation plan.

En(ev), the **enabling set** of an evolution ev, includes any elementary attack executed in a step of ev. This notion is focused on the attacks of an evolution rather than on how they are composed. All the evolutions with the same enabling set are stopped if one attack in the set is stopped. As a consequence, if E enables at least one evolution, we are not interested in enabling sets that includes E, because all the corresponding evolutions are stopped if we stop those enabled by E. An enabling set is **minimal** if none of its proper subsets is an enabling set as well. We can stop any evolution if we know any minimal enabling set. En(ev) is minimal if no intermediate state of an evolution in ev is a final one for another evolution.

A countermeasure C(A) for an attack A exploits any combination of the followings:

  − remove one of the vulnerabilities in V(A),
  − update dependencies to prevent users that execute A from achieving all the rights in post(A),
  − update the initial rights of some users,
  − increase the resources that A requires so that some user cannot implement it.

The application of C(A) stops A because either A fails or the user that executes A cannot own the rights in post(A). We say that a countermeasure stops an evolution anytime it stops at least one of the evolution attacks. In terms of attack graphs, C(A) cuts, i.e. removes, the arcs associated with A. **Static** countermeasures are applied before an attack occurs, **dynamic** ones are applied as the attack goes on to remove some user rights. Hence, they are strongly related to competition evolutions and will not be considered in the following. We assume that there is at least one static countermeasure for each attack. This is not a loss of generality because we can always update the infrastructure to remove some component vulnerabilities. Notice that the same countermeasure can stop several attacks.

A **complete** set S of countermeasures stops any concurrent evolutions or, equivalently, it stops at least one attacks in each enabling set. Hence, some users can acquire some rights because some elementary attacks may be successful, but no user will achieve any of its goals. From another point of view, only intermediate states of the attack automaton can be reached but no final one. In term of attack graphs, a complete set defines a cut set that partitions the graph so that no subgraph includes both an initial node and a success one. A complete set of countermeasures is **minimal** if none of its proper subsets is complete. A minimal set defines a smallest set of countermeasures because it stops at least one attack for each minimal enabling set. The computation of a minimal set is an NP-hard problem and several Montecarlo or approximated strategies may be applied and they can be generalized to compute any minimal set. The next section discusses how distinct minim! al set s result in alternative risk mitigation plans.

Assume now that, for each attack A, V(A) includes just one vulnerability and that any countermeasure removes just one vulnerability, so that countermeasures can be mapped into vulnerabilities and the other way around. In this case, we can evaluate the role of V in the evolutions through an index Cr(V) that is defined as the percentage of minimal sets that remove V, i.e. that stop the attack A where V(A)=V. As Cr(V) approaches one, it becomes more and more important to remove V to stop the evolutions. Cr(V) may be useful if V is a newly discovered vulnerability or if its introduction is planned because of cost efficiency reason.

# 4    Countermeasure Ranking

To rank countermeasure, first of all we notice that cost effective risk mitigation plans should consider minimal sets only and that distinct minimal sets result in alternative plans. We define a risk mitigation plan in two steps:

1. single ranking that defines a partial order for each minimal set,
2. global ranking that merges all the partial orders.

A partial order is adopted to rank sets of countermeasures rather than single ones. In this way, we consider disjoint evolutions or, from another perspective, distinct success paths of an attack graph that lead to the same final node. If disjoint equivalent evolutions for some users exist, stopping just some of these evolutions does not prevent the users from achieving the goal. This shows that countermeasure and vulnerabilities are correlated so that applying a counter-measure is useless if other vulnerabilities enable the user to achieve the same goal through distinct attacks. Hence, two countermeasures (vulnerabilities) are correlated if they stops attacks (are exploited by attacks) in disjoint equivalent evolutions. Hence, ranking correlated countermeasures may be inconsistent if the ranking is used to plan their adoption. Notice that countermeasures for attacks in equivalent but not disjoint evolutions are not correlated because these evolutions may be stopped by a count! ermeasure for any attack they share. The next two subsections show how our approach takes correlation into account.

## 4.1    Single Ranking

First of all we define non-redundant subsets. RM is a non-redundant subset of a minimal set of countermeasures M if, for any evolution e it stops, it also stops

any evolution equivalent to $e$ and if no proper subset of RM stops all the evolutions stopped by RM. Each non-redundant subset of M is the smallest subset
of M that has to be applied to stop all the evolutions enabling some users to
achieve some of their goals. Non-redundant sets play a critical role to define a
risk mitigation plan because, if we apply a redundant set of countermeasures,
some of its countermeasures are useless and a smaller, and hence less expensive,
set achieves the same result. In other words, the application of a set of countermeasures S has the same utility of the largest non-redundant set included
in S.

We consider the partially order set, poset, that orders all the non-redundant
sets of M according to set inclusion. The bottom of the poset is $\phi$ and the top is
M. Any maximal chain from $\phi$ to M of length n defines a n-1 steps risk mitigation
plan where the i-th step applies the countermeasures in the difference set between
the i-th set and the (i+1)-th one. Suppose $\{C1, C2, C3, C4\}$ is a minimal set and
that each of C1 and C4 stops all the evolutions that result, respectively, in the
goals g1 and g4. Instead, C2 and C3 stop two equivalent, and disjoint, evolutions
resulting in g23. Hence only by applying both countermeasures simultaneously
g23 cannot be achieved. The non-redundant sets are $\{C1\}$, $\{C4\}$, $\{C2, C3\}$,
$\{C1, C2, C3\}$, $\{C2, C3, C4\}$, $\{C1, C4\}$, $\{C1, C2, C3, C4\}$. In the poset in Fig.2
a), the chain $\{C4\}$, $\{C2, C3, C4\}$, $\{C1, C2, C3, C4\}$ defines the plan that applies
at first C4, then both C2 and C3 and, at last, C1.

## 4.2   Global Ranking

This step merges the partial orders into a single one. The bottom of the resulting
poset is $\phi$, while each minimal set is a maximum. Maximal chains of the poset
define all risk mitigation plans that can stop any evolution. The number of
maximal chains that include a non redundant set S depends upon the number
of minimal sets including S.

The choice of the most appropriate plan depends upon not only the maximal
chains but also financial parameters such as the amount of the resource to be
invested in countermeasures, the distribution in time of these resources and the
return of delaying an investment. The framework does not define a strategy to
choose one maximal chain and, consequently, one plan because these financial
parameters fully determine the optimal one. Hence, only the space of possible
plans is defined. Suppose, as an example, that the resources currently available
do not support the implementation of all the countermeasures in a minimal set
and little information is available on future investment. Here, we can privilege
those chains resulting in some degrees of freedom and adopt a least commitment
plan corresponding to those chains that cross all the subsets from where any
minimal set can be reached. In this case, the choice of a chain that leads to just
one minimal set may be inappropriate, because it is immediately freezes the set
of countermeasures to be implemented even if little information is available on
future investments. Any update to this plan implies the choice of a disjoint chain
but, in turns, this implies that some of the countermeasures previously applied
are redundant, i.e. useless, in the new plan. Instead, if accurate information

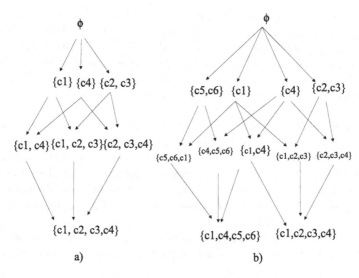

**Fig. 2.** Local and Global Ranking

about future investments is available, we can choose the optimal chain for the considered time distribution of the investment and neglect all the other ones.

Consider again the minimal set $\{C1, C2, C3, C4\}$ and assume that $\{C1, C2, C5, C6\}$ is another minimal set where C5 and C6 are countermeasures that stop the same evolutions of C3 and C4. The sets $\{C1\}$, $\{C3, C4\}$ and $\{C5, C6\}$ are some of the non-redundant sets in the global poset shown in Fig.2b). Any strategy that applies at first either $\{C5, C6\}$ or $\{C3, C4\}$ commits itself to one minimal set, instead those that at first apply either $\{C1\}$ or $\{C2\}$ can freely choose to apply any of the two minimal sets.

## 5   Taking Risk into Account

Till now we have neglected two important risk related issues, namely the impact and the probability of a successful attack. While the former can be estimated in a fairly accurate way, approximating the latter is a goal of the framework. Some preliminary considerations about risk have already been introduced when considering the resources an attack requires. In fact, by exploiting this information, we have to consider only the strategies that can be implemented by each user rather than any strategy as unconditionally security. This section shows that the introduction of risk into the framework further constrains evolutions that are considered.

At first, we introduce further attributes of an evolution to consider the corresponding risk. The first attribute is the impact of an evolution, i.e. the loss of the infrastructure owner if a user achieves the corresponding goal. We assume that there is an impact, i.e. a loss, if and only if a user achieves one of its goals. This is fully general, because the owner can pair an impact with any subset of rights owned by a user. The existence of equivalent evolutions implies that a user may exploit distinct strategies to achieve the same goal, i.e. the same impact. The benefit of a set of countermeasures is defined as the sum of the impacts the set avoids. If several users achieve the same goal, we assume that the corresponding impact is the maximum of those of each user. If a set of countermeasures does not stops all equivalent evolutions, then the corresponding impact does not contribute to the overall benefit.

A further attribute evaluates the evolution complexity, a non decreasing function of $n$, the numbers of evolution attacks, and of the complexity of each attack. Alternative definitions are the sum of the complexities, the average complexity multiplied by some function of $n$ and even the largest complexity of evolution attacks. The framework does not freeze this definition because distinct ones are appropriate in distinct contexts. Furthermore, the definition can consider any historical data about attacks.

To take risk into account, we prune evolutions occurring with a low probability because of their large complexity or low impact. Hence, we prune evolutions with

1. an impact lower than ImpT,
2. a complexity larger than OvCompT,
3. an elementary attack with a complexity larger than CompT,
4. a number of elementary attacks larger than MaxAtT.

The definition of the threshold values may exploit any statistics or historical data on attacks. After the pruning, we update both the minimal sets of countermeasures and the benefit of countermeasures by neglecting pruned evolutions. The corresponding minimal sets are denoted as a reduced minimal set, r-minimal set. The ranking of vulnerabilities and countermeasures does not change because it is independent of the definition of minimal set. An alternative definition of r-minimal sets considers the cost of countermeasures so that a set is r-minimal if its countermeasures have the lowest cost or the best cost-benefit ratio among all minimal sets.

# 6   Programming Tools

Automatic tools are important not only to reduce the time to implement the assessment, but also to guarantee that no evolution has been neglected. This is fundamental for infrastructure with a large number of components.

The two most complex steps of an assessment are the computations of all evolutions and of minimal, or r-minimal, sets of countermeasures. Both steps compute all the evolutions due to a single user through a backtracking mechanism. Instead, evolutions due to distinct users may be computed in parallel. Another important operator is the transitive closure of rights because it is applied for each evolution attack. We believe that the programming framework more appropriate to take all these features into account is the logic programming one that offers backtracking as a native feature and can handle graph data structure in a fairly simple way. In this framework, an evolution corresponds to a deduction in a theory that describes the infrastructure, the attacks, the initial set of rights and the goals of each user. Also the transitive closure of a user rights is the deduction, from the set of axioms describing the user rights, of all the theorems of the theory represented by the hy! pergra ph. This computation can be implemented in two different ways. One represents each hyperarc as a distinct clause of the logic program and applies the program to the initial set of rights. Instead, the other program version includes a set of hypergraph independent clauses that are applied to both the hypergraph and the user rights. This version implements an inference engine independent of the infrastructure that is one of the program inputs. The main advantage of the first solution is a better execution time but the program has to be updated anytime the hypergraph changes. Instead, the second version can be directly applied to the hypergraph without requiring an intermediate translation step. Now the clauses are more complex, but they do not change if the infrastructure is updated. However, both solutions exploits the built in backtracking to explore all the paths in the hypergraph and deduce all the rights of a user. The computation of evolutions heavily exploits backtracking as well because, for each state, it has to consider all elementary attacks. An optimal computation of evolutions works backward from the user goals to the initial state. A first prototype version of the inference engine to implement the deductions of interest has already been developed. A first version of the tools is under development and it will be available by the end of this year. This version will offer a friendly user interface and it will enable the user to configure those parameters that are not defined by our approach.

## 7   Conclusion

We have presented a framework to define risk mitigation plan based upon a ranking of set of countermeasures and that can handle equivalent attack strategies. Any plan that stops just one strategy and neglects equivalent ones is not cost effective because it cannot avoid all the impacts. Instead, risk mitigation plans should be defined as a sequence of sets of countermeasure, where each step stops all equivalent strategies.

Future developments concern an extensive experimentation of the prototype tools being developed with reference to real infrastructures, a detailed analysis of collusion and competition evolutions and the investigation of dependencies related to time or to state values of a component. A further problem is the application of the framework to interdependent infrastructures.

## References

1. C. Alberts, A.Dorofee, *Managing Information Security Risks.* Addison-Wesley, 2002.
2. P.Ammann, et al. *Scalable, Graph-based Network Vulnerability Analysis,* 9th ACM Conf. on Computer and Communications security, Nov. 2002, Washington, DC, USA

3. R.J. Anderson *Security Engineering A Guide to Building Dependable Distributed Systems*. John Wiley & Sons, 2001.

4. F.Baiardi, et al.*Constrained Automata: a Formal Tool for ICT Risk Assessment*, NATO Advanced Research Workshop on Information Security and Assurance, Marocco, June 2005

5. B.Barber, J. Davey, *The use of the CCTA risk analysis and management methodology CRAMM*. Proc. MEDINFO92, North Holland, 1589 pp.1593, 1992.

6. CORAS: A platform for risk analysis of security critical systems. IST-2000-25031, 2000.

7. J. Dawkins, C. Campbell, J. Hale, *Modeling Network Attacks: Extending the Attack Tree Paradigm*, Statistical and Machine Learning in Computer Intrusion Detection, June 2002.

8. L. Gordon,M. Loeb. The economics of information security investment. *ACM Trans. on Information and System Security* 5(4) 2002. pp.438-457.

9. R.P. Lipmann, K.W. Ingols, *An Annotated Review of Past Paper on Attack Graphs*, Project Report, Lincoln Lab. MIT, March 2005.

10. IEC 1025: 1990 Fault tree analysis (FTA).

11. S. Jha, O. Sheyner , J. Wing, *Two Formal Analysis of Attack Graphs*, 15th IEEE Computer Security Foundations Workshop , p.49, June 2002.

12. P. Moore, R. J. Ellison, R. C. Linger,*Attack modeling for information security and survivability*, CMU/SEI- 2001-TN001.

13. National Infrastructure Advisory Council, The Common Vulnerability Scoring System, Final Report and Recomandations, Oct. 2004

14. P. Ning, et al., *Constructing attack scenarios through correlation of intrusion alerts*, 9th ACM Conf. on Computer and Communications Security, Nov. 2002, Washington, DC, USA.

15. C. Phillips, L. Painton Swiler, *A graph-based system for network-vulnerability analysis*,Workshop on New Security Paradigms, p.71-79, Sept.1998.

16. R. Ritchey, et al., *Representing TCP/IP Connectivity For Topological Analysis of Network Security*, 18th Annual Computer Security Applications Conf, p.25, Dec. 2002.

17. S.Russell, P.Norving, *Artificial Intelligence: a Modern Approach*, Prentice Hall, 2003

18. O. Sheyner, et al., *Automated Generation and Analysis of Attack Graphs*, Proc. of the 2002 IEEE Symposium on Security and Privacy, May 12-15, 2002.

19. O. M. Sheyner, *Scenario Graphs and Attack Graphs*, CMU-CS-04-122,2004.

20. L.P. Swiler, C. Phillips, D. Ellis, S. Chakerian, *Computer-Attack Graph Generation Tool*, Proc. of the DARPA Information Survivability Conf, June 2001.

21. V.Swarup, S.Jajodia, J.Pamula, *Rule-Based Topological Vulnerability Analysis*, 3rd Int. Wor. on Math. Methods, Models and Arc. for Network Security, S.Petersburg Sept. 2005.

# Modelling Risk and Identifying Countermeasure in Organizations

Yudistira Asnar and Paolo Giorgini

Department of Information and Communication Technology
University of Trento, Italy
{yudis.asnar,paolo.giorgini}@dit.unitn.it

**Abstract.** Modelling and analysing risk is one of the most critical activity in system engineering. However, in literature approaches like Fault Tree Analysis, Event Tree Analysis, Failure Modes and Criticality Analysis focus on the system-to-be without considering the impact of the associated risks to the organization where the system will operate. The Tropos framework has been proved effective in modelling strategic interests of the stakeholders at organizational level. In this paper, we introduce the extended Tropos goal model to analyse risk at organization level and we illustrate a number of different techniques to help the analyst in identifying and enumerating relevant countermeasures for risk mitigation.

**Keywords:** risk analysis, countermeasure identification, goal modelling.

## 1 Introduction

Software systems are more and more part of our life (look how many computers and electronic gadgets are around us), and very often they have a strong influence in our daily life decisions. Considering software systems as integral and active part of the organization introduces the needs of including the software development as part of the organizational development. In this direction, some software engineering methodologies have been proposed (e.g., Tropos [1] and KAOS [2]) to capture relationships between system-to-be and the organizational setting since the early phases of software development. Traditional techniques for modelling and analysing risk, such as Fault Tree Analysis (FTA) [3], Event Tree Analysis (ETA) [3], Failure Mode Effect and Criticality Analysis (FMECA) [4], are commonly used in Reliability and Safety community. Unfortunately, these techniques are not conceived to model risks at organizational level and they focus mainly on risks at the system level.

In this paper we present a modelling and reasoning framework that considers risk (in more general *uncertain event*) at organizational level. Several models have been proposed in literature to represent the intentions of the stakeholders in an organization, such as Tropos/*i\** [1,5], KAOS [6], GBRM [7], and ERM-COSO [8]. We propose a framework, called Goal-Risk Model, that extends the

J. Lopez (Ed.): CRITIS 2006, LNCS 4347, pp. 55–66, 2006.

Tropos methodology [9,10] with three basic layers (i.e., goal, event, and treatment). The framework introduces also number of techniques to analyse risk and identify countermeasures. The rest of the paper is organised as follows. Section 2 overviews briefly about Goal-Risk framework introducing the London Ambulance Service (LAS) [11,12] case study, then using this framework we define several categories of countermeasures that can be applied as a part of the solution to protect an organization from its risks. We define the guidelines to choose and model them in Section 3 and draw an example in LAS and Vehicle company case study. Finally, we conclude the paper and outline the future work in Section 4.

## 2   Tropos Goal-Risk Framework

Tropos goal model [9,10] proposes a formal framework to do requirement analysis by refining stakeholders' goals and ending up with the elicitation of the requirements. The framework results in a number of goal models represented as graphs $\langle \mathcal{G}, \mathcal{R} \rangle$, where $\mathcal{G}$ are goals and $\mathcal{R}$ are relations (decomposition or contribution relations). In Tropos, a goal is defined as a strategic interest of a stakeholder that intended to be achieved [1].

Each goal has two attributes SAT- $Sat(G)$ and DEN- $Den(G)$ , which quantify the value of evidence for the goal being satisfied and denied, respectively[1]. The values of the attributes are qualitatively divided in the range of *(F)ull, (P)artial, (N)one*. These attributes can infer the probability of the goal to be satisfied and denied.

Goal analysis in Tropos starts with a number of top goals (i.e., ellipse in Fig. 1) of stakeholders and each of them is refined by decomposition (AND or OR) into subgoals. For example, consider in modelling the strategic objectives of London Ambulance Service (LAS) where an ambulance needs to reach the location of Accident and Emergency (A&E) in time (Fig. 1). The goal reach the location A&E in time can be achieved by distributing ambulance over the area or dispatching the closest ambulance from the A&E location to handle the accident. Moreover, distributing ambulance over area can be achieved either by organizing the movement of ambulance s.t. cover all the area or by building many ambulance pools all over the area. This decomposition and refinements will continue until the goals are considered tangible goals, i.e., when there is an actor that can fulfil the goal.

Moreover, Tropos goal analysis allows the analyst to model the influence of the satisfaction (denial) of a goal to the satisfaction (denial) of other goals. This influence can be positive or negative and is graphically indicated by "+/−" contribution relations. Tropos also has "++" and "−−" to express *strong positive contribution* and *strong negative contribution*, respectively. For example, the goal, applying dispatch to the closest ambulance from the A&E location to reach

---

[1] There is no relation between SAT and DEN, unlike Probability Theory P'(x) = 1 - P(x).

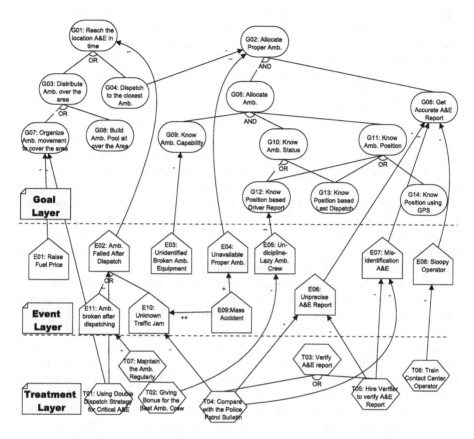

**Fig. 1.** London Ambulance Services (LAS) Case Study

the location in time, can result the assigned ambulance is not the most appropriate one, indeed the closest ambulance could be not equipped to handle that particular accident (i.e., dispatch to the closest ambulance from the A&E location gives "−" contribution to the achievement of goal allocate the proper ambulance).

We extend the Tropos goal model [9,10] introducing two new entities: event[2] (e.g., risk, opportunity) and treatment (e.g., tasks, countermeasure, and mitigations). This allows for modelling uncertain events, mainly risks, that can influence the fulfilment of one or more goals, and treatments that are needed to manage the effect of risks. Each entity has a separate layer of analysis as shown in Fig. 1: Goal layer, Event layer, and Treatment layer.

The analysis starts identifying a relevant event or an uncertain circumstance, depicted as pentagon in Fig. 1 that can influence the goal fulfilment in the goal layer. Top events are decomposed and related one to another with contribution

---

[2] A *risk* is defined as an uncertain event with negative impact and an *opportunity* with positive impact.

relations. A top-event is identified applying the approaches proposed in literature, such as obstacle analysis in KAOS [13], taxonomy-base risk identification [14], or Risk in Finance [15]. We represent *likelihood* as the level of evidence that supports or prevents the occurrence of an event (SAT or DEN), and the level of influence or *impact* of an event is encoded as the type of contribution relation between events and goals.

An event can influence more than one goal and one event can be considered as a risk for certain goals and, at the same time, as an opportunity for other goals. For instance, in LAS of Fig. 1 the risk of failure in contact centre computer system is a risk that obstructs the achievement of the goal allocate ambulance properly because LAS can not know the status of current ambulance. However, the event can also be seen as an opportunity for the goal having reliable manual standard operating procedure (SOP) for A&E, because it can give the opportunity to exercise the manual SOP. Events refinement continues until leaf-events are assessable (i.e., we can assess the likelihood of leaf-event) and the analyst ensures that each leaf-event is mutually exclusive. When a risk obstructs a goal, the denial evidence-DEN of being fulfilled is added.

Once the events have been analysed, the analyst identifies and analyses the countermeasures (denoted as hexagon in Fig. 1) to be adopted in order to mitigate the risks. We categorise a countermeasures into five categories: avoidance, prevention, alleviation, detection, and retention (the guidelines for choosing among the categories are presented in the next section). A countermeasure can be realised in two different ways: reducing the *likelihood* or reducing the *impact* [16]. In this work, we concentrate on modelling a countermeasure that reduces the likelihood of risk. Similarly for goals and events, we use SAT and DEN to represent the evidence that supports and prevents a treatment/countermeasure to be successfully executed, called success-rate. A countermeasure effects the event layer, and in particular risks. We represent the *effect* of a countermeasure as a relation, where its strength is expressed by the type of contribution relations. For instance in Fig. 1, the countermeasure maintaining ambulances regularly reduces the risk of having ambulance is broken after receiving A&E dispatch, which is denoted by "−" contribution. A countermeasure mitigates a risk by adding (propagating) evidence for the risk denial-DEN.

In our model, we also allow for relations between the treatment layer and the goal layer. This is useful to model situations where a countermeasure adopted to mitigate a risk has also a contribution (especially negative effects) to some goals. For instance in Fig. 1, the countermeasure double-dispatch ambulances for critical A&E can reduce the likelihood of the risk of ambulance failed to reach location after dispatch because there are 2 ambulances that dispatch to handle a critical A&E. This countermeasure leads to the difficulties in achieving the goal organizing the movement of ambulance s.t. cover all the area, because the countermeasure needs a greater number of ambulances than in the case of normal strategy.

The idea of model separation into 3 layers makes a flexibility in interchanging the model language in each layer, as far as the model still has the same intuition (e.g., model for goal layer is to represent the structure of the needs of the stake-holders). This flexibility helps the modeller that has already had prior experience in a particular modelling framework to reduce the learning cost. For instance, reliable engineers have been familiar with FTA [3] s.t. they can use FTA in event layer, or enterprise risk analysts are well train to build COSO-Objective model [8], then they can use that model instead of Tropos goal model. However, a semantic re-definition of relations between layers is needed to be done to adopt those modelling frameworks.

When the model has been fully developed, we start analysing the model and eliciting the most reasonable solution to fulfil the stakeholders' goals and satisfy certain preference (e.g., minimizing the total cost). A solution consists of the leaf-goals that need to be fulfilled, the treatments which need to be employed to manage the risks, and the total cost (leaf goals and treatments). The steps of analysis are the following:

**Find alternative solutions,** Stakeholders define their targets in terms of as-signment of SAT values to top-goals. Backward reasoning, as presented in [10], is used to search all the possible SAT/DEN values assignments for leaf-goals that satisfy the stakeholder's targets. These assignments are called alternative solutions.

**Evaluate alternative solutions against relevant risks,** Stakeholders de-fine the acceptable level of risk, in terms of assignment of DEN values to top-goals. Forward reasoning, as presented on [9], is used to propagate the SAT/DEN values of risk on the goal layer. If the level of risk of top-goals are below the acceptable level of risk (namely, if they produce DEN values for top-goals less than the DEN values specified by the stakeholders) then the alternative solution is considered as a candidate solution. Conversely, if the DENs of top-goals are higher than the acceptable level of risk, then we move to the next step.

**Assess countermeasures to mitigate risks,** Combinations of countermea-sures are identified to reduce the effects of risk of an alternative solution such that it becomes acceptable for the stakeholders. The alternative solution and the combination of countermeasure are considered as a candidate solution.

After identified "all" the candidate solutions, we evaluate them adopting the "minimal cost" criteria as a preference. The candidate solution with the cheapest cost, in terms of total cost of the leaf-goals and the necessary countermeasures, is the selected solution to be implemented. The complete framework of Tropos Goal-Risk (i.e., semantic definitions, reasoning mechanisms, analysis guidelines) has been defined in [17].

## 3   Countermeasure Identification

As mention before, in this paper we also provide the guidelines to identify coun-termeasures, in particular countermeasures that reduce the likelihood of risk. There are two ways to manage a risk: one can choose alternative goals with free of risk (avoidance) or trying to anticipate the risk with the countermeasures.

We categorise treatments into 5 categories of measure that can be used to manage the risk: *avoidance*[3], *prevention, alleviation, detection,* and *retention.* The
order of the categories can also be seen as the steps in eliciting the treatments.
First, the analysts try to find the way to *avoid* the risks; if it is not possible then
they should try to *prevent* the occurrence of the risks. If the prevention measures
are not adequate, then they try to identify the *alleviation* measures. If it is still
not adequate, then they have to identify the *detection* measures. Otherwise, the
organization should be prepared to *retain* the risk.

In the next sub-section section, we detail the measures by specifying the goal-
risk model characteristics that can lead the analyst in choosing the proper category of measure and what are the consequences (advantages and drawbacks) of
each category. In the model, goals, events and treatments are characterised as
follows:

- Goal (i.e., leaf goal in goal layer): the importance of a goal from the stakeholder point of view and its fulfilment type (i.e., achieve goal, maintain goal,
  and achieve-maintain goal [18]);
- Event (i.e., top event in event layer): the impacts and the likelihood of the
  event, the structure of event tree in event layer, and the type of risk (e.g.,
  avoidable, preventable, reducible);
- Treatment (i.e., leaf treatment in treatment layer), the success rate in mitigating the risk, the cost of the treatment, and the probability of cost.

### 3.1  Avoidance

It defines as an activity that tries to achieve the stakeholders' goals by choosing
a risk free alternative.

*Characteristics of the model.* The goal fulfilment results being very important for
the stakeholder, and most of the time the goal is categorised as a maintain goal
or an achieve-maintain goal (i.e., the goal that needs to be fulfilled from certain
time until the future). Thus, the analyst has to ensure its fulfilment during
the time. For example in Fig. 2, the stakeholder can fulfil the goal  knowing
ambulance position ($G_{11}$) by means of choosing  knowing ambulance position from
driver's report ($G_{12}$) or  knowing from Global Positioning System (GPS) ($G_{14}$).
In this scenario, the modeller chooses  $G_{14}$  instead of  $G_{12}$  because  $G_{11}$
needs to be fulfilled all over the time. However, this category of measure can not
always being elicited, while there could exist a circumstance where there are no
alternatives to fulfil the goal with risk-free.

*Consequences.* There is no need to introduce any treatment and/or additional
cost to use countermeasures. The only possible drawback of this category is that
the risk-free alternative could be more costly than the total cost for the risky
alternative and relative countermeasures. For instance, the cost of  $G_{14}$  is much
higher than the cost  $G_{12}$  and its treatment (e.g.,  $T_2$ ).

---

[3] Some works do not consider avoidance as a countermeasure.

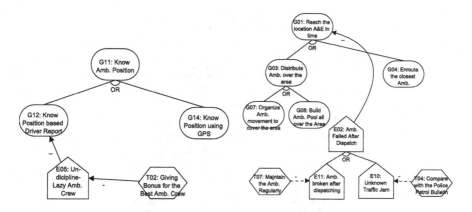

**Fig. 2.** Avoidance Means          **Fig. 3.** Prevention Means

## 3.2  Prevention

This category aims at preventing the risk occurrence by employing certain measures. Preventing risk means reducing the risk until an acceptable value for the fulfilment of stakeholders' goals. This measure operates mitigating leaf-events.

*Characteristics of the model.* The risk obstructs significantly the stakeholders' goals and it results unavoidable. This category of measure is carried on by reducing the likelihood of related leaf-events s.t. the likelihood of the top-event is also reduced. To identify the related leaf-events, we use the same technique that commonly used in defining minimal cut-set in FTA [3]. For instance in Fig. 3, $T_7$ and $T_4$ try to prevent $E_2$ occurrence by mitigating all the leaf-events of $E_2$ which are $E_{10}$ and $E_{11}$. This category is less efficient while meeting the risk/top-event with many alternative occurrences (or-decomposition), because the risk will be really reduced when we prevent all the leaf-events from risk (as we have seen in the example, we need to prevent two events in order to mitigate an event).

*Consequences.* Differently from avoidance, here it is not possible to guarantee 100% risk-free of the model since there is a chance that the treatment fails to mitigate the risk. This category is not suitable for mitigating the unlikely risk, because it has to be taken before the risk occurs, and frequently, the organization does this measure as part of their daily activity even the likelihood of risk is low.

## 3.3  Alleviation

This measure intends to reduce the risk/top-event by employing a countermeasure over the top-event. This measure does not intend to prevent the risk to be developed (i.e., the occurrence sub-events), it just mitigates top-events that impact directly to the goals fulfilment.

*Characteristics of the model.* The analyst can not find any measures from the previous categories and then introduces a new treatment. For instance in Fig. 4,

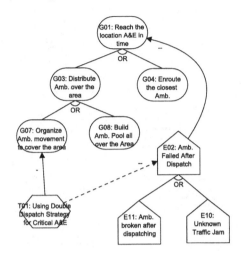

**Fig. 4.** Alleviation Means

$E_2$ can be caused by $E_{10}$ or $E_{11}$ and the analyst mitigates $E_2$ introducing $T_1$. In this scenario, the analysts can not prevent the occurrence of $E_{10}$ and $E_{11}$, and they argue that it is fine having high-risk at $E_{10}$ and $E_{11}$ as far as they can contain $E_2$ on low-risk. This type is suited for circumstances in which there are many leaf-events that need to be mitigated to prevent a top-event and thus the total cost of mitigating risk is not economical as we mention in prevention measure.

*Consequences.* Once the measure fails to mitigate the top-event than the top-event will impact to the goal layer severely without any mitigation. Unlike, in the prevention category, a failure in a countermeasure can be compensated by the effect of other countermeasures, because prevention measures, typically, are employed as a group. This measure is recommended to be applied when the analyst is really satisfied with the success-rate of the countermeasure in mitigating the risk. The probability of cost follows the likelihood of top-event/risk, which is usually less or equal than the likelihood of its sub-events. The measure is very suitable for the unlikely risks.

### 3.4   Detection

This category mitigates an intermediate event in the event tree so to reduce the risk/top-event. The advantage of applying this category is that there is a chance that several top-events share intermediate-event so mitigating an intermediate event can consequently reduce several risks/top-events at the same time.

*Characteristics of the model.* The event-trees of the risk layer share intermediate-event/sub-tree. Mitigating risks/top-events can be done employing a countermeasure over the shared intermediate-event and consequently, reducing several risks/top-events. Suppose, we are the managers of a vehicle testing plant (Fig. 5) and

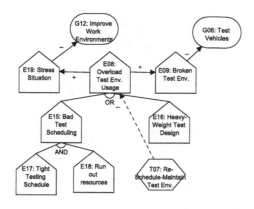

**Fig. 5.** Detection Means

we need to ensure that the plant performs test vehicle $(G_6)$ correctly. Moreover, we need to improve the situation of work environments $(G_{12})$ so to maintain quality of employees. As you see in Fig. 5, each goal has own risk, and interestingly there is a common sub-tree from these risks, namely overload test environment usage $(E_8)$. By re-schedule and maintain test environment $(T_7)$, it will reduce, hopefully, the likelihood of overload test environment usage $(E_8)$. Consequently, $E_8$ reduces the possibility of stress condition $(E_{19})$ for employees, which in turn can obstruct the achievement goal $G_{12}$. $E_8$ also reduces the chance of having broken test environment $(E_9)$ that could lead to the denial of goal $G_6$.

*Consequences.* Very bad consequences if the measure fails to reduce an intermediate event. Indeed, it results in the obstruction of one or more goals. Therefore, the analyst has to be aware of the final consequences if the countermeasure fails and how much the success rate of the countermeasure is, before choosing this type. The probability of cost of the detection measures follows the likelihood of its intermediate event (i.e., equal or higher than likelihood of top-events, and equal or less than likelihood of leaf-events).

### 3.5    Retention

It is the last alternative to deal with risks, once we can not find any treatments from the previous types.

*Characteristics of the model.* It is used when the organization does not have the capability to mitigate or control the risk (e.g., war, inflation, new competitor, natural disaster). The best thing that the organization can do is predicting the likelihood of risk and work for its consequences. For instance in Fig. 6, the risk of having new competitor $(E_7)$ is beyond the control of the company and it could obstruct the goal of having high specialized labour $(G_{15})$ because the competitors can give a better offer to the specialize labour. The only thing that the company can do is trying to give incentive for specialized labour $(T_5)$ s.t. the achievement of $G_{15}$ is maintained. Transferring the risk to an insurance company, restore the

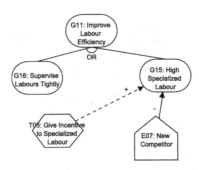

**Fig. 6.** Retention Means

obstructed goals, and design fault tolerance system can be categorised in this type, because they neither reduce the likelihood nor the effects of risks, rather they just repair the consequence of the risk.

*Consequences.* There will be a certain period of time where the goal might be un-satisfied before it is restored. Besides that, this measure can be seen as a mean to fulfil the goal besides as a treatment for the risk.

## 4   Conclusions

In this paper, we have presented a framework to model and reason about risk within the early phase of the system development. We have adopted and extended the Tropos goal modelling framework to analyse, evaluate, and select risk among the alternatives that are able to fulfil the stakeholders' goals and satisfies the preference (e.g., minimizing the total cost). The framework elicits a solution that is not only based on the stakeholders' goals but it also anticipates the existence of malicious events by introducing several treatments to manage their impacts. Therefore, the solution from 3-layers model is more robust compared to the solution that comes from the goal model.

The paper has also presented different categories of measures that typically are used to deal with the existence of risks in organizations. They are categorised as: avoidance, prevention, detection, alleviation, and retention. The analyst must understand the characteristics of the model before choosing them, especially prevention, detection, alleviation, and be aware of their consequences. Differently, an avoidance measure is usually chosen if it is feasible finding risk-free alternative, and a retention measure is the last option if there is no other type of measures which fits with the model.

The framework has been implemented as an extension of the Goal Reasoning Tool[4] (GR-Tool), shown in Fig. 7. The tool is graphical tool in which it is possible to draw the extended goal models and analyse them.

---

[4] http://sesa.dit.unitn.it/goaleditor/

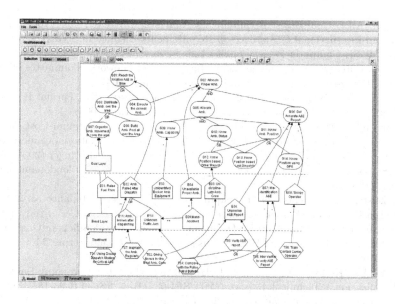

**Fig. 7.** Extended GR-Tool for Goal-Risk Modelling

Finally, as future work we want to propose also a quantitative reasoning mechanisms where evidence is expressed in term of probability model. The idea is to propose something similar to what have been already developed for the Tropos goal models.

## Acknowledgement

This work has been partly supported by the projects EU-IST-IP SERENITY 27587, FIRB-ASTRO RBNE0195K5_004, PAT-FU-MOSTRO n. 35 - (D.P.G.P. 1587 - date: 09/07/2004), and PAT-STAMPS.

## References

1. Bresciani, P., Perini, A., Giorgini, P., Giunchiglia, F., Mylopoulos, J.: Tropos: An Agent-Oriented Software Development Methodology. Autonomous Agents and Multi-Agent Systems **8**(3) (2004) 203–236
2. van Lamsweerde, A., Letier, E.: Handling Obstacles in Goal-Oriented Requirements Engineering. IEEE Transaction Software Engineering **26**(10) (2000) 978–1005
3. Stamatelatos, M., Vesely, W., Dugan, J., Fragola, J., Minarick, J., Railsback, J.: Fault Tree Handbook with Aerospace Applications. NASA (2002)
4. DoD: Military Standard, Procedures for Performing a Failure Mode, Effects, and Critical Analysis (MIL-STD-1692A). U.S. Department of Defense (1980)
5. Yu, E.: Modelling Strategic Relationships for Process Engineering. PhD thesis, University of Toronto, Department of Computer Science (1995)
6. Dardenne, A., van Lamsweerde, A., Fickas, S.: Goal-Directed Requirements Acquisition. Science of Computer Programming **20** (1993) 3–50

7. Anton, A.I.: Goal-Based Requirements Analysis. In: ICRE '96: Proceedings of the 2nd International Conference on Requirements Engineering, Washington, DC, USA, IEEE Computer Society (1996) 136

8. COSO: Enterprise Risk Management - Integrated Framework. Committee of Sponsoring Organizations of the Treadway Commission. (2004)

9. Giorgini, P., Mylopoulos, J., Nicchiarelli, E., Sebastiani, R.: Formal Reasoning Techniques for Goal Models. Journal of Data Semantics (2003)

10. Giorgini, P., Mylopoulos, J., Sebastiani, R.: Simple and Minimum-Cost Satisfiability for Goal Models. In: CAISE '04: In Proceedings International Conference on Advanced Information Systems Engineering. Volume 3084., Springer (2004) 20–33

11. LAS: London ambulance service - official website. http://www.londonambulance.nhs.uk/(2006)

12. Finkelstein, A.: Report of the inquiry into the london ambulance service. In: International Workshop on Software Specification and Design Case Study. (1995)

13. van Lamsweerde, A., Letier, E., Darimont, R.: Managing Conflicts in Goal-Driven Requirements Engineering. IEEE Transaction Software Engineering 24(11) (1998) 908–926

14. Carr, M.J., Konda, S.L., Monarch, I., UlrichCarr1993, F.C.: Taxonomy-Based Risk Identification. Technical Report CMU/SEI-93-TR-6, ESC-TR-93-183, Software Engineering Institute, Carnegie Mellon University (1993)

15. Holton, G.A.: Defining Risk. Financial Analyst Journal 60(6) (2004) 1925

16. Feather, M.S., Cornford, S.L., Dunphy, J., Hicks, K.: A quantitative risk model for early lifecycle decision making. In: Proceedings of the Conference on Integrated Design and Process Technology. (2002)

17. Asnar, Y., Giorgini, P., Mylopoulos, J.: Risk Modelling and Reasoning in Goal Models. Technical Report DIT-06-008, DIT - University of Trento (2006)

18. Fuxman, A., Kazhamiakin, R., Pistore, M., Roveri., M.: Formal Tropos: language and semantics. http://trinity.dit.unitn.it/~tropos/papers_files/ftsem03.pdf (2003)

# Modelling and Analysing Network Security Policies in a Given Vulnerability Setting

Roland Rieke*

Fraunhofer Institute for Secure Information Technology SIT, Darmstadt, Germany
rieke@sit.fraunhofer.de

**Abstract.** The systematic protection of critical information infrastructures requires an analytical process to identify the critical components and their interplay, to determine the threats and vulnerabilities, to assess the risks and to prioritise countermeasures where risk is unacceptable. This paper presents an integrated framework for model-based symbolic interpretation, simulation and analysis with a comprehensive approach focussing on the validation of network security policies. A graph of all possible attack paths is automatically computed from the model of an ICT network, of vulnerabilities, exploits and an attacker strategy. Constraints on this graph are given by a model of the network security policy. The impact of changes to security policies can be computed and visualised by finding differences in the attack graphs. A unique feature of the presented approach is, that abstract representations of these graphs can be computed that allow comparison of focussed views on the behaviour of the system. This guides optimal adaptation of the security policy to the given vulnerability setting.

**Keywords:** threats analysis, attack simulation, critical infrastructure protection, network security policies, risk assessment, security modelling and simulation.

## 1 Introduction

Information and communication technology (ICT) is creating innovative systems and extending existing infrastructure to such an interconnected complexity that predicting the effects of small internal changes (e.g. firewall policies) and external changes (e.g. the discovery of new vulnerabilities and exploit mechanisms) becomes a major problem. The security of such a complex networked system essentially depends on a concise specification of security goals, their correct and consistent transformation into security policies and an appropriate deployment and enforcement of these policies. This has to be accompanied by a concept to adapt the security policies to changing context and environment, usage patterns and attack situations. To help to understand the complex interrelations of security policies, ICT infrastructure and vulnerabilities and to validate security

---

* Part of the work presented in this paper was developed within the project SicAri being funded by the German Ministry of Education and Research.

goals in such a setting, tool based modelling techniques are required that can efficiently and precisely predict and analyse the behaviour of such complex interrelated systems. These methods should guide a systematic evaluation of a given network security policy and assist the persons in charge with finally determining exactly what really needs protection and which security policy to apply.

A typical means by which an attacker or his malware try to break into a network is, to use combinations of basic exploits to get more information or more credentials and to capture more hosts step by step. To find out if there is a combination that enables an attacker to reach critical network resources or block essential services, it is required to analyse all possible sequences of basic exploits, so called *attack paths*. Based on such an analysis, it is now possible to find out whether a given security policy successfully blocks attack paths and is robust against changes in the given vulnerability setting.

For this type of security policy analysis, a formal modelling framework is presented that, on the one hand, represents the information system and the security policy, and, on the other hand, a model of attacker capabilities and profile. It is extensible to comprise intrusion detection components and optionally a model of the system's countermeasures. Based on such an operational model, a graph representing all possible attack paths can be automatically computed. It is called *attack graph* in the following text. Now security properties can be specified and verified on this attack graph. If the model is too complex to compute the behaviour, then simulation can be used to validate the effectiveness of a security policy. The impact of changes to security policies can be computed and visualised by finding differences in the attack graphs. Furthermore, abstract representations of these graphs can be computed that allow comparison of focussed views on the behaviour of the system. If there are differences in the detailed attack graphs but no differences in the abstract representations thereof, this proves that the different policies are equally effective on the enforcement of security goals on the abstract level, even if variations in the attack paths are covered by different policy rules. The subsequent paper is structured as follows. Section 2 gives an overview of related work. The modelling approach is described in Sect. 3, while Sect. 4 presents an exemplary analysis of network security policy adaptation aspects in a given scenario. Finally, the paper ends with an outlook in Sect. 5.

## 2    Related Work

The network vulnerability modelling part of the framework presented in this paper is adopted from the approach introduced in [1] and is similar in design to an approach by Phillips and Swiler in [2] and [3]. A major contribution of [1] was the use of abstraction methods to visualise compact presentations of the graph and the inclusion of liveness analysis. Related work of Jha, Sheyner, Wing et al. used attack graphs that are computed and analysed based on model checking in [4] and [5]. Ammann et al. presented an approach in [6] that is focussed on reduction of complexity of the analysis problem by explicit assumptions of monotonicity. Recent work in this area by Noel, Jajodia et al. in [7] and [8] describes attack graph visualisation techniques while the work of Kotenko and Stepashkin in [9] is focussed on security metrics computations.

To model the ICT network, the vulnerabilities and the intrusion detection systems, a data model loosely resembling the formally defined M2D2 information model [10] is used. Appropriate parts of this model are adopted and supplemented by concepts needed for description of exploits, attacker knowledge and strategy and information for cost benefit analysis.

The model of the network security policies used in this paper is based on the Organisation Based Access Control (Or-BAC) model. A formal approach to use Or-BAC to specify network security policies was presented in [11]. This approach is used here to model the network security policies in the attack graph analysis framework.

The modelling framework is based on Asynchronous Product Automata (APA), a flexible operational specification concept for cooperating systems [12]. An APA consists of a family of so called elementary automata communicating by common components of their state (shared memory). The applied verification method is implemented in the SH verification tool [13] that has been adapted and extended to support the presented attack graph analysis methods.

Major focus of the combined modelling framework presented in this paper, is the integration of formal network vulnerability modelling on the one hand and network security policy modelling on the other hand. This aims to help adaptation of a network security policy to a given and possibly changing vulnerability setting. Recent methods for analysis of attack graphs are extended to support analysis of abstract representations of these graphs.

# 3   Modelling Critical ICT Infrastructures and Threats

The proposed operational model comprises, (1) an asset inventory including critical network components, topology and vulnerability attributions, (2) a network security policy, (3) vulnerability specifications and exploit descriptions, and (4) an attacker model taking into account the attackers knowledge and behaviour.

## 3.1   ICT Network Components

The set of all hosts of the information system consists of the union of the hosts of the ICT network and the hosts of the attacker(s). Following the M2D2 model, *products* are the primary entities that are vulnerable. A *host configuration* is a subset of products that is installed on that host and *affects* is a relation between vulnerabilities and sets of products that are affected by a vulnerability. A host is *vulnerable* if its configuration is a superset of a vulnerable set of products and the affected services are currently running.

In order to conduct a subsequent comparative analysis of attack paths, an asset prioritisation as to criticality or worth regarding relative importance of a host is required.

## 3.2   Network Security Policies

The model of the network security policies is based on the Organisation Based Access Control (Or-BAC) model. The approach to use Or-BAC to specify network security policies as presented in [11] is adopted here to model the network security policies in the attack graph analysis framework. The advantage of this choice is, that it is possible to link the policies in the formal model at an abstract level to the low level vendor specific policy rules for the policy enforcement points (PEPs) such as firewalls in the concrete ICT network. Please refer to [11] for such a transformation concept exemplified on the iptables packet filtering mechanism used in Linux.

Following the Or-BAC based concept, the network vulnerability policy is given at an abstract level in terms of *roles* (an abstraction of subjects), *activities* (an abstraction of actions) and *views* (an abstraction of objects). A *subject* in this model is any host. An *action* is a network service such as snmp, ssh or ftp. Actions are represented by a triple of protocol, source port and target port. An *object* is a message sent to a target host. Currently only the target host or rather the role of the target host is used for the view definition here. To specify the access control policy using this approach, *permissions* are given between role, activity and view.

To illustrate the concept described here, a small example scenario is given in Fig. 1(a). Modelling concepts and typical analysis outcome will be illustrated using this example scenario throughout the paper. One possible attack path is sketched in the scenario. The policy rules for the example scenario are defined by the table in Fig. 1(b).

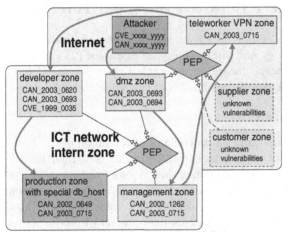

| Role (source) | View (target) | Activity (service) |
|---|---|---|
| *internet* | *internet* | *any* |
| *any* | *dmz* | *ssh* |
| *any* | *dmz* | *smtp* |
| *dmz* | *intern* | *ssh* |
| *intern* | *any* | *net* |
| *intern* | *internet* | *ftp* |
| *intern* | *internet* | *rsh* |
| *intern* | *dmz* | *ssh* |
| *db_host* | *production* | *rpc* |
| *teleworker* | *dmz* | *any* |

(b) Network security policy

(a) ICT network and vulnerabilities

**Fig. 1.** Scenario and network security policy

### 3.3 Vulnerabilities

Vulnerability specifications for the formal model are derived from the Common Vulnerabilities and Exposures (CVE/CAN) descriptions. The MITRE Corporation provides a CVE web site (http://www.cve.mitre.org/) with a list of virtually all known vulnerabilities. The CVE name is the 13 character ID used by the CVE standards group to uniquely identify a vulnerability. Additional information about the vulnerabilities also covers preconditions about the target host as well as network preconditions. Furthermore, the impact of an exploitation of a vulnerability is described. The specifications for the formal model of the vulnerabilities additionally comprise the vulnerability *range* and *impact type* assessments provided by the National Institute of Standards and Technology (NIST) (http://nvd.nist.gov/).

**Vulnerability Severity.** The Common Vulnerability Scoring System (CVSS) [14] provides universal severity ratings for security vulnerabilities. These ratings are used in the model as an example for a measure of the threat level. Another example for such a measure is the metric used by the US-CERT (cf. http://www.kb.cert.org/vuls/html/fieldhelp#metric). These measures are based on information about the vulnerability being widely known, reported exploitation incidents, number of infected systems, the impact of exploiting the vulnerability and the knowledge and the preconditions required to exploit the vulnerability. Because the approximate values included in those measures may differ significantly from one site to another, prioritising of vulnerabilities based on such measures should be used with caution.

To have a vulnerable product installed on some host, does not necessarily imply, that someone can exploit that vulnerability. A target host *is configured vulnerable*, if (1) the target host has installed a product or products that are vulnerable with respect to the given vulnerability, and (2) necessary other preconditions are fulfilled (e.g. some vulnerabilities require that a trust relation is established as for example used in remote shell hosts allow/deny concepts).

A second precondition to exploit a vulnerability is, that the target host *is currently running the respective products* such as a vulnerable operating system or server version. If a user interaction is required this also requires that the vulnerable product is currently used (e.g. a vulnerable Internet explorer).

The third necessary preconditions is, that the *network security policy permits* that the target host is reachable on the port the vulnerable product is using from the host the attacker selected as source.

### 3.4 Attacker and System Behaviour

**Attacker Knowledge.** The knowledge of exploits and hosts and the credentials on the known hosts constitute an attackers profile. Knowledge about hosts changes during the computation of the attack graph because the attacker might gain new knowledge when capturing hosts. On the other hand, some knowledge may become outdated because the enterprise system changes ip-numbers or other configuration of hosts and reachability. In case a vulnerability is exploited, the model has to cover the *effects for the attacker* (for example, to obtain additional user or root credentials on the target host) and also the *direct impact on the network and host* such as, to shut down a service caused by buffer overflow.

**Dynamic System Behaviour.** The information model presented so far covers the description of a (static) configuration of an ICT network and its vulnerabilities. In the formal model such a configuration describing the *state* of the ICT network is represented by *APA state components* (APA representation of an ICT network is covered in more detail in [1]).

To describe how actions of attacker(s) and actions of the system can change the state of the ICT network model, specifications of *APA state transitions* are used. These state transitions represent atomic exploits and optionally the actions that the ICT network system can take to defend itself or to implement vital services. Formally, a state transition can occur, when all expressions are evaluable and all conditions are satisfied. So called *interpretation variables* are used to differentiate the variants of execution of the same transition. All possible variants of bindings of interpretation variables from the state components are generated automatically. So for example for a transition modelling an exploit, all possible combinations of bindings of source and target host are computed and further evaluated.

**Attacker Behaviour.** Attacker capabilities are modelled by the atomic exploits and by the strategy to select and apply them.

A state transition modelling an exploit is constructed from, (1) a predicate that states that the attacker *knows* this exploit, (2) an expression to select source and target hosts for the exploit, (3) a predicate that states that the target *host is vulnerable* by this exploit, (4) an expression for the impact of the execution of this exploit on the attacker and on the target host as for example the shut down of services. Optional add-ons are, an assignment of cost benefit ratings to this exploit and intrusion detection checks.

Several different attackers can easily be included because an attacker is modelled as a role not a single instance and the tool can automatically generate multiple instances from one role definition.

Modelling of Denial of Service (DoS) attacks aiming to block resources or communication channels either directly or by side effects require a much more detailed model of the resources involved. This could be accomplished using the presented framework but is out of scope of this paper.

Some experiments have been made to generate a set of known exploits for the attacker(s) from a given algorithm. If for example it is assumed that the attacker knows 3 different exploits, then all combinations of 3 exploits from the set of all specified exploits have to be computed and further analysed. Another example for an attacker strategy is, that the attacker uses only exploits for vulnerabilities with a severity above a given threshold. This is based on the assumption, that the vulnerability severity reflects the probability of exploitation of a vulnerability.

**Composition of a Model and Computation of an Attack Graph.** The SH
verification tool [13] is used to analyse this model. It manages the components
of the model, allows to select alternative parts of the specification and automatically "glues" together the selected components to generate a combined model
of ICT network specification, vulnerability and exploit specification, network
security policy and attacker specification.

After an initial configuration is selected, the attack graph (reachability graph)
is automatically computed by the SH verification tool. Also, on the fly analysis
allows, to stop computation automatically when specified conditions are reached
(or invariants are broken), so called break conditions can be specified using
regular expressions. A violation of a security property for example, can in many
cases be specified as a break condition.

**Attack Graph of the Example Scenario.** The computed attack graph for
the simple example scenario (assuming the attacker knows all exploits) has 500
nodes and 4136 edges. Now we assume as a more realistic attacker behaviour,
that the attacker will only exploit vulnerabilities with a severity level above
a given minimum. In the example scenario, a severity level of 4 results in an
attack graph with 178 nodes and 1309 edges. This graph is still far too big
to inspect it manually. Figure 2 shows a small section of it. Nodes with circle shape depict states where the successors are completely shown, nodes with
rectangular shape depict nodes where the successors are cropped. For example the edge $M4 \longrightarrow M5$ depicts the application of an exploit where the ssh-
vulnerability $CAN\_2003\_0693$ was used and the edge $M4 \longrightarrow M6$ depicts an
exploit based on the same vulnerability but in this case operating stealth (not
detected).

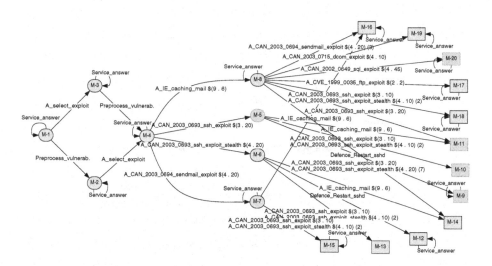

**Fig. 2.** Attack graph of example scenario (small section)

## 4   Evaluation of the Model

**Abstractions.** Abstract representations of the attack graph can be computed to visualise and analyse compacted information focussed on interesting aspects of the behaviour. The mappings used to compute the abstract representations of the behaviour have to be *property preserving*, to assure that properties are *transported* as desired from a lower to a higher level of abstraction and no critical behaviour is hidden by the mapping. Such properties, namely *simplicity*, are given in [15] and and a check for simplicity is implemented in the SH verification tool [13]. In some applications the SH verification tool already computed graphs of about 1 million edges in acceptable time and space. But it is impossible to visualise a graph of that size. So abstraction focussing on some interesting aspect is definitely a comfortable way to go in this case.

**An Example for the Usage of Behaviour Abstraction.** For this experiment, the vulnerability *range* and *impact type* assessments provided by NIST (cf. Sect. 3.3) are utilised. Range types of the vulnerabilities in the example scenario are *remote* (remotely exploitable) and *local* (locally exploitable). Impact types used here are *unspecific* (provides unauthorised access), *user* (provides user account access) and *root* (provides administrator access).

**Step 1 - Define a Mapping.** Figure 3 defines a mapping of all transitions representing the exploit of a vulnerability to the respective range and impact types of the vulnerabilities.

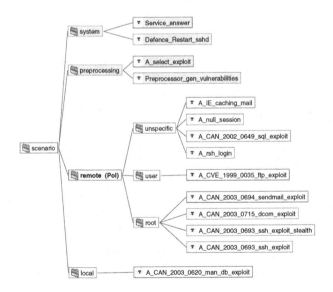

**Fig. 3.** Definition of an abstract representation of the attack graph

This mapping denotes, that all transitions (the leaves of the tree) are to be represented by their respective father nodes, namely *system*, *preprocessing*, *unspecific*, *user*, *root* and *local* in the abstract representation. The nodes *system* and *preprocessing* are coloured in grey, symbolising that they are mapped to $\epsilon$, that means the transitions represented by these nodes are invisible in the abstract representation. Please ignore the notation (*Pol*) at the node *remote* for the moment.

**Step 2 - Compute the Abstract Representation.** Figure 4 shows the computed abstract view focussing on the transition types *root*, *user*, *unspecific* and *local*. This graph with only 20 states and 37 edges was derived from the attack graph (cf. Fig. 2) with 178 states and 1309 edges. The simplicity of this mapping that guarantees that properties are preserved was automatically proven by the tool.

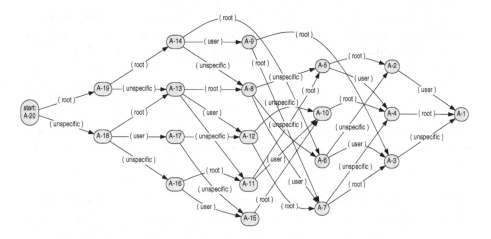

**Fig. 4.** Abstract view on an attack graph

**Step 3 - Optionally Refine the Mapping.** If you want to know for example, what policies are responsible to allow the attacks shown in Fig. 4 then a refinement of the abstraction defined in Fig. 3 is necessary. It is possible to "fine tune" the mapping so that the interpretation variables (cf. Sect. 3.4) stay visible in the abstract representation. In this case the binding of the interpretation variable *Pol* that contains the respective policy can be visualised. This is denoted by (*Pol*) in the node *remote* in Fig. 3. The corresponding refined abstract representation is a graph with 34 states and 121 edges when computed on the attack graph in Fig. 2. The initial nodes and edges of this graph are shown in Fig. 5(a). In comparison to the initial edges of the graph in Fig. 4 now the details on the related policies are visible.

(a) $(any\_role, dmz\_host, ssh/smtp)$          (b) $(any\_role, dmz\_host, smtp)$

**Fig. 5.** Details in the abstract view

**Step 4 - Adapt/Optimise the System Configuration.** Further analysis reveals, that, if the example policy given in Fig. 1(b) is changed to allow only *smtp* instead of *ssh* and *smtp* for *any_role* to *dmz_host* then the analysis yields a graph with only 94 states and 783 edges and performing the same steps as described above leads to the same graph (Fig. 4) in step 2 but a different one shown in Fig. 5(b) in the refinement step 3.

If alternatively the policy is restricted to allow only *ssh* instead of *ssh* and *smtp* in the above example, then again you get a different attack graph with 167 states and 1203 edges but the abstract view in step 2 is still the same.

This stepwise analysis demonstrates that there may be differences in the detailed attack graphs but no differences in the abstract representations thereof. This indicates that the different policies are equally effective (or not) concerning the enforcement of security goals on the abstract level, even if variations in the attack paths are covered by different policy rules.

**Using Predicates to Define Abstractions.** Let us now assume that the host *db_server* in the scenario is the most valuable and mission critical host in the ICT network. So we want to know if in the given scenario, (1) attacks to the *db_server* are possible, (2) on which vulnerabilities they are based, and, (3) what policy rules are directly involved.

The abstraction in Fig. 6(a) exemplifies how predicates can be used to define such a mapping. In this mapping the predicate $(T = db\_server)$ matches only those transitions that model direct attacks to the target host *db_server*. The remote transitions that don't match that predicate are mapped to $\epsilon$ and so are invisible.

Evaluating this abstraction on the attack graph from Fig. 2 above results in the simple graph given in Fig. 6(b). This proves that, (1) in the current policy configuration attacks to the *db_server* are possible, (2) those attacks are based on exploits of the vulnerability $CAN\_2002\_0649$, and, (3) they are utilising the policy rule $(intern\_hosts, any\_role, net)$. So to prevent this attack, it has to be decided, if it is more appropriate to uninstall the product that is hurt by this vulnerability or to restrict the internal hosts in their possible actions by replacing the above policy with a more restrictive one.

Many further uses of these attack graphs are possible, such as cost benefit analysis or analysis of intrusion detection configurations.

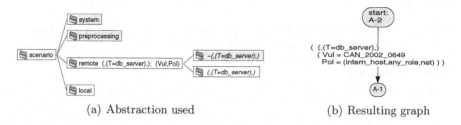

|  (a) Abstraction used | (b) Resulting graph |

**Fig. 6.** Focus on attacks to the host *db_server*

Liveness properties in this context reflect survivability and business continuity aspects. When a system's countermeasures and the behaviour of vital services the system provides are included in the model, then these effects and the system's resilience can be analysed. Please refer to [1] for an example.

## 5   Further Research Objectives

The work presented in this paper brings together, (1) attack graph computation technology, (2) state-of-the-art policy modelling, and, (3) formal methods for analysis and computation of abstract representations of the system behaviour. The aim is, to guide a systematic evaluation and assist the persons in charge with optimising adaptation of the network security policy to an ever-changing vulnerability setting.

To seamlessly integrate the methods and tool presented here into a network vulnerability analysis framework, a tool-assisted transformation of up-to-date ICT system configuration and vulnerability databases into a formal specification of the model is required. This should preferably be based on automatically updated information of network scanners because administration databases are typically out-of-date. Recent work by Noel, Jajodia et al. in [7] and [8] already covers this aspect but more work is needed to facilitate the transformation of descriptions from vulnerability databases into formal vulnerability and exploit specifications.

A summarisation of severity ratings for single security vulnerabilities as provided by CVSS or US-CERT (cf. Sect. 3.3) based on attack graphs has been addressed in recent work of Kotenko and Stepashkin [9]. Interesting questions in such an approach are, which attacker strategy or bundle of strategies to apply and how to "condense" the information in the graph into a comprehensive measure of the security of an ICT network. Consideration of *resilience against unknown attacks* could also contribute to such a measure.

An even more advanced objective is, to extend this framework to support *policy-based, automated threat response* that makes use of alert information. Such a self-adaptive response mechanism could substantially improve the resilience of policy controlled ICT systems against network attacks.

# References

1. Rieke, R.: Tool based formal Modelling, Analysis and Visualisation of Enterprise Network Vulnerabilities utilising Attack Graph Exploration. In: In U.E. Gattiker (Ed.), Eicar 2004 Conference CD-rom: Best Paper Proceedings, Copenhagen, EICAR e.V. (2004)
2. Phillips, C.A., Swiler, L.P.: A graph-based system for network-vulnerability analysis. In: NSPW '98, Proceedings of the 1998 Workshop on New Security Paradigms, September 22-25, 1998, Charlottsville, VA, USA, ACM Press (1998) 71–79
3. Swiler, L.P., Phillips, C., Ellis, D., Chakerian, S.: Computer-attack graph generation tool. In: DARPA Information Survivability Conference and Exposition (DISCEX II'01) Volume 2,June 12 - 14, 2001, Anaheim, California, IEEE Computer Society (2001) 1307–1321
4. Jha, S., Sheyner, O., Wing, J.M.: Two formal analyses of attack graphs. In: 15th IEEE Computer Security Foundations Workshop (CSFW-15 2002), 24-26 June 2002, Cape Breton, Nova Scotia, Canada, IEEE Computer Society (2002) 49–63
5. Sheyner, O., Haines, J.W., Jha, S., Lippmann, R., Wing, J.M.: Automated generation and analysis of attack graphs. In: 2002 IEEE Symposium on Security and Privacy, May 12-15, 2002, Berkeley, California, USA, IEEE Comp. Soc. Press (2002) 273–284
6. Ammann, P., Wijesekera, D., Kaushik, S.: Scalable, graph-based network vulnerability analysis. In: Proceedings of the 9th ACM conference on Computer and communications security, ACM Press New York, NY, USA (2002) 217–224
7. Noel, S., Jajodia, S.: Managing attack graph complexity through visual hierarchical aggregation. In: VizSEC/DMSEC '04: Proceedings of the 2004 ACM workshop on Visualization and data mining for computer security, New York, NY, USA, ACM Press (2004) 109–118
8. Noel, S., Jacobs, M., Kalapa, P., Jajodia, S.: Multiple Coordinated Views for Network Attack Graphs. In: IEEE Workshop on Visualization for Computer Security (VizSec'05), Los Alamitos, CA, USA, IEEE Computer Society (2005)
9. Kotenko, I., Stepashkin, M.: Analyzing Network Security using Malefactor Action Graphs. International Journal of Computer Science and Network Security **6** (2006)
10. Morin, B., Mé, L., Debar, H., Ducassé, M.: M2d2: A formal data model for ids alert correlation. In: Recent Advances in Intrusion Detection, 5th International Symposium, RAID 2002, Zurich, Switzerland, October 16-18, 2002, Proceedings. Volume 2516 of Lecture Notes in Computer Science., Springer (2002) 115–137
11. Cuppens, F., Cuppens-Boulahia, N., Sans, T., Miège, A.: A formal approach to specify and deploy a network security policy. In: Second Workshop on Formal Aspects in Security and Trust (FAST). (2004)
12. Ochsenschläger, P., Repp, J., Rieke, R., Nitsche, U.: The SH-Verification Tool Abstraction-Based Verification of Co-operating Systems. Formal Aspects of Computing, The International Journal of Formal Method **11** (1999) 1–24
13. Ochsenschläger, P., Repp, J., Rieke, R.: The SH-Verification Tool. In: Proc. 13th International FLorida Artificial Intelligence Research Society Conference (FLAIRS-2000), Orlando, FL, USA, AAAI Press (2000) 18–22
14. Schiffmann, M.: A Complete Guide to the Common Vulnerability Scoring System (CVSS) (2005) http://www.first.org/cvss/cvss-guide.html.
15. Ochsenschläger, P., Repp, J., Rieke, R.: Verification of Cooperating Systems – An Approach Based on Formal Languages. In: Proc. 13th International FLorida Artificial Intelligence Research Society Conference (FLAIRS-2000), Orlando, FL, USA, AAAI Press (2000) 346–350

# A Framework for Conceptualizing Social Engineering Attacks

Jose J. Gonzalez[1], Jose M. Sarriegi[2], and Alazne Gurrutxaga[2]

[1] Agder University College, Faculty of engineering and science,
Research Cell "Security and Quality and Organizations," Serviceboks 509,
4884 Grimstad, Norway
(and Gjøvik University College, NISlab, 2802 Gjøvik, Norway)
[2] Tecnun (University of Navarra), Manuel de Lardizábal 13,
20018 San Sebastian, Spain
jose.j.gonzalez@hia.no, jmsarriegi@tecnun.es,
A900348@alumni.tecnun.es

**Abstract.** At the highest abstraction level, an attempt by a social engineer to exploit a victim organization either attempts to achieve some specific target (denial of service, steal an asset, tap some particular information) or it wishes to maximize an outcome, such as to disable the organization by a terrorist attack or establish a permanent parasitic relationship (long-term espionage). Seen as dynamic processes, the first kind of exploit is a controlling ("balancing") feedback loop, while the second kind is a reinforcing feedback loop. Each type of exploit meets a first line of defense in control processes or in escalating ("reinforcing") processes of resistance. The possible combinations of the two modes of attack and the two modes of defense yield four archetypes of exploit and natural defense. Predictably, the social engineer would seek to outsmart the first line of defense; it is shown that each archetype implies a particular strategy to do so. Anticipation of these modes of attack must be the starting point for an effective multi-layered defense against social engineering attacks.

**Keywords:** Social engineering, critical infrastructure, pattern recognition, system archetype, system dynamics, information security.

## 1 Introduction

While the technical security of most critical infrastructure is high, it remains vulnerable to attacks from social engineers, whether outsiders or insiders. A report released in October 2004 by the Gartner Research Group concluded: «The greatest security risk facing large companies and individual Internet users over the next 10 years will be the increasingly sophisticated use of social engineering to bypass IT security defenses.» [Quoted in ref. 1, p. 152]. No exception for the vulnerability of critical infrastructure to social engineering attacks is made in this prediction or in recent assessments by other security expert groups. The recent study by Keeney et al. [2] on computer system sabotage in critical infrastructure sectors mentions examples of social engineering techniques (p. 27, 40).

J. Lopez (Ed.): CRITIS 2006, LNCS 4347, pp. 79 – 90, 2006.
© Springer-Verlag Berlin Heidelberg 2006

In the context of information security, social engineering is «the term that hackers give to acquiring information about computer systems through non-technical means» [3]. The Gartner Research Group defines social engineering as «the manipulation of people, rather than machines, to successfully breach the security systems.» [Quoted in ref. 1, p. 152] Wikipedia [4] defines it as «the practice of obtaining confidential information by manipulation of legitimate users.» It has been claimed that social engineers typically proceed by gathering information about people in the target organization, and then applying "neuro-linguistic programming" techniques (NLP) [5]. Harl in "People Hacking" [6] states succinctly: «social engineering is the art and science of getting people to comply to your wishes.» Social engineering is closely related to what magicians call "psychological forcing": An agent inserts surreptitiously grounds for false belief into the stream of consciousness of people; then they can be lead to make what they experience as free and rational decisions when it is the agent who controls their actions [7, p. 243]. Social engineers take advantage from existing security breaches or vulnerabilities (such as employees' poor training, ineffective segregation of duties or faulty supervision of tasks).

Much is found in the Internet, in magazines and newspapers about social engineering, because deception is central for innumerable phishing attacks, propagation of worms and even for spamming. However, there are comparatively few peer reviewed papers and books dealing with social engineering. Of particular interest is research documenting social engineering attacks from the perspective of the attacker. An early study by Winkler [3] described a social engineering attack against a company with their permission, demonstrating how easily unauthorized access can be obtained. Ten years later, this is still very much the case: A recent paper defining a metric for resistance to social engineering [8] concludes «our experiment shows that it is relatively cheap and easy to mount a large scale social engineering attack (or experiment) with a high success rate.» Are there strong reasons to exclude organizations and companies within the critical infrastructure from this gloomy prediction? From our personal experience as consultants and scientific researchers we would conclude that the danger to critical infrastructure from social engineering attacks is real and increasing.

Given the scarcity of strictly controlled scientific studies of social engineers assaults [3, 5, 8], the next best source are the books by Winkler [9, 10] and by Mitnick & Simon [11], which mostly consist of anecdotal evidence. The books have a plethora of details, but we argue that something is missing: A simple way to conceptualize social engineering attacks. Without a framework that allows to recognize attack patterns, the social engineering cases described in the books [9-11] read mostly like a game of check described in terms of moves of individual figures. While there is no yet general agreement about how chess masters think, it is widely agreed that pattern recognition is one of the crucial elements [12]. Master chess players think in terms of strategic patterns: *openings* (such as Caro-Kann Defense, English Opening, King's Pawn Opening, Sicilian Defense); *middlegame strategies* (such as forking, skewering, pinning, discovered checks, sacrifices); and *endgame studies*. We argue that descriptions of social engineering attacks in terms of system archetypes have qualities as strategic patterns: they conceptualize crucial aspects of the attack and defense process; they are cognitively simple; they are fairly easy to recognize and to interpret; they are modular and can be combined.

## 2    A Feedback View of Social Engineering

Dolan [13] characterizes the techniques used by social engineers to attack organizations in terms of action and outcomes that feed back on each other: «Social engineers use tactics to leverage trust, helpfulness, easily attainable information, knowledge of internal processes, authority, technology and any combination there of. They often use several small attacks to put them in the position to reach their final goal. Social engineering is all about taking advantage of others to gather information and infiltrate an attack. The information gained in a phone book may lead to a phone call. The information gained in the phone call may lead to another phone call. A social engineer builds on each tidbit of information he or she gains to eventually stage a final, deadly attack.» Accordingly, one way to

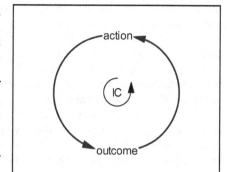

**Fig. 1.** From the perspective of the social engineer the intended consequence (IC) of the attack is to escalate the access to the target organization in a series of actions and outcomes feeding back on each other

conceptualize social engineering attacks is to capture the patterns of action and outcomes using feedback concepts.

A social engineer attempting to exploit an organization must manage a process of a certain temporal duration to achieve a particular outcome. Ambitious social engineering attacks against organizations would be accomplished over weeks, or even months [3]. Social engineers obtain «small amounts of access, bit for bit» from different employees in a firm [14]. The knowledge gained at each step is used skillfully by the social engineer to augment his credibility in his next move. The attack is a dynamic process where the outcome of an action is fed back to execute the next action, yielding a better outcome which again is fed back to execute another action, etc. Fig. 1 describes this idea as a feedback loop.

The reaction from the organization is the procedures and controls that are activated by the social

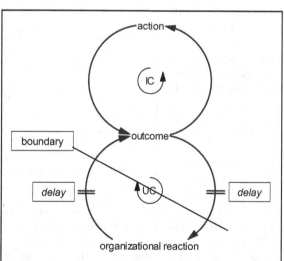

**Fig. 2.** From the perspective of the social engineer the intended series of outcomes in the attack activates the organizational defense as unintended outcome (UC)

engineer. From the point of view of the social engineer this reaction is an unintended consequence. The organizational defense is hidden behind "boundaries," creating difficulties for the social engineer. There might be delays in the organizational perception and reaction, indicated in Fig. 2.

Skilled social engineers anticipate the organizational reaction and devise their attack in such a way as to minimize or control the organizational defense (Fig. 3). For the attack to succeed, the series of outcomes obtained by the social engineer must contain information to penetrate the organizational boundaries (shown in the solution archetype as dashed line, to indicate the gain in boundary transparency for the social engineer).

At this level of abstraction, and seen as a dynamic feedback process, the approach of a social engineer can be described by system archetypes. Made popular in the early nineties by Senge [15] and Kim [16], system archetypes became a powerful tool with Wolstenholme's price winning paper [17] showing that all the known instances of system archetypes can be recast as one of four possible types, namely the 'underachievement', the 'out of control', the 'relative achievement' and the 'relative control' archetype.

A feedback loop can either be balancing (B) or reinforcing (R). Balancing feedback occurs when the series of actions and outcomes targets a desired value, such as launching a deadly attack or getting hold of a specific trade secret. Once this occurs, the social engineer's mission is accomplished. Reinforcing feedback could occur in a long-term parasitic relationship, e.g. when the social engineer is a spy updating an external organization on developments occurring

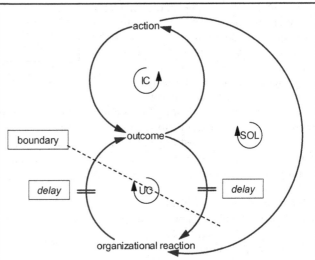

**Fig. 3.** From the perspective of the social engineer the solution loop (SOL) is to carefully devise each action to neutralize the organizational reaction while gradually making the defense boundaries more transparent (dashed line)

in the victim organization [10, p. 16]. There is no specific up-front goal, the outcome growing and accumulating as time passes, and the social engineer keeps on working as a mole 'for ever' – in principle; in practice, until the mole is caught or the parasitic relationship is no longer interesting. The four possible archetypes correspond to the possible ways to combine the two types of intended consequences (either as a reinforcing or a balancing feedback loop) with the two types of unintended consequences (either as a balancing or a reinforcing feedback loop).

System archetypes are powerful generic causal loop structures; they are responsible for generic patterns of behavior over time, particularly counter-intuitive behavior; they occur in many application domains, this isomorphic quality making them excellent tools to transfer insights from one domain to other and to accelerate learning in complex domains [15-18].

Wolstenholme [17, 18] emphasizes that there is a closed-loop "solution" archetype for each "problem" archetype. In the generic approach to social engineering attacks delineated above, the social engineer's problem archetype is shown in Fig. 2, while Fig. 3 describes the social engineer's solution archetype. Wolstenholme emphasizes also the role of organizational boundaries as an obstacle to recognize and to address the unintended consequence loop, implying the necessity to penetrate or to make the boundaries transparent in the closed loop solution (the transparent boundary is hinted at by a dashed line in Fig. 3).

The process described in Fig. 1, the feedback loop describing the intended consequence from the perspective of the social engineer, might trigger an organizational defense, which – again from the perspective of the social engineer – is an unintended, an undesired, consequence. Such unintended consequence is again a process of actions and outcomes, that is, a feedback loop. Keeping in mind that there are only two possible kinds of feedback loops, namely balancing (B) or reinforcing (R) loops, it follows that there are four basic combinations, namely BB, BR, RB, RR, of the two feedback loops; in other words, a feedback perspective describing the intended consequence of the social engineering attack and the unintended consequence as organizational defense results in four basic patterns. These basic patterns correspond to the four types of generic system archetypes proposed by Wolstenholme [17, 18]. Strictly speaking, they correspond to the *problem* archetypes. From the perspective of the social engineer, the challenge posed by the organizational defense must be countered by a dynamic process – again a feedback loop – that neutralizes or minimizes the organizational reaction. This last feedback loop is the element needed for a closed-loop "solution" in Wolstenholme's sense [17, 18]. Note that archetypes are qualitative models, but they can be extended to quantitative models that can be simulated. Two of us have e.g. developed simulation models for insider attacks [19, 20].

Using literature sources we identify in sections 3-6 four kinds of social engineering attacks and show that each type corresponds to one of the possible system archetypes [17, 18]. Our emphasis is on characterizing the attack type, the organizational defense and how the social engineer anticipates and neutralizes the organizational defense. The attack type is a balancing loop if the social engineer targets a specific goal and a reinforcing loop is the social engineer's activity is to achieve an "unbounded" outcome, such as maximum harm or a long-term parasitic relationship. The organizational defense is the security controls that would become activated, were it not that the social engineer deploys a "solution" loop to neutralize or mitigate the defense reaction.

Finally in section 7 we discuss the implications of our findings. A word of caution: We see system archetypes as idealized patterns describing at a high level of abstraction and aggregation the main modes of social engineering attacks. We do not claim that system archetypes do full justice to real cases. A system archetype is a way to conceptualize the most salient aspect of the attack and defense for some time interval. Returning to the analogy of a game of chess, an analysis in terms of specific strategic patterns, such as "King's gambit" opening, controlling space in the middlegame and "King and Pawn vs. King" endgame provides a useful, structured high-level description for various purposes (teaching chess strategy; developing counterstrategies; training for a championship, etc). Such strategic patterns are useful but there are additional relevant aspects (tactics, mental attitude, motivation, etc). System archetypes describing strategic patterns in social engineering must be seen in a similar perspective – to be complemented and supplemented.

## 3  External Social Engineer Targeting an Explicit Goal

The narratives about industrial espionage using social
engineering techniques [9] and
social engineering attacks by
external agents [11] describe
myriads of tricks to conduct
social engineering attacks. But
seen as instances of system
archetypes practically all cases
described in the famous book
by Mitnick and Simon [11]
condense to just one type,
namely the archetype
describing an external agent
using social engineering
techniques to achieve a
particular goal (denial of
service, steal specific assets,
obtain particular pieces of
information) that is opposed
by an organizational def-
ense. Ch. 6 of Winkler's book
provides a very good
and detailed description of
this kind of assault [9, p. 139-
151]. The intended
consequence IC (B) in this
kind of exploit is a
"controlling" (B: balancing)
feedback loop with an
explicit goal. The social
engineer's mission is finished
once the goal is achieved (i.e.
when the value of outcome,
say valuable knowledge
about the victim organization,
has become virtually equal to

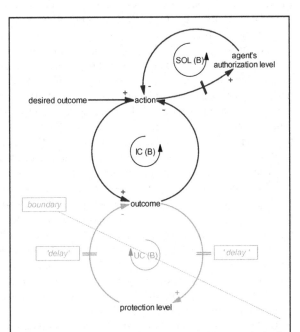

**Fig. 4.** The social engineer acts to achieve a desired outcome – a balancing or control loop, IC (B). The unintended consequence from the perspective of the social engineer is the activation of higher protection levels that compromise the outcome – a balancing loop, UC (B). A positive link + means that if the cause increases (decreases), the effect increases above (decreases below) what it would otherwise have been. A negative link - means that if the cause increases (decreases), the effect decreases below (increases above) what it would otherwise have been. To achieve the desired outcome, the social engineer shapes actions to pass as legitimate at high authorization level. This yields a balancing feedback loop that strengthens the primary process IC and mitigates the effect of the defense process (UC).

desired outcome), implying a limited time horizon. As the social engineer comes closer and closer to the desired outcome, the level of protection of the valuable asset is higher and higher. Hence, from the point of view of the social engineer the unintended (and undesired) consequence is a balancing feedback loop UC (B) compromising the outcome. The IC- and UC-feedback loops form the "problem" archetype from the perspective of the social engineer (Fig. 4). This kind of problem archetype is known as a "relative control" archetype [17]; it occurs often in specific settings that are known as "escalation" (or "the arms race") or the "drifting goals" archetype [15, 17].

To achieve the ultimate objective (desired outcome), the social engineer uses elements from the outcome to gain fake authority, e.g. by posing as senior manager, and thus to bypass the organizational defenses of high level of protection. The closed solution loop, SOL(B) is a balancing loop strengthening the primary process (IC) and mitigates the effect of the defense process (UC).

Note the line representing the organization boundaries obstructing the social engineer's work. To succeed with the closed loop solution attempt, the social engineer must direct the action-outcome sequence to get insight in the organizational structure. Such insight is represented as a dashed line, hinting a boundary that has become more transparent to the attacker.

## 4  Social Engineer Targeting a Long-Term Parasitic Relationship

Consider now the situation of the social engineer as mole within the organization, that is, as a malicious insider serving an external party. Rather than targeting a particular outcome, the social engineer's role is to provide the external party long-term access to more and more valuable assets. A very good description of such an assault is found in Winkler's book [9, Ch. 8, p. 185-211]. The malicious insider was extremely patient, spending years to gather his information [9, p. 205]. Being an insider, it was not so much the organizational security controls that limited the agent's endeavors (that is: caused the unintended

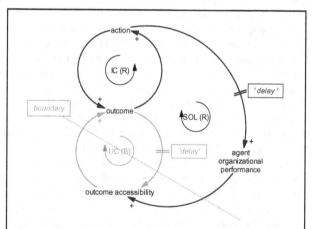

**Fig. 5.** The social engineer gathers more and more access over a long period of time, yielding an accumulating outcome – a reinforcing loop (R); this is the intended consequence, IC. The unintended consequence, UC, from the perspective of the social engineer is the necessity to reach farther and farther away for outcomes that are increasingly less accessible – a balancing or blocking (B) loop. Again from the perspective of the social engineer, the closed loop solution, SOL, is a reinforcing feedback loop whereby the social engineer, becoming a star performer, gains increasing access to more and more outcomes.

consequence loop). Rather, it was the necessity to identify and get access to trade secrets that was the stumbling block; a well-conceived security policy would, among other things, enact separation of duties and establish a multi- layered defense. Accordingly, the "problem" archetype – from the perspective of the social engineer/malicious insider – consists of a reinforcing intended consequence loop and a balancing (that is "blocking") unintended consequence loop (Fig. 5). This combination of intended and unintended feedback loops is known as an "underachievement" archetype [17].

In Fig. 5 the closed loop solution, SOL, from the perspective of the social engineer is a reinforcing (R) feedback loop: The malicious insider needs to become a start performer to bypass security controls and to obtain access to deeply guarded trade secrets (by understanding more and more of what is going on, to know who has valuable information and where it is located [9, p. 43 and p. 205]).

Again, the line representing the organizational boundaries is dashed – indicating that the social engineer, as part of the outcome, must get increased insight about the target organization's structure.

## 5   Disgruntled Insider as Social Engineer

A disgruntled insider might end planning a specific outcome, such as releasing a software time bomb that disrupts the organizational IT network; such outcome would have serious implications for critical infrastructure. We consider this situation explicitly in the next section. In this section the emphasis is on a disgruntled insider with strong motivation to take revenge and act to maximize some outcome – but without yet having formed a specific vision of the target. A series of actions produce escalating outcomes that are still unfocused in the sense that they are accompanied by "markers" or "precursors." If the insider is successful, in the sense that the outcome is achieved, the motivation to proceed increases, yielding a reinforcing (R) feedback loop; this is the intended consequence, IC, loop (Fig. 6). At this stage the insider is in danger to be caught if the organization does detect too much unusual behavior, such as markers or precursors; see Appendix and [21, 22] for markers, deliberate errors and precursors related to evolving insider attacks.

The unintended consequence loop, UC, describes what might happen if precursors are detected and the insider is warned or demoted – however, without management actually understanding the full implications of the insider's actions.[1] In such case, management's reprieve does not stop the insider's action to take revenge, but they increase the insider's disgruntlement and motivation to attack; there is a danger to the insider, though, in that the resulting reinforcing (R) loop, with its escalating pattern of behavior ultimately might lead to management to fire or in any other way to stop the insider before revenge has been accomplished. The "problem" archetype described by a reinforcing IC and a reinforcing UC loop is known as a "relative achievement" archetype [17].

From the perspective of the insider, the closed solution loop, SOL, is a careful self-control (*regulatory action*) that gives priority to focused actions targeting a major

---

[1] This was e.g. the case for the Tim Lloyd/Omega case, where management interpreted Lloyd's precursors as a threat to workplace climate, see ref. 19.

outcome in a covert way (in other words, by suppressing markers and precursors that might betray the insider's intention of a major revenge). In this case, the solution loop describes the transition from an unsophisticated insider to a social engineer stealthily buiding up a major strike. Evidence to the effect that insiders act to conceal activities and identities has been presented in the recent study of sabotage to critical infrastructure in the USA [2, p. 19].

As the insider targets a specific goal – say deve-loping a time bomb – a new kind of archetype describes the pattern of behavior (see the next section).

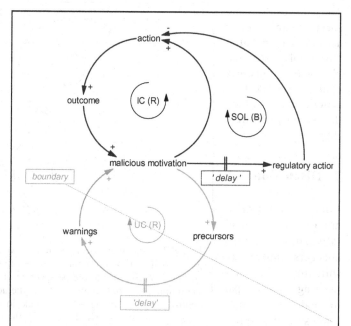

**Fig. 6.** The disgruntled insider seeks revenge: Actions resulting in successful outcomes increase the insider's malicious motivation; this is the intended consequence, IC, loop, which is a reinforcing (R) feedback loop. The unintended consequence, UC, from the perspective of the insider is a reinforcing loop. Whereas the accompanying markers and precursors result in warnings and demotions from management that enhance the insider's motivation to take revenge, such escalation of visible signs might lead to decisive managerial intervention (e.g. firing the insider). The insider needs to suppress precursor signals and concentrate on smart and stealth behavior (the closed solution loop, SOL, a balancing, B, feedback loop).

## 6   Insider Social Engineer Targeting a Massive Strike

An insider who is determined to launch a massive strike to damage an organization might act out of revenge or for terrorist purposes. Using generic findings from the recent study of sabotage to critical infrastructure in the USA [2] we propose the archetype depicted in Fig. 7. Again, the archetype must be seen from the perspective of the insider/social engineer. The social engineer acts to achieve a desired outcome – a balancing (B) or control loop; this is the intended consequence IC. From the perspective of the social engineer the unintended consequence, UC, is the activation of security controls that could compromise the outcome; this yields a reinforcing feedback loop (R).

The combination of a balancing intended consequence loop and a reinforcing unintended consequence loop is known as an out-of-control problem archetype [17].

To gain control the social engineer must activate a solution loop, SOL, using the obtained outcomes both to generate new actions and o weaken the security controls (Fig. 7).

## 7 Discussion

With improved technology to defend information assets, attackers might to shift to social engineering as principal method to compromise critical infrastructure. This paper suggests that recognition of dynamic patterns, rather than

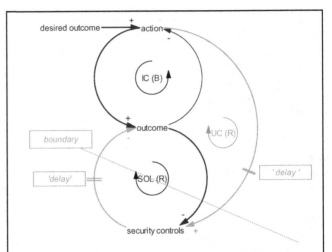

**Fig. 7.** The social engineer acts to achieve a desired outcome – a balancing (B) or control loop; this is the intended consequence, IC. From the perspective of the social engineer, the unintended consequence, UC, is the activation of security controls (a reinforcing, R, feedback loop). To achieve the ultimate objective (desired outcome), the social engineer must shape each action to reduce the impact of the security controls. This yields a reinforcing (R) solution feedback loop, SOL, that feeds back on an improved outcome.

of heaps of symptoms, should be a worthwhile addition to our methods to detect social engineering attacks. Experience with system archetypes teaches that they are easily assimilated and that they improve recognition of the causal structure leading to dynamic patterns [15-18]. Better pattern recognition means better detection of objects low in the radar screen. Better detection means improved efficacy of security controls.

In addition, system archetypes facilitate policy insight. Inspecting Figs. 4-7, it is evident that the social engineer has a big strategic advantage: The social engineer's combined strategy of a primary feedback intended consequence (IC) feedback loop with a solution (SOL) feedback loop outsmarts the single-loop organizational defense. Gragg [23] argues that social engineering attacks can be avoided by using multi-layered defenses; that is, even if an intruder were able to penetrate one level, there would still be more levels where he could be discovered and stopped. This might be too optimistic a view. Multi-layered defenses will not provide enhanced protection if the organizational defense still operates in terms of a single feedback loop. We conclude that system archetypes suggest an important research question for future work: How to design security controls that provide multi-layered feedback against the combined action of the social engineer's primary feedback intended consequence (IC) loop and the solution (SOL) loop.

# References

1. Greene, S., *Security Policies and Procedures: Principles and Practices*. 2006, Upper Saddle River, NJ: Prentice Hall.
2. Keeney, M., et al., *Insider Threat Study: Computer System Sabotage in Critical Infrastructure Sectors*. 2005, Carnegie Mellon, Software Engineering Institute: Pittsburgh, PA.
3. Winkler, I.S., *The non-technical threat to computing systems*. Computing Systems, 1996. 9(1): p. 3-14.
4. Wikipedia. *Social engineering (computer security)*. 2006 [cited 2006 May 13]; Available from: http://en.wikipedia.org/wiki/Social_engineering_%28computer_security%29.
5. Barrett, N., *Penetration testing and social engineering: hacking the weakest link*. Information Security Technical Report, 2003. 8(4): p. 56-64.
6. Harl. *The psychology of social engineering*. 1997 [cited 2006 May 13]; Available from: http://www.cybercrimes.net/Property/Hacking/Social%20Engineering/PsychSocEng/PsySocEng.html.
7. Dennet, D.C., *Freedom Evolves*. 2004, London: Penguin Books.
8. Hasle, H., et al., *Measuring resistance to social engineering*, in *Information Security Practice and Experience (Lecture Notes in Computer Science 3439)*, F.B. Robert H. Deng, Hwee Hwa Pang, Jianying Zhou, Editor. 2005, Springer: Heidelberg.
9. Winkler, I.S., *Corporate Espionage: what it is, why it is happening in your company, what you must do about it*. 1997, Rocklin, CA: Prima Publishing.
10. Winkler, I.S., *Spies Among Us*. 2005, Indianapolis, IN: Wiley Publishing, Inc.
11. Mitnick, K.D. and W.L. Simon, *The Art of Deception: Controlling the Human Element of Security*. 2003, New York: John Wiley & Sons.
12. Chabris, C.F. and E.S. Hearst, *Visualization, pattern recognition, and forward search: effects of playing speed and sight of the position on grandmaster chess errors*. Cognitive Science, 2003(27): p. 637-648.
13. Dolan, A. *Social Engineering*. 2004 [cited 2006 19 May]; Available from: http://www.sans.org/.
14. Granger, S. *Social engineering fundamentals, Part I: Hacker tactics*. 2001 [cited 2006 May 12]; Available from: http://www.securityfocus.com/infocus/1527.
15. Senge, P., *The Fifth Discipline*. 1990, New York: Doubleday/Currency.
16. Kim, D., *Systems Archetypes*. 1992, Cambridge, MA: Pegasus Communications.
17. Wolstenholme, E.F., *Towards the definition and use of a core set of archetypal structures in system dynamics*. System Dynamics Review, 2003. 19(7): p. 7-26.
18. Wolstenholme, E.F., *Using generic system archetypes to support thinking and modelling*. System Dynamics Review, 2004. 20(4): p. 341-356.
19. Melara, C., et al., *A system dynamics model of an insider attack on an information system*, in *From Modeling to Managing Security: A System Dynamics Approach*, J.J. Gonzalez, Editor. 2003, Norwegian Academic Press: Kristiansand, Norway.
20. Martinez-Moyano, I.J., et al. *Simulating Insider Cyber-Threat Risks: A Model-Based Case and a Case-Based Model*. In *The 23rd International Conference of the System Dynamics Society July 17-21*. 2005. Boston, MA: The System Dynamics Society.
21. Schultz, E.E., *A framework for understanding and predicting insider attacks*. Computers and Security, 2002. 21(6): p. 526-531.
22. Suler, J.R. and W. Phillips, *The Bad Boys of Cyberspace: Deviant Behavior in Multimedia Chat Communities*. CyberPsychology and Behavior, 1998. 1: p. 275-294.

23. Gragg, D. *A Multi-Level Defense Against Social Engineering.* 2003 [cited 2006 19 May]; Available from: http://www.sans.org/.
24. Gaudin, S. *Case Study of Insider Sabotage: The Tim Lloyd/Omega Case.* Computer Security Journal 2000 [cited 2006 19 May]; Available from: http://www.gocsi. om/pdfs/insider.pdf.

# Appendix

A famous and well-documented case of an insider attack is Tim Lloyd's vs. Omega Engineering Corporation [24]. Lloyd went from star to disgruntled employee as a result of Omega's expansion globally and Lloyd's position slipped from sole network administrator to member of team. Lloyd developed and executed a time bomb targeting software programs that were critical for Omega's manufacturing processes. The impact to Omega was loss of current version of critical software; derailed Omega growth with layoff of about 80 employees; and costs to Omega estimated at $10M.

There were important precursors that normally should have raised suspicion about Lloyd's intention: Lloyd requested and received sole copy of current backups; he centralized critical manufacturing programs on one file server, telling workers not to store them locally any longer; he wrote and tested three versions of the logic bomb prior to the attack, twice on dummy data and once on the real system; Lloyd's disgruntlement was conspicuous by his verbal and physical assaults on co-workers, his bottlenecking of projects for which he was not in charge, and his loading of fault programs to make co-workers look bad. Lloyd received verbal warning, he was written up twice, and demoted as a result of these actions. However, management did not perceive Lloyd as a threat to the information security; Lloyd was instead seen as a threat to workplace climate [19].

Admittedly, Lloyd had an easy game at Omega, since its management still trusted Lloyd as network administrator despite his overt disruption of workplace climate. In the case of a better protected company, the insider social engineer would have to activate a solution loop, whereby the obtained outcomes are used both to generate new actions and to weaken the security controls (designated SOL in Fig. 7).

# An Overview of R&D Activities in Europe on Critical Information Infrastructure Protection (CIIP)

Sandro Bologna[1], Giovanni Di Costanzo[1], Eric Luiijf[2], and Roberto Setola[3]

[1] ENEA
bologna@casaccia.enea.it
[2] TNO Defence, Security and Safety
eric.luiijf@tno.nl
[3] Università CAMPUS Bio-Medico, Complex Systems & Security Lab
r.setola@unicampus.it

**Abstract.** In recent years there has been an increasing R&D interest in critical infrastructures and their protection. However, this represents a still very immature field of research with very fuzzy and confused boundaries. This paper reports an initial overview of R&D activities in Europe on this topic to illustrate the state of art and to emphasize the major areas of research but also to identify the most relevant lacks.

## 1 Introduction

Contemporary societies are increasingly dependent on availability, reliability, correctness, safety and security (dependability) of many technological infrastructures, commonly referred to as Critical Infrastructures (CIs) [2]. For many economical, social, political and technological reasons, we observed a rapid change in their organizational, operational and technical structures in the last years. Until one decade ago, these infrastructures could be considered as autonomous vertically integrated systems. They are now tightly coupled with others and show a large numbers of dependencies and interdependencies [3].

Apart from many positive effects to society, the complexity of our infrastructures has increased introducing new and very dangerous vulnerabilities [4]. Due to the presence of links between the different infrastructures, an accidental failure or malicious event in one of them may easily spread across, amplifying its negative consequences. Such phenomena may affect remote users, both from the geographical and/or the logical point of views [5].

Moreover, the actual world socio-political situation emphasizes new classes of threats for these infrastructure, for instance those related to market liberalisation and international activism and terrorism.

These considerations have focused the attention of governments and international organizations on the need to improve dependability, robustness, resilience and plasticity of these infrastructures [2,6]. These strategies are usually referred

J. Lopez (Ed.): CRITIS 2006, LNCS 4347, pp. 91–102, 2006.
© Springer-Verlag Berlin Heidelberg 2006

to as Critical Infrastructure Protection (CIP) and as Critical Information Infrastructure Protection (CIIP) when the focus is on the ICT component of a critical infrastructure or the critical ICT-sector itself.

The related strategic approaches identify R&D cornerstone elements to face the problem. The US has recently released a specific CIP R&D programme [8] and also the EU Commission has explicitly included this topic in the Preparatory Action on Security Research (PASR) and in the forthcoming 7th Framework Programme (FP).

The EU Commission co-funded also some activities in the 6th FP. One of the project is CI$^2$RCO (Critical Information Infrastructure Research Co-ordination) [9]. CI$^2$RCO is a coordinated action devoted to: 1) snapshot the national and regional R&D initiatives about CIIP existing in the EU-25 countries plus the Associate Candidate Countries (ACC), 2) to identify possible research gaps or areas no adequately investigated and 3) to promote the creation of an European Research Area (ERA) on CIIP.

This paper reports some intermediate high-level results obtained by the CI$^2$RCO project. Details can be found in [10].

## 2   R&D Analysis

The first problem that has been considered in the analysis of CIIP related R&D initiatives, was the identification of valuable sources. Indeed, due to the broad scope of CIIP many and heterogeneous organizations are involved.

To this end, in a first step, 1155 possible *Point of Contacts* (POCs) were identified in the different EU-25 countries and ACC. Each of them have been contacted personally. On the base of their availability and competence, 89 POCs were selected as national and sector contacts for the CI$^2$RCO project. These belong to ministries (20%), research (52%), technology providers (3%), associations (3%), agencies (10%) and CI stakeholders (12%). These POCs, as shown in Figure 1, ensure a good coverage of the interested countries, although five nations are not covered. Moreover, while the large part of the POCs provided high quality and detailed information about R&D initiatives in their countries other POCs supplied less complete information (i.e., that related to their own activities).

Each POC was asked to fill in questionnaire(s) in order to collect information about national Critical Information Infrastructure Protection (CIIP) strategies and specifically about national and sector-specific CIIP-related R&D initiatives [11].

The CI$^2$RCO consortium initially collected 87 questionnaires which report information on about 135 projects: 77 national initiatives and 58 projects co-funded by EU-commission (for more information [11]). This set of projects was extended to a total number of 156 projects (88 national projects and 68 co-funded projects) with additional information collected from open documents and Internet researches.

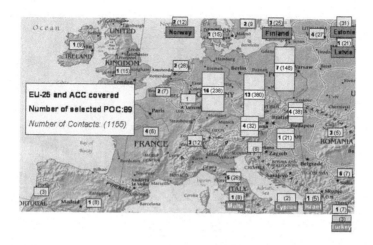

**Fig. 1.** Geographical allocation of contacted and selected POCs [11]

After a more detailed analysis, it became clear that many of these projects are not or only marginally related to CIIP. This is largely due to the confusion that still exists about this topic. Indeed, some POCs reported R&D projects focused on security of embedded systems, or projects devoted to specific technologies, such as biometrics or cryptography algorithms. This imposed the need to perform a selection of the projects in order to identify that specifically focused on CIIP. (for the definition of the criteria and the list of the selected projects see [10]).

This procedure identified 72 projects out of the original 156 as CIIP relevant. These projects comprise 44 national initiatives and 28 EU co-funded projects. Their geographical allocation[1] is shown in Figure 2. It is evident that there is inhomogeneity into the two sets with nations very active in the EU framework programs but with a very limited national effort and vice versa. Moreover, Germany and France looks to be present in nearly all the EU co-funded CIIP relevant projects.

A different, and more complete view, of national CIIP R&D related initiatives is reported in Figure 3.

According to the data collected, ten EU countries have released a strategic plan to improve the protection, security and availability of their critical infrastructures including their information infrastructures. Moreover, seven countries have set up specific R&D programmes on CIP/CIIP. However, only Germany, The Netherlands and Norway have promoted both strategic/political and research activities.

## 2.1 National Activities

The investigated projects span the period 2000 to 2013: 12 projects (28%) have just ended, while 19 (44%) are still on-going, of which 5 projects (12%) will end in

---

[1] An EU co-funded project is counted in country A if there is at least a team member of the country A involved in the EU project.

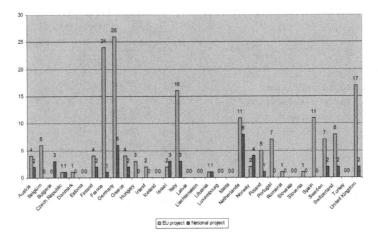

**Fig. 2.** Geographical allocation of the 44 CIIP-relevant national initiatives and of the 28 EU co-funded projects (these latter decomposed in accordance with the nationality of each partner)

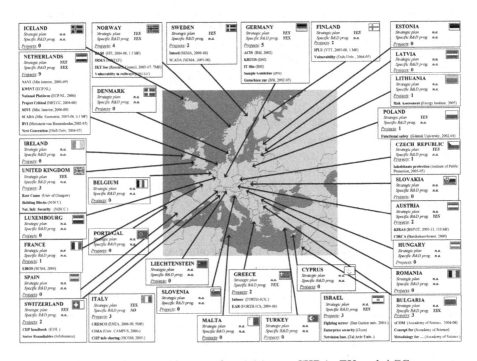

**Fig. 3.** Overview of national activities on CIIP in EU and ACC

2006. For 12 projects (28%) information is latching about their schedule. There is a large inhomogeneity in projects duration: some projects have a duration of only a few months, while others last a long period.

Looking to the team members of the different projects (see Figure 4), it is evident that there is a large participation by government institutions (35%) and specifically from those that are involved in national security (e.g., police, intelligence) which represent 15% of the actors. Research represents 43% with a slight predominance of *Research Institutions* (24%) in respect to *Academia* (19%). The direct participation of CI stakeholders as team member is very limited and quite exclusively related to Telecommunication and Information technology operators. By the way, a number of the national projects involve the participation of CII stakeholders on a voluntary basis, e.g., in a advisory role, not as partner.

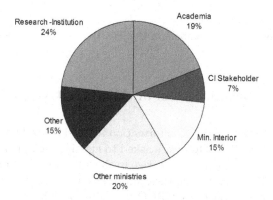

**Fig. 4.** Distribution of team members in the 44 CIIP-relevant national projects (N=94)

## 2.2 EU Co-funded Initiatives

EU co-funded projects are generally characterised by a large number of partners. The consortium composition is more heterogeneous (see Figure 5). Research entities (50%) represent still the most relevant actor with academia (22%) and research institutions (28%). There is some partner participation of CI stakeholders (13%) and also from technology providers (about 15%). The most relevant element is the limited participation of Ministries and government agencies (less then 2%).

The geographical distribution of the partners, reported in Figure 6, shows that 57% of the partners belong to only four countries (Germany, UK, France and Italy) and that seven countries (i.e. the previous four plus Spain, The Netherlands, and Sweden) represent the 74% of the involved partners.

Most of these projects have a project duration of two or three years. Of the projects identified, 15 projects (54%) have already ended, 11 projects (39%) are still on going, three will end in 2006. For two of the project we could not track down any information on their time schedule.

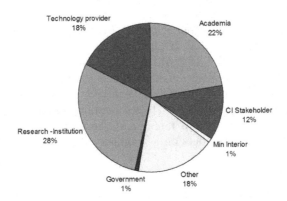

**Fig. 5.** Distribution of team members in the 28 CIIP-relevant EU co-funded projects (N=244)

## 3    Different Classifications of All Initiatives

The questionnaires collected also information about the R&D topics covered by each project. Specifically, POCs were asked to classify each project according to 42 topics grouped in nine main categories. In the following, for brevity, we will refer only to these latter main categories; information on single topics cab be found in documents available on the CI$^2$RCO web site [9]. The main categories are: Holistic system security; Risk management & vulnerability analysis; Prevention & detection; Incident response & recovery; Survivability of systems; Policies & legal environment; Fundamental research & development; Non technology issues compromising CIIP.

National initiatives, as illustrated in Figure 7, show a quite irregular distribution of interest for the different R&D topics, ranging from *Risk management* that is part of 89% of the projects to *Fundamental research* that is addressed by only 14% of the projects.

EU co-funded projects (Figure 8) are characterised by a more regular distribution with larger efforts on *Holistic system security* (53%), and a relatively less attention to *Prevention & detection, Incident response* and *Policies & legal* (all three categories with about 18%).

As shown in Figure 9 most national initiatives appear to consider, almost uniformly all the critical sectors with a very limited predominance for *Communication* and *Energy*, but with a limited *Overall* approach. On the other side, the EU co-funded projects, are largely oriented to consider *Overall* approaches. In any case, both these data appears incoherent with data collected about the consortiums composition, lack of stakeholders belonging to sectors different than electricity, communications and transportation.

Concerning the geographical aspect, national initiatives are (of course) mainly focused on the *National* level (20 projects, about 76%). But there are also projects with *Regional* (2 projects - 6%), *European* (5 projects - 15%), and

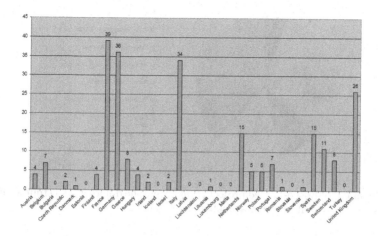

**Fig. 6.** Geographical distribution of the partners of the 44 CIIP relevant EU co-funded projects

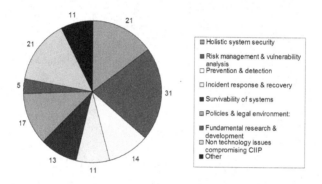

**Fig. 7.** Number of national initiatives that covers the different R&D topics (multiple answers admitted - information available for N=35 projects)

*International* (6 projects - 18%) focus. EU co-funded projects are exclusively focused on *European*-level.

A different, and for some aspects complementary, way to classify the projects is to consider their main focus in the research cycle proposed in [12]. The result is shown in Figure 10.

It is evident that while EU co-funded projects are more focused on *System Analysis* (and partially on *Dependability* and *Survivability*), national initiatives are more polarised on the *Risk Analysis* and *Vulnerability Assessment* topics. There is a limited activity on *Impact Assessment* and *Interdependency Analysis*, but the most surprising result is the absence of projects devoted to *Cost-Benefit Analysis* .

In Figure 11, the projects have been classified with respect to their hierarchical focus (i.e., component, infrastructure, (inter)dependent infrastructures, and national level) and with respect to the type of instrument adopted (i.e.,

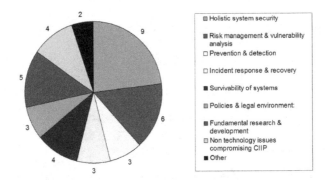

**Fig. 8.** Number of EU co-funded projects that covers the different R&D topics (multiple answers admitted - information available for N=17 projects)

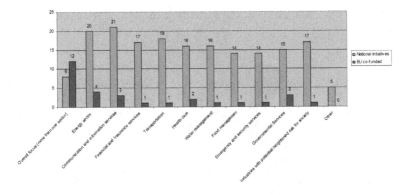

**Fig. 9.** Allocation of projects with respect to critical sectors (multiple answers admitted)

roadmap, assessment, method, and tool). National initiatives (filled square) are more present in the left-upper corner while EU co-funded projects are condensed in the lower-right corner (filled circle). In the graph are reported also other security related initiatives (empty square and circle, respectively) because this helps to better understand the global framework.

It is evident that the *infrastructure (inter)dependency* stripe is the less populated. There is, however, an other gap as well: the lower-left to upper-right diagonal appears to be empty. This can be explained considering that governments are mainly interested to understand if and how they are vulnerable in order to promote initiatives to reduce the negative consequences. Therefore, they are interested to assessment and risk analysis approach with a national view, and they pose very limited attention on solutions that are able to remove the causes of the problem. On the other hand, EU co-funded projects appear more devoted to technological innovation with a scope highly focused on components or on a single critical sector. This may be explained by the absence of a multi-domain

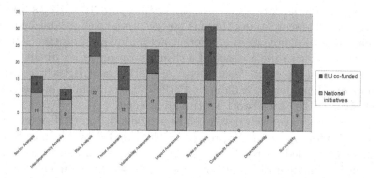

**Fig. 10.** Classification of the 78 CIIP relevant R&D projects with respect to specific research areas (multiple classification admitted)

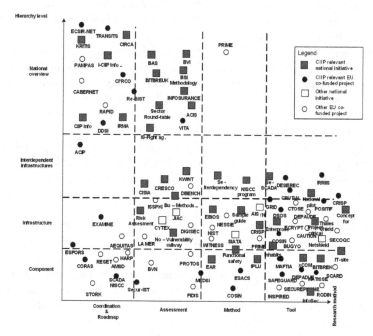

**Fig. 11.** Classification of projects with respect to hierarchy and instruments [12]

research community, by the limited interest from CI stakeholders, by the intrinsic complexity of the CIIP problem and also by the limited "market" and "proficiency" of strongly multi-disciplinary research communities.

## 4    Conclusions

In this paper we illustrate results obtained performing different type of analysis on the data collected by the CI²RCO project about CIIP R&D initiatives in the EU-25 countries plus ACC.

This analysis emphasises that, at least in Europe, CIP/CIIP is still a very immature field of research, and there is not yet a real well-established research community able to aggregate the different actors involved on the R&D topics. This is partially due to the absence of a clear European policy about CIP/CIIP and a clear vision on what "concretely" are CIP and CIIP, their objectives, constraints and boundaries. Building a CIIP R&D community in the European Research Area (ERA) framework is strongly needed.

Some initiatives have been developed or are ongoing on CIIP-relevant topics (we collected information on 72 projects) either funded by Member State governments or co-funded by EU Commission. However, aim and focus of the two types of projects appear different, and, for some aspects, complementary.

A great part of Member States has neither a strategic plan on CIIP nor a specific CIIP R&D program. CIIP related R&D activities are funded under different labels, from IT security to Border Control. Moreover, there is a set of different European and national agencies promoting this kind of initiatives, often with very limited coordination.

The majority of national initiatives are fragmented and of small economical dimension, with a short time span, with exception of very few countries (e.g. The Netherlands, Germany, UK, Sweden, and Austria). The lack of information about the economical dimension of different regional/national initiatives is common to more or less all of the projects, making it difficult to do any real comparison of the different initiatives. One of the reasons is that these projects either internally founded (e.g., aggregating manpower from various researches and stakeholders with no real money involved) or are commercial-sensitive contracts.

As discussed in Section 3, national initiatives are mainly focused on the risk analysis framework and on activities aimed to improve vulnerability and threat assessment. Inside these initiatives, an important role is played by government agencies and specifically by those involved in national security (e.g., police, intelligence) with a little involvement from CI stakeholders and little investment on R&D.

On the other hand, EU co-funded projects, at least the ones co-funded by the EU-IST Programme, are more focused on technological issues with some participation from CI-stakeholders but with the absence of government entities. In addition, the majority of the EU R&d funds is going to a limited number of nations (Germany, UK, Sweden) and research organizations.

In general, CI stakeholder involvement appears largely deficient. They expres some interests to better understand the phenomena, but they neither appear ready to play any active role nor are prepared to share their information and experience. They show a vision strongly related to their own infrastructure and business framework, with a limited attention on inter- and cross-sector interface elements and trans-domain consequences.

Because Critical Infrastructures owners and operators play a major role in CIIP, research programs and projects in this field must find effective ways to consider the perspectives of sector professional associations, sector councils, and other sources that understand the R&D needs of owners and operators.

Moreover, some important CI stakeholders appear not to be involved (e.g., the healthcare sector) and there is a very limited participation from infrastructure's component providers (e.g., SCADA providers).

With finite resources available to support CIIP R&D, setting a CIIP ERA would serve a unifying framework to ensure that CIIP R&D investments are coordinated and address the highest priorities based on risk assessment. This to ensure continuity of the essential infrastructures at the level of Member States and the EU.

An improved coordination is needed between sector-specific CIIP R&D plans and national and EU planning efforts, technology requirements, current and candidate CIIP R&D initiatives, and gaps between the CIIP R&D topics addressed in the current and candidate R&D initiatives.

A greater involvement is requested from the stakeholders of all critical sectors. Up to now, it appears that most of the CIIP R&D activities are sector-specific for the energy, communication, and information technology sectors.

In order to establish an operational and concrete co-operation between all actors involved in the topic of EU CIIP R&D, it would be desirable that they all produce program statements through different initiatives like CI$^2$RCO. The next step is to collect that data centrally at the EU, a first step to implement synergies and cross-fertilization through common CIIP R&D Programs and Projects.

## Acknowledgement

This work has been partially funded by the EU-project CI$^2$RCO (IST-2004-15818).

The authors would thank to the Ernst Basler + Partner AG, and specifically Daniel Bircher, Christof Egli, Connor Spreng and Tillmann Schulze, for the work done to collect the data.

## References

1. U.S. Government, *The National Strategy for The Physical Protection of Critical Infrastructures and Key Assets.* Washington, USA: The White House, Feb. 2003. www.whitehouse.gov/pcipb/physical.html
2. E.U. Commission, *Green Paper on a European Programme for Critical Infrastructure Protection COM(2005)576*, Brussels, 2005.
3. S. Bologna and R. Setola, "The Need to Improve Local Self-Awareness in CIP/CIIP," in *Proc. First IEEE International Workshop on Critical Infrastructure Protection (IWCIP 2005)*, Darmstadt, Germany, Nov. 3–4 2005, pp. 84–89.
4. E.A.M. Luiijf, and M.H.A. Klaver, "International interdependency of C(I)IP in Europe," in *Proc. of CIP Europe 2005 - Critical Infrastructure Protection*, GI CIS Forum, Bonn Germany, Sept. 19, 2005.
5. J. Moteff, C. Copeland, and J. Fischer, "Critical Infrastructures: What Makes an Infrastructure Critical?" in *Report for Congress RL31556*. The Library of Congress, Aug. 2002. www.fas.org/irp/crs/RL31556.pdf

6. M. Dunn and I.A. Wigert, *International CIIP Handbook*, A. Wenger and V. Mauer, Eds. Zurich: ETH, The Swiss Federal Institute of Technology, 2004. www.isn.ethz.ch/crn/publications/publications_crn.cfm?pubid=494

7. U.S. Government, *Interim National Infrastructure Protection Plan* . Washington, USA: The White House, Feb. 2005.

8. U.S. Government (The Executive Office of the President and the Office of Science and Technology Policy), *The National Plan for Research and Development in Support of Critical Infrastructure Protection*, Washington, USA, Apr. 2005. www.dhs.gov/dhspublic/interweb/assetlibrary/ST-_2004_NCIP_RD_PlanFIN%ALApr05.pdf

9. CI²RCO project - Critical Information Infrastructure Research Co-ordination - web page www.ci2rco.org

10. CI²RCO project delivery *D10 - Gap Analysis of existing CIIP R&D Programmes at Regional, National and EU Level*, www.ci2rco.org/downloadMaterial/IST-2004-15818%20-%20D10%20(V%201.3).pdf

11. CI²RCO project delivery *D3 - CIIP R&D Programmes, Projects and Actions Data Collection Overview*, www.ci2rco.org/downloadMaterial/IST-2004-15818%20-%20D3%20(V1.1).pdf

12. CI²RCO project delivery *D6 - Report on the analysis and evaluation of CIIP R&D programmes*, www.ci2rco.org/downloadMaterial/IST-2004-15818%20-%20D6%20(V%201.3.4).pdf

# Intelligent Network-Based Early Warning Systems

Karsten Bsufka, Olaf Kroll-Peters, and Sahin Albayrak

Technische Universität Berlin, DAI-Labor
{karsten.bsufka,olaf.kroll-peters,sahin.albayrak}@dai-labor.de

**Abstract.** In this paper we present an approach for an agent-based early warning system (A-EWS) for critical infrastructures. In our approach we combine existing security infrastructures, e.g. firewalls or intrusion detection systems, with new detection approaches to create a global view and to determine the current threat state.

**Keywords:** critical infrastructures, early warning system, multi agent systems, intrusion detection.

## 1   Introduction

Modern societies depend heavily on certain infrastructures, which are critical for existence and smooth operation of society. Examples for these critical infrastructures are:

- Transportation and traffic
- Telecommunications and information technology
- Finance and insurance services
- Supplies
  - Health care
  - Emergency services
  - Water supply
  - Energy supply
- Public administration and legal system [2]

With the dawning information age these infrastructures lose the independent character. The main reason for this loss of independence lies within the emergence of information technology infrastructures and the Internet.

Every critical infrastructure is based on its underlying networks. These separate networks are connected by Internet provider networks, see Figure 1.

Figure 1 is similar to a figure presented in [5], which shows how *bounded* networks reside within an *unbounded* domain. Generally speaking bounded networks are under single administrative control and adhere to known security policies. Unbounded networks on the other hand are under different administrative controls and there is no global visibility of the network. As a consequence, problems

J. Lopez (Ed.): CRITIS 2006, LNCS 4347, pp. 103–111, 2006.

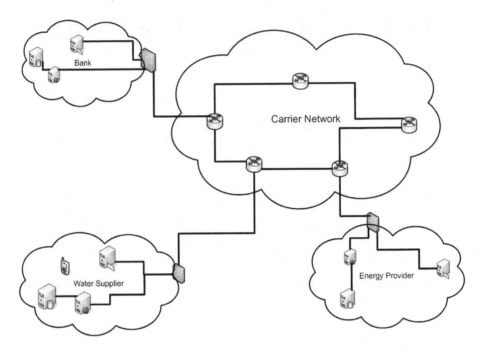

**Fig. 1.** Overview of CRITIS networks

occurring within one critical infrastructure, e.g. power failures caused by natural disasters or attacks are carried out against transport systems, will not be communicated to other critical infrastructures.

We propose an early warning system for critical infrastructures, which helps to relay information about threatened critical infrastructures. Before we go into details about our proposed agent-based early warning system for critical infrastructures, we first describe some potential scenarios for a breakdown of critical infrastructures, the role of IT systems and the potential effects in these situations.

## 2    Breakdown Scenarios for Critical Infrastructures

There are several potential causes for a breakdown or limited availability of a critical infrastructure. Obvious causes would be attacks (cyber or physical) or natural disasters, other reasons may include (labor) strikes, erroneous use or technical failures of IT systems or other systems. A detailed discussion of critical infrastructures can be found in [9].

The threats to critical infrastructures can be classified into the following different categories.

- Financial threats
- Material threats

- Immaterial threats
- Threats of living
- Social threats

We chose the following scenarios as examples for the effect on IT systems. First, we describe the dependence of other critical infrastructures from the telecommunication systems. Subsequently, we will describe possible threat scenarios for the chosen infrastructures.

## 2.1   Financial Payment Systems

Nowadays, financial transactions without IT support are unthinkable. IT systems are the foundation for processing global business (e.g. stock market transactions) and private business such as online banking or online tax declaration. IT systems are a fundamental infrastructure in this field.

Attackers can have different motivations for attacking a financial payment system. Foremost there is the possibility of gaining monetary benefits for themselves by attacking the infrastructure. For example, a potential attacker could transfer rounding errors from stock transactions to his own account.

## 2.2   Electric Power Systems

In contrast to financial payment systems, an electric power system is more susceptible to natural disasters and attacks, which try to damage the physical part of the infrastructure. As an example for natural disasters serves the winter of 2005/2006, where parts of Germany were without any electric power, because extremely cold temperatures caused power lines to collapse.

Electronic devices are employed in most activities of everyday life. In case of power failure all energy-dependent processes cease to function. Therefore power supply is also considered to be a basic infrastructure. Power failure will also cause the breakdown of other critical infrastructures, a general power failure for example would also cause the traffic systems to fail.

The effects of a power failure can be reduced by back-up systems, but they will only provide a reduced amount of electric power.

## 2.3   IT and Telecommunications

IT and Telecommunication infrastructure can be indirectly targeted by attacking the underlying electric power systems, but they also can be attacked directly. In both cases this will affect other critical infrastructures that use or are built upon an attacked IT or telecommunication infrastructure.

Control devices and communication in all other critical infrastructures require an underlying operational telecommunication network. In case of an attack, this infrastructure can be utilized to take preventive measures, issue an alert or initiate a responsive action.

For instance, if an attacker plans to reduce the market value of a company, he could spread falsified rumors about the company. Another possibility would be to cut off the access for customers to the e-business portal.

## 2.4  Common Themes in Attacks

All the aforementioned critical infrastructures exhibit the following character-istics: they require a running IT infrastructure, energy and they are all dis-tributed systems. All fields require electric power for operation consequently a running power infrastructure. They also need a running IT infrastructure to deliver results, to be controlled and coordinated. Distributed sensors, which in-clude the fields of IT and power supply, have to be employed to control and protect the systems. Therefore we describe an approach which is distributed as well.

## 3   Agent-Based Early Warning System

Currently, operators of a critical infrastructures are on their own when dealing with attacks or natural disasters. This may work as long as a problem, natu-ral disaster or cyber attack, affects only his infrastructure. Generally, critical infrastructures are interconnected. It certainly would enhance the survivability of critical infrastructures if early warnings of approaching problems could be issued, received and exchanged.

We propose an agent-based early warning system (A-EWS) for this task, see Figure 2 for high-level overview.

The general architecture depicted in Figure 2 is similar to the architecture presented in [12], but our proposed systems does not focus on networks alone, but also on hosts.

Currently, our research focuses solely on detecting cyber attacks, and we will describe the A-EWS in this context. Yet, we believe our approach can be ex-tended to cover natural disasters and technical failures as well. We are aware that an A-EWS raises a lot of privacy and policy issues for the co-operation be-tween different entities. We decided to focus our research on the technical aspects and to use the results of the technical solutions to identify specific privacy and policy requirements. These requirements will then be used for a revised A-EWS version.

The foundation of an A-EWS is its capability to detect attacks as early as possible. Known attacks can be detected by IDS, firewalls and anti-virus soft-ware. In general, these applications inform users or system administrators about detected events. Sometimes they do even less and store the knowledge about occurring attacks in log files.

An A-EWS will not help the current victim of an attack. If information con-cerning detected attacks is spread beyond the border of a single local network, it can help others in preparing for an attack. If, for example, anti-virus soft-ware attached to e-mail servers detects several e-mails with an attached viruses, it currently only cleans the e-mails. If it would also propagate the information about the virus attacks to other e-mail servers, they could start updating the anti-virus softwares signature database ahead of time.

To this end, one type of sensor in an A-EWS should be a wrapper for current security products capable of interpreting and reporting the detection results in a

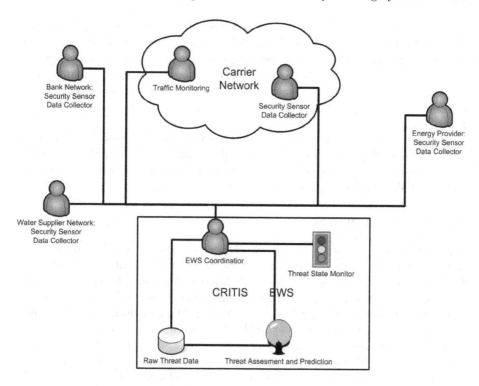

**Fig. 2.** Proposed agent-based EWS

common attack ontology. Another kind of sensor would use honey pots or honey nets as a sensor [8]. Sensors will be represented by agents that share common ontologies and use services for interaction with the A-EWS.

Our research focus is on three other types of sensors:

- Anomaly Sensors,
- Network Traffic Sensors and
- Attack Pattern Sensors.

### 3.1 Anomaly Sensors

In our work anomaly sensors are used to observe the behavior of hosts. Although the basic ideas and concepts could also be used to realize network traffic anomaly sensors, we are currently do not investigate that direction. For detecting anomalies we use two different approaches.

One approach uses unsupervised learning (Self Organizing Map — SOM) algorithms to learn the "normal" behavior of hosts [1]. Here we measure a selected set of features on host systems. For this approach to work well, the behavior of hosts should not be too erratic. It will be much more complicated to detect anomalies on PCs, used by students in a PC pool, than observing a PC used by a single secretary. The other approach is a host-based artificial immune systems (AIS). Both approaches work on the same set of observed features and can simultaneously observe the same host. Supervisor agents are capable or correlating observation results for one host produced by the AIS and SOM components. To reach a certain belief of the current threat state of a host, these agents also consider their beliefs and the known measurements results from neighboring hosts.

In general, the supervisor agents will act as the anomaly sensors for a critical infrastructure. Depending on the current global threat state or the local threat state, it should also be possible to propagate all anomaly sensor events to the global A-EWS system.

### 3.2 Network Traffic Sensors

Anomaly sensors can only report attacks, which have reached or breached a target system. Furthermore, the impact on the (global) threat state is very low for small numbers of breached systems. Unfortunately, it is be more or less to be expected, that a small number of systems will be infected.

It would make more sense to detect ongoing attacks before they fully reach their targets. A field of application for this is the network level. Here it is possible to detect threats during transmission and react to them. A carrier network, that connects critical infrastructures, would be very suitable. Networks for a specific critical infrastructure would be less suitable but still acceptable.

There are two types of network traffic sensors. One simply observes the traffic flow and could be used to detect denial-of-service attacks. The other type analyzes the traffic content, trying to identify known malware signatures. Currently our researches focuses on the latter.

The realization of network traffic sensors faces technical and social challenges. When the traffic content is analyzed, privacy considerations have to be taken into account. Current privacy laws prevent the use of network traffic sensors for analyzing traffic content in some countries. Legislators must weigh the gain in critical infrastructure survivability and security against the loss of privacy. Technically there are two main problems to address. In large networks it is infeasible to analyze traffic at every possible server and router. This means a method for identifying the minimum number of observation points and their locations must be found. The question of a minimum number of observation points is closely related to the second challenge, which deals with performance issues. Network traffic sensors must be capable of handling a huge amount of traffic in relatively short time frames. The amount of traffic and the time-frame of traffic analysis depends not only on technically issues, but also on the security and survivability goals for a critical infrastructure.

### 3.3 Attack Pattern Sensors

Sophisticated attacks contain a sequence of steps, where each step produces some sort of effects. Attack pattern sensors know a formal description of attack steps or effects [10]. An example for the former is an IP fragmentation attack on an IDS [11], were the order and properties of the IP fragments can be described; an example for the latter would be the installation (modifies the file system) and execution of a Trojan horse (increases the number of running processes and opens new network connections) by exploiting different bugs in e-mails and/or web browsers. These two very short examples also illustrate the fact that attack pattern sensors either can be deployed to monitor hosts or to monitor network traffic.

### 3.4   Sensor Placement and Cooperation

When selecting a location where a sensor is to be placed, its detection abilities must be taken into account. If a sensor agent is responsible for interpreting fire-wall log files, it should be attached to a firewall. It is not necessary to place network traffic sensor agents on every node in the network. They only need to be placed on nodes, which add additional information to their knowledge about the current network traffic flow. We are currently working with game–theoretic approaches for determining the optimal placement of sensors in a network.

One defining aspect of placement algorithms is whether sensors need communicate with other sensors. In general, our sensors do not need to cooperate directly with each other, they only need to report relevant events to coordinator or collector agents. We plan to build this A-EWS up on the JIAC framework [6]. JIAC is a Java-based environment for developing agent-based applications. It already offers yellow–page, security and communication services, which allow the discovery of other agents and the secure communication between agents. In order to build an early warning system with JIAC, the global EWS part will be connected to trusted remote platforms (at least one per connected critical infrastructure IT system), which will in turn host sensors in specific critical infrastructure IT systems. The concept of trusted remote platforms for JIAC, was introduced in the security target [4] for Common Criteria evaluation of JIAC [7,3].

### 3.5   Countermeasures

Anomaly sensors, network traffic sensors and attack pattern sensors are used by A-EWS to detect ongoing attacks. The simplest reaction to detected attacks is to inform human operators about it, e.g. by sending e-mails to a threat state monitoring tool.

We envision that an A-EWS also contains a prediction unit, capable of making educated guesses about the future development of the attack. These guesses will be used to send warnings and advices to administrators, prepare alternative transport mechanisms for important messages, e.g. converting e-mails to SMS messages if normal e-mail transport is not possible, or disconnect hosts or sub-networks.

## 4    Conclusions and Future Work

In order to enhance the survivability of IT systems for critical infrastructures. It is important to detect failures and attacks as early as possible. To this end, we propose an agent-based early warning systems, that on one hand builds upon already existing security products and on the other hand uses new agent-based sensors for hosts and networks.

Currently our work is conducted in an industry endorsed research project, which focuses on the development of the described agent-based sensors and the sensor placement. We envision the described A-EWS as an application and extension of our current work. An especially interesting research aspect, will be the correlation of anomaly detection results, with events from security appliances. At the moment we are only working on different correlation strategies between anomaly sensors.

## Acknowledgments

The authors wish to thank Katja Luther, Danie Christelle Mouapi Tientcheu, Rainer Bye, Christian Scheel, Stephan Schmidt, Tuvshintur Tserendorj, Robert Wetzker, Volker Eckert, Sebastian Linkiewicz, Thorsten Rimkus, Aubrey-Derrick Schmidt and Tansu Alpcan for supporting them during the creation of this paper and the productive work on the malware filtering project funded by the Deutsche Telekom AG.

## References

1. Sahin Albayrak, Achim Müller, Christian Scheel, and Dragan Milosevic. Combining Self-Organizing Map Algorithms for Robust and Scalable Intrusion Detection. In M. Mohammadian, editor, *Proceedings of InternationaInternational Conference on Computational Intelligence for Modelling Control and Automation (CIMCA 2005 Book 2)*, pages 123–130, Vienna, Austria, 2005.
2. Bundesamt für Sicherheit in der Informationstechnik. Critical infrastructures in state and society. `http://www.bsi.de/fachthem/kritis/kritis_e.htm` (2006-05-16).
3. Bundesamt für Sicherheit in der Informationstechnik. Certification Report BSI-DSZ-CC-0248-2005 for Java Intelligent Agent Componentware IV Version 4.3.11 from DAI- Labor Technische Universität Berlin. `http://www.bsi.de/zertifiz/zert/reporte/0248a.pdf`, 2005.
4. DAI-Labor. Security Target Java Intelligent Agent Componentware IV. `http://www.bsi.de/zertifiz/zert/reporte/0248b.pdf`, 2004.
5. R.J. Ellison, D.A. Fisher, R.C. Linger, H.F. Lipson, T. Longstaff, and N.R. Mead. Survivable Network Systems: An Emerging Discipline. Technical Report CMU/SEI-97-TR-013 ESC-97-013, Software Engineering Institute, Software Engineering Institute. Carnegie Mellon University. Pittsburg, PA 15213 USA, November 1997.

6. Stefan Fricke, Karsten Bsufka, Jan Keiser, Torge Schmidt, Ralf Sesseler, and Sahin Albayrak. Agent-based telematic services and telecom applications. *Communications of the ACM*, 44(4):43–48, April 2001.
7. Tim Geissler and Olaf Kroll-Peters. Applying Security Standards to Multi Agent Systems. In *The First International Workshop on Safety and Security in Multiagent Systems (SASEMAS) Part of AAMAS held at Columbia University New York City, 20 July 2004*, July 2004.
8. Cristine Hoepers, Klaus Steding-Jessen, Luiz E. R. Cordeiro, and Marcelo H. P. C. Chaves. A National Early Warning Capability Based on a Network of Distributed Honeypots. In *Proceedings of the 17th Annual FIRST Conference on Computer Security Incident Handling*, Singapore, June 2005.
9. John C. Knight, Matthew C. Elder, James Flinn, and Patrick Marx. Analysis of Four Critical Infrastructure Applications. Technical Report Computer Science Report No. CS-97-27, Department of Computer Science, University of Virginia, September 1998.
10. I. Kotenko. Active vulnerability assessment of computer networks by simulation of complex remote attacks. In *International Conference on Computer Networks and Mobile Computing, 2003. ICCNMC 2003*, pages 40–47, October 2003.
11. Antonio Merola. Intrusion Detection Systems-Interna. *hakin9*, (4), 2005. http://www.hakin9.org.
12. C. Zou, L. Gao, W. Gong, and D. Towsley. Monitoring and early warning for internet worms. In *Proceedings of the 10th ACM conference on Computer and communication security, ACM Press (2003)*, pages 190–199, 2003.

# Can an Early Warning System for Home Users and SMEs Make a Difference? A Field Study*

Urs E. Gattiker

CyTRAP Labs, Roentgenstrasse 49, 8005 Zurich, Switzerland
Critis06@CyTRAP.eu

**Abstract.** This paper outlines how early alert systems can help home users and SMEs in improving their security hygiene (culture of security). The viability of our framework and concepts are evaluated using www.CASEScontact.org as a case study. The latter offers its services to targeted groups of home users and SMEs supporting them in better protecting their information and data assets stored on, for instance, PCs or smartphones. As this paper shows, careful targeting of services (e.g., type of information and technical focus) and diligence (e.g., accurate and timely information is being provided) are a must for attaining users' trust and confidence. Only then may behavioral change follow that will, in turn, improve security hygiene (culture of security). As a result, we present conceptual and empirical evidence for the need to integrate marketing and information security elements to improve an early alert system's resource-advantage.

**Keywords:** awareness, critical infrastructure, critical infrastructure protection, crime, culture of security, cybercrime, CASEScontact.org, CyTRAP Labs, early warning system, EWS, freeware, identity theft, incident response, information assurance, information security, lessons learned, malware, phishing, patch management, prevention, public-private partnership, privacy, risk management, security assurance, security guide, threat, trust, US-CERT, virus, vulnerability, worm.

## 1 Introduction

In 2002, the OECD released a statistic that indicated that 4.9 percent of inhabitants had a broadband connection such as DSL, cable or ADSL. By 2004 this number had risen to 10.3 percent, while for 2005 the OECD reported a 13.2 percent average (EU15 = 14.2 percent) [1]. Based on June 2006 statistics the OECD reported that many countries in Europe have numbers in the high twenties (e.g., Belgium, Denmark & Switzerland) [2]. If we consider that a household may, on average, consist of two

---

* An earlier version of this paper was presented at the First International Workshop on CRITICAL INFORMATION INFRASTRUCTURES SECURITY (CRITIS'06) August 30 - September 2, 2006 Samos Island, Greece. A longer and more detailed version of this paper entitled "New threats and national warning systems - lessons to be learned" can be downloaded from http://cytrap.eu/blog/?p=30.

J. Lopez (Ed.): CRITIS 2006, LNCS 4347, pp. 112–127, 2006.
© Springer-Verlag Berlin Heidelberg 2006

people, it follows that in many EU Member States as well as OECD ones, 50% or more of a country's citizens have broadband access to the internet.

Also, a widely cited 2001 report by the CERT/CC [3] indicated that it had observed a significant increase in activity resulting in compromises of home user machines, specifically targeting those with cable modem and DSL connections. Recent data indicate that new type of threats than can spread ever faster continue to be a significant threat [4]. Unfortunately, home users have generally been the least prepared to defend against attacks, while often not updating their software or defence mechanisms as they should. Hence, detecting and resolving attacks on those systems is a real challenge.

For this reason, several Member States of the European Union and their representatives met with experts in July of 2002 to discuss how better awareness could result in improved prevention for home users and citizens, thereby being better protected against attacks. This resulted in the creation of the Cyberworld Awareness and Security Enhancement Structure or CASES for short (e.g., see CASEScontact.org, CASES-CC.org, and CASES.lu).

This paper tries to advance our knowledge of how early alert systems can help in improving prevention and security posture against malicious code and attacks for home-users and SMEs. This is accomplished by the application of generally accepted concepts that have been used regarding early warning systems for quite some time. The objectives of this paper are (1) to determine what structure must be used to reach target groups of users with warnings regarding threats, vulnerabilities and zero-day exploits, and (2) to assess whether such a tailored and targeted service (i.e., according to age, using different information distribution channels) can help in fostering better prevention by users to raise the protection level of their systems and data.

The article is organized as follows. First, the conceptual background is discussed; in particular, how an early warning system could help home-users and SMEs is outlined. Next, the requirements for an early warning system (EWS) to make it services valuable for home-users and SMEs are presented. Third, the framework offered is then analyzed using CASEScontact.org as a case study. Finally, we summarize key issues for early warning systems for home-users and SMEs, suggest ropes to skip and highlight management as well as policy implications.

## 2  Moving from Awareness to Active Defence

To reduce a health pandemic or the number of incidents caused by smokers falling asleep in bed, federal governments, public health offices and fire departments have, for a long time undertaken efforts to raise awareness about fire and health hazards. Hence, pamphlets and/or other information provide insights and checklists helping citizens to take the necessary steps for achieving effective fire prevention. Similarly, improving dental hygiene and reducing the spreading of infectious diseases requires that children are being taught early.

As well all know cleaning one's teeth regularly reduces the risk for dental decay. But this does not mean that we clean them them regularly after each meal as we should. Similarly, most users' know that one should refrain from just opening an attached file sent by somebody. This helps reduce the risk for having one's PC infected by a virus (see Table 1). However, it requires taking the precautionary step of confirming with the sender that he or she did actually send the message with that attachment. In turn, such cautious behaviour reduces one's risk for becoming a victim of a malicious user's attack that spoofed the sender's address to get one to open an attachment infected by a virus or a worm (see Table 1).

**Table 1.** From awareness to prevention

|  | Fire | AIDS | InfoSec |
|---|---|---|---|
|  | Information pamphlet from fire department | Information campaigns against AIDS | Information about malware in the media, updates to patch software vulnerabilities by vendors, public campaigns |
| Prevention – training and practice helps | Fire drill | Instructions about how to best use a condom | How to fine-tune a firewall or conducting a regular security update for the Windows operating system (using Automatic Update or other means) (http://CASEScontact.org/) |
| Behavioral change is a vital step on the road to better prevention | Practical rules mean behavioral change ➔ Don't smoke in bed | Do not have unprotected sex with strangers | User follows these three steps to minimize risks by: 1) making certain the originating person of the e-mail or instant messaging having a picture attachment is the person he or she claims to be; and 2) the attachment is being scanned by regularly updated anti-virus software before it will be opened. The user must understand that if the above two steps are not followed diligently, the risk for infection and possible damages could be quite high. Finally, every piece of equipment should have a: 3) correctly installed and properly working software-based firewall. |

**Note.** The key for successful prevention is getting users to take advantage of knowledge and applying their know-how to change their behavior accordingly.

In order to get people to change their behavior, however, information security must succeed in showing users that changing their behavior results in personal benefits (e.g., what benefits does better security mean for my family connecting to the Internet using the home PC?).

As Table 1 indicates, without increased awareness resulting in behavioral change, the risk for infections remains unnecessarily high. Hence, for better protecting the public against fire hazards and dangerous diseases, most countries have undertaken the necessary policy-related steps. These include launching awareness programs to make sure the public knows what needs to be done and how. If necessary, the public health nurse will be visiting schools teaching children about hygiene.

Table 2 summarises how governments have moved to active defence by putting a regulatory framework into place that helps reduce risks and accidents regarding fire prevention and better public health. Unfortunately, the regulatory framework in the information security domain is not as clear. For instance, most countries do not require through regulation that Internet Service Provider(s) (ISPs) must provide spam filtering as well as anti-virus services and firewall protection. Some ISPs may provide this on a voluntary basis or else for a fee to their clients.

**Table 2.** Successful prevention demands active defence

| Category | Fire | Food & Health | InfoSec |
|----------|------|---------------|---------|
| Regulatory framework & laws | Building code (i.e. certain materials cannot be used). | Public Health regulations stipulate how food must be stored | E-Commerce and Privacy Regulations outline consumers and sellers rights and responsibilities. |
| Active defense | Installing smoke detectors - reduce the risk for being caught in a fire | Refrigerators for food storage can help in reducing the risk for food spoilage | Protecting confidentiality and integrity of customer data. |
| Consequences for breaking the law or best practices | Insurance claim submitted is being adjusted downward | Repeated violation as discovered by on-site inspection of the restaurant, results in fine and/or closure of facility | Depending upon the country, privacy violations may result in fines for the enterprise. Insurance coverage for such events as identity theft may be adjusted downward if the user is unable to demonstrate having had state-of-the-art security protection installed on her PC that functions properly (e.g., anti-virus, firewall, etc.). |
| Developing appropriate automatisms | Before leaving the apartment, checking that all electrical devices are turned off | After going to the toilet, washing one's hands | User knows e-mail attachments should not be opened without having checked with the known and trusted sender beforehand that he or she actually sent it. Such careful behavior should become innate or automatized and, therefore, part of the user culture. |

**Note.** For the columns labelled fire and food/health, much of the regulatory efforts have to be put into practice by organizations, such as builders, construction companies, restaurants and catering firms. In turn, audits and control inspections are feasible. In contrast, information security and home PCs means that neither adequate regulatory efforts are in place nor can control inspections be undertaken if these regulations are adhered to by using the proper auditing procedures to assess compliance at the Internet Service Provider (ISP).

Insurance companies offer policies against identity theft. The price charged or acceptance into such an insurance program, however, depends upon having state-of-the-art anti-virus software installed as well as having a properly working software-based firewall running on one's PC [5].

As Table 2 would suggest, the greatest challenge is in convincing computer users that following 'best practices' regarding information security is to their advantage. In turn, it will reduce the risk for being infected by malware or having a malicious user taking control of one's smarthpone or tablet PC.

# 3  Defining Target Markets for an Early Warning System

In the above section we described that getting the user's attention and interest for improving his or her security posture is a not to be underestimated challenge. The key is that when awareness is hightened due to a security incident or media coverage, providing an effective solution for the user is the first step. The challenge is, however, to maintain the interest and to encourage the user to remain vigilant. This issue is addressed in more detail below.

## 3.1  Identifying Potential Market Segments

As pointed out in the previous section, Microsoft products (e.g., Excel, Powerpoint, Outlook and Word) and Windows compatible software are most widely used. Moreover, younger users are an important target group since they use the Internet extensively and differently compared to other age groups. For instance, research findings indicate that IM is primarily used for entertainment, chatting about private matters by over 70% of younger users [6].

## 3.2  Handling of Critical Security Incidents

A security incident is sometimes described as an event that violates an organization's security policies, user access policies or regulatory requirements. A security incident could also affect negatively the security of data such as confidentiality, integrity and availability. What follows is that a **security incident is an adverse event, whereby data and information security could be jeopardized** [7].

Based on the above, a distinction must be made beween *incidents versus security incidents*. Dictionaries tend to define an incident as an occurrence that might lead to an accident. However, an accident caused by an incident cannot just be categorized as being a security incident such as a flat tire causing a crash (safety versus security). To illustrate, if a user cannot connect to a hotspot, this is most certainly not a security incident [7]. Finally, while a system administrator of a large network may perceive scanning of the network as a security incident, a security service provider may classify the scanning of a network as an incident (see also Figure 1 below).

### 3.2.1  Monitoring and Detection of Security Incidents

Monitoring and detection has to assure that the threat mitigation service receives the information relevant for the target group of users. Hence, participation in various forums and online discussions, as well as the monitoring of other alert services, seems to be an important part of this work (see also Figure 1 below).

Because the malicious user may not finish working once office hours are over or during long weekends, the alert service must be able to monitor the Internet for emerging threats at those times as well. Put differently, while the monitoring at 3 am may not be vital, being not online for several days during a long weekend such as Easter (e.g., Good Friday and Easter Monday are public holidays in most European countries) may result in unacceptable delays until a response is being issued. Failing to manage this properly is, of course a threat to the level of trust users will be able to have in a service being on time, relevant and reliable.

### 3.2.2  Analysis and Detection of Critical Security Incidents

As illustrated in Figure 1, the 2nd step in an effective handling process system for security incidents is the analysis and decisions of security incidents. Performing well here requires the necessary human capital. The latter must be able to provide the know-how needed to analyze, sometimes rather sketchy information that is being discussed online about, for instance, a zero-day vulnerability.

Another important issue is that security incidents, threats and vulnerabilities that have been identified must be prioritized according to criticality. Similar to triaging[1] according to severity as done by medical doctors arriving at a car crash site, decisions must be made about which security incidents should not be investigated or analyzed.

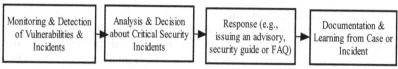

Copyright: CyTRAP Labs 2006

**Fig. 1.** Effective handling of security incidents for an early warning system or EWS for short. Managing the incident response process can involve several additional sub-steps that help further improve the managing of the response. Ultimately, learning should result in the EWS being successful in helping home users and SMEs improving their security posture further. This might occur through security guides, tips and/or tools that help reduce risks that could jeopardize privacy, confidentiality, reliability and dependability of their information assets.

Monitoring may involve such information sources as: 1) user or subscribers reporting suspicious incidents, 2) information  scanned from alerting services (e.g., vendors and CERTs), 3) IT and other staff,   4) automatic alarms (e.g., network sniffers).

Analysis requires that we have to use triage for deciding about a) security incidents, vulnerabilities and threats or zero-day exploits vs. others and, thereafter, b) analyzing what can be considered critical taking into careful consideration the subscriber and user base.

Ultimately, response is the opportunity for demonstrating to clients and subscriber that the output produced adds value. As importantly, it will make potential users aware about the service the EWS offers and its value for protecting their information assets (value-proposition).


Analyzing a security incident, threat or vulnerability will result in assigning both, a risk level for becoming a victim or being harmed as well as a worry index regarding the possible damages if the infection mightoccur. In turn, the risk and worry indices should help in deciding what type of response is required. The severety of the threat may depend if the users subscribing or being serviced by an early alert system. How prevalent is the software that is being reported as having a vulnerability that is classified as being a zero-day exploit (see also below).

### 3.2.3  Type and Form of Response

Sometimes an advisory may have to be issued not because it is a critical security incident but, unfortunately, due to the media hyping it up unnecessarily.

---

[1] Triage derives from the French word meaning to sort. Process of prioritizing the evacuation of the injured by the medical or ambulance staff at the casualty site.

Alerts or advisories are important and they are most certainly effective attention grabbers as far as users and the media are concerned. But as pointed out in Table 2, active defence efforts undertaken by the user should help to reduce the probability for such attacks in succeeding. Hence, to reduce the vulnerability of becoming a victim requires that users are provided with security guides. The latter help users with the efforts that must be undertaken to reduce the risks for getting infected by malicious software when using, for instance, IM. Similarly, providing advice on how to use free software for discovering rootkits that have been installed on their PC by a worm or a malicious program (e.g., the Sony BMG case see [8]) may help resolve a problem today). As importantly, such advice can help improve the user's security posture as well, thereby reducing the risk for infection by a rootkit sometime in the future.

### 3.2.4  Documentation and Learning

Once the decision about what type of response is most appropriate has been made and executed, the final step is the documentation of the security incident. In the case documentation does include assessing through webpage and other statistics how much users have taken advantage of the information provided.

As far as learning is concerned, the advisory has to be linked to efforts that help prevent users from being vulnerable to a similar threat in the near future. This may require that a guide is being prepared that helps subscribers in reducing their risk for becoming a victim of a phishing attack. Accordingly, the learning triggered by a security incident for the early warning team must, of course, result in additional documentation and/or tools for users empowering them to better protect themselves.

## 4   Assessing Market Competence: Using CASEScontact.org as a Case Study

In the previous sections we outlined how awareness raising should ultimately result in better prevention for home users and employees. Furthermore, a security incident handling framework was provided in figure 1 and, as importantly, an early warning system for users was sketched out. In this section we describe such a system using CASEScontact.org as the example and provide information regarding how the framework and concepts outlined can be applied in practice.

CASEScontact.org is one node in a network of nodes. It is a private and vendor neutral initiative that offers security advisories and various content (see http://CASEScontact.org/subscribe_all.php) As the name would suggest, other nodes such as www.CASES.public.lu are publicly funded initiatives that collaborate and exchange information with CASEScontact.org and other nodes.

### 4.1  Extant and Potentially Available Resources

To enable CASEScontact.org to produce effectively services that have value for its primary market segment(s) (see Section 4.2), it had to narrow down its offerings from the start. An opportunity for providing services grounded in identifying and analyzing high-impact threats and vulnerabilities was identified as well as focusing on:

1. attacks on those systems that may result in their misuse for launching attacks against the network infrastructure or other systems;
2. providing advice for better protecting smaller systems against software vulnerability exploits (e.g., zero-day exploits); and
3. helping users in better protecting their systems against attacks and social engineering exploits that involve new vulnerabilities, scams, techniques and tools.

## 4.2 Selecting the Target Markets

Based on its financial and human resource constraints as outlined in the previous section and, most importantly, to provide services that met its targeted groups' needs, CASEScontact.org was launched in late 2004 with a particular focus on younger users. This group included and continues to target today teenagers and those 35 years and younger. Services focus on SMEs as well [10].

Target groups were further narrowed by offering services and tools for those users with hardware and software running on the Windows operating system's platform, using Microsoft Office programs and compatible software.

Table 3 outlines some of the issues that we addressed regarding focus of our services. In particular, we began by targeting younger Internet users that have been shown to take advantage of the latest technology, software and the internet. For instance, this is particularly true for their extensive use of social networking, instant messaging (IM) and voice over IP (VoIP) services [6]. But focusing on younger respondents may also create synergies. For instance, when looking at households it is obvious that improving teenagers' security behavior may create positive effects for other household members as well. Teenagers are often the most tech savvy members of the family but might, unfortunately, also take the greatest risks. Helping teenagers to better manage those risks, while improving their security posture, is likely to benefit other users of the family PC as well.

As Table 3 indicates, we began by simply providing advisories and security guides for home-users and SMEs regardless of location. This allowed us to begin with English content only[2]

Because of our expansion and history as well as demands by our subscribers[3] we decided to issue security guides in German (i.e. called Ratgeber) besides English beginning mid-December 2005. About 20 percent of our users (e.g., web page visitors and subscribers to e-mailed content) come from Germany and Switzerland. Approximately 50 percent of subscribers or registered users come from such countries as: Belgium, Denmark, Finland, Greece, Italy, Netherlands, Norway, Slovakia,

---

[2] Teenagers are also most likely to come from a generation that knows the English language fairly well as a second language (e.g., Denmark, Germany, The Netherlands). Hence, reaching this target group using English was possible, thereby avoiding further demands on scarce resources.

[3] Because CASEScontact.org was launched in Luebeck (Germany) and Copenhagen (Denmark), the focus was primarily on these countries when we began. With further activities in Switzerland (opening of a CyTRAP Lab office in Zurich) things changed and services expanded. This was another reason why we began offering some content in German (e.g., security guides in late 2005). Some services are also prepared for third parties for a fee.

**Table 3.** Target markets

| Categories | Definition | Advisories | Security Guides | What user data reveal |
|---|---|---|---|---|
| Countries | World *Benelux *Denmark *Germany | Alerts are released in English | Guides are published in German and English | Alerts have been of particular interest to SME system administrators and security experts from large organizations. |
| Age group | 35    and under | 20-50 or older | 20 or older but quite popular with younger clientele | Younger users appear to take a particular interest in improving their security posture with the help of the security guides. |

Slovenia and Spain. A smaller but still significant number of subscribers are located in the Persian Gulf States as well as Canada.

Recently we have also succeeded in getting others to subscribe to our services for a fee. In such instances, the party may distribute these to either their employees (i.e. in case of an employer or ISP), or else to citizens in case of national service.

### 4.3  Handling of Critical Security Incidents

Based on the above section, handling security incidents for younger adults and teenagers as well as SMEs requires the development of a system and process management that allows issuing advisories that are relevant to this target audience.

#### 4.3.1  Monitoring and Detecting of Security Incidents

CASEScontact.org participates in the CASES network of nodes as well as in various forums and expert groups. It also tries to assure that the Internet is being monitored during a long weekend such as Easter (e.g., Good Friday and Easter Monday are public holidays in most European countries) to avoid unacceptable delays until a response is being issued[4].

#### 4.3.2  Analysis and Detection of Critical Security Incidents

As illustrated in Figure 1, the 2nd step in an effective handling process system for security incidents is the analysis and decisions of security incidents. CASEScontact.org's dedicated staff work together with volunteers (e.g., CyTRAP Labs and members of www.EICAR.org) to provide technical insights and analyses required for quality service.

---

[4] It has been documented that over public holidays and long weekends some EWS systems are quite slow in responding [11]. CASEScontact.org has discovered that especially in instances of zero-day exploits[11], however, many home-users check out our advisories quickly after they have been released (e.g., afternoon of Good Friday - a public holiday in Europe).

**Table 4.** Monitoring and detection of critical security incidents

| Category | Description | Advisories | Tips / Security Guides | Comments |
|---|---|---|---|---|
| Risks | Windows MS Office Compatible software | Patch Tuesday Zero-Day | Limiting risks by better protecting hardware & information | CASEScontact.org/risk.php provides a definition what requirements must be met for assigning a high risk score |
| Worry & Impact | Windows MS Office Compatible software | Patch Tuesday Zero-Day | Limiting possible impact by better protecting hardware & information better | CASEScontact.org/worry.php provides a definition when a threat is assigned a high impact and worry score |

**Note.** Certain events require an advisory (e.g., the Firefox browser and Thunderbird e-mail vulnerabilities (see CASEScontact.org/alerts/110058) even though the user should have simply set his or her preferences such that these programs would check for updates regularly. Here the key is to get the user to change these options accordingly, thereby making certain that next time this happens, an automatic update helps in reducing a risk quickly for the user. This improves prevention while making it unnecessary for the user to have to do work as outlined in an alert when a patch or software update is issued.

The first hurdle is if a security matter is significant to CASEScontact.org's target group of subscribers. Hence if it affects Windows or Microsoft Word the vulnerability reported is surely of interest. Furthermore, a zero-day exploit of a just discovered vulnerability regarding Excel is certainly critical for CASEScontact.org's target group. In cases, where such newly discovered vulnerabilities relevant to our user group are reported, they are analyzed regarding their risk level and worry index level.

In summary, Table 5 below explains further the vulnerabilities or threats relevant to our subscribers. In particular, if these can be considered coming with a high risk for the user and, as importantly, with a high impact if the damage occurs (e.g., possibly loosing data if the vulnerability is being exploited by a malicious user), then the particular threat or vulnerability exploit must be analyzed. As importantly, a decision has to be made what type and form of response is appropriate.

## 4.4 Type and Form of Response

If a security incident, vulnerability or threat is being assigned both, a high impact as well as a high risk level (or highly critical as others would call it), releasing an advisory as a response is being put in motion. CASEScontact.org does neither have the human nor financial resources to offer a 24x7x365 type of service. Nonetheless, weekends and long holidays are covered in contrast to some much better funded efforts elsewhere (see also [11]).

CASEScontact.org has succeeded in providing alerts to its target group usually around the same time as such organizations as US-CERT, and De Waarschuwingsdienst. Sometimes we manage to be quicker, especially during public holidays and long weekends. While releasing advisories timely does, most certainly, raise trust and confidence in the service's quality by our target groups, we do not

**Table 5.** Responding to critical incidents

| Categroy | Description | Advisories | Tips / Security Guides | Additional offerings |
|---|---|---|---|---|
| Type of distribution channel[1] | * Web<br>* E-mail[2]<br>* RSS[3]<br>* Podcast<br>* Blog<br>* Printed news | Without podcast | German and English podcasts available | podcast.CyTRAP.eu is offering additional information regarding podcasts (CyTRAP Labs radio) and their downloads in various formats (e.g., iTunes) |
| Format | Online or offline viewing, text in point form with bullets | Hyperlinks for downloading patches or instructions for implementing work arounds | Hyperlinks to more detail including checklists, installation guides, etc. | Additional tools and free downloads are hyperlinked to and described in more depth in EU-IST's blog located at blog.CyTRAP.eu and Wincurity the blog for Windows users at blog.CASEScontact.org |

**Note.** Different communication channels are being used. Most important here is that people that may get the advisory via RSS may not subscribe to any other content. Put differently, a blog subscriber may receive information about alerts or guides from CASEScontact.org via a blog post referring to the alert or the security guide. Accordingly, overlap between e-mail subscribers of the various.

People may choose to receive the podcasts via e-mail subscription, RSS feed or visiting the web site directly.

[1] RSS offers a short summary of alerts and tips. E-mail subscribers can choose between a short summary or full text in ASCII format or html. Podcasts in German and English have increased in length from about 2 minutes to about 5 minutes, thereby allowing the providing of more depth and detail.

[2] Subscribers may register themselves to receive advisories and tips via e-mail. Additionally, blogs also offer an e-mail alert telling a subscriber about new postings. EU-IST News offers subscribers a weekly newsletter via e-mail. The e-zine includes all postings made during last week.

Statistics show that subscribers of content that is delivered via e-mail rarely take advantage of more than one service, such as receiving blog postings and advisories via e-mail. Instead, they tend to choose one or two but rarely is it three or more.

[3] The RSS feed is creating far less traffic and clickthroughs than we expected. In fact, viewers seem to prefer to visit the Web site directly by being alerted using robot-type software alerting them about changes on the  website or having the website open in one of their browser's windows.

strive to be the fastest but being timely, instead. Moreover, for our specific target markets we are generally the ones providing the most comprehensive information the quickest. Confirmation for this we have received by attaining the greatest distribution and attention with advisories that were released just before or during long weekends. What has helped us here compared to others, is that our staff are usually monitoring events during weekends. Other services may not be able to respond before Wednesday or Thursday the coming week for reasons beyond the scope of this paper.

If a security incident is classified as being critical, of high risk and with a high worry or impact rating as well as relevant to CASEScontact.org's user group (e.g., it affects Word or Firefox software running on Windows and possible Mac), an advisory is being issued. Once a month a security guide is issued in German and English. The primary objective of the guides is to help users improve their system's security with easy to follow measures as well as free and easy to operate tools and/or software.

### 4.5  Documentation and Learning

CASEScontact.org documents how much use subscribers or viewers have made of the advisory. One way can be by looking at usage statistics, such as click through rates from RSS subscribers or from the Webpage. Advisories are important to protect users against newly and rapidly spreading malware that exploit vulnerabilities that cannot be patched at this time. However, better protection to minimize one's risk against new yet to be discovered threats requires prevention.

### 4.6  Documentation and Learning

CASEScontact.org documents how much use subscribers or viewers have made of the advisory. One way can be by looking at usage statistics, such as click through rates from RSS subscribers or from the Webpage. Advisories are important to protect users against newly and rapidly spreading malware that exploit vulnerabilities that cannot be patched at this time. However, better protection to minimize one's risk against new yet to be discovered threats requires prevention.

To foster learning from past advisories, CASEScontact.org tries to take this information and transfer those insights into its security guides. The latter may be revised or due to new types of threats invite a revision (e.g., Sony BMG rootkits [8] see http://CASEScontact.org/tips/210002) or suggest the write-up of a new security guide (e.g., using public hotspots at your favourite coffee shop http://CASEScontact.org/tips/210020).

## 5  Evaluation and Refinement of Current Strategies: Seven Lessons Learned

During the process of running CASEScontact.org and following an action research approach we learned much about the ropes others might want to skip. While the seven lessons outlined below were important milestones in our learning process, things may be different for organizations that have a trusted brand (e.g., US-CERT). Nonetheless, for most others, our lessons might be of considerable interest and, most importantly, skipping those will help save scarce resources including money and time.

*Lesson 1 – Targeting markets is the first step on the long and hard journey to success.* Different user groups have different needs and must be served with different types of content. We decided to focus on younger users at home and SME employees. Whenever we have strayed away from this particular focus, response has indicated that we erred a bit. Hence, whilst we have technical experts and older folks that subscribe to our content, our message is targeted toward younger people.

*Lesson 2 – Value proposition must be clear.* Serving younger people also required that to stay relevant for a large group, we had to focus on the Windows Operating System, Microsoft Office and compatible software. In time we learned that our alerts had to also state if the vulnerability affected Macs or Linux systems. Moreover, telegram style description of the vulnerability including what it meant to be infected or exploited by not patching was asked for by subscribers. Other feedback also let us include equipment that is highly popular with the younger folks such as iPods and such software as iTune. Again all this increased the relevance of our content and the value for subscribers.

*Lesson 3 – Give user a choice for type of content and how it is being delivered.* When we began we offered the information on our Webpage only. Lateron because of the hype about RSS, we took the effort and made our content available this way as well. Unfortunately, response has been far from great. Instead, e-mail delivery seems to be the preferred choice even for younger users. Even SMS does not appear to be as desirable from our subscribers' point-of-view (we tried for some time without much success).

Best practice regarding online subscription procedures requires that certain procedures are being followed. Nonetheless, we learned that many of our users (remember, younger, impatient and tend to know what they prefer, while wanting to use technology without having to bother too much about security) did not appreciate this very much. In fact they complained or else did not complete the registration process. Hence, we have begun with a so-called quick subscribe procedure that allows users to register from within an advisory, blog posting or security guide by just entering an e-mail address (see also: http://CASEScontact.org/subscribe_all.php).

*Lesson 4 – Being relevant and not too frequent to get attention.* We always knew that being relevant (see also Lessons 1 & 2) would be the key. However, in the last 12 months we have also discovered that we should issue advisories scarcely and when needed only. Moreover, we have come to issue one security guide in English and German about each month only.

A critical issue is that we have to be clear and consistent when to issue an alert regarding a zero-day exploit with Microsoft Office and when not [12]. We learned that if we issue an advisory about a particular zero-day exploit regarding Powerpoint one week but fail to do so the next time a zero-day exploit happens regarding Powerpoint, we better be able to justify and explain our decision succinctly.

Another thing we learned was that our subscribers wanted more than just 'Today is Patch Tuesday, go and look at the Microsoft web site for more information....' Instead additional beef was expected and some hints and suggestions for further improving security posture was an expected ad-on that our subscribers seemed to demand from our advisories (e.g., http://blog.casescontact.org/?p=164).

*Lesson 5 –Developing the CASEScontact.org brand – it takes time and quality to secure subscribers' trust in the quality of our service(s).* We knew that without providing our service as a government agency or as part of a large vendor's offerings, our brand recognition would be near zero for all practical purposes for the first couple of years. Even after just about two years we still feel that we have a brand that is known to a few users only. Nonetheless, dedication and diligence means that progress must and is being made during this journey.

Our data indicate that on average subscribers tend to visit the site at least three times each month. Another indicator is that external deep links to our content are increasing slowly but surely. For instance high traffic sites may add links to particular security guides (en.Wikipedia.org) or a Sicherheits Ratgeber (de.Wikipedia.org). Moreover, other CASES sites and affiliates may link to our home page or deep link to particular advisories and guides (e.g., www.CASES.public.lu).

Links from others, such as Answer.com (Free Online Dictionary, Encyclopedia, Thesaurus and much more) or Mitre may not just provide traffic but also add credibility, since they themselves have brand recognition. Links from smaller blogs may just add traffic (security.megablog.org).

*Lesson 6 – Serving clients better requires continuous improvement.* When we started we believed that we would be able to design, program and implement the service at fairly sophisticated level. But we learned that improvements and innovation result in continous adjustments and improvements of the services provided (e.g., see how to subscribe as discussed under Lesson 3 above).

Whilst we do not get suggestions from our subscribers very often, whenever we do, we try to assess and discuss them with various stakeholders. In fact, our subscribers are a critical part of our quality assurance (QA) efforts. Subsequently we might very likely implement a subscriber suggestion. That this approach is highly effective is reflected by the few, mostly positive responses we get and sometimes this triggers more insightful suggestions for improvements[5].

*Lesson 7 – Finding and exploiting resource advantages.* We pointed out that both, human and financial resources are limited for CASEScontact.org in comparison to most other players. However, the efficiency advantage is such that we can produce market value at lower cost than some others. Additionally, by focusing on a specific sub-segment of the market (narrow focus of services), our offerings are perceived as being more valuable than some competitors´offerings. The latter provides us with a so-called effectiveness advantage [13].

## 6  Conclusion

This article discussed first, how an early warning system could help home-users and SMEs better protect their PCs and information assets. Next, the requirements for an early warning system to make it services valuable for home-users and SMEs were

---

[5] For instance, some subscribers felt that our EU-IST News – Information Security this Week newsboard (published since Nov. 2000) and particularly the newsletter were simply not that nice looking and sometimes outright hard to read (e-mail sent in ASCII format only). September 2006 we began improving the newsletter by using our own plug-in for Word Press, the open source blogging software. Not only does the newsletter look much nicer but, most importantly, reader response has been very positive. As well, the once again increasing numbers of requests for subscriptions to this newsletter could in part be attributed to this face lift (see http://blog.CyTRAP.eu).

discussed. Third, a framework was presented (see also Figure 3) and analyzed using CASEScontact.org as a case study. Last we summarized the seven lessons we learned in the process and how efficiency-seeking and effectiveness-seeking marketing success can be fostered by better leveraging limited resource-advantages [14].

In conclusion, knowing how to use a public hotspot safely and securely and following the 10 commandments for more secure online banking are important milestones on the journey to better security for home PCs. Naturally, experts must be up-to-date about the latest exploits, malware pandemics and threats. In contrast, citizens want to know primarily about those threats and malware exploits that may affect their security and privacy directly. The acid test for a successful awareness campaign will be how much and often people refer to guides regarding IT security prevention. In turn, such efforts help in further minimizing users' risks for becoming victims of phishing attacks, losing valuable data that might result in identity theft, or having malicious users taking control of their systems. CASEScontact.org will continue to, hopefully, play an important part in this theatre of operations.

**Acknowledgments.** The author would like to thank Francois Thill (www.CASES. public.lu) and Martine Ducobu for their insightful comments made about an earlier version of this paper. Thanks also to the CRITIS reviewers. All omissions or misunderstandings are, of course, the author's sole responsibility.

# References

1. OECD Broadband Statistics. OECD, Paris (Dezember 2005). [Online] (Available: http://casescontact.org/euist_view.php?newsID=4019 Last access: May 22, 2006)
2. Gattiker, U. E. Digital divide is dead but keeping broadband competition alive remains a challenge. CyTRAP Labs, Zurich (October 2006). [Online] (Available: http://cytrap.eu/blog/?p=66. Last access: October 20, 2006).
3. CERT/CC Overview Incident and Vulnerability Trends. Cert Coordination Center, Pittsburgh, PA (2001). (http://www.cert.org/present/cert-overview-trends/module-5.pdf Last access: May 21, 2006).
4. Gattiker, U. E. Blended threats - are the computer security's new nemesis? CyTRAP Labs, Zurich (August 2006). [Online] (Available: http://cytrap.eu/blog/?p=23. Last access: October 20, 2006).
5. Gattiker, U. E. Identity theft, anti-virus protection: Insurance plans for professionals. CASEScontact.org, Zurich (May 2002). [Online] (Available: http://casescontact.org/euist_view.php?newsID=2564 Last access: June 15, 2006).
6. Lenhart, A., Madden, M., & Hitlin, P. Teens and technology: Youth are leading the transition to a fully wired and mobile nation Report Family, Friends & Community. Pew Internet & American Life Project, Washington, DC (July 27, 2005). [Online] (Available: http://www.pewinternet.org/report_display.asp?r=162 Last access: June 13, 2006).
7. Terena Incident Taxonomy and Description Working Group. Taxonomy of the computer security incident related terminology (Work in Progress). Author, Amsterdam (not dated) [Online] (Available: http://www.terena.nl/activities/tf-csirt/iodef/docs/i-taxonomy_terms.html Last access: June 14, 2006)

8. Sony BMG rootkit. CyTRAP Labs: getting the security jargon right. CyTRAP Labs, Copenhagen (2006) (http://cytrap.org/RiskIT/mod/glossary/view.php?id=13&mode=entry&hook=284 Last access: 2006, August 2).

9. Burnett P. & Gattiker, U.E. An information sharing vision for improving internet security: Building a warning, advice and reporting point (WARP). CASES network, Copenhagen, DK (November 2002). [Online] (Available: http://casescontact.org/euist_view.php?newsID =2869 Last access: 2006, June 8).

10. Gattiker, U. E. Best Practices Guide - Instant Messaging (IM) audit - managing IM communication securely & successfully CASEScontact.org, Zurich (May 2006). [Online] (Available: http://casescontact.org/euist_view.php?newsID=3981 Last access: June 15, 2006).

11. Gattiker, U. E. CyTRAP Labs–national alert systems are needed since today's mechanisms do not appear to work. CyTRAP Labs, Copenhagen (June 2006) [Online] (Available: http://casescontact.org/euist_view.php?newsID=4030 Last access: 2006, June 8).

12. Zero-day exploit. CyTRAP Labs: Getting the security jargon right. CyTRAP Labs, Zurich (2006) (http://cytrap.org/RiskIT/mod/glossary/view.php?id=2&mode=entry&hook=7 Accessed: May 23, 2006).

13. Commission of the European Communities. COM(2002) 263 final COMMUNICATION FROM THE COMMISSION TO THE COUNCIL, THE EUROPEAN PARLIAMENT, THE ECONOMIC AND SOCIAL COMMITTEE AND THE COMMITTEE OF THE REGIONS - eEurope 2005: An information society for all An Action Plan to be presented in view of the Sevilla European Council, 21/22 June 2002, 23 pages (28.5.2002) [Online] (Available: http://casescontact.org/euist_view.php?newsID=2779 Last access: 2006, June 8).

14. Hunt, S. D., Arnett,D. B.: Does marketing success lead to market success? J. of Business Research 59 (2006) 820-828.

# Protection of Components Based on a Smart-Card Enhanced Security Module

Joaquín García-Alfaro[1], Sergio Castillo[1], Jordi Castellà-Roca[2],
Guillermo Navarro[1], and Joan Borrell[1]

[1] DEIC-UAB, 08193 Bellaterra (Catalonia), Spain
{jgarcia,scastillo,gnavarro,jborrell}@deic.uab.es
[2] DEiM-ETSE-URV, 43007 Tarragona (Catalonia), Spain
jordi.castella@urv.net

**Abstract.** We present in this paper the use of a security mechanism to handle the protection of network security components, such as *Firewalls* and *Intrusion Detection Systems*. Our approach consists of a kernel-based access control method which intercepts and cancels forbidden system calls launched by a potential remote attacker. This way, even if the attacker gains administration permissions, she will not achieve her purpose. To solve the administration constraints of our approach, we use a smart-card based authentication mechanism for ensuring the administrator's identity. Through the use of a cryptographic protocol, the protection mechanism verifies administrator's actions before holding her the indispensable privileges to manipulate a component. Otherwise, the access control enforcement will come to its normal operation. We also show in this paper an overview of the implementation of this mechanism on a research prototype, developed for GNU/Linux systems, over the *Linux Security Modules* (LSM) framework.

## 1 Introduction

The protection of network security components, such as *Firewalls* and *Intrusion Detection Systems*, is a serious and important problem which must be solved. Otherwise, whenever a remote adversary manages to compromise the security of these components, she may obtain the control of the system itself. Contrary to many other elements of a network, security components are almost always working with special privileges to properly execute their tasks [6]. This situation is very likely to lead remote attackers to acquire these privileges in an unauthorized manner. For instance, the existence of programming errors within the code of these components, the illicit manipulation of their related resources (such as processes, filesystem, and so on), or even the increase of privileges though operating system's errors, are just a few examples regarding means in which a remote adversary can bypass traditional security policy controls.

In [4,5] we presented an enhanced protection module integrated into the kernel of an attack prevention system intended to intercept and cancel forbidden system calls launched by a remote attacker. Specifically, the mechanism presented in [4,5] prevents a privilege escalation attack on the prevention system itself – through an enhanced access control scheme which handles the protection of the system's elements. This strategy introduces, however, some administration constraints, since the administrators are not

J. Lopez (Ed.): CRITIS 2006, LNCS 4347, pp. 128–139, 2006.

able to throw system calls which may suppose a threat to the protected system. To solve these constraints, we present in this paper an extended version of our approach which includes a smart-card based authentication mechanism, which acts as a reinforcement of the kernel-based access control. The objective of this complementary mechanism is twofold. First, it holds to the administrator the indispensable privileges to carry management and configuration activities just when she verifies her identity through a two-factor authentication mechanism. Second, it allows us to avoid those attacks focused on getting the rights of the administrative entity, such as dictionary-based attacks or buffer overflows.

The rest of this paper is organized as follows. Section 2 summarizes some related works. Section 3 shows an overview of our protection strategy. Section 4 takes a closer look at the development of the proposed mechanism. Section 5 presents our smart-card based authentication protocol intended to solve the administration constraints introduced by the protection mechanism. An evaluation concerning the efficiency of our proposal is then presented in Section 6. Finally, Section 7 closes the paper with a list of conclusions.

## 2   Related Work

There are two main approaches to safely execute processes with special privileges on modern operating systems. A first approach, as the one presented in this paper, is to apply a kernel-based access control to the outcoming system calls. A second approach is the creation of restricted environments, in which the processes will be executed and controlled outside the trusted system space.

Regarding the first approach, the proposals closest to ours are the protection mechanisms presented in [9] and [11] for the creation of enhanced access control mechanisms integrated in the kernel of the GNU/Linux operating system. The main goal behind these two proposals is to reinforce the complete system by controlling the system calls and ensuring which process or user does the system call and against what it will be done. The ability to control the access to the resources allows to protect the security components and to avoid that nobody (including an attacker with administrator privileges) can disable them.

Nevertheless, both approaches differ from ours in a number of ways. First, and to our best knowledge, neither [9] nor [11] do not address the management of administration constraints, as our proposal does through the two-factor authentication mechanism we present in Section 5. Second, our approach, entirely based on the *Linux Security Modules* (LSM) framework [13], guarantees the compatibility with previous applications and kernel modules without the necessity of modifications. However, both [9] and [11] require the rewriting of some features of the original Linux kernel to properly work. This situation may force to recompile existing code and/or modules in order to obtain the new security features. Although it exists a LSM-based prototype for the approach presented in [9], it does not seem to be actively maintained for the current Linux-2.6 kernel series.

Regarding the second approach, we find in [8] a protection mechanism for the creation of restricted environments within Unix setups. The authors in [8] present the use of a special system call to restrict the access to a specific area of the file system. This specific area is intended just for the processes that are executed under each restricted environment. Then, this system call properly changes the root directory to the given path. This way, the process remains in a safe space from where it is not possible to escape – even if the component is compromised, the whole system will remain safe since the illicit activities are caught within the replicated file system. This proposal requires, however, a replicated file system tree for each environment. Hence, the administrator in charge of the system must reproduce the original file system tree to include, for example, shared libraries or configuration files, and copy them to the new path. Other disadvantage of this proposal is that it does not guarantee the correct execution flow of a process, i.e., the behavior of a process can be modified by using, for example, a buffer overflow. Hence, the attacker can overwrite the configuration or logs files of such a process by simply using an arbitrary code execution attack – since these files remain in the same environment of the protected security component process.

Extended versions of the previous model, as the one presented in [7], may also offer support for access control to resources and guarantee the integrity of the security component's resources. Nonetheless, these extended proposals do not protect from vulnerabilities placed outside the trusted environment. A simple bug in a privileged service, or even the use of stolen passwords, may lead the attacker from the external environment to attack the component and its resources.

## 3   Our Proposal

As introduced in Section 1, our main motivation is the protection of network security components, such as *Firewalls* and *Intrusion Detection Systems*, which, if successfully attacked, are very likely to lead an intruder to get the control of the whole system. This problem leads to the necessity for introducing a protection mechanism on the different elements of each component, keeping with their protection and mitigating – or even eliminating – any attempt to attack or compromise the component's elements and their operations. This way, even if an attacker compromises the security of the component, she would not be able to achieve her purpose.

We consider the protection of the elements carried by the kernel of the operating system as a proper solution for such a protection. First, the protection at kernel level avoids that potentially dangerous system calls (e.g., *killing* a process) could be produced from one element against another one. This protection is achieved by incorporating an access control mechanism into the kernel system calls. This way, one may allow or deny a system call based on several criteria – such as the identifier of the process making the call, some parameters of the given call, etc. The kernel's access control allows to eliminate the notion of trust associated to privileged users, delegating the authorization for the execution of a given system call to the internal access control mechanisms. In addition, and contrary to other approaches, it provides a unified solution, avoiding the implementation of different specific mechanisms for each component. This mechanism allows us, moreover, to enforce the compartimentalization principle [12]. This principle is based in the segmentation of a system, so several elements can be protected independently one from another. This ensures that even if one of the elements is compromised, the rest of them can operate in a trusted way.

In our case, several elements from each component are executed as processes. By specifying the proper permission based on the process ID, we can limit the interaction between these elements of the component. If an intruder takes control of a process associated to a given component (through a buffer overflow, for example), she will be limited to make the system call for this given process.

It is not always possible, however, to achieve a complete independence between the elements. There is a need to determine which system calls may be considered as a threat when launched against an element from the component. This requires a meticulous study of each one of the system calls provided by the kernel, and how they can be misused. On the other hand, we have to define the access control rules for each one of these system calls. For our approach, we propose the following three protection levels to classify the system calls: (1) critical process protection; (2) communication mechanisms protection; and (3) protection of files associated to the elements.

The first level of protection (critical processes) comprises actions that can cancel the proper execution of the processes associated to a component, either by interaction over them by signals, or the manipulation of the memory space. Some examples are: execution of a new application already in memory, manipulation of the address space and process traces, and so on. The second level (communication mechanisms protection) includes the protection of all those processes that allows an attacker to modify, generate or eliminate any kind of messages exchanged between component's elements. Finally, the third level of protection (protection of files associated to the elements) takes into account all those actions that can maliciously address the set of files used by the elements of the component, such as executable, or configuration files.

## 4    Prototype Implementation

In this section we outline the current implementation of SMARTCOP (which stands for *Smart Card Enhanced Linux Security Module for Component Protection*). In accordance with the protection scheme proposed in Section 3, it consists of a kernel-based access control mechanism, and its development has been done over the *Linux Security Modules* (LSM) framework for *GNU/Linux* systems [13]. The LSM framework does not consist of a single specific access control mechanism; instead it provides a generic framework, which can accommodate several approaches. It supplies several hooks (i.e., interception points) across the kernel that can be used to implement different access control strategies. Such hooks are: *Task hooks, Program Loading Hooks, File systems Hooks* and *Network hooks*. These LSM hooks, can be used to provide protection at the three levels pointed out above. Furthermore, LSM adds a set of benefits to our implementation. First, it introduces a minimum load to the system when comparing it to kernels without LSM, and does not interfere with the detection and reaction processes (cf. Section 6). Second, the access control mechanism can be composed in the system as a module, without having to recompile the kernel. And third, it provides a high degree

of flexibility and portability to our implementation when compared to other proposals for the Linux kernel, such as [9] and [11], where the implementation requires the
modification of some features of the original Linux-2.6 kernel series.

The LSM interface provides an abstraction, which allows the modules to mediate
between the users and the internal objects from the operating system kernel. To this
effect, before accessing the internal object, the hook calls the function provided by the
module and which will be responsible to allow or deny the access. This can be seen
in Figure 1. There, a module registers the function to make a check over the *inodes* of
the file system. At the same time, LSM allows to keep the *discretionary access control*
(DAC) provided by the kernel Linux, by standing between the discretionary control and
the object itself. This way, if a user does not have permissions in relation to a given file,
the DAC of the operating system will not allow the access and no call to the function
registered by the LSM will be made. This architecture reduces the load of the system
when compared to an access control check centralized in the operating system call
interface, which always gets used for all the system calls.

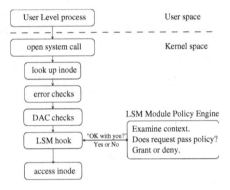

**Fig. 1.** Linux Security Modules (LSM) Hooks

The component's elements will be allowed to make operations only permitted to
the system administrator (e.g., as packet filtering and process). This implies that the
system processes associated to each element will be executed by the administrator. On
the contrary, if we associate the processes to a non privileged user, the discretionary
access control of Linux will not allow the execution of some specific calls. The internal
access control mechanisms at the kernel is based in the process identifier (PID) that
makes the system call, which will be associated to a specific element. Each function
registered by a LSM module, determines which component is making the call from the
PID of the associated process. It then, applies the access control constraints taking also
into account the parameters of the system call. Thus, for example, a given element can
access its own configuration files but not configuration files from other elements.

An important issue in the implementation is the administration of the access control
mechanisms and the management of each one of the elements. As pointed out in previous sections, the administrators should not be able to throw a system call, which may

suppose a threat to the component. This prevents an intruder doing any harm to the component even if she could scale her privileges to the administrator ones. This contrasts with the administration of the component, since, if an administrator can not interact with the elements of the component, she will not be able to carry out any management or configuration process and activities. To solve this hazard, we propose a smart-card based authentication mechanism. Specifically, we use the functionality of a smart-card for ensuring the administrator's identity. Through the use of an authentication protocol, the LSM module verifies administrator's actions before holding her the indispensable privileges to manipulate the component. Otherwise, the access control enforcement will come to its normal operation. In the following section, a detailed description of such a mechanism is given.

## 5   Smart-Card Based Authentication Mechanism

Traditional user authentication, also known as single-factor authentication, relies on user's knowledge of some secret – for instance, a password or a PIN. Then, using this knowledge as the only requirement, the user may proof his identity. Nevertheless, single-factor authentication is not secure enough – the existence of password attacks, man-in-the middle techniques, etc., is a proof of that. A two-factor authentication mechanism, on the other hand, solves most of these problems. Two-factor authentication mechanisms require to prove both the knowledge of some secret and the possession of some characteristic. This characteristic must be unique, and not easily replicable (e.g., a smart-card).

Therefore, to better assure the administrator's identity in our protection scheme, we propose the use of a two-factor authentication mechanism based on the cryptographic functions of a smart-card. This mechanism is intended for authenticating the administrator to the LSM modules and holds with the following requirements:

– The actions must be authorized by the use of a smart-card;
– The smart-card only authorizes one action iff the PIN is correct;
– The LSM module only authorizes the action iff the smart-card response is valid, i.e., the cryptographic operation is correct.

According with these requirements, just when the smart-card is connected to the system, and the authentication protocol's result is satisfactory, the administrator is able to hold the indispensable privileges to manipulate the node. On the contrary, when the device is retired or the authentication protocol fails, the access control enforcement, presented in Section 4, comes to its normal operation.

### 5.1   Protocol Description

We give in the following a detailed description of the cryptographic protocol that leads our smart-card based authentication mechanism. Let us recall that the cryptographic engine of such a smart-card is capable of performing several cryptographic functions, such as symmetric key generation, symmetric cryptographic algorithms execution, etc.

**Protocol 1**

*1. The system administrator opens a new console and she requests an action $X$. It is assumed that $X$ must be authorized by using the smart-card;*

*2. The module receives the request from the console and does the following steps:*
   *(a) Open a connection to the smart-card reader device;*
   *(b) Print a message in the console, asking for the smart-card insertion to the smart-card reader device;*
   *(c) While the smart-card has not been inserted do;*
       *i. Detect the insertion of the smart-card;*
   *(d) Print a message in the console asking for the operation PIN;*

*3. The system administrator types the operation PIN in the keyboard;*

*4. The module does the following steps:*
   *(a) Obtain the operation PIN;*
   *(b) Obtain a NONCE value at random;*
   *(c) Compute the Message Authentication Code (MAC) of NONCE with the shared key $K$, $\mu_1 = MAC(K, NONCE)$;*
   *(d) Execute the Procedure 1 inside the smart-card using the operation PIN and the NONCE, and obtain a response $\mu_2$;*
   *(e) Print a message in the console to remove the smart-card from the smart-card reader device;*
   *(f) While the smart-card has not been removed do;*
       *i. Detect the removing of the smart-card;*
   *(g) if $\mu_2$ is ERROR the LSM module does not authorize the action $X$;*
   *(h) else do:*
       *i. if $\mu_1 \neq \mu_2$ the module does not authorize the action $X$;*
       *ii. if $\mu_1 = \mu_2$ the module authorizes the action $X$;*

As we can see in Protocol 1, an *operation PIN* and one *administration password* are used in our protocol. The operation PIN is at least six digits long. We use the operation PIN in order to authorize the actions. On the other hand, the administration password is used to change the operation PIN and other management tasks. The system administrator has three consecutive chances to enter the operation PIN. In the third chance if the smart-card receives an incorrect operation PIN it blocks itself. The smart-card only can be unblocked with the administration password. Again, there are three chances to enter the correct administration password. If the smart-card is blocked with the administration password the smart-card becomes useless.

The security parameters of the LSM module are properly initialized when it is installed. The system administrator inserts a smart-card in the reader device and the cardlet application is downloaded to the smart-card. Once the applet has been download and registered, the system administrator introduces the administration password and the operation PIN. The LSM module then sends the shared key $K$ – it stores the shared $K$ in a secure file, so the file can be read exclusively by the LSM module.

Then, the smart-card and the LSM module share a secret key $K$. In Step 1 of such a protocol, the system administrator requests an action to the LSM module which, in turn, blocks the communication channel between the smart-card reader and the LSM module (cf. Step 2a). The data sent between the LSM module and the smart-card can not be sniffed because the channel is blocked. The protocol avoids the smart-card remains in the smart-card reader when is not necessary. In Step 2c, the LSM module waits until the smart-card insertion, and in Step 4f the LSM module does not proceed since the smart-card has been removed.

In Step 3 the operation PIN travels in a secure way from the keyboard because the LSM module has blocked the channel between the keyboard and the module itself. Then, the LSM module sends a NONCE obtained at random and the PIN in Step 4d. The smart-card returns a Message Authentication Code (*MAC*) of the NONCE computed with the shared key $K$. In the last Step, i.e., Step 4h, the LSM module verifies whether the MAC has been properly computed.

Let us finally show the following procedure (cf. Procedure 1), which is executed within the smart-card to validate the operation PIN. If the operation PIN is correct, it computes the MAC of NONCE with the shared key $K$.

**Procedure 1** *[PIN, NONCE]*

1. *Check if the card is blocked;*
2. *If the card is not blocked do:*
   (a) *Validate the operation PIN;*
      i. *If the operation PIN is correct do:*
         A. *Compute the Message Authentication Code (MAC) of NONCE with the shared key $K$, $\mu_2 = MAC(K, NONCE)$;*
         B. *Reset to 0 the attempts counter;*
         C. *Return $\mu_2$;*
      ii. *If the operation PIN is not correct do:*
         A. *Increase the attempts counter;*
         B. *If the attempts counter is greater than 3 block the smart-card;*
         C. *Return* ERROR;
3. *If the card is blocked do:*
   (a) *Return* ERROR;

## 5.2 Security Considerations

To ensure the proper execution of both Protocol 1 and Procedure 1 (cf. Section 5.1), we must consider the protection of the entities and the channels involved in such a process, avoiding attacks like impersonation or channels data manipulation. The lack of ability to avoid these attacks and their impact makes our proposed protection mechanism usefulness. Regarding the different entities that take part in the protocol, we suggest in this section the following considerations.

First, the possible console attacks could be directed to the binary executable file and the console process in execution time. If this happens, an overwrite of the executable console's file using malicious code could lead an attacker to take the control of the authentication process, giving her the possibility to complete the protocol and get the control of the system – and even to steal the smart-card's PIN. To eliminate this attack, the LSM module guarantees that the binary file of the console can not be overwritten by anybody (even the administrator), remaining the permissions as read-only.

Second, the binary executable of the administration console is compiled in a static fashion. This allows us to reduce the complexity of the protection's console process, since we do not need to consider extra tasks introduced by the loading of shared libraries and its associated files. At the same time, it enables us to centralize and reduce the failure points that could be used by an intruder to tamper the console's process. Thus, and to protect the process associated to the console, the LSM module controls that each system call launched by some process can not be dangerous for the correct execution flow of the console process, such as keyboard key capture, cancellation, or debugging process system calls.

Regarding the exchange of information between the elements involved in the authentication mechanism, let us recall that the communication channels can not be manipulated by any opponent. To achieve this purpose, the LSM mediates between the system calls related with the communication channels and the entities that take part within the protocol (the LSM module, the smart-card, and the console process). On the other hand, and as pointed out in [2], the LSM module does not need to be directly protected since we can assume the kernel environment as a trusted area – since it is mandatory for the kernel security model of our prototype's operating system.

One final consideration is the consequence of the smart-card robbery by a possible attacker. If so, the attacker will need to know the operation PIN in order to use it in the system. Even so, and for further security measures, we assume that the stolen key should be removed as an administration key from the SMARTCOP nodes. This operation will normally be carried out off-line as a security measure.

## 6   Evaluation

This section describes the performance evaluation of SMARTCOP for GNU/Linux systems based on the *Linux Security Modules* (LSM) framework. We show the outcome of several tests steered towards measuring the penalty introduced by the installation of SMARTCOP as a LSM module, over the normal operation of the system. We do not take into account in this evaluation, the performance penalty during administrative tasks. That is, operations carried out by the system administrator making use of the authentication scheme presented in the previous section.

The set of tests is based on the use of the Strace [1] tool and the LMbench [10] package. Strace is a debugging tool, which allows us to trace the system calls made after the execution of a given process. This can be used to analyze and evaluate the time taken by these calls. On the other hand, LMbench is used to perform *microbenchmarks*, which are used to take more precise measures of the time taken for file access, memory access, etc.

The evaluation was carried out on a single machine with an Intel-Pentium M 1.4 GHz, with 512 MB of RAM memory and an IDE hard disc of 5400 rpm, running a Debian GNU/Linux operating system and ext3 file system. The objective of these tests is to compare the performance of the system using a Linux 2.6.15 kernel without LSM support against the performance of the same system and kernel with LSM support and the SMARTCOP module loaded.

| Test Type | 2.6.15 | 2.6.15 + sm artcop | % Overhead with sm artcop |
|---|---|---|---|
| null call | 0.255 | 0.255 | 0% |
| kill | 231.10 | 241.65 | 4.6% |
| stat | 1.99 | 2.03 | 2% |
| open/close | 2.96 | 3.02 | 1.9% |
| select TCP | 18.63 | 18.86 | 1.2% |
| sig inst | 0.9 | 0.9 | 0% |
| sig handl | 1.85 | 1.88 | 0.1% |
| fork proc | 95.61 | 96.52 | 0.9% |
| exec proc | 100.50 | 103.86 | 3.3% |
| sh proc | 2227 | 2302 | 3.3% |

Process tests, time in $\mu$seconds

| Test Type | 2.6.15 | 2.6.15 + sm artcop | % Overhead with sm artcop |
|---|---|---|---|
| pipe | 1342 | 1338 | 0.2% |
| AF Unix | 1334 | 1320 | 1% |
| TCP | 1088 | 1078 | 0.9% |
| file read | 1330 | 1308 | 1.6% |
| mmap read | 1480 | 1425 | 3.8% |
| mem bcopy | 5278 | 5277 | 0.01% |
| mem bzero | 4548 | 4548 | 0% |
| mem read | 25600 | 25590 | 0.03% |
| mem write | 24888 | 24869 | 0.07% |

Local communication bandwidth in MB/s

| Test Type | 2.6.15 | 2.6.15 + sm artcop | % Overhead with sm artcop |
|---|---|---|---|
| 0K file create | 193 | 193 | 0% |
| 0K file delete | 489 | 489 | 0% |
| 10K file create | 175 | 176 | 0.5% |
| 10K file delete | 658 | 668 | 1.5% |
| mmap latency | 2348 | 2348 | 0% |
| par mem | 1.26 | 1.26 | 0% |
| page fault | 0.974 | 0.981 | 0.8% |

File and VM sytem latencies, time in $\mu$seconds

**Fig. 2.** Performance evaluation of SMARTCOP

The results of the tests are shown in Figure 2. They are organized in three tables depending on the three protection levels stated in Section 3. As it can be appreciated in the results, the penalty introduced by SMARTCOP has a minimum impact on the performance of a standard GNU/Linux 2.6.15 system. The first table (*Process tests*) shows the latency in microseconds for a set of operations related to the execution of processes and system calls such as process creation through *fork()*, *fork()+exec()* and *sh()*, process cancellation through *kill()*, descriptor waiting through *select()*, opening and closing files through *open()/close()*, signal installation and management, etc. This first category of tests shows that more than the 50% of the tests indicate a performance penalty below 2%. For example, the process creation with *fork()* is scarcely penalized with a 0.9%. The same can be noticed for process creation with *fork()+exec()* and *sh()*, which have an approximate penalty of 3.3%. On the other hand, the higher performance penalty is presented by the process cancellation through the system call *kill()* with a 4.6%. This higher penalty is produced by the access control verifications of SAMRTCOP at kernel level, during the identification checks of the process, system call parameters, etc.

The second set of tests shown in the second table of Figure 2, present the bandwidth of operations related to communication issues such as reading, writing and copy of memory sections through *read()* and *mmap()*, Inter Process Communications (IPC) using TCP, pipes and sockets of the Unix address family (*AF Unix sockets*), etc. Again, the results show a minimum penalty in the performance. In this case the greater penalty (3.8% approx.) is found in the reading and summing of a file via the memory mapping *mmap()* interface.

Finally, the set of tests from the third table (Figure 2) shows the latency found in operations related to file and memory manipulation. The performance penalty of the system is also minimum. The greater penalty being introduced by the file elimination due to the verifications performed by SMARTCOP during the associated system calls.

## 7  Conclusion

In this paper we have presented an access control mechanism specially suited for the protection of network security components, such as *Firewalls* and *Intrusion Detection Systems*. Whenever one of these components, or one of its elements, is compromised by an attacker, it may lead her to obtain the full control of the network. The protection of these components is not easy, specially when dealing with distributed setups, made up of different elements distributed over a complex network. Like for example, the attack prevention platform presented in [3].

The solution we provide in this paper proposes the protection of the components by making use of the LSM system in the Linux kernel over GNU/Linux systems. The mechanism we have developed, called SMARTCOP (*Smart Card Enhanced Linux Security Module for Component Protection*), works by providing and enforcing access control rules at system calls, and is based on a protection module integrated into the operating system's kernel, providing a high degree of modularity and independence between elements. The use of LSM allows our protection system to be used in new components and elements, by just considering its environment and its interactions (regarding access control). It reinforces the modularity of the system and provides an easy and generic way to introduce new elements without having to consider each component separately.

Thus, we consider that our proposal provides a high degree of scalability. The introduction of new components provides a minimum performance penalty, because the LSM framework and the access control scheme do not introduce an excessive computational complexity. We have measured the penalty introduced by the use of SMARTCOP against the usual performance of the system. The results show the minimum performance impact of SMARTCOP. To reinforce the protection mechanism itself, SMARTCOP provides a complementary authentication method, based on smart-cards. This additional enhancement is based both on a secret (smart-card PIN) and a physical token (the smart-card itself). This way, we can prevent some logical attacks (e.g., password forgery) against the protection mechanism proposed in this paper.

For all these reasons, we can finally conclude that the enhanced access control provided by SMARTCOP, and integrated inside the operating system's kernel, offers a good degree of transparency to the administrator in charge, and it does not interfere directly with user space's processes.

## Acknowledgments

J. García-Alfaro, S. Castillo, G. Navarro, and J. Borrell are partially founded by the Spanish Government project *TIC2003-02041*, and the Catalan Government grant *2003-FI126*. J. Castellà-Roca is partly supported by the Spanish Government project SEG-2004-04352-C04-01.

# References

1. W. Akkerman. Strace, `http://liacs.nl/~wichert/strace/`
2. M. Borchardt, C. Maziero, and E. Jamhour. An architecture for on-the-fly file integrity checking. In *Latin American Symposium on Dependable Computing*, 117-126, Brazil, 2003.
3. J. García, F. Autrel, J. Borrell, S. Castillo, F. Cuppens, and G. Navarro. Decentralized publish/subscribe system to prevent coordinated attacks via alert correlation. In *6th Int. Conf. on Information and Communications Security*, 223–235, Spain, 2004.
4. J. García, S. Castillo, G. Navarro, and J. Borrell. ACAPS: An Access Control Mechanism to Protect the Components of an Attack Prevention System. In *Journal of Computer Science and Network Security*, 5(11):87-94, November 2005.
5. J. García, S. Castillo, G. Navarro, and J. Borrell. Mechanisms for Attack Protection on a Prevention Framework. In *39th Annual IEEE International Carnahan Conference on Security Technology*, 137–140, Spain, October 2005.
6. D. Geer. Just How Secure Are Security Products? *IEEE Computer*, 37(6):14–16, June 2004.
7. A. Herzog and N. Shahmehri. Using the Java Sandbox for Resource Control. In *7th Nordic Workshop on Secure IT Systems (NORDSEC 2002)*, Linköpings universitet, Linköping, Sweden, 2002.
8. P. Hope. Using Jails in FreeBSD for Fun and Profit. *Login; The Magazine of Usenix & Sage*, 27(3):48–55, June 2002.
9. P. Loscocco and S. Smalley. Integrating Flexible Support for Security Policies into the Linux Operating System. In *11th FREENIX Track: 2001 USENIX Annual Technical Conference*, USA, 2001.
10. L. McVoy. LMbench, Portable Tools for Performance Analysis. In *1996 USENIX Annual Technical Conference*, USA, 1996.
11. A. Ott. The Role Compatibility Security Model. In *7th Nordic Workshop on Secure IT Systems*, Sweden, November 2002.
12. J. Viega, and G. McGraw. *Building Secure Software - How to Avoid Security Problems the Right Way*. Addison-Wesley, September 2002.
13. C. Wright, C. Cowan, S. Smalley, J. Morris, and G. Kroah-Hartman. Linux Security Modules: General Security Support for the Linux Kernel. In *11th USENIX Security Symposium*, USA, 2002.

# Revisiting Colored Networks and Privacy Preserving Censorship

Yvo Desmedt[1,3,*], Yongge Wang[2], and Mike Burmester[3,**]

[1] University College London, UK
y.desmedt@cs.ucl.ac.uk
[2] UNC Charlotte, USA
yonwang@uncc.edu
[3] Florida State University, USA
burmester@cs.fsu.edu

**Abstract.** Reliable networks are obviously an important aspect of critical information infrastructures. *Dolev-Dwork-Waarts-Yung* linked research on reliable point-to-point networks with privacy and authenticity. In their threat model the adversary can only take over a number of nodes bounded by a threshold $k$. Hirt-Maurer introduced the concept of an adversary structure (i.e. the complement of an access structure). Kumar-Goundan-Srinathan-Rangan and Desmedt-Wang-Burmester generalized Dolev-Dwork-Waarts-Yung scenarios to the case of a general adversary structure.

Burmester-Desmedt introduced a special adversary structure, now called a color based adversary structure. Their argument in favor of their model is that using automated attacks (such as worms), a vulnerability can be exploited on all computers in the network running the same platform (color). In their model the adversary can control all nodes that use up to $k$ different platforms (or colors).

We will demonstrate one of the limitations of their model. Although the family of color based adversary structures has a trivial representation which size grows polynomial in the size of the graph, we will demonstrate in this paper that deciding reliability issues and security issues are co-**NP**-complete.

In most societies censorship is common. Indeed, for centuries it has often been viewed by authorities as an essential security tool. We apply the computational complexity result to study censorship. Authorities may require network designers to demonstrate the capability to censor the internet. We present a zero-knowledge interactive proof for the case of a color based adversary structure.

**Keywords:** network security, Byzantine threats, secret sharing, adversary structure, censorship, unconditional security, zero-knowledge.

---

\* A part of this work has been funded by CCR-0209092. The author is BT Professor of Information Security. He is also courtesy professor at Florida State University.
\*\* A part of this work has been funded by CCR-0209092.

J. Lopez (Ed.): CRITIS 2006, LNCS 4347, pp. 140–150, 2006.

# 1  Introduction

The research on how to achieve reliable networks is well known [11,20]. After Dolev-Dwork-Waarts-Yung [12] extended the research on reliable networks by also addressing privacy issues, a lot of research has been done on this topic (see e.g. [15,1,13,27,9,23,2,7,8]). This research has been partially motivated by the importance of securing networks both against a denial of service attack as well how to achieve privacy and authenticity at the same time.

Another important issue is to guarantee that the infrastructure built cannot be exploited to undermine society. Although, the topic of censorship is taboo in the West, it has been used extensively during centuries. There are many examples over the centuries, and even today, that censorship was used in Western societies. As a first example, consider the recently recovered "Gospel of Judas" [24]. It has been used as an occasion to reflect back on how the church censored "non-traditional" gospels [19]. As a second example, today in many countries books remain censored. A well known example is Hitler's "Mein Kampf." As a third example, in the US, the Rolling Stones performance during the 2006 superbowl on February 5 was censored. Finally, texts describing in details the construction of atomic bombs, or other classified information, are also censored.

Whether censorship in a limited format is in the benefit of mankind or not, is a non-scientific topic, and therefore not discussed. Information, such as books, are passed on through a network, e.g. a distribution network, involving bookstores, etc. The communication of gossip can be modeled using social networks [26]. Whether the edges in this network are virtual or physical communication links seems irrelevant. However, as we now discuss, this conclusion may be wrong.

In the *classical model* for communication networks nodes are treated equally. So when a limited adversary (or a censor in our prior example) wants to undermine communication, it is natural to assume that there is an upperbound $k$ of the number of nodes the adversary (or censor) can control. The first to dispute this homogeneous viewpoint was Hirt and Maurer [21]. Their paper introduces the concept of an adversary structure (i.e. the complement of an access structure [22]). An adversary structure is a list of subsets the adversary can control. Before performing the attack the adversary must choose one of these subsets. However, Hirt and Maurer do not specify how to choose such an adversary structure. Burmester-Desmedt [5] introduced a method to address this, we now discuss. Burmester-Desmedt partition the nodes in a network based on the platform used to operate the node, e.g. the router. The mapping from node to platform is modeled using a node coloring. To take into account the ease of automated attacks using computer viruses and worms, they view that the difficulty for an adversary to control one node running one platform is approximately the same as the difficulty to control all nodes running the same platform. A limited adversary corresponds in their setting to one that can control all nodes that have up to $k$ different colors. The resulting adversary structure is called a color based adversary structure.

We believe that color based adversary structures are worth studying in more details for the following reasons:

1. It was revealed at the Blackhat 2005 conference that the operating system used on Cisco routers has serious vulnerabilities [28] (note the paper in the proceedings was pulled due to pressure by Cisco). So, a color based adversary structure corresponds to reality.
2. The family of color based adversary structures has a representation which size grows polynomial in the size of the graph. This is not the case for the general case of adversary structures, making them completely impractical to use on large graphs.

In this paper we will demonstrate that although the family of color based adversary structures has a short representation, the complexity of deciding whether a given colored graph allows to achieve reliability and/or privacy are co-**NP**-complete problems. So, the question which colors to shut down to censor such a priorly described colored network is **NP**-complete. As is well known, the equivalent problem for the classical model is in **P**.

When a point-to-point network is built the designer may be asked by the authorities whether it can be censored by controlling $k$ platforms. This can be achieved by building trapdoors in these $k$ platforms (for a discussion on this issue, see e.g. [25]). Evidently, it should be hard for an adversary to find these $k$ colors. To answer this question, we present a zero-knowledge interactive proof.

The paper is organized as following. In Section 2 we survey what is known about security (privacy and authenticity) and reliability in point-to-point networks with a color based adversary structure. We also briefly survey the concept of zero-knowledge interactive proof. In Section 3 we prove the computational complexity. In Section 4 we give a zero-knowledge interactive proof for knowledge of up to $k$ colors that will cut the colored graph. Finally we conclude with some remarks and open problems in Section 5.

## 2   Background

We survey the work on colored networks with a color based adversary structure. We also briefly discuss the concept of zero-knowledge interactive proof. We start by some definitions.

### 2.1   Definitions

**Definition 1.** *[21] Let $V$ be a finite non-empty set. An adversary structure $\mathcal{A}_V$ for $V$ is a subset of the power set $2^V$ such that if $B \in \mathcal{A}_V$ then subsets of $B$ are also in $\mathcal{A}_V$.*

In our context, $V$ will be vertices in a graph.

**Definition 2.** *A vertex-colored graph is a tuple $G = G(V, E, C, f)$, with $V$ the node set, $E$ the edge set, $C$ the color set, and $f$ a map from $V$ onto $C$. The structure*
$$\mathcal{Z}_{C,k} = \{Z \mid Z \subset V \text{ and } |f(Z)| \leq k\}.$$

*is called a k-color adversary structure. Let $A, B \in V$ be distinct nodes of G. $A, B$ are called $(k+1)$-color connected for $k > 1$ if for any color set $C_k \subseteq C$ of size k, there is a path p from A to B in G such that the nodes on p does not contain any color in $C_k$.*

It should be noted that color connectivity is unrelated to the issue of vertex disjoint paths. Indeed take the graph in Figure 1. $A$ and $V$ are 3-color connected, but not 4-color connected, as is easy to verify using an exhaustive search. However, the simple paths from $A$ to $B$ are not vertex disjoint. If one removes nodes to make them vertex disjoint, the resulting graph is no longer 3-color connected.

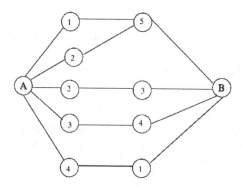

**Fig. 1.** A 3-color connected graph

**Definition 3.** *Let $G(V, E)$ be a directed graph, $A, B$ be nodes in $G(V, E)$, and $\mathcal{Z}$ be a an adversary structure on $V \setminus \{A, B\}$.*

- *$A, B$ are $\mathcal{Z}$-separable in G, if there is a set $Z \in \mathcal{Z}$ such that all paths from A to B go through at least one node in Z. We say that Z separates A and B.*
- *$A, B$ are $(\mathcal{Z}+1)$-connected if they are not $\mathcal{Z}$-separable in G.*

**Definition 4.** *[7] If $\mathcal{Z}_1$ and $\mathcal{Z}_2$ are adversary structures for $\mathcal{P}$, then $\mathcal{Z}_1 + \mathcal{Z}_2 = \{Z_1 \cup Z_2 : Z_1 \in \mathcal{Z}_1, Z_2 \in \mathcal{Z}_2\}$. $2\mathcal{Z}$ and $3\mathcal{Z}$ are the adversary structures $\mathcal{Z} + \mathcal{Z}$ and $\mathcal{Z} + \mathcal{Z} + \mathcal{Z}$ respectively.*

Obviously, $\mathcal{Z}_1 + \mathcal{Z}_2$ is also an adversary structure for $\mathcal{P}$.

## 2.2   Survey of the Known Results

We now survey the state of the art on the research of security and reliability in point-to-point networks with a general adversary structure.

**Theorem 1.** *A necessary and sufficient condition for A and B to privately communicate in a point-to-point network in the presence of a Byzantine adversary, in the case all communication links (edges in the graph) are:*

**two-way** *is that $A, B$ are $(2\mathcal{Z} + 1)$-connected in $G$ [23]).*
**one-way without feedback,** *is that $A, B$ are $(3\mathcal{Z} + 1)$-connected in $G$ [7].*

We say that we have $\mathcal{Z}$-reliable message transmission from $A$ to $B$ if a protocol exists which will guarantee that a message $M^A$ sent by $A$ arrives correctly with 100% success, even if a Byzantine adversary chooses a subset of nodes $Z$ such that $Z \in \mathcal{Z}$.

**Theorem 2.** *[7] Let $G = G(V, E)$ be a directed graph, $A, B$ be nodes in $G$, and $\mathcal{Z}$ be an adversary structure on $V \setminus \{A, B\}$. We have $\mathcal{Z}$-reliable message transmission from $A$ to $B$ if, and only if, $A, B$ are strongly $(2\mathcal{Z} + 1)$-connected in $G$.*

Note that the issue of privacy without reliability will be addressed in the final paper of [7].

The above results for the case of color based adversary structure trivially become:

**Corollary 1.** *Let $G = G(V, E, C, f)$ be a vertex-colored graph and $A, B \in V$. A necessary and sufficient condition for $A$ and $B$ to privately communicate in a point-to-point network in the presence of a $k$-color adversary in the case all communication links (edges in the graph) are:*

**two-way** *is that $A, B$ are $2k + 1$-color connected in $G$*
**one-way without feedback,** *is that $A, B$ are $3k + 1$-color connected in $G$.*

*Moreover, reliable message transmission from $A$ to $B$ with such an adversary is possible if, and only if, $A, B$ are $2k + 1$-color connected in $G$.*

## 2.3   Zero-Knowledge Interactive Proof

**Interactive protocols.** Following [18], an *interactive Turing machine* is a Turing machine with a public input tape, a public communication tape, a private random tape and a private work tape. An *interactive protocol* is a pair of interactive Turing machines sharing their public input tape and communication tape. The *transcript* of an execution of an interactive protocol (P,V) is a sequence containing the random tape of V and all messages appearing on the communication tape of P and V.

**Interactive proof systems.** An interactive proof system for a language $L$ is an interactive protocol in which, on an input string $x$, a computationally unbounded prover P convinces a polynomial-time bounded verifier V that $x$ belongs to $L$. The requirements are two: completeness and soundness. Informally, completeness states that for any input $x \in L$, the prover convinces the verifier with very high probability. Soundness states that for any $x \notin L$ and any prover, the verifier is convinced with very small probability. A formal definition can be found in [18].

**Zero-knowledge proof systems in the two-party model.** A zero-knowledge proof system for a language $L$ is an interactive proof system for $L$ in which, for any $x \in L$, and any possibly malicious probabilistic polynomial-time verifier V', no information is revealed to V' that he could not compute alone before running the protocol. This is formalized by requiring, for each V', the existence of an efficient simulator $S_{V'}$ which outputs a transcript "indistinguishable" from the view of V' in the protocol. There exists three notions of zero-knowledge, according to the level of indistinguishability: computational, statistical, and perfect. The reader is referred to [18] for the definitions of computational, statistical, and perfect zero-knowledge proof systems. In this paper, we will only deal with computational zero-knowledge proof systems.

## 3    Computational Complexity

In this section we are interested in the computational complexity of deciding whether a given vertex-colored graph can achieve privacy and reliability against a $k$-color adversary structure. From Corollary 1 we know that the issue of $k + 1$ (or $2k + 1$, or $3k + 1$)-color connectivity is essential.

So, from a computational problem it is sufficient to focus on the case of $k$-connectivity. We now prove that this problem is co-**NP**-complete. We focus on the complementary problem, which is trivial to see to correspond to the following. We call it the color separable problem. We first define, as a special case of Definition 3, the following.

**Definition 5.** *Let $G = G(V, E, C, f)$ be a vertex-colored graph and $A, B$ be nodes in $G(V, E)$. $A, B$ are $k$-color separable in $G$, if there is a set $V' \subseteq V$ such that all paths from $A$ to $B$ go through at least one node in $V'$ and $f(V') \leq k$. We say that $V'$ is a $k$-color separator of $A$ and $B$.*

INSTANCE: A vertex-colored network $G = G(V, E, C, f)$, two nodes $A, B \in V$, and a positive integer $k \leq |C|$.
QUESTION: Are $A$ and $B$ $k$-color separable?

**Theorem 3.** *The color separable problem is* **NP**-*complete.*

*Proof.* It is straightforward to show that the problem is in **NP**. Thus it is sufficient to show that it is **NP**-hard. The reduction is from the Vertex Cover (VC) problem. The VC problem is as follows (definition taken from [16]):

INSTANCE: A graph $G = (V, E)$ and a positive integer $k \leq |V|$.
QUESTION: Is there a vertex cover of size $k$ or less for $G$, that is, a subset $V' \subseteq V$ such that $|V'| \leq k$ and, for each edge $(u, v) \in E$, at least one of $u$ and $v$ belongs to $V'$?

For a given instance $G = (V, E)$ of VC, we construct a vertex-colored network $G_c = (V_c, E_c, f, C)$ as follows. First assume that the vertex set $V$ is ordered as in $V = \{v_1, \ldots, v_n\}$. Let

$$V_c = \{A, B\} \cup \left\{ e^1_{(v_i, v_j)}, e^2_{(v_i, v_j))} : (v_i, v_j) \in E \text{ and } i < j \right\}$$
$$E_c = \left\{ (A, e^1_{(v_i, v_j)}), (e^1_{(v_i, v_j)}, e^2_{(v_i, v_j)}), (e^2_{(v_i, v_j)}, B) : (v_i, v_j) \in E \right\}$$
$$C = \{c_v : v \in V\}$$
$$f = \left\{ f(e^1_{(v_i, v_j)}) = c_{v_i}, f(e^2_{(v_i, v_j)}) = c_{v_j} : (v_i, v_j) \in E, i < j \right\}$$

In the following, we show that there is a vertex cover of size $k$ in $G$ if and only if there is a $k$-color separator for $G_c$.

Without loss of generality, assume that $V' = \{v'_1, \ldots, v'_k\}$ is a vertex cover for $G$. Then it is straightforward to show that $C' = \{c_{v'_i} : v'_i \in V'\}$ is a color separator for $G_c$ since each incoming path for $B$ in $G_c$ contains both colors of the corresponding edge's end-vertices.

For the other direction, assume that $C' = \{c_{v'_i} : i = 1, \ldots, k\}$ is a $k$-color separator for $G_c$. Let $V' = \{v'_i : c_{v'_i} \in C'\}$. By the fact that $C'$ is a color separator for $G_c$, for each edge $(v_i, v_j) \in E$ in $G$, the path $(A, e^1_{(v_i, v_j)}, e^2_{(v_i, v_j)}, B)$ in $G_c$ contains at least one color from $C'$. Since this path contains only two colors $c_{v_i}$ and $c_{v_j}$, we know that $v_i$ or $v_j$ or both belong to $V'$. In another word, $V'$ is a $k$-size vertex cover for $G$. This completes the proof of the Theorem.

# 4   Privacy Preserving Censorship

## 4.1   Introduction

As we discussed in the introduction, deciding whether one can censor a network using limited resources is straightforward under the classical network problem. However, it is no longer under the vertex-colored graph model. The problem is **NP**-complete.

When a network is designed, the authority may want to ask whether it is possibly to censor traffic in the network by only controlling nodes running on at most $k$ platforms (colors). To allow the network designer to prove this censoring capability, the network designer will prove to the authority the existence of such $k$ platforms (colors). To avoid an outsider to take control of the network the set of these $k$ platforms (colors) should remain secret. Therefore we present a zero-knowledge interactive proof for above problem. Inspired by [10] we present a zero-knowledge interactive proof for above.

## 4.2   A Difficulty

Many zero-knowledge proofs for NP-complete problems [3,17,4] consists of committing in a first stage. Then the verifier asks a binary question. The prover then either opens all the commitments or reveals other information such that if both questions would had been asked, the secret would leak.

The problem of designing an efficient zero-knowledge proof seems rather trivial. Indeed, the prover could in the first step permute all the vertices, and permute all the colors and commit to these. The verifier then asks a question. If the question is 0, the prover opens all commitments, else reveals a set $V'$ that separates $A$ and $B$ in this isomomorphic graph. In the first case, the verifier checks the commitment. In the else case, the verifier checks that the number of colors in $V'$ is at most $k$ and checks $V'$ indeed separates.

Unfortunately, the above protocol is not zero-knowledge. Indeed, it leaks the size of $V'$, which it should not. The knowledge of the size of $V'$ may help the verifier to find the $k$ colors. Moreover, it also leaks the multiplicity of each color, etc.

### 4.3   Avoiding This Problem

To solve this problem, we prove the following lemma.

**Lemma 1.** Let $G_c = G_c(V, E, C, f)$ be a vertex-colored graph. Let $C' \subseteq C$ be such that $|C'| = k$ and $V' = \{v'_i : f(v'_i) \in C'\}$ separate $A$ and $B$. Let $k'$ be the maximum number of vertex disjoint paths in $(V, E)$ ignoring the colors. Let $P_1$, $P_2$, ..., $P_{k'}$ be these vertex disjoint paths. We then have that for each of these path $P_i$: $P_i \cap V' \neq \emptyset$. So, on each path $P_i$ there exists a node of a color in $C'$.

*Proof.* The proof follows trivially by contradiction.

We now use this lemma to provide a zero-knowledge interactive proof.

### 4.4   The Protocol

Let $G = G(V, E, C, f)$ be a vertex-colored graph and $m = |C|$. For simplicity we assume $C = (1, 2, \ldots, m)$. Let $C'$ and $V'$ be as in Section 4.3.

First the verifier and the prover (separetely) compute:

- $k'$, i.e. the maximum number of vertex disjoint paths ignoring colors.
- $k'$ vertex disjoint paths $P_1, P_1, P_2, \ldots, P_{k'}$.

This can be done in polynomial time [6]. So both prover and verifier obtain the same $k'$ vertex disjoint paths. Let $l_i$ be the length of the path $P_i$ minus one, and let us call the vertices, except $A$ and $B$, on this path $v_{(i,1)}, v_{(i,2)}, \ldots, v_{(i,l_i)}$.

Then they repeat the following steps $n$ times, where $n$ is specified later. The randomness in each run is chosen independently.

Step 1. The prover chooses a permutation $\pi$ of the colors, so $\pi \in_R sym$ $(\{1, \ldots, m\})$. For each of the aforementioned paths $P_i$:
- the prover chooses a permutation $\rho_i \in_R sym(\{1, \ldots, l_i\})$, permutes the vertices (ignoring $A$ and $B$) on the path $P_i$ and sends the verifier a commitment for the permuted coloring of the permuted vertices, so formally, sends:

$$E_{(i,j)} = commit(\pi(f(v_{(i,\rho_i(j))})), r_{ij}) \text{for } j = 1, \ldots, l_i,$$

where $r_{ij}$ is chosen independently uniformly random, and

- for each $c_h \in C'$ ($h = 1, \ldots, k$) sends $E'_h = commit(\pi(c_h), r'_h)$, where $r'_h$ is chosen independently uniformly random.

Step 2. The verifier flips a coin $q_1$ and also chooses randomly a value $q_2 \in_R$ $\{1, \ldots, k'\}$ and sends the prover the query $(q_1, q_2)$.

Step 3. If $q_1 = 0$, then the prover reveals $\pi$, all $\rho_i$ and opens all commitments of the type $E_{(i,j)}$ (Note the prover does not open $E'_{h \cdot}$),

else the prover decommits one (of the) permuted colors of the vertex set: $P_{q_2} \cap V'$. This is done by opening:
- exactly one $E_{(q_2, j')}$, and
- exactly one $E'_h$

such that $f(v_{(q_2, \rho_{q_2}(j'))}) = c_h$. (Note $\pi$ is not opened, and neither is $\rho_{q_2}$

Step 4. If $q_1 = 0$, then the verifier verifies that $\pi$ and all $\rho_i$ are permutations and all the decommitted values,

else the verifier checks that the two opened commitments and checks that they correspond to the same color.

**Theorem 4.** *When $n$ is chosen such that $((k'-1)/k')^n$ is negligible, the protocol is a computational zero-knowledge interactive proof system for the color separable problem assuming that the commitment function* commit *is secure.*

*Proof.* (**Sketch**) We have perfect completeness, which is indeed trivial. We now prove soundness. Suppose that the graph is not $k$-color separable. Then a separator will have at least $k + 1$ different colors. However, the prover only commits to $k$ colors by using the commitments $E'_h$ in the zero-knowledge proof. The prover could try to commit incorrectly to $E_{(i,j)}$ or choose $\pi$ and $\rho_i$ that are not commitments. However, the prover would be caught with probability $1/2$ if this was the case. Assume now that $\pi$, $\rho_i$ and $E_{(i,j)}$ are correct. The best case for the dishonest prover occurs when we have that for all, except one, path $P_i$ there is a color on the path that is in the one of the $k$ colors committed in $E'_h$. The conditional probability the verifier does not catch this is $1/k'$. Thus, the conditional probability the dishonest prover fools the honest verifier is $(k' - 1)/k'$. However, since the protocol is repeated independently sufficiently many times, the probability the dishonest prover convinces the verifier of an untruth is negligible.

We now prove zero-knowledge. The simulator first guesses a query $(q'_1, q'_2)$ with the same probability distribution as a honest verifier. We now explain the simulation of Step 1. If $q'_1 = 0$, the simulator chooses random permutation $\pi'$ and $\rho'_i$ and makes commitments for these. The simulator also chooses a subset of $k$ colors and commits to these. In the case $q'_1 = 1$, the simulator chooses a uniformly random color $c'$. Then the prover chooses $k - 1$ other colors. He creates commitments for these $k$ colors and call these $E'_h$. All the colors of the type $E_{(i,j)}$ are chosen randomly, except for one $j$ and for $i = q'_2$ for which the color $c'$ is chosen.

The commitments are presented to the verifier who sends $(q_1, q_2)$. If $(q_1, q_2) \neq (q'_1, q'_2)$, then the simulator rewinds. Otherwise the simulator continues. He is able to answer the query correctly, as is trivial to verify. Due to the assumption on the commitment function, the zero-knowledge is computational.

This proved the theorem.

# 5    Conclusion

In practice the connectivity of a network may be small and then the research has only theoretical value. However, when wifi technology is used, this may no longer be true. Unfortunately, the results in this paper are for point-to-point communication. The work by [14,13,27,9] has demonstrated that even for an adversary bounded by a threshold, the problem of reliability and security in partial broadcast communication is much more complex. We believe that generalizing our results for a color based adversary structure to partial broadcast networks is a true challenge.

# Acknowledgment

The first author thanks those who asked him how research on color based adversary structures could be used in settings where one wants censorship or prevent censorship.

The authors acknowledge one of the referees for finding several typos.

# References

1. A. Beimel and M. K. Franklin. Reliable communication over partially authenticated networks. In M. Mavronicolas and P. Tsigas, editors, *Distributed Algorithms, 11th International Workshop, WDAG '97 (Lecture Notes in Computer Science 1320)*, pp. 245–259. Springer-Verlag, 1997. Saarbrücken, Germany, September.
2. A. Beimel and L. Malka. Efficient reliable communication over partially authenticated networks. *Distributed Computing*, 2005. In press.
3. M. Blum. How to prove a theorem so no one else can claim it. In *Proceedings of the International Congress of Mathematicians*, pp. 1444–1451, August 3–11, 1987. Berkeley, California, U.S.A., 1986.
4. G. Brassard, D. Chaum, and C. Crépeau. Minimum disclosure proofs of knowledge. *Journal of Computer and System Sciences*, 37(2), pp. 156–189, October 1988.
5. M. Burmester and Y. G. Desmedt. Is hierarchical public-key certification the next target for hackers? *Communications of the ACM*, 47(8), pp. 68–74, August 2004.
6. T. H. Cormen, C. E. Leiserson, and R. L. Rivest. *Introduction to Algorithms*. MIT Press and Mc. Graw-Hill, 1990.
7. Y. Desmedt, Y. Wang, and M. Burmester. A complete characterization of tolerable adversary structures for secure point-to-point transmissions without feedback. In X. Deng and D. Du, editors, *Algorithms and Computation, 16th Annual International Conference, ISAAC 2005, (Lecture Notes in Computer Science 3827)*, pp. 277–287, 2005. December 19 - 21, 2005, Sanya, Hainan, China.
8. Y. Desmedt, Y. Wang, R. Safavi-Naini, and H. Wang. Radio networks with reliable communication. In L. Wang, editor, *To appear in: Computing and Combinatorics, 11th Annual International Conference, COCOON 2005 (Lecture Notes in Computer Science 3595)*, 2005. Kunming, Yunnan China, August 16-19, 2005.
9. Y. Desmedt and Y. Wang. Perfectly secure message transmission revisited. In L. Knudsen, editor, *Advances in Cryptology — Eurocrypt 2002, Proceedings (Lecture Notes in Computer Science 2332)*, pp. 502–517. Springer-Verlag, 2002. Amsterdam, The Netherlands, April 28–May 2.

10. Y. Desmedt and Y. Wang. Efficient zero-knowledge protocols for some practical graph problems. In *Third Conference on Security in Communication Networks '02 (Lecture Notes in Computer Science 2576)*, pp. 296–308. Springer-Verlag, 2003. Amalfi, Italy, September 12-13, 2002.

11. D. Dolev. The Byzantine generals strike again. *Journal of Algorithms*, 3, pp. 14–30, 1982.

12. D. Dolev, C. Dwork, O. Waarts, and M. Yung. Perfectly secure message transmission. *Journal of the ACM*, 40(1), pp. 17–47, January 1993.

13. M. Franklin and R. Wright. Secure communication in minimal connectivity models. In K. Nyberg, editor, *Advances in Cryptology — Eurocrypt '98, Proceedings (Lecture Notes in Computer Science 1403)*, pp. 346–360. Springer-Verlag, 1998. Espoo, Finland, May 31–June 4.

14. M. Franklin and M. Yung. Secure hypergraphs: Privacy from partial broadcast. *SIAM J. Discrete Math.*, 18(3), pp. 437–450, 2004.

15. M. K. Franklin and M. Yung. Secure hypergraphs: Privacy from partial broadcast. In *Proceedings of the twenty seventh annual ACM Symp. Theory of Computing, STOC*, pp. 36–44, 1995.

16. M. R. Garey and D. S. Johnson. *Computers and Intractability: A Guide to the Theory of NP-Completeness.* W. H. Freeman and Company, San Francisco, 1979.

17. O. Goldreich, S. Micali, and A. Wigderson. Proofs that yield nothing but their validity or all languages in NP have zero-knowledge proof systems. *Journal of the ACM*, 38(1), pp. 691–729, July 1991.

18. S. Goldwasser, S. Micali, and C. Rackoff. The knowledge complexity of interactive proof systems. *SIAM J. Comput.*, 18(1), pp. 186–208, February 1989.

19. Gospels of Matthew, Mark, Luke, and John written. http://www9. nationalgeographic.com/lostgospel/timeline_04.html.

20. V. Hadzilacos. *Issues of Fault Tolerance in Concurrent Computations.* PhD thesis, Harvard University, Cambridge, Massachusetts, 1984.

21. M. Hirt and U. Maurer. Player simulation and general adversary structures in perfect multiparty computation. *Journal of Cryptology*, 13(1), pp. 31–60, 2000.

22. M. Ito, A. Saito, and T. Nishizeki. Secret sharing schemes realizing general access structures. In *Proc. IEEE Global Telecommunications Conf., Globecom'87*, pp. 99–102. IEEE Communications Soc. Press, 1987.

23. M. Kumar, P. Goundan, K. Srinathan, and C. Rangan. On perfectly secure communication over arbitrary networks. In *Proceedings of the Annual ACM Symposium on Principles of Distributed Computing (PODC)*, pp. 193–202, 2002.

24. B. Meier and J. N. Wilford. How the gospel of Judas emerged. The New York Times, http://www.nytimes.com/2006/04/13/science/13judas.html, April 13, 2006.

25. NSA access codes have been secretly built into windows. http://ureader.co.uk/ message/792934.aspx.

26. Social networks, quarterly journal.

27. Y. Wang and Y. Desmedt. Secure communication in broadcast channels. In J. Stern, editor, *Advances in Cryptology — Eurocrypt '99, Proceedings (Lecture Notes in Computer Science 1592)*, pp. 446–458. Springer-Verlag, 1999. Prague, Czech Republic, May 2–6.

28. K. Zetter. Cisco security hole a whopper. http://www.wired.com/news/privacy/ 0,1848,68328,00.html?tw=wn_tophead_2, July 27, 2005.

# PROSEARCH: A Protocol to Simplify Path Discovery in Critical Scenarios

Cristina Satizábal[1,2], Rafael Páez[1], and Jordi Forné[1]

[1] Telematics Engineering Department. Technical University of Catalonia
C/Jordi Girona 1-3, C3, 08034 - Barcelona (Spain)
{isabelcs,rpaez,jforne}@entel.upc.edu
[2] Engineering and Architecture Department. Pamplona University
Km 1 via a Bucaramanga, Pamplona (Colombia)

**Abstract.** Authentication is a strong requirement for critical information systems, and Public Key Infrastructure (PKI) is widely used to provide this service. Peer-to-peer PKIs are quite dynamic and certification paths can be built although part of the infrastructure is temporarily unreachable, which is quite common after disasters or network attacks. However, certification path discovery is one of the main drawbacks of peer-to-peer PKIs that strongly affects their scalability. We propose a protocol to build a virtual hierarchical PKI from a peer-to-peer PKI, since certification path construction in hierarchical PKIs is straightforward. Our protocol does not require to issue new certificates, facilitates the certification path discovery process and it is adaptable to the characteristics of users with limited processing and storage capacity. Results show that the execution time of this protocol is short in critical scenarios.

**Keywords:** Public Key Infrastructure (PKI), hierarchical trust model, peer-to-peer trust model, certification path discovery, critical information systems.

## 1  Introduction

As communication networks have increased their importance in our daily lives, our dependency upon their underlying infrastructure has grown too. Unfortunately, at the same time, hostile attacks on the infrastructure have increased in number and impact. Thus, networks become increasingly vulnerable and it is essential to guarantee the security of information which is considered of critical importance, from a political, economic, financial or social standpoint.

Secure connectivity is a requirement of communication networks in many critical scenarios. Some critical information systems require the rapid deployment of a secure connected network, in which each node has a path to every other node in the network and they can authenticate each other. Hierarchical Public Key Infrastructures (PKIs)[1] are widely used in distributed applications to provide the authentication service because are scalable and certification path construction is straightforward. Nevertheless, there are many situations where a static hierarchical PKI cannot operate, because part of the infrastructure is not available. On the other hand, peer-to-peer PKIs are quite dynamic and certification paths can be built although part of the

J. Lopez (Ed.): CRITIS 2006, LNCS 4347, pp. 151–165, 2006.
© Springer-Verlag Berlin Heidelberg 2006

infrastructure is temporarily unreachable, which is quite common after disasters or network attacks. However, certification path discovery is difficult in peer-to-peer PKIs because there can be multiple certification paths between two entities and all the options do not lead to the target entity.

In this paper, we propose a protocol to establish a virtual hierarchy among the CAs of a peer-to-peer PKI called PROSEARCH (Protocol to Simplify the Certification Path Discovery Constructing a Hierarchy). Thus, we take advantage of the efficiency in the path discovery process offered by hierarchical architectures, where trust relationships are unidirectional and paths are easy to find. Using this protocol, nodes of critical information systems can find easy and rapidly the certification paths to the other nodes and in case that some node fails due to a disaster or attack, it is possible to establish a new hierarchy in a short time.

Unlike the previous works, our protocol does not require to generate new certificates to establish a hierarchy among the entities of the PKI. In addition, PROSEARCH sets a maximum certification path length to be adaptable to users with limited capacities.

This paper is divided into six sections. Section 2 gives the concept of certification path and the characteristics of peer-to-peer and hierarchical PKIs. Also, it explains the certification path discovery process and some solutions to increase its efficiency in decentralized architectures. In section 3, we describe how our protocol establishes a hierarchical architecture in a peer-to-peer PKI. Section 4 contains a practical example of PROSEACH in a critical scenario. In section 5, we show the obtained results in the simulation of our protocol. Finally, section 6 concludes.

## 2   Background

### 2.1   PKI Trust Models and Certification Paths

PKI uses Trust Third Parties (TTPs), known as Certification Authorities (CAs), to digitally sign data structures called Public Key Certificates (PKCs). A PKC binds a particular public key with the identity of a certain user. Thus, certificates, and the keys they contain, give the communicating parties information about the owner of the certificate and the entity that issued it.

Before trusting the content of a certificate, the user must check its signature. When the same CA issues the certificates of communicating parties, one can easily verify the signature of the other's certificate using the public key of this authority. However, to verify the signature of a certificate issued by another CA, it is necessary a continuous chain of trust points between the two parties. These chains of trust are called certification paths.

A *certification path* [2] is a chain of public key certificates through which a user can obtain the public key of another user. Paths are traced from the trusted CA of the verifier to the target entity's certificate. Therefore, the certification path length is equal to the number of CAs in the path plus one: a certificate for each CA and the target entity's certificate.

Certification architectures or trust models describe how the trust relationships among the entities of a PKI and the necessary rules to find and to cross the certification paths are built. The most popular PKI trust models are hierarchical and peer-to-peer (see [3], [4])

### 2.1.1 Hierarchical Model

This is the most common model. In this configuration, all users trust the same root CA (RCA). That is, all the users of a hierarchical PKI begin their certification paths with the RCA's public key. In general, the root CA does not issue certificates to users but only issues certificates to subordinate CAs. Each subordinate CA may issue certificates to users or another level of subordinate CAs, if it is permitted by the certification policies. In a hierarchical PKI, trust relationships are unidirectional, that is, subordinate CAs do not issue certificates to their superior CAs (Fig. 1).

Hierarchical PKIs are scalable. Certification paths are easy to build and the longest path is equal to the depth of the tree less one because RCA's certificate is not part of the path, since it is known by all entities in the architecture.

The drawbacks of the hierarchical model result from the reliance on a single trust point. The compromise of the RCA's private key results in a compromise of the entire PKI. In addition, transition from a set of isolated CAs to a hierarchical PKI may be logistically impractical because all users must adjust their trust points.

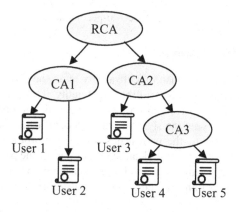

**Fig. 1.** Hierarchical model

### 2.1.2 Peer-to-Peer Model

It is also known as cross-certificate or mesh architecture. In the peer-to-peer model, all the CAs can be trust points because they are autonomous. Autonomy refers to the fact that the CA does not rely on a superior CA in a hierarchy. An autonomous CA can perform cross-certification with other autonomous CAs. Thus, a pair of certificates describes their bidirectional trust relationship (Fig. 2). However, the trust relationship may not be unconditional. If a CA wishes to limit its trust, it must specify these limitations in the certificates issued to its peers. All certificate validation, by clients within an autonomous CA, starts with the local CA's self-signed certificate.

Peer-to-peer PKI can easily incorporate a new community of users and although the management cost is high, there is not a single point of failure since it counts on different trust points and they can have multiple paths between two users. In addition, a peer-to-peer PKI can easily be constructed from a set of isolated CAs because the users do not need to change their trust point.

The drawback of peer-to-peer model is that the number of trust relationships is directly proportional to the number of CAs (n), that is, the number of trust relationships is equal to $n*(n - 1)$, what causes scalability problems. The maximum length of a certification path in a peer-to-peer PKI is the number of CAs in the infrastructure.

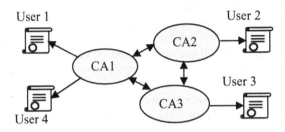

**Fig. 2.** Peer-to-peer model

## 2.2 Certification Path Discovery

The verifier must check the signature and validity of all the certificates in a certification path in order to trust the public key of the target entity. This process is called *certification path validation* and involves: discovering the certification path, retrieving the certificates in the path, verifying the signature of each certificate, and checking the expiration and revocation state of the certificates. Since our protocol tries to simplify the certification path discovery, we will detail only this part of the path validation process.

Discovering a certification path is to build a trusted path between the trusted CA of the verifier (trust anchor) and the target entity based on the trust relationship among the CAs of the PKI.

According to Elley et all[5], there are two basic ways to build certification paths:

- *Forward direction:* When the certification path is built from the target entity to a trust anchor. It is used when certificates are stored with the subject. The verifier starts by retrieving all the certificates in the target entity's directory entry. Each of these is a possible candidate certificate, so the verifier selects one of them and retrieves all the certificates from the directory entry of this certificate's issuer. This procedure continues until find the trust anchor.
- *Reverse direction:* When a certification path is built from a trust anchor to the target entity. It is used when certificates are stored with the issuer. This time, the verifier starts by retrieving all the certificates in the trust anchor's directory entry and looks for the path toward the target entity.

In the hierarchical trust model, building in the forward direction is more effective because each entity has a certificate issued by its superior CA and there is only one path between two entities. On the other hand, in a peer-to-peer trust model, it is better to validate the certification path as it is being built, so building in the reverse direction is more effective because it allows rejecting more quickly the certificates that are not useful in constructing a valid certification path. In addition, building in the reverse direction allows processing more effectively name constraints, policies, signatures and CRL-based revocation.

### 2.3 Related Works

There are different proposals which increase efficiency of path discovery and certification path validation in decentralized architectures using a hierarchical model.

Marchesini and Smith [6] propose a virtual hierarchy formed in a peer-to-peer network, that allows verifying certification paths in an efficient manner, because trust chains are loop-free, and splits the secrets (private keys) in multiple fragments, so that the compromise of one of them does not affect all the architecture, obtaining resilient trust chains. Thus, resulting nodes are virtual CAs, formed by several authorities that share a portion of a private key.

Pan et al. [7] propose a scheme of merging multiple PKIs, which is based on a hierarchical structure too. This scheme selects a root CA and remaining authorities are subordinate CAs that must apply to the root CA for a new certificate. New certificates still use the previous public keys. Thus, the merging process is quick and low-cost and certification path processing is much more simple and efficient than using cross-certification. Unfortunately, root CA selection process is not clearly defined.

Unlike these proposals, our protocol uses the existing trust relationships among PKI entities to create the virtual hierarchy, so it is not necessary to issue new certificates, adjust the trust points or create new nodes during the protocol execution. In addition, since validation of long paths is difficult for verifiers with limited processing and storage capacity, PROSEARCH sets a maximum certification path length whose value can be established taking into account the features of the users' terminals.

## 3   PROSEARCH (Protocol to Simplify the Certification Path Discovery Constructing a Hierarchy)

### 3.1 Protocol Description

In this section, we describe PROSEARCH operation. This protocol establishes a virtual hierarchy from the leaves to the root (upwards) in a peer-to-peer PKI, based on the trustworthiness level of the participant CAs. PROSEARCH facilitates the certification path discovery process and can be adapted to users with limited capacities.

Some aspects of our protocol are inspired on the algorithm proposed by J. Hernandez-Serrano et al in [8], although the application area is different. Table 1 shows the notation used in this paper.

We divide PROSEARCH in two phases to understand it better.

- *Trustworthiness order among CAs:* In this phase, the neighboring CAs are arranged from the less trustworthy to the most trustworthy.
- *Construction of the hierarchy:* In this phase, it is established a hierarchical trust relationship among the CAs of the peer-to-peer PKI.

**Table 1.** Notation

| Notation | Meaning |
|----------|---------|
| $L_{MAX}$ | Maximum path length allowed |
| $CA_i$ | Certification Authority i |
| $L_i$ | Number of certificates from the leaves to authority i |
| $IN_i$ | Number of CAs which $CA_i$ trusts (received certificates) |
| $OUT_i$ | Number of CAs that trust $CA_i$ (issued certificates) |
| $CA_0$ | Current authority |

### 3.1.1  Trustworthiness Order Among CAs

The protocol begins when an authority $CA_0$ declares to its neighboring CAs (authorities that issued a certificate to $CA_0$ and authorities that $CA_0$ issued a certificate) that it wants to establish a hierarchical trust relationship with them. In addition, $CA_0$ must propose a maximum certification path length ($L_{MAX}$) based on the processing and storage capacity of its users. Thus, $CA_0$ sends a request message to its neighbors containing the value of $L_{MAX}$. These messages and all the messages sent among the CAs along the protocol must be authenticated at the receiver.

Each neighbor can accept or refuse to collaborate in the establishment of that hierarchy, sending to the demanding entity an acceptance or rejection message.

Once $CA_0$ receives the responses from all its neighbors, it determines the number of authorities that issued a certificate to $CA_0$ and want to be part of the hierarchy ($IN_0$), and the number of authorities that received a certificate from $CA_0$ and want to participate in the hierarchy ($OUT_0$). Then, $CA_0$ sends these values to its participant neighbors in an information message and these neighbors send to $CA_0$ their own values $IN_i$ and $OUT_i$. We assume that there is a secure system by which each entity always sends truthful information to its neighbors.

Later, $CA_0$ compares $OUT_0$ with the received $OUT_i$ values and puts them in order from the lowest to the highest. The authority with the lowest $OUT_i$ is the less trustworthy, that is, the neighbor that less the other participants trust. If there are two or more authorities with the same $OUT_i$, they are arranged in accordance with the $IN_i$ value from the lowest to the highest too. For the sake of simplicity, we have not considered other parameters to put in order the authorities such as existing policy mapping or distance between them, but these can be considered if parameters $OUT_i$ and $IN_i$ are the same for two or more authorities. Thus, each CA puts in order its neighbors, determining which of them are less trustworthy and more trustworthy than itself. At the beginning of the protocol, $L_i=0$ for all the CAs.

### 3.1.2  Construction of the Hierarchy

In this phase of the protocol, participant CAs act from the less trustworthy to the most trustworthy in accordance with the order established at the first phase. Therefore, the less trustworthy authority in the neighborhood acts first and the other CAs must wait for the intervention of their less trustworthy neighbors.

The objective of the second phase is that each authority chooses a superior CA among the participant neighbors that issued it a certificate (trusted neighbors). Thus, when an authority $CA_0$ acts (current authority), it looks for the most trustworthy CA of its trusted neighbors, based on the trustworthiness order established at the first phase of the protocol, and chooses this neighbor like superior CA. If $L_0$ is greater than $L_i$ of superior CA and ($L_0$ +1) is less than or equal to ($L_{MAX} - 1$), $L_i$ of superior CA takes the value of ($L_0$ +1). In case that ($L_0$ +1) is greater than ($L_{MAX} - 1$), the current authority must choose like superior CA the next trusted neighbor, according to the trustworthiness order, provided that this neighbor is more trustworthy than $CA_0$. $CA_0$ checks again if $L_0$ is greater than $L_i$ of the new superior CA and so on until $CA_0$ finds a suitable superior CA. Nevertheless, it can be possible that none of the trusted neighbors that are more trustworthy than $CA_0$ can be used like superior CA. Thus, when $CA_0$ concludes this procedure, it sends an association message to its neighbors informing the identity of its superior CA or a failure message if it was not possible to choose a superior CA.

Later, the following less trustworthy CA in the neighborhood, according to the order established at the first phase, repeats the procedure and so on until all authorities act, except for the most trustworthy CA of the neighborhood that must not carry out this procedure because there is not a neighbor more trustworthy than it. Thus, when this authority acts, it sends a root_CA message to its neighbors.

The authorities that did not choose a superior CA in this phase of the protocol, including the most trustworthy CA, are considered root CAs. If there are more than one root CA at the end of the second phase that share some trust relationship among them, the protocol must be repeated, considering only the certificates issued among them to determine the new value of $OUTi$ and $IN_i$ parameters. Thus, the root CA of the neighborhood will start the repetition of the protocol, if it receives some failure message from its neighbors. $L_i$ maintain the value that they obtained at the second phase of the protocol. In addition, when the protocol is repeated, the value of $L_i$ can be less than or equal to $L_{MAX}$ in the second phase, instead of $L_{MAX}$ -1.

Even so, hierarchy can have more than one root CA after the repetition of the protocol. In this case, the root CAs must find the shortest path among them using an alternative method.

Root CAs send their public key certificate to all the CAs below them in the hierarchy once the protocol has concluded (root_CERT message).

### 3.1.3  A New Authority Joins the Hierarchy
If a new CA gets into the network and wants to be part of the hierarchy, it must request the value of $L_{MAX}$ to one of its neighbors in the hierarchy. Then, the new authority and its neighbors carry out the protocol.

The changes in the hierarchy will depend on the trustworthiness level of the new authority, so if this authority is the less trustworthy among its neighbors, the other CAs will not modify their superior CA.

### 3.1.4  An Authority Leaves from the Hierarchy

If an authority leaves from the hierarchy, the changes will depend on its trustworthiness level. Thus, if this authority is not a superior CA, the hierarchy will not be modified. On the contrary, when the authority that leaves from the hierarchy is a superior CA, its children must carry out the protocol with their neighbors.

## 4  Practical Example

Fig. 3 shows a peer-to-peer network with 10 nodes. Arrows represent the certificates issued from one node to another.

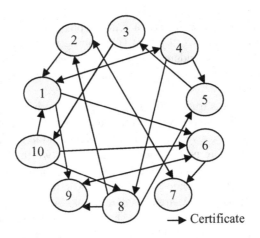

**Fig. 3.** Scenario A: peer-to-peer network

In the first round, node 1 wants to carry out the protocol, so it sends a request message to its neighbors (2, 4, 6, 9 and 10) and proposes a maximum path length $L_{MAX}=3$.

We define a *round* as the set of messages that are sent or received at the same time slot. Round time will depend on processing time, network speed, latency, etc.

In the second round, if node 2 wants to collaborate with node 1, it sends an acceptance message to 1 and a request message containing the value of $L_{MAX}$ to its other neighbors (7 and 8).

For the sake of simplicity, we suppose that all nodes want to be part of the hierarchy. Therefore, also in the second round, node 4 sends an acceptance message to node 1 and a request message to nodes 5 and 8; node 6 sends an acceptance message to node 1 and a request message to nodes 7, 9 and 10; node 9 sends an acceptance message to node 1 and a request message to nodes 6 and 8; and node 10 sends an acceptance message to node 1 and a request message to nodes 3, 6 and 8.

In the third round, node 7 sends an acceptance message to nodes 2 and 6; node 8 sends an acceptance message to nodes 2, 4, 9 and 10, and a request message to node 5; node 5 sends an acceptance message to node 4, and a request message to nodes 3 and 8; node 3 sends an acceptance message to node 10 and a request message to node

5; node 6 sends an acceptance message to nodes 9 and 10; node 9 sends an acceptance message to node 6; and node 10 sends an acceptance message to node 6.

Finally, in the fourth round, node 3 sends an acceptance message to node 5. At the same time, node 5 sends an acceptance message to nodes 3 and 8; and node 8 sends an acceptance message to node 5.

When nodes receive response to their request messages, they must determine their $OUT_i$ and $IN_i$ values and send them in an information message to their neighbors in the fifth round. Table 2 shows the parameters of each node.

**Table 2.** Parameters of the nodes

| $i$ | 1 | 2 | 3 | 4 | 5 | 6 | 7 | 8 | 9 | 10 |
|---|---|---|---|---|---|---|---|---|---|---|
| $OUT_i$ | 3 | 2 | 1 | 3 | 1 | 2 | 1 | 3 | 1 | 3 |
| $IN_i$ | 3 | 2 | 1 | 1 | 2 | 3 | 2 | 2 | 3 | 1 |

Once each node obtains the parameters of its neighbors, puts them in order from the less trustworthy to the most trustworthy. Thus, for node 1 the trustworthiness order is: 9, 2, 6, 4, 10, **1**. When parameters $OUT_i$ and $IN_i$ are the same, we use the identifier of the nodes to put them in order.

Likewise, the other nodes determine their trustworthiness order, for node 2 is: 7, **2**, 8, 1; for node 3 is: **3**, 5, 10; for node 4 is: 5, **4**, 8,1; for node 5 is: 3, **5**, 4, 8; for node 6 is: 7, 9, **6**, 10, 1; for node 7 is: **7**, 2, 6; for node 8 is:5, 9, 2, 4, 10, **8**, for node 9 is: **9**, 6, 8, 1; for node 10 is: 3, 6, **10**, 8, 1.

According to this order, nodes 3, 7 and 9 act first, then nodes 2, 5 and 6, next nodes 4 and 10, and finally nodes 1 and 8 are the most trustworthy of their neighborhood.

Node 3 chooses node 5 like superior CA because it is its most trusted neighbor. Since, $L_3=L_5=0$ and $(L_3+1) <= (L_{MAX}-1)$, $L_5=L_3+1=1$. Then, node 3 sends an association message to its neighbors with the identity of its superior CA, in the sixth round.

In the same round, node 7 chooses node 6 like superior CA and $L_6=1$; and node 9 among its trusted neighbors (1, 6, and 8) chooses node 1 like superior CA and $L_1=1$.

In the seventh round, node 2 chooses node 8 like superior CA and $L_8=1$; node 5 also chooses node 8 like superior CA. Since $L_5>L_8$ and $L_5+1=L_{MAX}-1$, $L_8=L_5+1=2$; and node 6 chooses node 1 like superior CA and $L_1=2$.

Next, in the eighth round, node 4 chooses node 1 like superior CA. $L_1$ value is not increased since $L_1> L_4$. On the other hand, the nodes that are more trustworthy than node 10 (1 and 8) do not issue certificates to node 10, so this node can not choose a superior CA and sends a failure message to its neighbors (1, 3, 6, and 8) indicating that its association process failed.

Finally, in the ninth round, nodes 1 and 8 send a root_CA message to their neighbors.

Thus, the protocol must be repeated with the resulting root CAs (1, 8 and 10).

When the protocol is repeated, they are taking into account the certificates among the root CAs. In this case, node 10 issues a certificate to nodes 8 and 1, and there are not more certificates among nodes 1, 8 and 10. Therefore, in the tenth round, nodes 1, 8 and 10 send their new parameters: $OUT_1=0$, $IN_1=1$; $OUT_8=0$, $IN_8=1$; $OUT_{10}=2$,

$IN_{10}$=0. Thus, the trustworthiness order for node 1 is: **1**, 10; for node 8 is: **8**, 10; and for node 10 is: 1, 8, **10**.

In the eleventh round, node 1 and 8 choose node 10 like superior CA. Since $L_1$ and $L_8$ are greater than $L_{10}$=0 and $L_1$+1 and $L_8$+1 are equal to $L_{MAX}$, $L_{10}$=3 at the end of the second phase. Fig. 4 shows the established hierarchy.

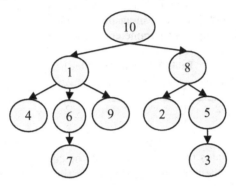

**Fig. 4.** Established hierarchy

### 4.1 Discovering a Certification Path

Node 9 in Fig. 3 wants to build a certification path to node 3. If node 9 looks for the path through node 1, it can find the following paths: 1-6-9/ 1-6-7-2-7/ 1-6-7-2-1/ 1-4-1/ 1-4-5-3/ 1-4-8-2-1/ 1-4-8-2-7-2/ 1-4-8-5-3/ 1-4-8-9.

If node 9 looks for the path through node 6, it can find the following paths: 6-7-2-7/ 6-7-2-1-9/ 6-7-2-1-6/ 6-7-2-1-4-1/ 6-7-2-1-4-5-3/ 6-7-2-1-4-8-2/ 6-7-2-1-4-8-5-3/ 6-7-2-1-4-8-9.

Finally, if node 9 looks for the path through node 8, it can find the following paths: 8-5-3/ 8-2-7-2/ 8-2-1-9/ 8-2-1-6-9/ 8-2-1-6-7-2/ 8-2-1-4-8/ 8-2-1-4-5-3/ 8-2-1-4-1.

Therefore, node 9 has 25 possible paths of which 6 are successful paths that is 76% of the paths do not lead to node 3.

On the other hand, after our protocol (Fig. 4), node 9 only has one possibility: 10-8-5- 3. Therefore, the path discovery process is easier and more rapidly.

### 4.2 Dynamic Reconfiguration After a Disaster

Some critical scenarios, such as systems for disaster relief or military applications, require the rapid deployment of a secure connected network, in which each node has a path to every other node in the network and they can authenticate each other. Thus, we can suppose that due to a natural disaster, such as an earthquake, nodes 1, 2, 7 and 10 of the network shown in Fig. 3 fail. Therefore, the remaining nodes must carry out PROSEARCH among them to reestablish the hierarchy. Fig. 5 shows the network without nodes 1, 2, 7 and 10, and the parameters of each node ($IN_i$ and $OUT_i$) sent in the first phase of the protocol. This phase takes five rounds.

The trustworthiness order for node 3 is: **3**, 5; for node 4 is: 5, **4**, 8; for node 5 is: 3, **5**, 4, 8; for node 6 is: **6**, 9; for node 8 is: 5, 9, 4, **8**; and for node 9 is: 6, **9**, 8. Therefore, in the second phase of the protocol, nodes 3 and 6 act in the sixth round, nodes 5 and 9 act in the seventh round, node 4 acts in the eighth round , and finally, node 8 acts in the ninth round.

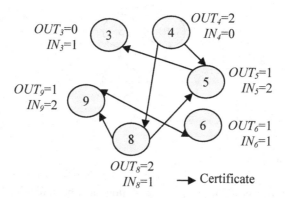

**Fig. 5.** Scenario B: peer-to-peer network after a disaster

Node 3 chooses node 5 like superior CA and $L_5= L_3+1=1$. At the same time, node 6 chooses node 9 like superior CA and $L_9 =L_6+1=1$.

Then, node 5 chooses node 8 like superior CA and $L_8 =L_5+1=2$. At the same time, node 9 chooses node 8 like superior CA and $L_8=2$.

Node 4 can not choose a superior CA because it does not have trusted neighbors; therefore, the protocol must be repeated among nodes 4 and 8. During the repetition of the protocol, nodes 4 and 8 send their information messages in the tenth round, and in the eleventh round, node 8 chooses node 4 like superior CA and $L_4 =L_8+1=3$. Fig. 6 shows the established hierarchy.

Table 3 shows the number of messages among the nodes needed to establish the hierarchy in Scenario A (Fig. 3) and Scenario B (Fig, 5).

**Table 3.** Number of messages to establish the hierarchy

| Type of message | Scenario A | Scenario B |
|---|---|---|
| Request Messages | 21 | 7 |
| Acceptance Messages | 21 | 7 |
| Information Messages | 38 | 12 |
| Association Messages | 30 | 10 |
| Failure Messages | 4 | 2 |
| Root_CA Messages | 14 | 5 |
| Root_CERT Messages | 9 | 5 |
| **TOTAL** | 137 | 48 |

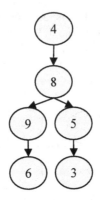

**Fig. 6.** New hierarchy

## 5  Evaluation

The outcomes shown in the figures of this section have been obtained, calculating the average of 50 iterations by each combination of the following parameters:

- Number of CAs: from 10 to 200, ten at a time.
- Relation ratio values: 0,2; 0,4; 0,6.
- Maximum path length allowed: 3 ($L_{MAX}$=3).
- Percentage of failure in the network: 30%.

The relation ratio (*rel*) is the probability that one entity trust another entity in the network, that is to say, the possibility that one entity receives a certificate from any other entity in the network.

The percentage of failure in the network means that 30% of the CAs fail after the protocol, so we reconfigure the hierarchy without these CAs. They were chosen randomly.

Fig. 7 compares the number of rounds needed to carry out PROSEARCH, with all the CAs operating correctly (without failures) and after a disaster, with 30% of the CAs failing (with failures). We can see that the number of rounds needed to reconfigure the hierarchy is lower than the number of rounds needed to establish the hierarchy the first time, thus the run time of our protocol depends on the number of CAs (a less number of CAs implies a less number of rounds). Also, Fig. 7 shows that the number of rounds increases with the relation ratio value, since authorities have bigger neighborhoods, so they must wait for more CAs to act in the second phase.

On the other hand, Fig. 8 shows the number of root CAs in each case. We can see that the number of root CAs without failures and with failures is almost the same for the three relation ratio values considered. Thus, the hierarchy obtained after a disaster will be as functional as the previous one. In addition, the number of root CAs decreases insofar as the relation ratio increases, because it is easier to find a path when the relation ratio is high.

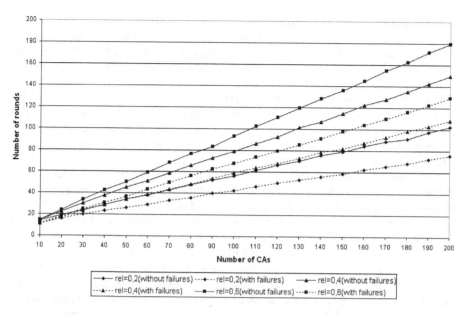

**Fig. 7.** Number of CAs vs. number of rounds

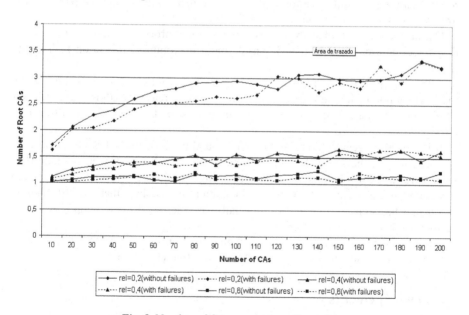

**Fig. 8.** Number of CAs vs. number of root CAs

# 6  Conclusions

Authentication is a strong requirement for critical information systems, and Public Key Infrastructure (PKI) is widely used to provide this service. Although peer-to-peer

PKIs are quite dynamic and certification paths can be built in critical scenarios where part of the infrastructure is temporarily unreachable, discover the certification paths is not an easy task since there can be multiple paths between two entities and all the options do not lead to the target entity. This is not the case of hierarchical PKIs, where there is only one path between two entities.

In this paper, we describe PROSEARCH, a protocol that establishes a virtual hierarchy in a peer-to-peer PKI, based on the trustworthiness of the participant CAs. The level of trustworthiness of each authority is determined in accordance with two parameters: the number of issued certificates ($OUT_i$) and the number of received certificates ($IN_i$).

An advantage of our protocol is that it does not establish new trust relationships among the CAs but it takes the existing relationships to establish the hierarchy. Thus, it is not necessary to issue new certificates or adjust the trust points.

The practical example of section 4 shows that our protocol can be reconfigured easily when some of the nodes of the network fail due to a disaster or other critical situations. Also, thanks to unidirectional trust relationships of the established hierarchy, a verifier can discover easier and faster the paths than in a peer-to-peer model.

Section 5 shows that the number of rounds of necessary to reconfigure the hierarchy after a disaster tends to decrease, since the run time of PROSEARCH depends on the number of CAs and the trust relationships among them. In addition, the number of root CAs after the reconfiguration is almost the same than the number of root CAs before the disaster, so the new hierarchy is also functional.

Our protocol is also adaptable to users with limited processing and storage capacities, since hierarchy is established considering a maximum certification path length ($L_{MAX}$).

Although PROSEARCH not always finds a single root CA, this does not involve that there is not a path among the authorities. For that reason, in those cases, we advise to use alternative methods to find the shortest path among the resulting root CAs.

It is worthy to remark that the hierarchy found by our protocol is not always the best solution, in the sense that the minimum path length is not ever guaranteed or some existing trust relations in the P2P PKI might be lost. However, in our opinion this is not an important drawback since simulation results show that in most cases an acceptable hierarchy is found, and especially considering that the simplicity of the protocol makes it easy-to-implement.

Future wok will be centered on the implementation of our protocol for different devices, and the evaluation of its development in different scenarios.

## Acknowledgements

This work has been supported by the Spanish Research Council under the project ARPA (TIC2003-08184-C02-02). The authors also would like to thank the anonymous reviewers and the audience at the CRITIS workshop for their comments and suggestions.

# References

[1]  ITU-T, "Recommendation X.509: Information Processing Systems - Open Systems Inter-connection - The Directory: Authentication Framework (Technical Corrigendum)", International Telecommunication Union, 2000.

[2]  R. Housley, W. Polk, W. Ford and D. Solo, "RFC3280 - Internet X.509 Public Key Infrastructure Certificate and Certificate Revocation List (CRL) Profile", 2002.

[3]  W. T. Polk and N. E. Hastings, "Bridge Certification Authorities: Connecting B2B Public Key Infrastructures", NIST, 2000.

[4]  R. Perlman, "An Overview of PKI Trust Models", *IEEE Network*, 1999, vol. 13, pp. 38-43.

[5]  Y. Elley, A. Anderson, S. Hanna, S. Mullan, R. Perlman and S. Proctor, "Building Certification Paths: Forward vs. Reverse", *Network and Distributed System Security Symposium (NDSS 2001)*, 2001.

[6]  J. Marchesini and S. Smith, "Virtual Hierarchies - An Architecture for Building and Maintaining Efficient and Resilient Trust Chains", *7th Nordic Workshop on Secure IT Systems (NORDSEC 2002)*, Karlstad (Sweden), 2002.

[7]  H. Pan, J. Li, Y. Zhu and D. Wei, "A Practical Scheme of Merging Multiple Public Key Infrastructure in E-commerce", *Networking and Mobile Computing: 3rd International Conference (ICCNMC 2005)*, Springer-Verlag, Zhangjiajie (China), 2005, pp. 1287-1294.

[8]  J. Hernandez-Serrano, J. Pegueroles and M. Soriano, "GKM over large MANET", *IEEE International Workshop on Self Assembling Wireless Networks (SAWN2005)*, 2005, pp. 484-490.

# Applying Key Infrastructures for Sensor Networks in CIP/CIIP Scenarios

Cristina Alcaraz and Rodrigo Roman

Computer Science Department,
University of Malaga,
29071 - Malaga, Spain
{alcaraz,roman}@lcc.uma.es

**Abstract.** It is commonly agreed that Wireless Sensor Networks (WSN) is one of the technologies that better fulfills features like the ones required by Critical (Information) Infrastructures. However, a sensor network is highly vulnerable against any external or internal attacks, thus network designers must know which are the tools that they can use in order to avoid such problems. In this paper we describe in detail a procedure (the KMS Guidelines), developed under our CRISIS project, that allows network designers to choose a certain Key Management System, or at least to know which protocol need to improve in order to satisfy the network requirements.

**Keywords:** Critical Information Infrastructures, Sensor Networks, Key Management, Key Infrastructures.

## 1 Introduction

According to the European Commission, *Critical Infrastructures* consist of *"those physical and information technology facilities, networks, services and assets which, if disrupted or destroyed, would have a serious impact on the health, safety, security or economic well-being of citizens or the effective functioning of governments in the Member States."* [1]. These infrastructures depend on a spectrum of highly interconnected national (and international) software-based control systems for their smooth, reliable, and continuous operation. This information infrastructure underpins many elements of the aforementioned Critical Infrastructures, and is hence called *Critical Information Infrastructures* (CII).

CII are characterized by unique requirements for communications performance, including timing, redundancy, centers control and protection, and equipment control and diagnostics. One of the technologies that can fulfill these requirements are *Wireless Sensor Networks* (WSN)[2]. However, these networks are highly vulnerable against physical and logical attacks from a malicious adversary. Therefore, it is essential for a network designer to have the right set of tools and protocols for protecting the Wireless Sensor Network itself.

One of these tools are the *Key Management Systems* (KMS), which distributes some security credentials (i.e. keys) along the nodes of the network. However,

J. Lopez (Ed.): CRITIS 2006, LNCS 4347, pp. 166–178, 2006.

due to the great number of existent KMS, it is not clear which KMS is suitable for a certain scenario. The purpose of this paper is to introduce the KMS CRISIS Guidelines, a tool that will help network designers into choosing the right KMS for its WSN in a C(I)IP environment. The rest of this paper is organized as follows. In section 2 we explain in more detail the challenges of protecting a CII and its relationship with WSN. In section 3 we introduce our KMS CRISIS Guidelines, and explain the procedure for choosing a certain KMS. Afterwards, in section 4, we will describe and apply our Guidelines to some actual and possible C(I)IP scenarios. Finally, we conclude the paper in section 5.

## 2    The Importance of WSN for C(I)IP

### 2.1    CIIP Challenges

In a Critical Infrastructure, the interconnected nature of networks means that single, isolated disturbances can cascade through and between networks with potentially disastrous consequences. Therefore, it is indispensable to have a resilient and robust information infrastructure that could deal with any situation, being a physical or computational attack to the system or an abnormal behavior of any component inside the overall system. Such infrastructure must be able to issue alerts and warnings in order to help human users and the information subsystems to react against adverse scenarios. Those alerts could be issued even in the case that a problem is not taking place but the context seems to be slowly changing into a problematic situation. In a worst-case scenario, the information infrastructure must be able to react and protect itself in real time, and to assure the seamless continuation of its services.

As any Information infrastructure, the CII must be thoroughly tested in order to assure that the system and its response mechanisms will work under any kind of context. However, it is usually not feasible to test and obtain results about a CII without endangering the operation of the entire system itself. As a result, it becomes imperative to create models and simulations that show how the system should behave in presence of problems. As an input to these models and any decision-making tools, it is also of vital importance to analyze an infrastructure and quantify the possible problems in order to correctly model the protection system.

In all these processes, it is essential to guarantee the security of information that is considered of critical importance, from a political, economic, financial or social standpoint. Adding Information Security provisions such as authorization, authentication, encryption, and other basic security services is not enough to manage these complex scenarios and applications, due to the complex and dynamic nature of these infrastructures. Finally, since these Information Infrastructures compose a very heterogeneous environment, it is crucial to provide a set of policies and methods to allow an effective and secure interaction of the elements of a CII, both internal and external.

As we have seen, CII are characterized by unique and complex requirements, and are vulnerable to many different types of disturbances. Although strong centralized control is essential to reliable operations, CII require multiple high-data-rate communication links, a powerful central computing facility, and an elaborate operations control center. All of them are especially vulnerable when they are needed most - during serious system stresses or disruptions. Therefore, intelligent distributed control is strongly required to keep parts of the network operational. Such intelligent control, alongside with other features, can be provided by Wireless Sensor Networks.

## 2.2   The Importance of Wireless Sensor Networks

Both the scientific community and the governments around the world have recognized the importance of Wireless Sensor Networks as an integral part of the protection of Critical (Information) Infrastructures. In the 2004 National Plan for Research and Development in Support for CIP [3], the U.S. Department for Homeland Security stated that one of the strategic goals was *"to provide a National Common Operating Picture (COP)"* for Critical Infrastructures, where the core of the systems would be an intelligent, self-monitoring, and self-healing sensor network. As a result, many projects regarding sensor networks and C(I)IP are being funded by the different U.S. agencies. Moreover, the Research Network for a Secure Australia (RNSA) has launched a major R&D initiative called the Cooperative Research Center for Security (CRC-SAFE), which aims to develop research and commercialization opportunities for CIP in Australia. One of the research programs of that initiative, Electronic Systems Security, will examine and develop solutions to security problems that arise in systems that are utilized in the critical infrastructure environment, including Wireless Sensor Networks [4].

A Wireless Sensor Network can be abstracted as the "skin" of a computer system, where hundreds or thousands of inexpensive and intelligent nodes ("cells") are able to sense the physical events of their surroundings, such as temperature, humidity, light intensity, radiation, and others. They can be also connected to any external system, acquiring, processing, and supplying information about its status. Every node is battery-powered, communicates with the other using a wireless channel, and is totally independent. The Sensor Network, as a whole, is connected to one or many central systems ("brains") called Base Stations, which provides an interface for accessing the data collected by the network.

An interesting property of the Sensor Network is that every node has computational capabilities, thus the network can work autonomously if the circumstances requires so. A typical sensor node such as MICAz [5] has a 8Mhz microprocessor with 128Kb of program flash memory and 512Kb of serial flash memory. Regarding their communication capabilities, nowadays most of the existing sensor nodes follows the IEEE 802.15.4 standard for Personal Area Networks, with a maximum data throughput of 250 Kbps.

As a sensing system, the tasks of a Wireless Sensor Network are focused on sensing the events of its surroundings, and providing that information to a set of users, being humans or machines or both. Those tasks include the following: Alerting (a Sensor Network is able to feel whether a problematic situation is either going to happen or actually happening, and alert any user), Monitoring (a Sensor Network is able to continuously monitor its environment, adapting itself to the ever-changing context), Querying (a Sensor Network is also able to provide information "On-Demand"), and Distributed Computing (it is also possible to use the network as a distributed computing platform under extreme circumstances).

Both these tasks and the ability to work under severe conditions render Wireless Sensor Networks as an essential component in the overall scheme of protecting a Critical (Information) Infrastructure. A Sensor Network is capable of offering a redundant and resilient system that can provide an accurate diagnosis of a certain context, feeding systems such as Early Warning Systems. It can also provide the foundation of an intelligent distributed control system, both monitoring and supervising parts of the system even in situations where there is no central management available.

Moreover, due to its computational and wireless capabilities, a Sensor Network can be easily set up in a physical context where it is needed. For example, in case a control system is faced with a serious disruption that renders the operation of its subsystems unusable, a sensor network can be deployed "on the spot" that would provide reliable and robust information about the physical infrastructure or the status of any component.

## 2.3   CRISIS and Key Management

Although Wireless Sensor Networks can be regarded as an integral part of the protection of Critical (Information) Infrastructures, it has many problems and open issues by itself. Due to the extreme constraints of the network infrastructure, a sensor network is highly vulnerable against any external or internal attack, thus the infrastructure and protocols of the network must be prepared to manage these kinds of situations. Protecting the information flow not only requires a set of power-efficient encryption schemes, but also an effective key infrastructure in terms of key storage policies, key distribution procedures and key maintenance protocols. Collecting the information from a static or dynamic set of nodes and routing it through the error-prone, unreliable network is a difficult task as well. Moreover, the network should be able to monitor over any failures or security breaches in any of its members while self-configuring and self-healing itself.

We have recently started a project, named CRISIS (CRitical Information Infrastructures Security based on Internetworking Sensors) [6], that tries to solve some of the previous problems in the context of a Critical Information Infrastructure. This on-going project focuses on the design of security solutions for Critical Information Infrastructures by means of the development of protection, control and evaluation mechanisms, where Wireless Sensor Networks are introduced as a main technological platform for this task.

More concretely, one of the areas of the project pursues the definition and design of *Advanced Authentication Services*, where, at low level, a network designer must choose a Key Management System (KMS) for the Sensor Network. In a

Wireless Sensor Network, Key Management is an essential part of its core behavior, since the wireless nature of the communication flow allows any malicious
adversary to easily get access to the information of the network, eavesdropping
or injecting packets. Therefore, a node must negotiate with its peers (offline
or online) some security credentials in order to set up a secure communication
channel.

The creation of a secure an optimal KMS is one of the most prolific areas in
WSN research, spanning multiple research branches [7]. However, at present, a
network designer has no means to know whether a certain protocol is suitable
for its needs. For example, the requirements for a KMS in a sensor network that
monitors a nuclear power plant are not the same that the requirements of a sensor
network that is deployed after a radiation leak. As a result, we have studied the
existent protocols and developed a manual (the KMS CRISIS Guidelines) that
allows a network designer to choose a certain existent KMS, or at least to know
which protocol needs to improve in order to satisfy the network requirements.

## 3   KMS CRISIS Guidelines

In this section we present the KMS CRISIS Guidelines (henceforth known as
"The Guidelines"). Such Guidelines classifies the KMS according to their properties, rather than their features or the underlying mechanisms employed in their
construction, such as Key Pools or Combinatorial Designs. This classification differs from other papers that survey the area, such as [7], in that is oriented to
help a network designer on choosing or constructing a certain KMS based on the
properties of the network. Due to the extension of the Guidelines, we will only
provide the protocols and main properties for configurations that could relevant
in the protection of Critical (Information) Infrastructures.

### 3.1   Main Properties of a KMS

The main purpose of a Key Management System is to allow the nodes in a
sensor network to securely negotiate a set of pairwise keys, which will be used
in creating secure communications channels via security primitives like RC5
or Skipjack in TinySec [8] or AES in the 802.15.4 standard. However, every
KMS give some priority to certain objectives, optimizing certain properties while
neglecting others. Those properties are the following:

**Memory footprint.** In a context where a sensor node is usually very constrained in terms of memory (a MICAz mote has only 4KB of RAM and 512KB
of Flash memory [5], whereas a TMoteSky mote has 10KB of RAM and 1024KB
of Flash memory [9]), it is essential for certain applications to reduce the memory
footprint as much as possible. Many protocols are designed to reduce the memory space reserved to the security credentials (i.e., keys), primarily by reducing
the number of keys to be used for bootstrapping the entire infrastructure.

**Security.** The purpose of any KMS is to provide the nodes in the network
with some security credentials that the cryptographical primitives need for their

operation. The whole process of distributing the keys must be secure by default. However, in certain scenarios, there are extra security requirements that must be fulfilled. *Confidentiality* is one of those requirements, because in some protocols it is necessary to bootstrap the security credentials.

**Network resilience.** In order to provide the right data, a sensor node must be located near the source of the possible events. However, this also implies that any node is vulnerable against physical capture, revealing its security credentials. In order to avoid the disruption of the network services, some protocols are designed to increase the network resilience, that is, the ability to cope with stolen credentials and rogue nodes.

**Connectivity.** This network property is related to the chance of two sensor nodes sharing the same security credentials. In scenarios where the location of a sensor inside the network is unknown before the deployment, or where the sensor can change its position inside the network, it is essential to have a high connectivity. There are protocols that tries to provide the maximum connectivity while having a decent memory footprint or network resilience.

**Scalability.** It is widely believed that someday there will be sensor network deployments of thousands of nodes, even hundreds of thousands. Besides, it is sometimes necessary to increment the number of nodes inside a network to increase the sensing (or communication) coverage. For those reasons, a key distribution protocol should be able to negotiate the security credentials regardless the number of nodes in the network (*Scalability*), or to include new nodes after the deployment finishes (*Extensibility*).

**Communication Overhead.** In most KMS, the nodes must negotiate with its peers the security credentials that they will share. Due to the size of the data included inside the negotiation packets and the retransmissions that could happen during those negotiations, there are some protocols that are specialized in decreasing the overall communication overhead.

**Energy.** A sensor node relies on batteries for powering itself, thus it must minimize its internal operations (sensing, communication,...) in order to live as much time as possible. Since the negotiation of the security credentials is a time-consuming and energy-consuming task (inferring the security credentials, sending/receiving data to/from other peers,...), it is the purpose of some protocols to minimize the energetic impact of their operations.

**Processing Speed.** Sensor nodes are also constrained in terms of computing power. For example, both MICAz motes and TMoteSky motes feature a 8Mhz microprocessor. Most KMS, but not all, are not very computationally expensive, and the time spent in negotiating the pairwise keys is usually spent in sending and receiving messages through the wireless channel.

## 3.2   The Guidelines

The Guidelines, as is, is a table composed of three columns. The first column specifies the main property of the protocols shown on its right. The second column specifies the name of the protocol in our Guidelines ($AT$-number), followed by the "official" name of the KMS. The third column shows the advantages ($\checkmark$) and disadvantages ($\times$) of every protocol, that is, which properties does and does not fulfill a certain protocol.

Due to space restrictions, the description of every advantage and disadvantage is reduced to the following nomenclature:

- Every property is abbreviated: Memory Footprint (Mem.), Security (Sec.), Network Resilience (Res.), Connectivity (Conn.), Scalability (Sca.), Extensibility (Ext.), Communication Overhead (Comm.), Energy (En.), Speed (Sp.).
- Some protocols have special requirements for being applied: i) The location of the nodes is known prior to the deployment ($LOC$). Also, when the requirements/properties of a certain protocol are affected by the variables used on its design, we use: $DES\{\alpha\}$.

For applying the Guidelines, a network designer must first find out which properties are essential for a KMS in its scenario (we will call them main properties), and which properties are not essential but important (we will call them secondary properties). After that, he must consult the protocols whose first column are equal to one of the main properties, and seek a protocol that has all the properties in the advantages and none in the disadvantages. If no protocol suits his needs, he can still know the weak points of the existents protocols and construct a new one.

The Guidelines itself are shown in Table 1, at the end of the paper. This way, it will be more easy for network designers to consult and apply the Guidelines.

## 4    C(I)IP Scenarios

There have been a large number of C(I)IP scenarios that involve sensor network technology in their operations, such as control of physical infrastructures, control of industrial machinery, monitoring of gas and oil transportation, and homeland security. Even so, these are just a fraction of the possible scenarios where sensor networks could be applied. In this section, we will present both scenarios where sensor networks are being applied or could be applied, and we will make use of our Guidelines in order to suggest a certain KMS to be employed or improved for an specific scenario.

### 4.1    Actual C(I)IP Scenarios

These are some of the actual projects where Sensor Networks have been or are being applied to areas related to Critical (Information) Infrastructure Protection.

**Monitoring of Ageing Infrastructures.** The Smart Infrastructure KIC (Knowledge Integration Community) [10] is a community of researchers at Cambridge and MIT. This community grew out from the "New technologies for condition assessment and monitoring of ageing infrastructure" project, where the research team was invited to develop and deploy a prototype wireless sensor network system to monitor the condition of a stretch of London Underground tunnel, which has some tunnels over 75 years old. In this trial, sensors transmitted the data to the Base Stations located in the columns, and then the data was forwarded to a central database.

**Detecting Equipment Vibration.** Intel is conducting a trial deployment of a wireless sensor network to monitor the health of semiconductor fabrication equipment in one of its plants in Oregon [11]. Specifically, the network senses the vibration signature of water purification equipment, providing data for early warning systems. In this deployment, groups of up to six sensors connect to battery-powered wireless motes form clusters, and a Crossbow Stargate computer, equipped with IEEE 802.11 (Wi-Fi) connectivity, serves as a cluster head. The deployment of wireless sensor networks, which can be installed inexpensively and provide more frequent and more reliable data, could decrease the response time in case of an emergency, reducing both the equipment and the service downtime.

**Management of Mobile Assets.** As on 2004, BP had a fleet of some 12,000 freight railcars transporting a range of products as diverse as polypropylene and natural gas liquids. Their journeys can be relatively short or cross-border, delivering products from its manufacturing plants to customers. Due to the hazardousness of some of these products, it is necessary to know about the status of the cars and its contents. BP, together with Intel [11], ran a trial where each car carried sensors to measure the temperature of the contents, the weight of the load, accelerometers to record impact, and a GPS transponder to give location. Every sensor was connected to a central station, where the data was transmitted using to a geostationary satellite, for onward relay to BP's control center. The trial was a success, and nowadays BP is expanding the trial with new services such as 'pinging' the cars - interrogating them from mobile devices such as laptop computers and cell phones.

**Identifying hazards to safety-critical structures.** The DISCOVERY (Distributed Intelligence, Sensing and Coordination in Variable Environments) project, developed by CSIRO (Commonwealth Scientific and Industrial Research Organisation), Australia's national science agency, aims to create fully autonomous underwater sensor networks to protect critical infrastructure and water resources [12]. Ultimately these networks, that can be deployed either on demand or in advance, will be used to identify hazards to safety-critical structures such as off-shore oil rigs, to respond to contamination of water supplies such as oil spills, to track oil spills to their sources (in a three-dimensional environment) and to establish absorption perimeters. The sensor network should be able to optimally distribute and coordinate sensing, computation, and actuation, providing efficient multi-agent communication and information fusion.

## 4.2   Potential C(I)IP Scenarios

The scenarios described in the previous section are only a subset of what could be accomplished using Wireless Sensor Networks for Critical (Information) Infrastructure Protection. In this section we preview some possible new scenarios yet to be developed.

**Self-Powered Communication and Diagnosis System.** In moments of crisis (e.g. a network failure inside a chemical plant), the control systems that form a Critical Information Infrastructure must react timely and effectively, providing the users with the appropriate information about the source and the extent of the problem. However, these control systems are also vulnerable by itself: their information networks can fail, and they can be unavailable in scenarios involving power loss. In such cases, Sensor networks can behave as a self-powered redundant communication and diagnosis system, routing both information about the computer it monitors and information about its physical environment to any existent control system.

**Testing of Existent Sensor Systems.** Some Critical Information Infrastructures, such as the radiation detection subsystem inside a power plant, must provide accurate data about the physical state of its environment. As a result, it is essential to test the behavior of the system as frequently as possible in order to prevent false alarms or failures in times of crisis. Due to its features, a Wireless Sensor Network can be a valuable asset for this purpose. A sensor network can be easily set up in the same places where the sensors of the CII system are located, automatically creating an information network which allows the system administrators to discover and take measures against any anomalies in the actual sensing system.

### 4.3   Applying the Guidelines to C(I)IP Scenarios

In this section we will apply the Guidelines for every scenario described above. As a result, we will obtain a KMS that can be immediately used to provide security credentials to the sensor nodes in a real environment. Note that, in certain scenarios, there is no KMS that can fulfill all the requirements of that scenario.

**Monitoring of Ageing Infrastructures.** In this scenario, the main property a KMS must fulfill is Connectivity (Sensors are working in a hard to deploy, hostile environment), while the secondary properties are Resilience and Security (Due to the importance of the infrastructure). Applying the Guidelines, the protocol that best suits those needs is *AT-4*, although *AT-25* could be applied, too.

**Detecting Equipment Vibration, Management of Mobile Assets.** In these scenarios, the main properties a KMS must fulfill are Connectivity (Sensors are working in a hostile environment - an industrial machine) and Resilience (Due to the importance of the data's reliability), while the secondary properties are Security (In the case that the deployment area is not totally secure) and Energy. Applying the Guidelines, the protocol that best suits those needs is *AT-1* if the deployment site is totally secure. If not, the best protocol should be *AT-13* or *AT-23*.

**Identifying hazards to safety-critical structures.** This scenario is fairly complex, since all the properties are essential being Connectivity (due to the mobile nature of the nodes) and Resilience (due to the importance of the data) primary ones. There is no protocol that can suit perfectly to this scenario, although *AT-4* could be applied if such scenario must be deployed immediately.

**Self-Powered Communication and Diagnosis System.** In this scenario, the main properties a KMS must fulfill are Resilience (Due to the "public" nature of the node), Connectivity (Sensors are working in a hostile environment) and Scalability (The network itself can grow if required), while the secondary property is Security (In the case that the deployment area is not totally secure). Applying the Guidelines, the protocols that best suits those needs could be *AT-13* and *AT-25*.

**Testing of Existent Sensor Systems.** In this scenario, the main properties a KMS must fulfill are Resilience (Due to the "public" nature of the node and the importance of the data), Connectivity (Sensors are working in a hostile environment), Scalability (Due to the staggered deployment), and Communication (Also due to the staggered deployment). Applying the Guidelines, the protocols that best suits those needs could be *AT-24* if the nodes know their deployment location, or *AT-13* and *AT-25*.

## 5   Conclusion

We have discussed why Wireless Sensor Networks are essential for protecting Critical (Information) Infrastructures, and how such technology is not exempt of security problems. As a step into developing secure WSN for C(I)IP in real scenarios, in this paper we have presented the KMS CRISIS Guidelines, a tool that allows network designers to either choose a certain Key Management System or discover which protocols could use as a foundation for its own protocol.

As a final note, while developing the KMS CRISIS Guidelines, we have discovered that most of the Key Management Protocols i) have no step for allowing the maintenance of the keys, ii) does not allow the introduction of new nodes, and iii) are not designed with a certain scenario in mind. We conclude that security experts should take these three considerations into account. The third one is interesting: Evidently, there is an inherent risk of designing too many KMS, but since WSN are scenario-centric, the resulting networks will be much more secure.

## References

1. Commission of the European Communities. *Communication from the Commission to the Council and the European Parliament: Critical Infrastructure Protection in the Fight Against Terrorism*, COM (2004) 702 final, Brussels, 20 October 2004.
2. I. F. Akyildiz, W. Su, Y. Sankarasubramaniam, E. Cayirci. *Wireless sensor networks: a survey.* Computer Networks: The International Journal of Computer and Telecommunications Networking, Vol.38, No. 4, pp. 393-422, March 2002.

3. *2004 US National Plan for Research and Development in Support for CIP*. April 8, 2005. Retrieved from http://www.dhs.gov/interweb/assetlibrary/ ST_2004_NCIP_RD_PlanFINALApr05.pdf

4. D. Bopping. *CIIP in Australia*. 1st CI2RCO Critical Information Infrastructure Protection conference. Rome, March 2006.

5. Crossbow Technology, Inc. Wireless Measurement Systems. http://www.xbow.com.

6. J. Lopez, J. A. Montenegro, R. Roman. *Service-Oriented Security Architecture for CII based on Sensor Networks*. 2nd International Workshop on Security, Privacy and Trust in Pervasive and Ubiquitous Computing (SecPerU 2006), Lyon (France), June 2006.

7. A. Camtepe, B. Yener. *Key distribution mechanisms for wireless sensor networks: a survey*. Rensselaer Polytechnic Institute, Computer Science Department, Tech. Rep. 05-07, March 2005.

8. C. Karlof, N. Sastry, D. Wagner. *TinySec: a link layer security architecture for wireless sensor networks*. In Proceedings of 2nd International Conference on Embedded Networked Sensor Systems (SensSys'04), November 2004.

9. Moteiv Corporation. http://www.moteiv.com.

10. *Smart Infrastructure*. The Cambridge-MIT Institute. http://www.cambridge-mit.org/smartinfrastructure

11. *Sensor Nets / RFID*. Intel Corporation. http://www.intel.com/research/exploratory/wireless_sensors.htm

12. *Distributed Intelligence, Sensing and Coordination in Variable Environments*. CSIRO. http://www.ict.csiro.au/page.php?cid=97

13. L. Eschenauer, V.D. Gligor. *A key-management scheme for distributed sensor networks*. Proceedings of the 9th ACM conference on Computer and communications security (CCS '02), ACM Press, November 2002, pp 41-47.

14. W. Du, J. Deng, Y. S. Han, P. Varshney. *A Key Predistribution Scheme for Sensor Networks Using Deployment Knowledge*. In IEEE Transactions on Dependable and Secure Computing, Vol. 3, No. 2, pp 62-77, January-March 2006.

15. W. Du, J. Deng, Y.S. Han, P.K. Varshney. *A pairwise key pre-distribution scheme for wireless sensor networks*. Proceedings of the 10th ACM conference on Computer and communications security (CCS '03), ACM Press, October 2003, pp 42-51.

16. R.D. Pietro, L.V. Mancini, A. Mei. *Random key-assignment for secure Wireless Sensor Networks*. Proceedings of the 1st ACM workshop on Security of ad hoc and sensor networks (SASN '03), ACM Press, October 2003, pp 62-71.

17. H. Chan, A. Perrig, D. Song. *Random Key Predistribution Schemes for Sensor Networks*. In 2003 IEEE Symposium on Security and Privacy, pp. 197-213, May 2003.

18. J. Lee, D.R. Stinson. *Deterministic Key Predistribution Schemes for Distributed Networks*. 11th International Workshop on Selected Areas in Cryptography (SAC 2004). Canada, August 2004. Revised Selected Papers published in Lecture Notes in Computer Science 3357 (2005), pp 294-307.

19. D. Liu, P. Ning, R. Li. *Establishing Pairwise Keys in Distributed Sensor Networks*. ACM Transactions on Information and System Security, Vol. 8, No. 1, pp. 41-77, February 2005.

20. R.J. Anderson, H. Chan, A. Perrig. *Key Infection: Smart Trust for Smart Dust*. Proceedings of the 12th IEEE International Conference on Network Protocols (ICNP 2004), October 2004, pp 206-215.

21. D. Liu, P. Ning. *Improving Key Pre-Distribution with Deployment Knowledge in Static Sensor Networks*. ACM Transactions on Sensor Networks (TOSN), Vol. 1, No. 2, pp. 204-239, November 2005.
22. A. Camtepe, B. Yener. *Combinatorial Design of Key Distribution Mechanisms for Wireless Sensor Networks*. Proceedings of the 9th European Symposium on Research Computer Security (ESORICS'04), September 2004, pp 293-308.
23. D.D. Hwang, B. Charles Lai, I. Verbauwhede. *Energy-Memory-Security Tradeoffs in Distributed Sensor Networks*. Proceedings of the 3rd International Conference on Ad-hoc Networks and Wireless (ADHOC-NOW 2004), July 2004.
24. J. Hwang, Y. Kim. *Revisiting Random Key Pre-distribution Schemes for Wireless Sensor Networks*. Proceedings of the 2nd ACM workshop on Security of Ad Hoc and Sensor Networks (SASN '04), ACM Press, October 2004, pp 43-52.

**Table 1.** KMS CRISIS Guidelines - Reduced Version

| | | |
|---|---|---|
| **Memory** | AT-8 - Basic Probabilistic Key Predistribution [13] | ✓: Mem., Sca. |
| | | ×: DES{Comm., Conn., Mem., Res.} |
| | AT-16 - Key Predistribution by using Deployment Knowledge [14] | ✓: Conn., Mem., Res., Sca. |
| | | ×: LOC, DES{Comm., Conn., Res.} |
| | AT-13 - Blom Key Predistribution [15] | ✓: Comm., Conn., Mem., Res., Sca. |
| | | ×: Ext., DES{Mem., Res., Sca.} |
| **Security** | AT-11 - Co-operative Pairwise Key Establishment [16] | ✓: Sec., Res. |
| | | ×: Comm., En., Sp. |
| | AT-05 - Random Pairwise Key [17] | ✓: Sec., Sca. |
| | | ×: Ext., DES{Conn., Mem., Res.} |
| **Network Resilience** | AT-13 - Blom Key Predistribution [15] | ✓: Comm., Conn., Mem., Res., Sca. |
| | | ×: Ext., DES{Mem., Res., Sca.} |
| | AT-14 - Multiple Space Key Predistribution [15] | ✓: Mem., Res., Sca. |
| | | ×: En., DES{Comm., Conn., Mem.} |
| | AT-07 - Q-Composite [17] | ✓: Res. |
| | | ×: En., DES{Comm., Conn., Mem., Res.} |
| | AT-21 - Deterministic Multiple Space Blom DMBS [18] | ✓: Mem., Sca., Res. |
| | | ×: DES{Comm., Conn., Mem.} |
| | AT-25 - Polynomial Based Key Predistribution [19] | ✓: Comm., Conn., Ext., Mem., Res., Sca., Sec. |
| | | ×: Sp., En., DES{Mem., Res., Sca.} |
| | AT-24 - Grid Based Key Predistribution [19] | ✓: Comm., Conn., Mem., Res., Sca. |
| | | ×: LOC, En., Ext., Sp., DES{Mem., Sca.} |
| | AT-01 - Key Infection [20] | ✓: Conn., Mem., Res., Sca., DES{En., Sp.} |
| | | ×: Ext., Sec., DES{Comm.} |
| **Connectivity** | AT-16 - Key Predistribution by using Deployment Knowledge [14] | ✓: Conn., Mem., Res., Sca. |
| | | ×: LOC, DES{Comm., Conn., Res.} |
| | AT-23 - Closest Pairwise Key Predistribution, Extended [21] | ✓: Comm., Conn., Mem., Res., Sec. |
| | | ×: LOC, Ext., Sca. |
| | AT-24 - Grid Based Key Predistribution [19] | ✓: Comm., Conn., Mem., Res., Sca. |
| | | ×: LOC, En., Ext., Sp., DES{Mem., Sca.} |
| | AT-03 - Symmetric Design [22] | ✓: Comm., Conn., Mem., Sp. |
| | | ×: Ext., Res. |
| | AT-04 - Hybrid Designs - Generalized Quadrangle [22] | ✓: Conn., Mem., Sca., Sp. |
| | | ×: DES{Conn., Ext., Sca.} |
| **Scalab.** | AT-18 - Multiple ID-Based one-way Function [18] | ✓: Conn., Mem., Sca., Sp. |
| | | ×: Comm., Ext., Res., DES{Conn.} |
| | AT-04 - Hybrid Designs - Generalized Quadrangle [22] | ✓: Conn., Mem., Sca., Sp. |
| | | ×: DES{Conn., Ext., Sca.} |
| **Comm.** | AT-23 - Closest Pairwise Key Predistribution, Extended [21] | ✓: Comm., Conn., Mem., Res., Sec. |
| | | ×: LOC, Ext., Sca. |
| | AT-10 - Cluster Key Grouping [23] | ✓: Comm., Mem., Sca. |
| | | ×: Sp., DES{Comm., Conn., Mem., Res.} |
| **Energy** | AT-01 - Key Infection (for small networks) [20] | ✓: Conn., Mem., Res., Sca., DES{En., Sp.} |
| | | ×: Ext., Sec., DES{Comm.} |
| | AT-17 - Transmission Range Adjustment (for small networks) [24] | ✓: Conn., Mem. DES{En.} |
| | | ×: Comm., Sec., Sp., DES{Conn., En., Res.} |

# Trust Establishment in Ad Hoc and Sensor Networks

Efthimia Aivaloglou, Stefanos Gritzalis, and Charalabos Skianis

Information and Communication Systems Security Laboratory,
Department of Information and Communication Systems Engineering,
University of the Aegean, Samos, Greece
{eaiv,sgritz,cskianis}@aegean.gr

**Abstract.** Ad hoc and sensor networks highly depend on the distributed cooperation among network nodes. Trust establishment frameworks provide the means for representing, evaluating, maintaining and distributing trust within the network, and serve as the basis for higher level security services. This paper provides a state-of-the-art review of trust establishment frameworks for ad hoc and sensor networks. Certain types of frameworks are identified, such as behavior-based and certificate-based, according to their scope, purpose and admissible types of evidence. Moreover, hierarchical and distributed frameworks are discussed, based on the type of ad hoc and sensor networks they are designed for. The review is complemented by a comparative study built both on criteria specific to each category and on common criteria, grouped into three distinct classes: supported trust characteristics, complexity and requirements, and deployment complexity and flexibility.

**Keywords:** Trust establishment, trust evaluation, ad hoc networks, sensor networks.

## 1  Introduction

Mobile ad hoc networks are temporary wireless networks, formed dynamically by a set of mobile nodes without relying on any central infrastructure. Ad hoc networks are characterised by randomly changing topologies, distributed control and cooperative behaviour. Sensor networks, as a special case of ad hoc networks, are composed of inexpensive, small and resource constrained sensor nodes, densely spread over sensing fields. The distributed and dynamic nature of these types of networks are highly desirable properties when considering the design of security solutions for Critical Information Infrastructures (CIIs). CIIs, offering information and communication services which are significantly affecting quality of life, safety, and economic activities, may thus include ad hoc and sensor network technologies not only for the provision of context-rich services, but also for their protection in crisis situations.

The design of secure ad hoc and sensor networks is an active research area. Securing ad hoc and sensor networks generally entails ensuring the confidentiality

J. Lopez (Ed.): CRITIS 2006, LNCS 4347, pp. 179–194, 2006.
© Springer-Verlag Berlin Heidelberg 2006

and integrity of the data communicated, providing the means for node authentication and access control, along with lower level security issues like secure routing and node grouping. However, several works (e.g., [1,2,3,4]) argue that the conventional view of security does not suffice provided the unique characteristics of ad hoc networks, that are susceptible to a variety of node misbehaviours. From compromised nodes acting as internal attackers to legitimate nodes that act selfishly or maliciously, internal misbehaving nodes are a vulnerability that can not be tackled using authentication and cryptography alone. This vulnerability, along with the cooperative nature of ad hoc and sensor networks, rise the necessity for assessing the trust relationships among the network nodes. The trust relationships established between network nodes could be used for the provision of higher level security solutions, such as trusted key exchange or secure routing. However, the trust evaluation requirements and challenges posed by ad hoc networks are substantially different from the case of traditional wired networks. The existence of trusted third parties used as intermediaries for establishing trust relationships cannot be taken for granted, trust relationships change frequently due to the dynamic topology, while trust evaluation may be based on uncertain and incomplete evidence due to connectivity problems. To tackle the aforementioned new challenges, trust establishment frameworks have been proposed for representing, evaluating, maintaining and distributing trust among ad hoc network nodes.

The rest of the paper is organised as follows: Section 2 discusses the notion of trust in ad hoc and sensor networks and the challenges and requirements related to trust establishment. Section 3 presents a selection of the trust establishment frameworks, separated into two categories according to their scope and purpose, and compared according to criteria specific to each category. Section 4 contains the comparative evaluation on issues that are common for all frameworks presented, and discusses issues related to the applicability on sensor networks. Finally, Section 5 concludes the paper and suggests future directions.

## 2    The Notion of Trust in Ad Hoc Networks

The notion of trust, as used in different research areas like trusted computing, trusted platforms, trusted code and trust management, has received various interpretations [5]. Throughout this work, we study the in-network trust relationships that can exist between network entities. We use the notion of trust as "The quantified belief by a trustor with respect to the competence, honesty, security and dependability of a trustee within a specified context" [6]. A trust relationship is established by two parties, the trustor and the trustee, also referred to in this work as the trust issuer and the target. The *trust establishment* process includes the specification of valid types of evidence, and its generation, distribution, collection and evaluation [7].

*Trust evidence*, which form the basis for establishing trust relations, may be uncertain, incomplete, stable and long-term [8]. *Trust evaluation* is performed by applying context-specific rules, metrics and policies on the trust evidence. The result of the process is the *trust relation* between the trustor and the trustee, usually represented as a certificate or as a numeric value, either discrete or in a continuous range. Trust relations can be *revoked* on the basis of newly obtained evidence. Trust is *transitive* if it can be extended beyond the two parties between whom it was established, allowing for the building-up of trust paths between entities that have not directly participated in a process of trust evaluation. In general, the problem of formulating evaluation rules and policies, representing trust evidence, and evaluating and managing trust relationships is referred to as the *trust management* problem [9].

Provided that ad hoc networks highly depend on the distributed cooperation among network nodes, while being susceptible at the same time to node misbehaviour, the formation of trust relationships within the network could serve as the basis for higher level security solutions. However, the inherent properties of ad hoc and sensor networks both at node and network level pose challenges unique for the trust management area. Ad hoc, and especially sensor nodes, have constrained energy, memory, computation and communication capabilities. The wireless nature of communications, the dynamically changing topology and membership, and the lack of fixed infrastructure are also parameters that affect the design of trust evaluation frameworks for ad hoc and sensor networks. The lack of centralised monitoring and management points preclude the use of trusted intermediaries, such as trusted third parties or certification authorities (CAs) for trust establishment. Each node needs to manage trust relationships with other nodes individually. Due to the vulnerability of wireless links and the frequent topology changes, connectivity can not be assured, and thus stable hierarchies of trust relations can not be supported. Moreover, because of the varying connectivity and the dynamic topology, trust establishment needs to support evidence that may be uncertain and incomplete, since it can only be sporadically collected and exchanged for each node under evaluation [7,8].

The susceptibility to node misbehaviour can affect not only network operations, but also the trust evaluation framework itself. Especially for frameworks that require cooperative trust evaluation, it is crucial that the nodes are willing to cooperate by making recommendations or evidence that they may hold for the target node available. However, this is not the case in ad hoc networks, since nodes may behave selfishly to preserve resources. Malicious nodes may also perform bad mouthing attacks against legitimate nodes to spread bad reputation, either by directly spreading false evidence or by pretending to be victims of mad mouthing themselves to make a legitimate node look malicious [10].

An additional requirement that mainly applies to sensor networks, is that pre-established and stable trust relationships must be supported. Some sensor nodes may be clustered by deployment so that trust relationships within the cluster may be assumed long-term and stable. For body sensor networks, for example, it is unlikely that a node may misbehave or be compromised. Within such predefined clusters, trust relationships do not need to be continuously evaluated.

As a result, trust establishment protocols for ad hoc and sensor networks should:

- Be decentralised, not based on on-line trusted parties. Instead, they should support distributed, cooperative evaluation, based on uncertain evidence.
- Support trust revocation in a controlled manner.
- Scale to large deployments and be flexible to membership changes.
- Entail acceptable resource consumption, especially for sensor networks.

# 3    Trust Establishment Frameworks for Ad Hoc Networks

The trust establishment frameworks proposed for ad hoc and sensor networks can be classified into two categories according to their scope, purpose and type of evidence that trust evaluation is based on.

Certificate-based frameworks aim to define mechanisms for pre-deployment knowledge on the trust relationships within the network, usually represented by certificates, to be spread, maintained and managed either independantly or cooperatively by the nodes. Trust decisions are mainly based on the provision of a valid certificate, that proves that the target node is considered trusted either by a certification authority or by other nodes that the issuer trusts. It is generally outside the scope of certificate-based frameworks to evaluate the behaviour of nodes and base trust decisions on that evaluation.

In behavior-based frameworks, each node performs trust evaluation based on continuous monitoring of the behavior of its neighbors, in order to evaluate how cooperative they are. Although a mechanism that determines the identities of the nodes is usually assumed to exist, it is generally outside the scope of behavior-based trust establishment models to securely authenticate other nodes and to determine whether they are legitimate members of the network. In that sense, behavior-based models are more reactive than certificate-based models. As an example, if a node makes unauthorised use of the network and behaves selfishly or maliciously, it will not manage to gain or retain a trust level that will allow it to cooperate with other nodes, and it will be thus isolated.

Alternatively, the frameworks are characterised as hierarchical or distributed, according to the type of ad hoc or sensor networks they were designed for. Hierarchical frameworks assume the existence of a hierarchy among the nodes, based on their capabilities or level of trust. These frameworks may specify, for example, that certification authorities or trusted third parties provide on-line or off-line evidence. Distributed frameworks assume that there is no fixed infrastructure, and the responsibility of acquiring, maintaining and spreading trust evidence is equally spread among the network nodes. This distinction mainly applies for certificate-based frameworks, since the behavior-based are all designed for distributed networks.

## 3.1    Certificate-Based Trust Establishment

The most widely used approach for certificate-based trust establishment is the traditional, hierarchical, public key infrastructure model formed as an organisation of certification authorities. The use of on-line certification authorities for ad hoc networks, however, is problematic for connectivity and service availability reasons. Three generic approaches for certificate-based trust establishment have been proposed, two of which are hierarchical and one is distributed. In the first hierarchical approach, trust is represented by certificates signed by offline trusted third parties, whose public keys the trustors need to possess to verify the signatures. The second is a fully distributed self-organised public key management scheme, where trust is evaluated using certificate chains. The third one utilises secret sharing mechanisms to distribute trust to an aggregation of nodes that can collaboratively provide certification authority services. This is considered to be a hierarchical approach, since trust is distributed among a subset of network nodes, that are designated to represent a certification authority.

**Hierarchical Trust Frameworks.** A hierarchical progressive trust negotiation scheme for ad hoc networks is introduced by Verma et al. [11]. Off-line trusted third parties are set responsible both for issuing the certificates required for each node, including a network address certificate and at least one identity certificate, and for issuing certificate revocation lists. The model includes the notion of certificate release policies that are used to enforce a negotiating strategy for each node, in order for the disclosure of information to be controlled during trust negotiation. Each node in the network stores the certificates of the third parties and the certificate revocation lists they have issued, along with the local certificates to be used in trust negotiation. Trust negotiation is carried out by incrementally exchanging certificates.

In [12], Davis proposes a scheme that similarly uses certificates based on a hierarchical trust model to manage trust, and also enables explicit revocation of certificates without input from trusted third parties. The only task in the scheme that is not performed locally at each node is the issuing of certificates. Any node $j$ is considered trusted by any node $i$ once it presents a certificate that has not expired, has not been revoked, and $i$ can verify using the public key of a third party. Nodes have to maintain locally their private keys and the public keys of the third parties.

To handle certificate revocation without input from third parties, nodes maintain certificate status tables and profile tables that contain information about the behaviour profile of each node in a network, which is used to determine whether or not a given certificate should be revoked. The profile tables kept by all nodes in the network should be consistent. In case inconsistencies are found by any node, accusations are broadcasted for the nodes that sent the inconsistent data. The two tables of all nodes are updated when an accusation is broadcasted, thus the accused node's certificate is revoked and network access is denied. In order to defend against bad mouthing attacks, the authors propose the final decision on certificate revocation to be based on a sum of weighted accusations from independent nodes.

**Distributed Trust Frameworks.** In contrast to the hierarchical frameworks, where certificates are issued by trusted third parties, distributed frameworks provide mechanisms for trust evaluation between network nodes in a cooperative, self-organised manner. The Pretty Good Privacy model (PGP) [13] was the first to enable users to act as independent certification authorities, expressing their trust on other users (the confidence on their identity) by validating their public keys. The public key certificates of this so-called "web of trust" approach are assigned with trust levels and confidence levels. However, although certificates are issued by the users, publicly accessible certificate directories are required for their distribution, which makes the model inapplicable for ad hoc networks.

A framework that uses the "web of trust" approach of the PGP model, without requiring certificate directories for the distribution of certificates, is proposed by Hubaux et al. [14]. The relationships between users are modeled as a directed graph, called trust graph, whose edges represent public key certificates. Each user maintains a subset of the trust graph as a local repository of certificates issued by himself or other users in the system. A subgraph selection algorithm is proposed, which is called Shortcut Hunter Algorithm. When a user $i$ wants to obtain the public key of user $j$, they merge their subsets of trust graph stored in their repositories and $i$ tries to find a trust route in the form of a certificate chain from $i$ to $j$ in the merged repository.

To deal with dishonest users issuing false certificates, an authentication metric is introduced as a function that takes two users $i$ and $j$ and a trust graph as inputs and returns a value that represents the assurance with which $i$ can obtain the authentic public key of $j$ using the trust graph. In the general case, however, it is assumed that the requester nodes trust the nodes in the generated certificate chains. Moreover, it is considered that this framework is practically inapplicable for ad hoc networks because it requires extensive public-key operations for constructing certificate chains [15,3].

The distributed trust establishment framework proposed by Eschenauer et al. [8] takes a broader view on the inputs required for node trust decisions by accepting as trust evidence not only certificates and public keys, but also information like identities, locations, or independent security assessments. The type of information required depends on the policy and the evaluation metric each node uses to establish trust. Trust metrics are used to assign confidence values to available pieces of evidence that may be uncertain or incomplete, while policy decisions are defined as a local procedures that, based on the evidence and the confidence assigned to it, output a trust decision.

The framework is fully distributed. Any node can generate trust evidence about any other node and make it available to others through the network, as long as it signs it with its private key and specifies its lifetime. The evidence is then replicated within the network to ensure availability. Evidence revocation is supported through revocation certificates and by the generation and distribution of contradictory evidence. To protect against bad mouthing attacks, when evidence revocation occurs, it is proposed that the policy decisions require redundant pieces of evidence from independent sources to proceed to the evaluation.

**Distributed Certification Authority Frameworks.** The use of secret sharing to distribute the CA functionality among a set of nodes in ad hoc networks was first proposed by Zhou and Haas [16]. Their Distributed Public Key Model takes advantage of redundancies in the network topology to achieve availability of the CA service, that is provided by an aggregation of nodes that trust is distributed to. The model uses threshold cryptography to distribute the private key of the CA over a number of network nodes $n$, that share the ability to perform cryptographic operations. The scheme allows for any $t+1$ out of $n$ nodes to combine their partial keys to collaboratively generate the secret key of the service and sign certificates, whereas this would be unfeasible for any $t$ nodes.

For an adversary to acquire the secret key, at least $t+1$ of the designated nodes must be compromised. In order to tolerate mobile adversaries, the authors make their threshold cryptography scheme proactive by using share refreshing. This enables the designated nodes to derive new partial keys from the old ones in collaboration, without having service secret key disclosed to any of them.

The Mobile Certificate Authority framework, presented by Yi and Kravets [17], similarly uses threshold cryptography to distribute trust. Provided that heterogeneity is expected to exist among ad hoc network nodes, the nodes that are assigned with CA functionality, called MOCAs, are selected according to criteria like computational power, physical security or risk of compromise. The framework includes a communication protocol that client nodes are equipped with in order to correspond with MOCAs for certification services, by contacting at least $t+1$ MOCAs and receiving at least $t+1$ replies.

The framework deals with trust revocation through certificate revocation lists, stored at each node, at the MOCAs, or at a set of specially designated nodes. For a certificate to be revoked, each MOCA signs a revocation certificate with its partial key and broadcasts it. When revocation certificates are gathered from least $t+1$ MOCAs, the certificate revocation list is updated. Bad mouthing attacks could thus only be successful if $t+1$ MOCAs are compromised.

**Summary and Remarks.** The PGP-like distributed trust frameworks are considered to offer more flexibility than the hierarchical frameworks, but may not be suitable for applications where high degrees of accountability and security are required [12]. The main reasons are that they are less structured and more prone to attacks by malicious agents, since it does not have any central management point like a CA, enforcing strict policies on trust assessment.

The Distributed Certification Authority Frameworks are considered are quite robust, but are the ones that impose the greater deployment complexity and have the higher communication requirements per evaluation request. Moreover, it is considered that threshold cryptography is too computationally expensive to be used in ad hoc networks. Finally, these frameworks require cooperation of ad hoc network nodes that may behave selfishly to preserve resources [14,12]. For these reasons, the applicability of secret sharing schemes in ad hoc networks is considered limited.

### 3.2   Behaviour-Based Trust Establishment

The behaviour-based trust models view trust as the level of positive cooperation between neighboring nodes in a network. Trust is evaluated both independently

**Table 1.** Characteristics of Certificate-Based Trust Frameworks. For each framework, the *type of evidence* that is required for trust evaluation of node $j$ by node $i$ is caterised as: (C/PK)-Certificate/Public Key, (RI)-Trust Revocation Information like Certificate Revocation Lists (CRLs) or similar structures, (CD)-Context-Dependent information like location, identity, etc., (CF)-Confidence Factor on Evidence/Recommendations, (TD)-Time-Dependency of Evidence or Recommendations. The *evidence provision* column presents the input required by the evaluation mechanism performed by $i$ from each of the parties involved in the evaluation. The *pre-configuration* column includes the information each node $x$ in the network must posses before entering the network. The representations used are: $(K_x)$-Private key of node $x$. $(C_x^y)$-Certificate issued for $x$ by $y$. $A$ represents the certification authority. The set $N$ represents all nodes in the network.

| Trust Framework | C/PK | RI | CD | CF | TD | Parties Involved | Evidence Provision | Pre-Configuration |
|---|---|---|---|---|---|---|---|---|
| Hierarchical Trust Frameworks | | | | | | | | |
| [11] | + | + | | | | $i,j,n$ CAs | $i{:}C_A^A \& n$ CRLs, $j{:}C_j^A$ | $C_x^A, K_x, nC_A^A$ s |
| [12] | + | + | | | | $i,j,n$ offline CAs | $i{:}C_A^A \& \mathrm{RI}, j{:}C_j^A$ | $C_x^A, K_x, nC_A^A$ s |
| Distributed Trust Frameworks | | | | | | | | |
| [14] | + | | | | | $i,j$ | $i{:}REP_i, j{:}REP_j$ | $K_x, REP_x{:}nC_{y\in N}^{z\in N}$ s |
| [8] | + | + | + | + | + | $i,j$, any other | $j$, any other | Keys, Policy, Metrics |
| Distributed Certification Authority Frameworks | | | | | | | | |
| [16] | + | | | | | $i,j,t+1$ partial CAs | $i{:}C_A^A$, CAs$:C_j^A$ | $x{:}K_x$, CAs$:K^{partial}_{t\in CAs}$ |
| [17] | + | + | | | | $i,j,t+1$ partial CAs | $i{:}C_A^A \& \mathrm{RI}$, CAs$:C_j^A$ | $x{:}K_x$, CAs$:K^{partial}_{t\in CAs}$ |

by each node based on observations and statistical data that is being continuously accumulated by monitoring the network traffic, and cooperatively through sharing recommendations and spreading reputation. The basic aim of these behaviour-based models is to isolate the nodes that either act maliciously because they have been compromised, or selfishly in order for example to preserve resources, by assigning and recommending low levels of trust.

The result of the independent evaluation is called *direct trust*, since it is based on the direct experience the trustor node may have on the trustee node. There have been several works on monitoring the behaviour of neighboring nodes in ad hoc networks, such as intrusion detection systems (a survey can be found in [18]), from which many aspects are borrowed by the behaviour-based frameworks. The evidence collection mechanisms are usually placed below the application layer, in order to evaluate routing behaviours and information integrity. In the context of sensor networks, even the raw data communicated could be evaluated for consistency among neighboring nodes [1]. What should be noted however is that monitoring the network traffic is very resource consuming, in terms of computation, memory and energy. For example, the radio on each node needs to be continuously enabled, while the trust values of all neighboring nodes need to be stored and continuously updated as interactions occur.

*Indirect trust* is derived using recommendations from other nodes, which usually are their trust values for the target node. Selection criteria may be applied for the neighboring nodes that will provide the recommendations [2]. The indirect trust derivation process may include weighting the recommendations of other nodes based on how trusted they are [7,1,2], or providing confidence values along with the recommendations [7]. The result of the recommendations exchange for computing indirect trust is that node reputation is spread through the network, enabling the formation of a connected trust graph. The most important factor that could hinder this process is node selfishness and unwillingness to spread reputation information. Including node cooperation on reputation spreading for the calculation of direct trust is one of the countermeasures.

The functions that are specified in most behaviour-based trust frameworks in order to evaluate the trust value of the trustor network node $i$ to the trustee network node $j$ are:

- A function $DT(i, j)$ for calculating the direct trust value, based on previous interactions and network traffic monitoring metrics. This function is considered implementation dependent and, as such, it is not explicitly defined in the trust evaluation frameworks that are studied.
- A function $IDT(i, j)$ for calculating the indirect trust value based on recommendations from neighboring nodes.
- A function $T(i, j)$ for calculating the final trust decision through balancing the relationship between direct and indirect trust. The result of this calculation is compared against a trust threshold to reach the final decision on node cooperation. Frameworks like [4] also include context and action specific metrics for computing $T$.

The factors being used by the trust frameworks in this section regarding the computation of the direct and indirect trust and the final decision are enlisted in Table 2. The symbols representing the factors in the table are also being used for the representation of the trust evaluation functions. For uniformity reasons, the functions presented in the following paragraphs use a set of symbols that are different from those used on the original forms.

**Behaviour-Based Frameworks.**    Yan et al. [4] proposed one of the first behaviour-based trust evaluation frameworks for ad hoc networks. It defines a trust evaluation matrix for each network node to store the knowledge derived through both network traffic monitoring and recommendations. While the framework does not include functions for direct trust computation or indirect trust combination, it proposes a linear function that computes the trust value for an action $a$ based on the evaluation parameters in the trust matrix and the preferences of the trustor node. The preferences are expressed as factor rates $r_x(i, j, a), x \in \{NTM, R, CAd, CAo\}$, each used for weighting a factor as expressed in Table 2. Factors $CAd$ and $CAo$ represent the importance of the communication data and other parameters like energy left, frequency of routing request, etc. Trust of node $i$ to node $j$ for an action $a$ is evaluated as:

$$T_a(i, j) = [r_{NTM}(i, j, a) * DT(i, j) + r_{CAd}(i, j, a) * V_{CAd}(i, j)$$
$$+ r_R(i, j, a) * IDT(i, j) + r_{CAo}(i, j, a) * V_{CAo}(i, j)] * V_{BL}(i, j) \qquad (1)$$

Functions $V_x(i, j), x \in \{CAd, CAo, BL\}$ are the functions that evaluate the corresponding factors. Function $V_{BL}(i, j)$ returns a value in $(1, 0)$ of the intrusion detection black list, thus enforcing zero trust level for the nodes included in it.

**Table 2.** Evaluation Parameters of Behaviour-Based Trust Frameworks. Parameters are: (NTM)-Network Traffic Monitoring, (WCE)-Weighted Combination On Event Significance, (WFE)-Freshness as as Weight Factor for the Events, (BL)-Black Lists, (R)-Recommendations From Neighboring Nodes, (RCF)-Confidence Factor on Recommendations, (WCR)-Weighted Combination of Recommendations, (WCDI)-Weighted Combination of DT - IDT, and (CA)-Context and Action Specific Metrics like value of data, energy left, QoS, etc.

| | Direct Trust Evaluation | | | | Indirect Trust Evaluation | | | Comb. & Final Decision | |
|---|---|---|---|---|---|---|---|---|---|
| Trust Framework | NTM | WCE | WFE | BL | R | RCF | WCR | WCDI | CA |
| [4] | + | | | + | + | | | + | + |
| [3] | + | + | | | | | | | |
| [7] | + | | | | + | + | + | | |
| [1] | + | | + | | + | | + | | |
| [2] | + | | | | + | | + | + | |

A trust model for finding trustworthy routes in ad hoc networks that is entirely based on direct trust evaluation is proposed by Pirzada and McDonald [3]. In their model, they make use of independent trust agents that reside on network nodes, each one gathering network traffic information in passive mode by applying appropriate taps at different protocol layers. The information gathered from these events is classified into trust categories, so that the *situational trust* $TS(i, j, x)$ for node $j$ can be computed using the information of trust category $x$. Moreover, weights $W_i(x)$ are assigned according to the utility and importance of each trust category to $i$. The general trust is thus computed as the trust that the trustor node $i$ assigns to the trustee node $j$ based upon all previous transactions in all situations, according to their significance:

$$T(i, j) = DT(i, j) = \sum_{x=1}^{n} [W_i(x) * TS(i, j, x)] \qquad (2)$$

A different view on trust evaluation is proposed by Theodorakopoulos and Baras [7], who mainly focus on the evaluation of indirect trust as the combination of opinions from neighboring nodes, assuming that some mechanism exists for these nodes to assign their opinions based on local observations. The process of indirect trust evaluation is formulated as a shortest path problem on a weighted directed graph, where graph nodes represent network nodes and edges represent trust relations. The edges are weighted with the trust value the issuer node has on the target node and the confidence value it assigns on its opinion, depending on the number of the previous interactions and positive direct evaluations. The theory of semirings is being used for formalising two versions of the trust inference problem: finding the trust-confidence value that node $i$ should assign to node $j$, based on the trust-confidence values of the intermediate nodes, and finding a sequence of nodes that has the highest aggregate trust value among all trust paths from $i$ to $j$. The authors define path and distance seminarings for computing the trust distance along trust paths from the issuer to the target, and a computation algorithm that is an an extension to Dijkstra's algorithm.

Ganeriwal and Srivastava [1] propose a different framework for the evaluation of indirect trust, that is designed for wireless sensor networks. The Reputation-based Framework for Sensor Networks (RFSN) includes a watchdog mechanism for monitoring the behaviour of neighboring nodes in terms of data forwarding and raw sensing data consistency. Each sensor node maintains reputation for other nodes in the form of a probabilistic distribution, and trust is obtained by taking its statistical expectation. Reputation $R_{i,j}$ is built based on the results of the watchdog mechanism (direct reputation) in combination with second hand information for deriving the indirect reputation $IDR_{i,j}$. The following equation is defined for computing the indirect reputation by weighting the second-hand information from the neighboring nodes of $i$, denoted as $N_i$:

$$IDR_{i,j} = IDR_{i,j} + \{g(R_{i,k}) * R_{k,j}\} \forall k \in N_i \tag{3}$$

Within the framework of RFSN, the authors propose an example system based on a Bayesian formulation for representing reputation and trust evolution. What is of special interest is the incorporation of exponential averaging when combining reputation information in order to place more weight on recently obtained information. Moreover, they propose propagation of good reputation information only to protect against bad mouthing attacks. In order to discourage adversaries from changing identities or creating virtual nodes, the initial reputation of each node is a null value and has to be gradually built.

Huang et al. [19] developed a similar trust evaluation model, one extension of which is the requirement for an authentication mechanism to ensure that all identities are trustworthy. Except from the Bayesian formulation, the authors also propose the Dempster-Shafer Theory of Evidence for combining evaluations.

A Trust-Domain based security architecture for mobile ad-hoc networks is proposed by Virendra et al. [2]. It includes a behaviour-based trust evaluation framework that is used both as the basis for key establishment decisions and for secure node grouping that can enable distributed control in the network. Trust evaluation is based both on direct and indirect knowledge. For computing direct trust, network monitoring parameters related to traffic volumes and information integrity are listed and a traffic statistics function is presented but not precisely defined. Four schemes are proposed for combining indirect trust information, the most sophisticated of which is is the double weighted approach:

$$IDT(i,j) = \frac{\sum_{k \in O} T(k,j) / \sum_{m \in O} T(m,j) * T(i,k)}{\sum_{k \in O} T(i,k)} \tag{4}$$

The set $O$ appearing in the equation is the set of nodes in the range of both $i$ and $j$, that $i$ trusts above a certain threshold. Function $T(i,j)$ for calculating the final trust decision balances the relationship between direct and indirect trust through utilising weighting factors.

**Summary and Remarks.** It can be observed from the frameworks presented above that, several formalizations of different complexity have been proposed, from weighted average to the use of probabilistic distributions and semirings, for the most interesting function in trust evaluation, the one for calculating the indirect trust value based on recommendations. The exchange of recommendations enables the view of the network as a connected trust graph, where trust is gradually built for each node through good reputation, but also gradually revoked as a result of malicious behaviour. In the presence of intrusion detection mechanisms issuing black lists, only the framework proposed by Yan et al. [4] enables immediate trust revocation. It is also noted that none of the frameworks supports pre-established and stable trust relationships, since they do not include any bias with respect to the identity of the node under evaluation.

## 4   Comparative Evaluation

The comparison of the trust establishment frameworks that were presented in the previous sections is based on the following three criteria: The characteristics of trust that each framework supports, the complexity and resource requirements it would impose, and its deployment complexity and flexibility. The applicability of each framework in sensor networks is separately discussed. Emphasis here is given on common issues for behavior-based and certificate-based frameworks, since those that are specific for each category are already discussed at the corresponding sections. Table 3 presents the evaluation of each framework for the following categories of criteria:

**Supported Trust Characteristics** include support for uncertain evidence, transitivity of trust and trust revocation. The use of uncertain evidence is characterised as controlled for frameworks that support assignment of confidence values to evidence supplied for trust evaluation, including recommendations from other nodes. Transitivity of trust, if supported, is considered controlled if trust values from third parties are weighted according to the trust relationship the requester has with the third party, before being used for trust evaluation. For frameworks that support trust revocation, it is considered controlled if either trust is revoked only by trusted third parties or some mechanism exists to protect from bad mouthing attacks. Moreover, trust revocation is characterised gradual if trust is not revoked explicitly, but as the result of bad reputation spread gradually due to node misbehaviour.

**Complexity and Requirements** in memory, computational power and communications. Due to the lack of homogeneity among the frameworks in the data structures used as evidence, the algorithms and functions used as primitives for trust evaluation, and the communication patterns during the trust establishment process, the evaluation on these criteria is somewhat subjective. It is considered that a model has high memory requirements if each node needs to store information about every other node in the network, or maintain detailed information about previous interactions and events. High computational power would be required to perform frequent public key operations, or for continuously monitoring surrounding nodes and re-evaluating trust relationships based on every event monitored. Communication requirements increase the more messages need to be exchanged between the interested nodes or third parties for a trust relationship to be established or revoked, and the more broadcasts that are required, either for trust revocation or for initialisation when a new node enters the network.

**Table 3.** Comparative Analysis of Trust Establishment Frameworks for Ad Hoc Networks The evaluation criteria are: (UC)-Uncertainty of Evidence, (TR)-Trust Transitivity, (RC)-Trust Revocation, (MEM)-Memory Requirements, (CMP)-Computational Complexity, (CMN)-Communication Requirements, (PC)-Pre-Configuration Required, (SE)-Scalability and Extensibility. The values are: (C)-Controlled, (U)-Uncontrolled, (N)-Not Supported, (G)-Gradual, (I)-Immediate, (H)-High, (M)-Medium, (L)-Low.

| Trust Framework | Supported Trust Characteristics | | | Complexity and Requirements | | | Deployment Issues | |
|---|---|---|---|---|---|---|---|---|
| | UC | TR | RC | MEM | CMP | CMN | PC | SE |
| Certificate-Based Trust Frameworks | | | | | | | | |
| [11] | U | N | C, I | M | M | H | M | H |
| [12] | U | N | C, I | H | H | H | M | M |
| [14] | U | U | N | M | H | M | M | M |
| [8] | C | C | C, I | M | M | M | H | H |
| [16] | U | N | N | M | H | H | H | H |
| [17] | U | N | C, I | H | H | H | H | H |
| Behaviour-Based Trust Frameworks | | | | | | | | |
| [4] | U | U | U, G/I | M | M | M | M | M |
| [3] | U | N | U, G | M | L | L | L | H |
| [7] | C | C | U, G | L | M | M | L | M |
| [1] | U | C | C, G | L | M | M | L | M |
| [2] | U | C | U, G | H | M | M | L | H |

**Deployment Issues** include pre-configuration, scalability and extensibility issues. The amount and complexity of the required pre-configuration is characterised as high when detailed trust policies and metrics need to be defined for each node, or when the keying material each node needs to be supplied with requires special selection or generation algorithms. Scalability and extensibility decisions are based on how the model would scale on large deployments, and how easily new nodes could be added. For example, low scalability and extensibility is assigned for models that require each node to maintain information for all other nodes, and update it every time a new node enters and broadcasts its information.

An issue that is not included in Table 3 is the additional *battery power consumption* the application of each model would impose to ad hoc network deployments. The issues included in the complexity and requirements category affect the energy requirements in different degrees. However, although behaviour-based trust evaluation models appear less complex, they would probably be more energy consuming because they require nodes to keep their radio constantly on in order to monitor their neighbors.

Concerning the *representation of trust*, none of the frameworks uses discrete values, since it is considered too restrictive. Behaviour-based evaluation frameworks represent trust in a continuous range and compare its value with a trust threshold to decide on node cooperation. Certificate-based frameworks base the decision on node cooperation on the provision of a trusted certificate, i.e. a certificate that either is valid since it is signed by a (distributed or centralised) trusted third party, or a trusted certificate chain that includes it can be formulated.

None of the behaviour-based models supports *pre-established and stable trust relationships*. From the certificate-based frameworks, pre-established trust could be supported by [8] through introducing identity related bias in the trust metrics and policies of the nodes. For the framework introduced by Hubaux et al. [14], this requirement could be satisfied if the certificate repositories of nodes were configured to include the certificates of trusted nodes that each issuer should maintain direct and stable trust relationships with.

The issue of tackling *node selfishness*, that is especially important for frameworks that entail node cooperation, either for reputation spreading or for providing CA functionality, is not sufficiently addressed in the frameworks studied. In the model proposed by Weimerskirch and Thonet [15], incentives and punishment mechanisms are specified for recommendating nodes.

**Applicability on Sensor Networks.** The main issues that need to be taken into account for assessing the applicability of the presented frameworks on sensor networks are related to their complexity and resource requirements. As explained in Sect. 2, sensor nodes are severely constrained regarding their energy, memory, computation and communication capabilities. Behaviour-based trust evaluation frameworks utilize techniques similar to the ones of intrusion detection schemes, which are considered expensive in terms of memory, energy and communications requirements [20]. Both the need for nodes to keep their radio constantly on in order to monitor their neighbors, and the need for continuous evaluation of their trust values, are unrealistic for the constrained sensor nodes.

The same constraints in memory and computational capabilities pose concerns on the applicability of the certificate-based trust frameworks, that utilise asymmetric cryptography. Traditional asymmetric cryptography is considered too expensive for sensor nodes [10,21]. However, Elliptic Curve Cryptography, that has recently emerged as an attractive alternative to traditional public key generation, is considered to be efficient enough to be attained and executed on resource-constrained sensor nodes, mainly due to the fact that it can offer equivalent security with smaller key sizes [21].

It is our belief, however, that both the behaviour-based and the certificate-based frameworks compared are better targeted for ad hoc than for sensor networks. The main reasons are that they do not exploit the pre-deployment knowledge that will usually be available in sensor network deployments, and they do not allow for pre-established, stable trust relationships. A possible way for the trust establishment frameworks to be applied in sensor networks is by using the intrusion detection systems paradigm: as services by a subset of the nodes, e.g. the cluster heads, so as not to consume the resources of the entire network.

## 5   Conclusions

The discussion on the behaviour-based and certificate-based trust establishment frameworks and their comparison both in common and in category-specific criteria has highlighted the different approaches taken in the representation and evaluation of trust, and their pros and cons in terms of complexity, requirements and scalability. The differences in scope and purpose between the two categories of frameworks show that they should not be viewed as alternative approaches, but as supplementary. It would be possible, for deployments that require high levels of accountability ans security, to combine a certificate-based with a behaviour-based trust framework to benefit both from the representation of pre-deployment trust relationships as certificates and from the continuous behaviour-based evaluation of trust.

What the comparison has also shown, however, is that the more sophisticated a trust establishment framework is in terms of supported trust characteristics and resilience to node compromise, the more complex and resource consuming it becomes. The computational complexity of the certificate-based and the energy requirements of the behaviour-based trust evaluation frameworks raise concerns related to their applicability on resource constrained sensor nodes. At the same time, none of the frameworks studied aims to fulfill the special requirements of sensor networks on the representation and evaluation of trust relationships. In the future, it would be interesting to see less complex frameworks, especially targeted for sensor node relationships.

# References

1. Ganeriwal, S., Srivastava, M.B.: Reputation-based framework for high integrity sensor networks. In: Proceedings of the 2nd ACM workshop on Security of ad hoc and sensor networks (SASN'04), ACM Press (2004) 66–77
2. Virendra, M., Jadliwala, M., Chandrasekaran, M., Upadhyaya, S.: Quantifying trust in mobile ad-hoc networks. In: IEEE International Conference on Integration of Knowledge Intensive Multi-Agent Systems (KIMAS'05). (2005) 65–71
3. Pirzada, A.A., McDonald, C.: Establishing trust in pure ad-hoc networks. In: Proceedings of the 27th conference on Australasian computer science (CRPIT'04), Australian Computer Society, Inc. (2004) 47–54
4. Yan, Z., Zhang, P., Virtanen, T.: Trust evaluation based security solution in ad hoc networks. In: Proceedings of the Seventh Nordic Workshop on Secure IT Systems. (2003)
5. Gollmann, D.: Why trust is bad for security. In: Electronic Notes in Theoretical Computer Science. Volume 157., Elsevier (2006) 3–9
6. Grandison, T.: Trust management for internet applications. PhD thesis, Department of Computing, University of London (2003)
7. Theodorakopoulos, G., Baras, J.S.: Trust evaluation in ad-hoc networks. In: Workshop on Wireless Security. (2004) 1–10
8. Eschenauer, L., Gligor, V.D., Baras, J.S.: On trust establishment in mobile ad-hoc networks. In: Security Protocols Workshop. (2002) 47–66
9. Blaze, M., Feigenbaum, J., Lacy, J.: Decentralized trust management. In: IEEE Symposium on Security and Privacy, IEEE Computer Society (1996) 164–173
10. Shi, E., Perrig, A.: Designing secure sensor networks. Wireless Communication Magazine 11(6) (2004) 38– 43
11. Verma, R.R.S., O'Mahony, D., Tewari, H.: Ntm - progressive trust negotiation in ad hoc networks. In: Proceedings of the 1st Joint IEI/IEE Symposium on Telecommunications Systems Research. (2001)
12. Davis, C.R.: A localized trust management scheme for ad hoc networks. In: 3rd International Conference on Networking (ICN'04). (2004) 671–675

13. Garfinkel, S.: PGP : Pretty Good Privacy. OReilly & Associates (1995)
14. Hubaux, J.P., Buttyán, L., Capkun, S.: The quest for security in mobile ad hoc networks. In: MobiHoc '01: Proceedings of the 2nd ACM international symposium on Mobile ad hoc networking & computing, New York, NY, USA, ACM Press (2001) 146–155
15. Weimerskirch, A., Thonet, G.: A distributed light-weight authentication model for ad-hoc networks. In: Proceedings of the 4th International Conference Seoul on Information Security and Cryptology (ICISC'01), Springer-Verlag (2002) 341–354
16. Zhou, L., Haas, Z.J.: Securing ad hoc networks. IEEE Network **13**(6) (1999) 24–30
17. Yi, S., Kravets, R.: Moca: Mobile certificate authority for wireless ad hoc networks. In: Proceedings of 2nd Annual PKI Research Workshop. (2003)
18. Djenouri, D., Khelladi, L., Badache, N.: A survey of security issues in mobile ad hoc and sensor networks. Communications Surveys & Tutorials, IEEE **7**(4) (2005) 2–28
19. Huang, L., Li, L., Tan, Q.: Behavior-based trust in wireless sensor network. In: APWeb Workshops, Springer Berlin (2006) 214–223
20. Perrig, A., Stankovic, J., Wagner, D.: Security in wireless sensor networks. Commun. ACM **47**(6) (2004) 53–57
21. Arazi, B., Elhanany, I., Arazi, O., Qi, H.: Revisiting public-key cryptography for wireless sensor networks. IEEE Computer **38**(11) (2005) 103 – 105.

# Enforcing Trust in Pervasive Computing with Trusted Computing Technology*

Shiqun Li[1,2], Shane Balfe[2,3], Jianying Zhou[2], and Kefei Chen[1]

[1] Dept. of Computer Science and Engineering, Shanghai Jiaotong University
Shanghai 200240, China
{sqli, chen-kf}@cs.sjtu.edu.cn
[2] Institute for Infocomm Research
21 Heng Mui Keng Terrace, Singapore 119613
jyzhou@i2r.a-star.edu.sg
[3] Royal Holloway, University of London
Egham, Surrey, TW20 0EX, United Kingdom
s.balfe@rhul.ac.uk

**Abstract.** Pervasive computing as a concept holds the promise of simplifying daily life by integrating mobile devices and digital infrastructures into our physical world. These devices in a pervasive environment would establish dynamic ad-hoc networks to provide ubiquitous services. The open and dynamic characteristics of pervasive environments necessitate the requirement for some form of trust assumptions to be made. Trust in this context not only includes authentication, confidentiality and privacy but also includes the belief that the devices and smart environment behave as expected. In this paper, we propose a trust enforced pervasive computing environment using the primitives provided by a TPM (Trusted Platform Module). The application scenario shows how critical information infrastructure such as services and data can be protected. In this smart environment, a person carrying a device authenticates to the environment in order to utilize its services. In this context the device and the smart environment can also test and check each other's behaviors to better perform trust negotiation.

## 1   Introduction

Pervasive computing as a concept holds the promise of simplifying daily life by integrating mobile devices and digital infrastructures into our physical world. It is envisioned that, in pervasive computing environments, devices carried by people will be able to spontaneously interact with other devices in order to achieve the user's communication, computation and entertainment needs. These devices would be capable of establishing dynamic ad-hoc networks in order to provide ubiquitous services.

---

* This work is partially supported under NFSC 60273049, 60303026 and 60473020. Both the primary and secondary authors' work was done during their attachment to the Institute for Infocomm Research under its sponsorship.

From a national viewpoint, pervasive computing environment is part of the critical information infrastructure. As the critical information infrastructure protection requested [3], both the infrastructure owners and the individual users of critical infrastructure services expect all services to be constantly available and trustworthy. However, a pervasive environment is an open and dynamic space. The devices and the environments in which they operate may or may not know each other and there may be no pre-configured settings that would aid in the establishment of trust relationships. Moreover, trust is subjective and changeable in these environments. So clearly stated security policies and trust models are needed to convince users (and by extension their devices) and the environments to trust each other. Here trust not only includes authorisation but also includes confidentiality, privacy and the belief that a counterpart behaves as expected.

In this paper, we are concerned with the trust establishment between devices and pervasive environments. By using TPM-enabled platforms and the primitives they provide [24], we propose a trust enforced pervasive computing environment. In this context, a person carrying a (TPM-enabled) device authenticates to an environment allowing them enter a 'smart space' and access its utilities and services. In this regard, the devices and the environment would be assured of each other's behavior is as expected.

The remainder of this paper is organised as follows: Section 2 reviews previous work in the area of trust management and authorisation. Security mechanisms for pervasive computing environments are also reviewed. A brief overview of Trusted Computing technology is given in Section 3. This section also shows how TPM-enabled platforms can be used for trust management in pervasive computing. In Section 4, we propose a trust enforced pervasive computing environment using Trusted Computing technology and briefly discuss the implementation issues of the proposal. Section 5 covers our conclusions and suggests some future research directions.

## 2   Related Work

Pervasive computing is indicative of devices operating in potentially unknown environments. In this sense there may be no prior trust relationship between either the devices themselves or between the devices and the environment in which they operate. On the other hand, trust is seen a prerequisite for the interaction between devices and environments. So mechanisms and trust models are needed to convince devices that the services provided by the environment are both trusted and trustworthy.

Although trust is important, it is a notoriously difficult concept to define. From a soteriological perspective, trust is what humans use to promote positive interaction and accept risk when partial information is available. McKnight et al. held an intensive survey on trust and defined a cohesive set of conceptual and measurable constructs across several disciplines [18]. They defined trust as the situation where one is willing to depend, or intends to depend, on another party with a feeling of relative security, in spite of lack of control over that party, and even though negative consequences may arise.

Trust models are an attempt to formalize definitions (such as the one mentioned above) to provide trust for computer systems [1]. Existing trust models typically represent trust using a security policy which explicitly permits or prohibits actions [22]. PGP (Pretty Good Privacy) [26] is a famous trust model in security circles. It was designed to send secure messages using what is defined as a 'web of trust model'. In this model trust is defined as a measure of establishing the authenticity of the binding between a user and her/his public key. In the Abdul-Rahmans approach [2], trust management is performed using a distributed trust model and recommendation protocol similar to PGP. Matt Blaze proposed another distributed trust model PolicyMaker [8]. The decentralised trust model determines whether particular credentials satisfy certain policies. PolicyMaker is able to interpret policies and answer questions regarding user access rights. KeyNote [9,7] is the successor of PolicyMaker which focuses more on standardization and ease of its integration into applications. Another trust model is the Simple Public Key Infrastructure (SPKI) [12], a proposed standard for distributed trust management to address some of the complexity that arises in traditional PKI systems. In SPKI, certificates can be issued by anyone with certain authorisation. Access rights can also be delegated by forming a chain of certificates.

Apart from these credential based trust models, trust formalization approaches were proposed to deal with trust management. Marsh proposed an approach [17] which focused on situational trust by using subjective variables to calculate a trust value. Beth's approach [6] is based on a formal methodology for trust evaluation which is used for granting authorization for sensitive tasks. It is an extension of [16] and has been the basis for [1]. Jøsang [13,15,14] described methods for computing authenticity based on certificates, on key bindings, and on trust relationships. It uses an opinion and evidence driven model to represent trust. A European project, SECURE [10,22], presents trust and risk frameworks to enable secure collaboration between ubiquitous computer systems. Almenßrez et al. [4] presented a decentralized trust management model for pervasive computing environments. Their model, PTM (Pervasive Trust Management Model), aims to establish a trust model between autonomous entities without central servers.

The above trust management models provide basic trust formalizations for distributed systems. However, in such systems, the users and the devices have to assume the system would perform 'trusted' operations. In this paper, we prefer the definition of trust from Peter Neumann [19]. "An object is trusted if and only if it operates as expected. An object is trustworthy if and only if it is proven to operate as expected". So we adopt Trusted Computing platform and the functions such as secure storage, attestation, trusted channels and paths to provide trust negotiation for pervasive computing.

## 3   Trusted Computing

Trust is perhaps one of the most over-utilized words in the security practitioners' lexicon, making a precise meaning difficult to define. A large proportion of this difficulty stems from the truism that trust is a contextually dependent homonym. This paper will examine the definition of trust as specified by the TCG (Trusted Computing Group), namely, 'a system that behaves in an expected manner for a particular purpose' in a pervasive deployment scenario.

The concept of trust in Trusted Computing centers around an integrated chip that resides on a platform's motherboard. This chip, or TPM (Trusted Platform Module), acts as a root for measuring, storing and reporting integrity events within a platform. The mechanisms and components through which this is achieved are a relatively modest set of isolated immutable functions.

### 3.1   Measurement

Measuring events on a platform is a multi-stage process that begins with an *extend* command. This command, more commonly referred to as 'extending the digest', appends a hash of the event being measured to one of a number of Platform Configuration Registers (PCRs) located internally to the TPM. These PCRs store a representative hash of all the events generated so far to form a picture of the current platform state or configuration. This digest extension process can be illustrated as follows, where $PCR_x$ is the digest being updated, $\|$ means concatenation and the *measuredvalue* is some representation of embedded data or program code:

$$PCR_x = HASH(PCR_x \parallel measured\ value)$$

The other phase in this process is the writing of the events reflected in a particular PCR to non-volatile storage. This writing to permanent storage, or logging, of integrity altering events within a platform occurs in the Stored Measurement Log (SML). The SML (alternatively referred to as the event log) maintains sequences of events (of which their hashes are reflected in PCRs) to which new events are appended. Due to storage constraints this log will typically be located external to the TPM. The two most important properties abstracted from the brief discussion above is that, firstly, atomicity of extensions be ensured and secondly, that updates be noncommutative. That is to say, updates should follow an all or nothing semantic and order in which extension events occur matters.

### 3.2   Storage

Storage within the definitions provided by Trusted Computing refers to two distinct concepts. The first, which is covered above refers to the intermediary step between measurement and reporting. The second, which we will discuss here, refers to the protection of keys and data within a TPM. The responsibility for protection of said elements with a TPM falls under the purview of the Root of Trust for Storage (RTS). The RTS maintains a small area of volatile memory used for performing cryptographic operations or storing opaque data. Due to the limitations in available memory, much like the SML, it will be necessary to move inactive keys into off-chip storage areas. This process is managed by the Key Cache Manager (KCM) which forms part of the TCG Core Services (TCS) of the Trusted Software Stack (TSS). Inactive keys are first encrypted into a blob using a key controlled by the Storage Root Key (SRK). This blobs are opaque outside of the TPM and are bound to the platform on which the TPM resides.

The SRK forms the root of all keys stored on a TPM key tree of which every node has an attribute designation as well as a key type. Attribute designations in the context of a 'TPM_Key' help to define key mobility. A key can be designated either migratable or non-migratable. Keys with either of these two designations are capable of leaving a TPM (under the encrypted blob semantics outlined above) except for non-migratable keys which are inextricably bound to a single platform. Key types are used to define what particular operations a TPM_Key is capable of performing.

### 3.3   Reporting

Reporting in the form of platform attestation is perhaps one of the singly most important features of a TPM-enabled platform. The basic steps involved in an attestation are as follows:

1. An external entity requests one or more PCR values.
2. A platform agent culls the SML for the events responsible for generating the requested PCR values.
3. The TPM signs the requested registers using an Attestation Identity Key (AIK) by calling the TPM_Quote [25, pp.155] command.
4. The agent then obtains various credentials (the platform credential, the conformance credential, attestation identity credential) that vouch for the TPM. These credentials, along with the relevant portion of the SML and the requested signed PCR values are returned to the Integrity Measurement Verifier.
5. The verifier then examines the credentials, checks signatures and compares a hash of the SML entries to the attested PCR values. If they match the verifier can be sure as to the current state of the Integrity Measurement Collector's platform.

Recently there have been a number of proposals [11,20] to improve this mechanism over worries with Digital Rights Management (DRM) and certain inflexibility when dealing with heterogenous computing environments. However, for the remainder of this paper we will deal exclusively with the method presented above.

### 3.4   Delegation and Certified Migration

Delegation and Certified Migration are new features that were added to version 1.2 of the specification and will be important to our discussion of trust enforced pervasive computing.

The delegation model used in TPM v1.2 aims to address some of the concerns surrounding the 'super-user' like privileges previously afforded to TPM_Owner. If a situation were to arise that necessitated the revelation of authorisation to perform a certain operation; delegation previously followed an all or nothing semantic. In order to better apply 'the principle of least privilege' a new model was introduced. The model centers around creating new authorisation data and to delegate certain owner privileges to it using an access control matrix like structure. Within this structure it is possible to enforce PCR constraints on delegated rights. So, for example, an owner could delegate a right to a process only when that process conforms to a predetermined state. The delegatee could be local to the platform or even a remote entity.

Certified Migration is also a new concept introduced in the TPM v1.2 specifications. Certified Migration is an operation that permits the secure transfer of migratory keys from one TCG compliant platform to another in such a manner as to allow the new platform full usage of the migrated key. The notion of a migratable key in Trusted Computing can be divided into two categories, the Migratable Keys (MKs) and the Certified Migratable Keys (CMKs). MKs are keys that, while not bound to a specific TPM, can be transferred to another TPM if appropriate authorisation is provided. CMKs are similar insofar as they also require appropriate authorisation in order to migrate, however, their migration is conditional on receiving permission from a relevant Migration Authority (MA).

## 4    Enforcing Trust in Pervasive Computing

### 4.1    Application Scenario

Here, we describe an application scenario illustrative of the Trusted Computing-enforced pervasive computing environment we propose (see Fig. 1). Before we begin we will briefly introduce the dramatis personae. Alice is a project manager for a large organization. Bob, a consultant, has been hired to advise one of the departments that Alice oversees. The scenario we consider begins when Bob arrives for the first time at the company's premises to work on the project that is indirectly under Alice's control. Upon entry to the building Bob meets the company's security agent who hasn't been informed of Bob's arrival. As the agent is unaware of Bob's role in the organization it denies him access by default.

According to the security policy, Alice is capable of delegating certain access rights to those whom she trusts. As Bob is in a state of limbo in the reception area he sends a message to Alice requesting credentials that would permit him entrance to the building. Alice forwards Bob the requisite credentials, as per his request, along with any additional credentials she thinks he will require to adequately perform his job function.

After Bob gains entrance to the building and presents his credentials to the security agent, he may wish to enter rooms such as the 'smart office' or the 'smart conference' room. He also would like to use the services provided by these rooms. Thus he interacts with the devices in these rooms to obtain their services. The

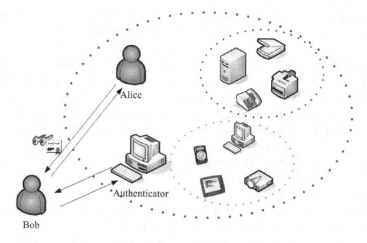

**Fig. 1.** The trust enabled pervasive computing environment

'smart rooms', and by extension the devices within, may permit him access to certain services whilst denying access to others.

Before Bob interacts with the service providing devices within a smart room he wishes to assure himself that the services provided are 'trusted'. For example, when he uses a printing service, he does not want the device to maintain a copy of the submitted document or misuse it in any way. Conversely, the smart space also wants to make sure Bob's behavior can be trusted. Bob may acquire some sensitive documentation to complete his project, the smart room may require him not to misuse it or copy the plaintext to other platforms.

To provide such a pervasive computing environment, the following assumptions are required:

- We assume each device in the pervasive computing environment is equipped with TPM as defined in TCG specifications. The smart environment is also equipped with devices that control the entrance of the smart building and smart rooms [5].
- The organization has its own CA for issuing public key certificates.
- Privacy issues are not explicitly specified in our system. However, it could possibly be addressed by use of DAA (Direct Anonymous Attestation) mechanisms provided by TCG specification.

## 4.2   Security Requirements

As mentioned in Section 1, a pervasive computing environment is an open and dynamic space where both devices and environments may be unknown to each other. Wireless technology may be used for communication in which data transmitted is easily eavesdropped upon, intercepted, injected or altered. In this setting, mechanisms are needed to ensure the devices and the environment in which they operate can trust each other, especially with regard to the mutual belief that a counterpart's behavior will be as expected. We summarize the security requirements of our pervasive computing environment as follows.

1. *Authentication and authorisation.* The infrastructure needs to trust that the valid user is authenticated and authorised before being allowed to access a protected objects. Moreover, to avoid insidious software attacks such as spoofing, man-in-the-middle, eavesdropping and modification attacks, the client platform should provide mechanisms to prevent other applications from accessing the object.
2. *Confidentiality.* The data transmitted and stored should be encrypted to avoid eavesdropping and misusing.
3. *Control after distribution.* In traditional systems, once information is released to a client there may be no further control. As required, a server may need to trust a client not to release an object illegally.
4. *Trusted services.* In traditional systems, the client has to assume the services provided by the environment are 'trusted'. While in pervasive computing environments, the client needs to ensure that the service provider behaves as it expected.

For the time being we are investigating the use of the hardware-based Trusted Computing technology to design and develop secure enterprise applications. These mechanisms may also be extended to protect other critical information infrastructure.

## 4.3   Authentication and Authorisation

As in the application scenario described above, Bob first wants to enter the smart space and then access the facilities and services (illustrated in Fig. 2).

Traditionally, authorisation relies on Access Control Lists (ACLs) stored in a resource server to express an access policy. Each subject is associated with a tuple in an ACL indicating the actions that the subject can exercise upon an object. ACLs usually require the server domain to maintain accounts and other administrative support for users. Thus ACLs may not provide satisfactory quality of security management when there are many subjects and objects, which is common for pervasive computing environments. An alternative approach is a capability-based access control system. Each subject has a capability list for each object. With capabilities, it is easy to determine the privilege set of a subject. In this sense, the choice of a capability-based approach affects the efficiency of authorisation revocation upon deletion of either subjects or objects [21]. This represents an advantage in distributed systems since it avoids repeated authentication of a subject. In this paper we use a combination of capability certificates and ACLs for access control. However, we focus on a capability-based approach to constrain subject actions. The use of a capability certificate in this context provides a short lived certificate specifying a user's rights to use the facilities and services in the pervasive computing environment. Once the certificate expires, the user must ask for a new certificate to access facilities and services. Correspondingly, ACLs can be used for generic access

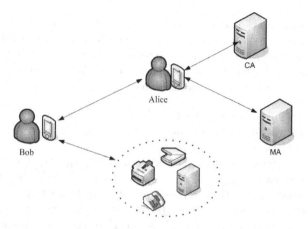

**Fig. 2.** Authentication and authorisation in the pervasive environment

control where a subject's rights to interact with an unknown object will be determined by the subject's current state. Here an ACL-based approach is indicative of a state-based access control system.

There are two phases in authorisation, *Credential Acquirement* that enables Alice to delegate access rights to Bob, and *Access Control* that enables Bob to enter the smart space and enjoy services as specified by his credential.

In the credential acquirement phase, Trusted Computing affords multiple different enrollment facilities. However, the presence of certain infrastructure components will dictate the precise service offered to an enrollment function.

The presence of a Privacy CA per environment/organisation will allow Bob to obtain a credential for an AIK key (see Section 3.3) that both authenticates the integrity metrics purported by Bob's platform during an attestation challenge as well as potentially authenticating Bob himself (depending on the presence of personally identifiable information within the credential). However, this approach alone cannot be used to constrain the operations that Bob may perform within an environment (except with ACL usage). In order to achieve this function we require the addition of an SKAE CA [23] that will provide an X.509 certificate for a TPM resident non-migratable key. This certificate contains extensions that describe the security properties of a TPM key. The use of a general purpose X.509 certificate in this setting allows the inclusion of capability attributes that will further constrain the operation of the private key corresponding to the key referenced in the certificate.

An alternative option to this approach is Certified Migration. Here Alice creates a CMK and migrates it from her platform to Bob's platform. During this process she also applies for a capability certificate binding the CMK to specify Bob's rights for accessing the necessary facilities and services. The use of a non-migratable or CMK key in this context is due to concerns with key provenance. We want to avoid the situation that may arise with migratable keys where a key migrated to Bob's platform my be further migrated to an un-trusted destination. In either case, Bob should end up with a certified key pair ($TPM\_Key_{bob}$) that both identifies him to the environment as well as constraining his behaviour to a set of pre-approved tasks as defined in his capability certificate $TPM\_Bob\_Cert$.

The access control phase enables Bob to enter the organization's smart rooms and use the services provided as his certificate having the specified privilege[1]. To enter the smart room, Bob and the smart space interact as follows.

1. Bob's device submits its request to the smart space.
2. The authentication server of the smart room generates a random number $R_S$ and sends back[2].
3. Bob's device generates another random number $R_B$ and sends $\{ TPM\_Sign_{TPM\_Key_{bobpriv}} (H(R_S \parallel R_B)) \parallel R_B \parallel TPM\_Bob\_Cert\}$ to the authentication server. Here $H()$ is a one-way hash function.
4. The authentication server verifies the signature and the capability list of the $TPM\_Bob\_Cert$ as well as its validation. If all these verifications pass, the authentication server allows Bob to enter the smart room.

In the smart room, Bob can simply provide his capability certificate to the service provider and access the service if the certificate has the specified rights. Alternatively, devices can interact with each other in an ad-hoc fashion depending on conformance with ACL-based state appraisal functions.

### 4.4   Trust Services

As described in the above application scenario, the smart environment may have policy restricting client's use of some confidential data. For example, the server needs a confidential document to be downloaded and bound only to Bob's platform. This can be addressed by sealing mechanism as specified by TCG. $TPM\_Seal$ and $TPM\_Unseal$ are used to encrypt and decrypt opaque data. The data is wrapped to particular TPM and can only be revealed by the TPM providing the platform is in a certain state. Whereas it is difficult for a remote platform to confirm whether the data was actually sealed. In our solution, we use $TPM\_CreateWrapKey$ and $TPM\_CertifyKey$ commands to make the platform binding more applicable. The document can only be opened by Bob's PDA and other platform cannot decrypt and view it. Even if Bob's PDA was lost, other people without knowledge of the authorisation data cannot open it.

### Controlling Access After Distribution

Fig. 3 illustrates the (simplified) procedures for application to restrict client's use of data. The details of the process is described as follows[3]:

1. $A_b \to S$: Request for document $Doc$.
2. $S \to A_b$: $R_S \parallel S_{pubkey}$.

---

[1] A system that enables mobile devices to access both physical and virtual resources is described in [5].

[2] We do not consider the authentication of the smart space to Bob. We also do not consider man in the middle attack as Bob is just in front of the smart room.

[3] Not all TPM commands are shown.

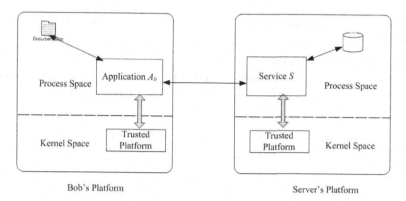

Bob's Platform                                    Server's Platform

**Fig. 3.** Restricting client's use of data

3. $A_b \rightarrow TPM$: $TPM\_CreateWrapKey(TPM\_Auth\_Always,$
   $digestAtCreation, digestAtRelease)$.
4. $TPM \rightarrow A_b$: $TPM\_Key_{legacy}$.
5. $A_b \rightarrow TPM$: $TPM\_CertifyKey_{TPM\_Key_{bob}}(TPM\_Key_{legacy})$.
6. $TPM \rightarrow A_b$: $TPM\_Certify\_Info$.
7. $A_b \rightarrow S$: $S_{pubkey}(R_S \parallel R_b \parallel TPM\_Certify\_Info \parallel TPM\_Key_{pubkey}) \parallel$
   $TPM\_Sign_{TPM\_Key_{bobpriv}}(H(R_S \parallel R_b \parallel TPM\_Certify\_Info \parallel$
   $TPM\_Key_{legacy-pub})) \parallel TPM\_Bob\_Cert$.
8. $S \rightarrow A_b$: $TPM\_Key_{legacy-pub}(K_{Doc}) \parallel K_{Doc}(Doc) \parallel S_{privkey}(H(K_{Doc} \parallel R_b))$.
9. $A_b \rightarrow TPM$: View request with authorisation data and its running integrity measurement.
10. $TPM \rightarrow A_b$: $Doc$.

The procedure is initialized when Bob requests a document $Doc$ from server $S$ by application $A_b$ in step 1. In step 2, $S$ sends a challenge together with its public key to the requestor $A_b$. In step 3, the request application instructs $TPM$ of the platform it runs on to generate a pair of asymmetric keys by $TPM\_CreateWrapKey$ command. This step is to generate non-migratable keys as described in Section 3. In step 4, the TPM returns a $TPM\_Key$ key structure. The key structure contains flags indicating that it is non-migratable and includes the PCR digests at key creation and the PCR digests required for key release. These constraints can be used to ensure the service provider that the client platform, and by extension the applications of the platform, would use the information as specified. In step 5, $A_b$ has the generated public key to be certified by $TPM$. The certified public key can further assure service provider's trust on the client application. In step 6, the TPM returns the $TPM\_Certify\_Info$ structure describing the newly certified key. In step 7, $A_b$ responses to $S$ the public key along with the signature, a new challenge and the capability certificate $TPM\_Bob\_Cert$. In step 8, $S$ verifies the response and sends $A_b$ the encrypted document $Doc$ and the encryption key provided the verification is OK. In step 9, $A_b$ requests to $TPM$ to view the document. In step 10, if current platform state matches the requirements and the authorisation data is valid, $TPM$ unseals the document.

**Trusted Printing Service**

In the following, we illustrate how TCG can be used to enhance the user's trust of the services provided by the pervasive computing environment.

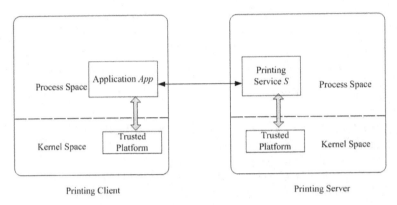

**Fig. 4.** Trusted printing service

Here Bob wants to print a confidential document using a printing service in the smart environment[4]. The following process can ensure him that the printing service behaves as he expected (Fig. 4), i.e. the printing service will not maintain a copy of the document or misuse it:

1. $App \rightarrow S : TPM\_Sign_{TPM\_Key_{bobpriv}}(R_b) \parallel R_b \parallel TPM\_Bob\_Cert.$
2. $S \rightarrow App : AIK_{privkey}(PCRs) \parallel SML \parallel TPM\_Key_{privkey}(R_b) \parallel TPM\_Key_{pubkey}.$
3. $App \rightarrow S : TPM\_Key_{pubkey}(K_{Doc}) \parallel K_{Doc}(Doc).$

In step 1, the client application requests server's attestation with a challenge and the $TPM\_Bob\_Cert$. In step 2, the server checks the validation of the certificate and responses to the challenge with its running integrity measurement, a signature, the public key and the related certificate. In step 3, the client application checks the signatures and compares a hash of the SML (event log) entries to the attested PCR values. If they match the client application sends the encrypted document to the printer for printing.

### 4.5 Discussions

As the information infrastructure, computing and networking are now becoming ubiquitous utilities like electricity or water. The security of those critical

---

[4] Here we assume Bob has got the valid PCR values from Alice. We also assume Bob trusts Alice.

information infrastructure is therefore of increasing concerns. Trusted Computing technologies promise to provide roots of trust on which secure applications can be developed. It is designed for a distributed and dynamic, open environment wherein 'trusted' application software can be executed and protected from interference from other software on the same platform. Standard such as TNC (trusted network connect) from TCG aims to release an open architecture and a growing set of standards for endpoint integrity. The TNC architecture would enable network operators to enforce policies regarding endpoint integrity at or after network connection. Trusted Computing technologies also seek to protect data in creation, processing, storage, and transfer which are required by the critical information infrastructure protection.

TCG is based on public key crypto-systems, so as the approach in this paper, which is not common for pervasive computing environments that are expected to be completely open and not to be restricted to a single CA domain. While in the application scenario of this paper, it is reasonable to assume the organization has a single CA domain to provide security services.

## 5   Conclusions

We presented a trust enforced pervasive environment by using Trusted Computing technology to realise trust-based services. In this environment, the devices and the environment can evaluate each other's behavior with primitives provided by TCG. Although the proposed setting cannot address all the problems related to pervasive computing environments, it can fill some of the void current proposals and methodologies leave. We have only scratched the surface of the possibilities of what pervasive computing environment can achieve. Our further research will be adding policies to the trust enabled pervasive computing environment to enforce its security. And how to efficiently implement the proposal is also a future concern.

## References

1. Alfarez Abdul-Rahman and Stephen Hailes. A distributed trust model. In *NSPW'97: Proceedings of the 1997 Workshop on New Security Paradigms*, pages 48–60, New York, NY, USA, 1997. ACM Press.
2. Alfarez Abdul-Rahman and Stephen Hailes. Supporting trust in virtual communities. In *HICSS'00: Proceedings of the 33rd Hawaii International Conference on System Sciences-Volume 6*, page 6007, Washington, DC, USA, 2000. IEEE Computer Society.
3. Isabelle Abele-Wigert and Myriam Dunn. *International CIIP Handbook 2006 (Vol.II)*. Center for Security Studies, ETH Zurich, 2006.
4. Florina Almenßrez, Andres Marn, Celeste Campo, and Carlos Garcia. Ptm: A pervasive trust management model for dynamic open environments. In *PSPT'04: Proceedings of the 1st Workshop on Pervasive Security, Privacy and Trust in conjuntion with Mobiquitous 2004*, 2004.

5. Lujo Bauer, Scott Garriss, Jonathan M. McCune, Michael K. Reiter, Jason Rouse, and Peter Rutenbar. Device-enabled authorization in the grey system. In *ISC'05: Proceedings of the 8th Information Security Conference, LNCS 3650*, pages 431–445, Singapore, 2005. Springer-Verlag.

6. Thomas Beth, Malte Borcherding, and Birgit Klein. Valuation of trust in open networks. In *ESORICS'94: Proceedings of the 3rd European Symposium on Research in Computer Security*, pages 3–18, London, UK, 1994. Springer-Verlag.

7. Matt Blaze, Joan Feigenbaum, John Ioannidisand, and Angelos D. Keromytis. The keynote trust-management system, version 2. 1999.

8. Matt Blaze, Joan Feigenbaum, and Jack Lacy. Decentralized trust management. In *SP'96: Proceedings of the 1996 IEEE Symposium on Security and Privacy*, page 164, 1996. IEEE Computer Society.

9. Matt Blaze, Joan Feigenbaum, and Angelos D. Keromytis. Keynote: Trust management for public-key infrastructures (position paper). In *Proceedings of the 6th International Workshop on Security Protocols, LNCS 1550*, pages 59–63, 1999. Springer-Verlag.

10. E. Gray, P. O'Connell, C. Jensen, S. Weber, J. Seigneur, and C. Yong. Towards a framework for assessing trust-based admission control in collaborative ad hoc applications, 2002.

11. Vivek Haldar, Deepak Chandra, and Michael Franz. Semantic remote attestation: A virtual machine directed approach to trusted computing. In *USENIX Virtual Machine Research and Technology Symposium*, May 2004.

12. IETF. Simple public key infrastructure (SPKI). February 2001.

13. Audun Jøsang. The right type of trust for distributed systems. In *NSPW'96: Proceedings of the 1996 Workshop on New Security Paradigms*, pages 119–131, New York, NY, USA, 1996. ACM Press.

14. Audun Jøsang. An algebra for assessing trust in certification chains. In *NDSS'99: Proceedings of the Network and Distributed Systems Security*, 1999.

15. Audun Jøsang and S. Knapskog. A metric for trusted systems. In *Proceedings of the 21st National Security Conference*, pages 16–29, 1998.

16. B. Klein, R. Yahalom, and T. Beth. Trust relationships in secure systems - a distributed authentication perspective. In *RSP: IEEE Computer Society Symposium on Research in Security and Privacy*, 1993.

17. S. Marsh. Formalising trust as a computational concept. 1994.

18. D. Harrison McKnight and Norman L. Chervany. Trust and distrust definitions: One bite at a time. In *Trust in Cyber-societites, Integrating the Human and Artificial Perspectives*, pages 27–54, London, UK, 2000. Springer-Verlag.

19. Peter G. Neumann. Architectures and formal representations for secure systems. Technical report, June 1996.

20. Ahmad-Reza Sadeghi and Christian St. Property-based attestation for computing platforms: caring about properties, not mechanisms. In *NSPW'04: Proceedings of the 2004 Workshop on New Security Paradigms*, pages 67–77, New York, NY, USA, 2005. ACM Press.

21. Pierangela Samarati and Sabrina De Capitani di Vimercati. Access control: Policies, models, and mechanisms. In *FOSAD'00: Revised versions of lectures given during the IFIP WG 1.7 International School on Foundations of Security Analysis and Design on Foundations of Security Analysis and Design*, pages 137–196, London, UK, 2001. Springer-Verlag.

22. Brian Shand, Nathan Dimmock, and Jean Bacon. Trust for ubiquitous, transparent collaboration. *Wirel. Netw.*, 10(6):711–721, 2004.
23. Trusted Computing Group. *TCG Infrastructure Workgroup Subject Key Attestation Evidence Extension*, 1.0 edition, June 2005.
24. Trusted Computing Group. *TPM Main: Part 1 Design Principles*, 1.2 edition, 2005.
25. Trusted Computing Group. *TPM Main: Part 3 Commands*, 2005.
26. Philip Zimmermann. *PGP source code and internals*. MIT Press, Cambridge, MA, USA, 1995.

# Proposals on Assessment Environments for
# Anomaly-Based Network Intrusion Detection Systems

M. Bermúdez-Edo, R. Salazar-Hernández, J. Díaz-Verdejo, and P. García-Teodoro

Dpt. of Signal Theory, Telematics and Communications, University of Granada
E.T.S. Ing. Informática y Telecomunicación, C/ Periodista Daniel Saucedo Aranda, s/n
18071 – Granada (Spain)
mbe@ugr.es, rsalaza@correo.ugr.es, jedv@ugr.es, pgteodor@ugr.es

**Abstract.** One of the key challenges that researchers should face when propos-
ing a new intrusion detection approach (IDS) is that of demonstrating its
general validity. This fact goes necessarily through the disposal of a real set of
intrusion (as well as non-intrusion) related events, from which to compare and
thus validate the performance of the novel proposed techniques. However, this a
priori simple issue is far to be obvious because of the lack of a commonly accepted assessment methodology. In this line, the authors discuss a set of basic
requirements that an intrusion-oriented framework should fulfill in order to deal
with the normalization of the evaluation process in IDS environments. In its
current preliminary state, the work is mainly focused to analyze, specify and
manage traffic databases for developing and validating NIDS.

**Keywords:** Network security, Intrusion event, IDS, Assessment.

## 1 Introduction

As the social acceptance of communication systems has grown, especially by means
of Internet, the dependence on ICT technologies has become more and more critical.
Moreover, the increasing relationships and complexity of current ICT-related systems
make global information and communication infrastructures highly vulnerable [1] [2].
A prominent aspect of such vulnerability concerns the dramatic increase of the
number of security incidents in last years [3]. In this context, one of the most adopted
tools to improve security in internetworking facilities is that of intrusion detection
systems (IDS) [4].

IDS' can be classified according to several criteria [5]. One of them regards the
type of analysis to be performed, from which an IDS can be either a signature-based
intrusion detection system (S-IDS) or an anomaly-based one (A-IDS). In the first case
attack patterns are specified, and the system will signal an intrusion event when a
match between the monitored events and one of the patterns in the signature database
is observed. In the anomaly-based IDS approach, the normal behavior of the target
system is captured and modeled, and an alarm rose if the behavior of the monitored
environment does not comply, within an accepted range, the expected one.

The main advantage of the S-IDS approach lies on the control of known attacks.
On the contrary, the main disadvantage of this approach is the impossibility of

J. Lopez (Ed.): CRITIS 2006, LNCS 4347, pp. 210–221, 2006.
© Springer-Verlag Berlin Heidelberg 2006

detecting unknown attacks, even if they are quite similar to a known one. On the other hand, the advantage of the A-IDS methodology is its hypothetical capacity to detect previously unobserved intrusive events; whilst the main disadvantage is related to the fact that an alarm will be triggered every time an "abnormal" event is accomplished, even if it is legitimate (false positives). Regarding this last point, it is important to indicate that false positives rate can be reduced through the so-called "specification-based" IDS approach, where a model is derived from formal protocol specifications.

One more accepted classification for IDS depends on the origin of the data to be analyzed: either the network or a host. The first case corresponds to a network-based IDS (NIDS), that is, the data to be analyzed is related to communication protocols and payloads. Instead, the approach is called host-based IDS (HIDS) when host events, such as processes, users, system calls, etc., are indeed the analyzed events.

Any combination of these techniques can be used to improve the effectiveness of the detection, like signature and anomaly detection based, or HIDS and NIDS [7], or anomaly based and specification based [8].

Because of the increasing impact of attacks in ICT, the intrusion detection technology is continuously evolving to improve the security and protection of systems and infrastructures. However, one of the main challenges that researchers face, when trying to implement and validate a new intrusion detection method, is to asses it, and to compare its performance to that of the currently available approaches. This is due to various reasons. First of all to data privacy, that forbids the real databases to be shared among researchers; on the other hand, the use of synthetic networking events has been widely criticized [9]. The second main obstacle concerns the lack of a methodology to use event databases for testing the new model, and benchmarking it with the existing ones [10].

At the present time, IDS methods are validated without any rigor from an objective technical point of view. Generally, every researcher has his/her own methodology for testing the work done, and hence, it is very difficult to actually decide on which technique performs better than another. In this line, and due to the relevance of the subject, the aim of this paper is to point out a number of issues to define equivalent frameworks to accomplish the assessment of IDS environments. Thus, every researcher could create his own real traffic database and use it with guaranty about the reliability of the obtained results. We will center the attention on the database management, preparing the real dataset for properly testing an IDS, and the steps followed in the process. The methodology to be described will be preliminary applied to a specific environment developed by the authors, which is mainly characterized by the use of a hybrid NIDS solution: signature-based detection, and anomaly-based detection (complemented with some specification-based aspects) are combined to take advantage of the two approaches.

The paper is organized as follows. In Section 2 already existing methodologies to assess IDS environments are described, and their main limitations discussed. Section 3 introduces a methodology for validating anomaly-based IDS, and how to manage the traffic databases for that. After that, Section 4 proposes and discusses a practical method to solve the implementation problems emphasized in the previous section. Section 5 describes the specific framework developed by the authors to test their own IDS approaches. Finally, main conclusions and future related work are given in Section 6.

## 2  Background in IDS Assessment

In 1998 DARPA (Defense Advanced Research Project Agency) started a program in the MIT Lincoln Labs with the aim of providing a complete and realistic benchmarking environment for IDS [11]. Before that program few works gave a solution for evaluation of NIDS, but none of them became as popular as the DARPA project. Most of them consist of creating a simulated network with background traffic and malicious activities interlaced.

The DARPA project was reviewed in 1999, so that the resulting 1999 DARPA/Lincoln Laboratory intrusion detection evaluation data set (IDEVAL) became a widely used benchmark tool containing synthetic network traffic [12].

Some contributions in the literature have raised questions about the accuracy of the IDEVAL simulation [9] [13], identifying its major shortcomings and offering clues to improve the assessment environment. The main reported problem is that the simulated traffic was unrealistic, even at the time it was developed. Nowadays the problem is even bigger because: (a) the types of attacks have changed since the creation of the database in 1999, and (b) the data rate is not comparable with that in current real networks. Despite these limitations, so far, no other IDS environment has displaced the famous IDEVAL.

In 2001 DARPA, in collaboration with other institutions, started the LARIAT (Lincoln Adaptable Real-time Assurance Test-bed) program [14]. Unfortunately, LARIAT is restricted to military USA environments and some academic organizations under special circumstances.

Some recent works have spotted the problem of evaluating IDS', but most of the solutions found were on the line of generating artificial databases [15]. However, our point, and that of many researchers, is that databases ought to be real, avoiding the subjectivity of the programmers and their interpretation of attacks, as well as the use of only well-known attacks that may bias the results.

There have been made some efforts in the line of sharing real traffic databases, like the Internet traffic archive [16] and web-caching [17]. However, all of them are quite old, and therefore the traffic is not realistic compared with that of current networks. Furthermore, the specifications of said datasets have not been described in detail.

One of the principal concerns with real traffic databases is the privacy of the data. Some papers proposed anonymity through IP address masquerading [18], taking the advantage of real traffic and avoiding the problem of privacy. This is a good approach, but sometimes the masquerading process is done without any consideration about the information kept in the IP address, workload or URI, what could be useful for some IDS systems. Therefore, it should be a good practice to change the IP addresses in a way that the relationships between the real addresses and the masqueraded addresses are one to one. The same applies to the other masqueraded information: user-ID, URI, etc. Most of the times these basic rules are not obeyed, and the masqueraded databases become useless. All of these works were focused on data privacy, but none of them deal with the problem of standardizing the acquisition and use of real traffic for validating IDS environments.

Summarizing, the problems with current intrusion databases are that either they come from synthetic traffic, which may lead to bias the results, or they come from real traffic, but they are old, with serious doubts about the usefulness for current networks. Moreover, the specifications of the databases are not well documented in terms of topology, data rate, location of the sensors, amount of captured data or applied filters. Furthermore, the validation of the IDS methods has been done without any regulation. In this context, the authors propose in what follows a methodology for the management of real traffic databases oriented to train and validate IDS approaches.

## 3   Database Management Requirements

As stated above, our research work is mainly focused on network-based hybrid IDS, where signature-based and anomaly-based approaches are jointly used. Because of the "deterministic" nature of the signature-based schemes, especially by the nearly unanimous use of Snort, we are going to emphasize the anomaly-based NIDS part in what follows. A-NIDS methods pursuit to model the "normal behavior" of the target network environment to be protected under "free-of-attack" conditions. Once the normality model is estimated, the anomaly detection process will analyze traffic events in order to determine a deviation degree with respect to that (normal) expected one.

The main requirement for an intrusion detection system is to be effective; that is, it should detect a substantial percentage of intrusions into the supervised system, while still keeping the false alarm rate at an acceptable level. At the same time it should be efficient, having a quick real time response and consuming few computer resources.

False alarms (alarms due to rare, although valid observations) are one of the main problems in current A-NIDS. When the system is running in the wild, it should not raise any alarm as far as the captured behavior of the system looks like, within a given range, that of the training data used to define the normality model. Thus, every model trained with a set of data becomes dependent of that set of data, as it is easily comprehensive.

The success in developing A-NIDS' requires getting a good model for the behavior of the monitored environment under normal circumstances, which implies both a good modeling approach and an adequate training stage. Therefore, the first step to create an A-NIDS is to implement a program which somehow simulates the normal states or behavior of the system. Then, the program will be trained running with an attack-free traffic database to estimate the model.

Hence, the model represents the statistics that an event, a transition and/or a sequence of packets, occurs under ideal conditions, i.e., without attacks. Once the model is trained, it must to be tested. This task goes through running the model over a database containing known attacks, and following the evolution of the system in order to analyze its deviation from the expected behavior. The test process should be used to improve our model in a feedback way.

After testing a validation stage is recommended. This last step should be performed with a new database because the results obtained with the former datasets were used to tune the model. This means that the system will become specially sensible to attacks appeared in previous data, and the chances to detect them "artificially" high. But, we still do not know how the detector will react against new attacks, unobserved in the test database. Therefore, the definition of a new database is "objectively" mandatory.

In summary, developing an A-NIDS system goes through the acquisition of a network traffic database consisting of real traffic, and fulfilling some important requirements:

1. *Normal / attack traffic partitioning.* An attack-free traffic set is necessary, as well as an attack-based set, and an event set of attacks interlaced with background "clean" traffic. This all is due to the types of traffic needed for the various steps regarding training, test and validation of the IDS, as explained above. The attacks should be labeled in order to account for proper detection and false positive rates.

2. *Training / test / validation partitioning.* It is also necessary to have got a traffic set for training, another one for testing, and a last one for validating the IDS. The training database has to be attack free, while both test and validation datasets have to include labeled attacks and normal traffic events. On the other hand, the proportions between attack and normal packets within the test and validation partitions have to be equal to that in the whole database; in other case, a bias in false positive rates may appear.

3. *Representativeness.* Another relevant requirement concerns the acquisition of the traffic database. The amount of data contained has to be sufficient to guaranty the modeling of the patterns of the system, and to test and validate it afterward. As in every statistical model, the samples should be enough to represent the regular behavior of the whole community including allowed and not allowed events.

Therefore, so far, three different datasets or partitions of the whole traffic database are going to be created (*see* Fig. 1.c). The first one is the training set (*Tr*), which has to be attack-free. The second and third compose, respectively, the testing set (*Te*), and the validation dataset (*Va*), which must contain some attack-free traffic and some labeled attacks (either as separate or interlaced instances).

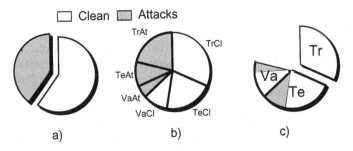

**Fig. 1.** Partitioning procedure: a) first step, b) second step, c) third step

## 4   A Method for Practical Database Partitioning

As mentioned in the previous section, three datasets (Tr, Te and Va) are going to be used, some parts with attacks and others without them. In the beginning we have a single traffic database sniffed from a real network, and hence, it may contain some attacks interlaced with attack-free traffic. At this point two main issues arise. The first one is how to label the attacks, and the second how to effectively divide the database

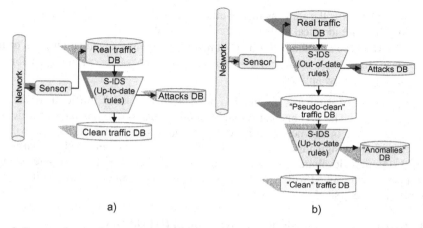

a)                                                          b)

**Fig. 2.** Proposed procedure to obtain suitable traffic databases: a) clean traffic and labeled attacks; b) clean traffic, labeled attacks and anomalous traffic

according to the already discussed requisites. The labeling process could be carried out by manually identifying the attacks in the database. However, this solution has two main drawbacks. First, it is almost unfeasible as the database has to be big enough to be representative. Second, it is an error prone method.

Therefore, in order to obtain the three desired datasets with their especial requirements, we propose a three-step procedure:

1. *Attack / normal classification.* First, we need to make a partition of the real traffic database to obtain clean (attack-free) traffic ($Cl$), and attack traffic ($At$) –Fig. 1.a –. To make this partition we could use a S-NIDS tool (Fig. 2.a), and assume that: (a) the clean traffic set is when said tool does not detect any attack, and (b) the attack traffic set is that for which said tool has detected some attack event. An arguable drawback is that we can not assure that the so-labeled clean database is indeed 100% attack-free. The main advantage of this procedure is that the classification is made automatically and error-free according to the attack ruleset considered by the S-IDS, while all known attacks are labeled properly if the ruleset is up to date.
2. *Training / test / validation partitioning.* Once the traffic instances are labeled as either attack or non-attack, the resulting clean traffic set is divided into three smaller databases according to some proportions (Fig. 1.b). The obtained datasets will be used for training ($TrCl$), testing ($TeCl$) and validating ($VaCl$) the system. After that, we operate in the same way and with the same proportions with the attack traffic set, thus obtaining $TrAt$, $TeAt$ and $VaAt$. As there is no need to train any attack model, the training attack partition, $TrAt$, will be useless.
3. *Merging and final partitioning.* Finally, the partitions for training, testing and validation are obtained as follows (Fig. 1.c):

   - The training dataset, $Tr$, is the training partition of the clean part: $Tr=TrCl$.
   - The testing database, $Te$, is obtained by merging the testing parts corresponding to clean and attack subsets: $Te=TeCl\cup TeAt$. As the proportion between the clean

set and *TeCl* is the same as that of attack set and *TeAt*, the relative sizes of *TeCl* and *TeAt* are identical to that in the original database.

- The validation database, *Va*, is obtained by merging the validation parts of the clean and attack subsets: $Va = VaCl \cup VaAt$. The same reasoning as for the testing database applies.

Despite this set of databases designed to have clean and attack traffic, there are still two open issues. The first one is that we have only clean traffic and attack traffic, but anomalous traffic is also needed. The term "anomalous" identifies traffic that will not be detected by a signature-based tool, but that should raise an A-NIDS alarm if a hybrid system is developed. A second issue concerns the fact that the sample size is a handicap in IDS trained with real traffic, since it is very difficult to have a good set of samples for every single type of attack.

### 4.1 Extension for Anomaly-Based Detection in Hybrid IDS

To solve the first issue point out above we propose to artificially create anomalous traffic according to the following methodology.

We thought on filtering the traffic twice (see Fig. 2.b). The first time an old set of rules of an S-NIDS tool is ran, thus detecting the attacks classified as such by said tool and rules. Two outputs are generated by this filter: attacks and "pseudo-clean" traffic. Obviously, this output is not real clean traffic in the sense defined in previous sections, because we used the signatures known some time ago instead of the newest ones. Then, we take said "pseudo-clean" traffic and filter it again using an up-to-date set of rules for the same tool. From this second filter we obtain two traffic subsets: new attacks, which will be used as "anomalous-traffic", and "clean-traffic".

Despite the premise that it is impossible to assure having clean traffic in a real traffic database, we assume that there are finally three sets of traffic: clean, anomalous and attacks. This assumption, although not real at the present time, allows the use of the database to train, test and validate the A-IDS module of a hybrid NIDS.

### 4.2 Improving the "Robustness" of the Datasets

In order to give response to the issue regarding the hypothetical small size of the training sample (see the last paragraph before subsection 4.1), we propose to use the well-known *leaving-k-out technique* [19]. This is a statistical method for reducing the error confidence interval of a classification procedure, when the size of the sample is small to be representative of all the number of possible classes. In other words, the leaving-k-out method can be interpreted as an attempt to increase the "robustness" of the estimated probability. The idea is to artificially increase the effective size of the data available for training and testing, by using every single data for both training and testing stages.

In a more formal way, for a given model and a sample size *n*, a classifier (or new model) is generated by using *(n-k)* cases or partitions, and tested with the remaining *k* cases. This can be repeated as many times as the number of combinations of *n-k* elements taken out of *n* elements, thus obtaining a different classifier each time. Thus, every element in the sample will be used as a test instance in some of the experiments, as well as a training instance in the remaining cases. The final results will be the

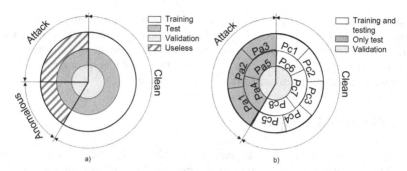

**Fig. 3.** Database partitions: a) for A-NIDS, and b) applying the leaving k-out technique in training and testing datasets

average of all the experiments. Therefore, the significance of the samples increases and the error tolerance decreases; i.e., the "robustness" of the whole process becomes higher.

Leaving-k-out not only improves the reliability of the results obtained during the evaluation of a system, but also allows regaining the up to now useless partitions for testing and validation (*see* Fig. 3.a and 3.b). This fact will be also of advantage to improve the representativeness of the sample.

To conclude this subsection, it is important to notice that the leaving-k-out method requires a high level of resources (both computational and storage-related). However, it is of application only during the training and testing processes, which can be carried out in lab conditions, with non real-time requirements.

### 4.3 Model Update

An underlying problem in hybrid NIDS deployment is related with the updates of both the signatures for the S-IDS module and the normality models for the A-IDS part. The update of signatures can be made by simply applying new up-to-date rules. However, updating models is a bit more complex, since it is necessary to re-train them. Nevertheless, this can be done if the newest and old rulesets are considered. To explain the point, consider three rulesets and the underlying philosophy in our hybrid NIDS deployment. The A-IDS part can become obsolete in some sense once the potential new attacks (detected as anomalies) are included in an updated ruleset of the S-IDS subsystem. This problem can be solved by shifting the rulesets used to classify the traffic: the up-to-date rules become the out-of-date rules, and the new rules become the up-to-date rules. By using this procedure, the A-IDS can be automatically adapted to the evolving context. Furthermore, it is necessary to incrementally add new data to the database, as, in any other case, the size of the anomaly-based partitions will decrease and the database itself can render obsolete.

The review of previous works in the literature deserves some comments. First, Mahoney and Chan already used a version of an S-IDS in their system LERAD to label attacks [20]. Nevertheless, we have gone one step further and used different versions of a S-IDS tool, not only for labeling attacks, but also for getting clean and anomalous traffic. Second, there exists a problem concerning the assumption of clean traffic from a real database. The lack of really clean traffic has been solved in LERAD by dividing the real traffic into 10 one-week periods, and testing each week after training with the previous week. An attack in the training dataset might mask a similar attack in the test dataset, but at least the first attack ought to be detected in the previous training/test pair. In our proposal, this problem is approached by the continuous update of the rules and the normality model.

## 5  A Practical Example

Beyond the specific A-NIDS approaches developed by the authors, this section describes a preliminary application of the proposed procedures for IDS assessment. Two traffic databases have been captured in both typical scenarios: the input link to a DMZ enterprise (ENTDB) segment, and the input link to a university (UNIDB). Hence, we are working with real data taken from real environments. At this point, we are not concerned with the size and representativeness of the databases, as the example is just oriented to check the proposed procedures for partitioning them.

The traffic data has been captured as-is (*tcpdump* format) by using Snort [21] and tcpdump as the sensing units. On the other hand, the NIDS of choice for filtering attacks is Snort, which simplifies the operation because the same tool can be used to capture packets, filter them and label those classified as attacks.

The sensors have been deployed at the access router for ENTDB and in a computer attached to the network, operating in promiscuous mode, for UNIDB. The main statistics of the captured data are shown in Table 1.

**Table 1.** Traffic classification using different VRT Snort rules

| Database | ENTDB | | UNIDB | |
|---|---|---|---|---|
| # of total packets | 3107295 | | 5439014 | |
| VRT rules used | VRT1 | VRT1 and VRT2 | VRT1 | VRT1 and VRT2 |
| Attack packets | 4154 | 4154 | 12375 | 12375 |
| Anomalous packets | - | 50 | - | 58 |
| Clean traffic | 3103091 | | 5426581 | |

**Table 2.** Sets of VRT to be used with Snort

| Feature\Rules | VRT1 | VRT2 |
|---|---|---|
| Date of release | 07/27/05 | 03/29/06 |
| # of rules | 3191 | 4392 |

**Table 3.** Final partition sizes without leaving-k-out method

| | Tr | | | Te | | | Va | | |
|---|---|---|---|---|---|---|---|---|---|
| | *TrCl* | *TrAt* | *TrAn* | *TeCl* | *TeAt* | *TeAn* | *VACl* | *VaAt* | *VaAn* |
| **ENTDB** | 930927 | 1246 | 15 | 1241237 | 1662 | 20 | 930927 | 1246 | 15 |
| **UNIDB** | 1627974 | 3712 | 17 | 2170633 | 4951 | 24 | 1627974 | 3712 | 17 |

As proposed, the first step to partition both databases is to classify the packets as normal (clean), attack or anomalous. For this, we need various signature files or rules for the S-NIDS (Snort in our case). In this line, two VRT (Vulnerability Research Team) rulesets, each of them corresponding to a different date, have been used. The details of the rulesets are shown in Table 2.

From the rulesets, the database is partitioned according to the three steps described in Section 4:

- Step 1: *Normal / anomalous / attack traffic partitioning*. The classification has been carried out by considering VRT1 (old rules) followed by VRT2 (up-to-date rules). The results obtained are shown in Table 1 too.
- Step 2: *Training / test / validation partitioning*. We chose to use 30% of the data for training, 40% for testing, and the remaining 30% for validation. Each normal, attack and anomalous sets are split in this way, yielding 9 subsets. Thus, only a 30% of the attacks and 30% of the anomalies will be dismissed (*TrAt and TrAn*). The corresponding statistics are shown in Table 3.
- Step 3: *Merging*. The validation sets (*VaCl, VaAt* and *VaAn*) are merged, as explained in Section 4 to obtain the final partition for validation, *Va*. On the other hand, the clean sets (*TrCl* and *TeCl*), the attack sets (*TrAt* and *TeAt*) and the anomalous sets (*TrAn* and *TeAn*) are also merged in the training and test sets.

At this point, the three obtained sets (*Cl, At, An*) can be divided into $n$ parts each to deal with the application of the leaving-k-out technique to train the normality model. As a mere example, let's imagine that we have divided the *Cl, At* and *An* sets into 5 parts each, and the leaving-2-out technique is applied. That means: we train the model with 3 parts of the *Cl* set, and test it with the remaining 2 parts of the *Cl*, with 2 parts of the *At* and 2 parts of the *An*. Then, we repeat the experiment the number of combinations of 3 elements taken out of 5 elements, thus obtaining a different classifier each time. Through this process, the *TrAt* and *TrAn* sets have been reused, whilst the final result will be the average of all the experiments. The only thing that it rests to do is validating the model, for which the *Va* set is used.

To conclude this Section as it was started, it should be noticed that none A-NIDS model has been developed. This fact is due to the nature of the available databases: neither ENTDB nor UNIDB are suitable, as concluded from its statistics.

# 6  Conclusions

A set of proposals oriented to normalize IDS assessment has been presented in this paper. The work is focused on the management of the traffic databases used to train, test, and validate this type of systems. In special, the authors propose and discuss a method to automatically prepare the database to accurately train, test and evaluate hybrid (signature+anomaly-based) NIDS'. The database partitioning involves three steps to obtain various datasets: normal/attack traffic, train/test/validation set, and merging and final set.

Furthermore, we have dealt with some practical problems with the proposal. First, the acquisition of anomalous traffic, which has been solved through the artificial generation of anomalous traffic by using two different rulesets of Snort. Second, the significativeness of the sample can be improved by considering the well-known *leaving-k-out* scheme.

We have also proposed the adaptation of the system, taking into account the evolution of the new reported attacks. Hence, we take advantage of the updates of the rulesets of Snort to apply the newest set of rules to our traffic with the aim of creating new partitions for clean, anomalous and attack traffic. In the same line, we propose to re-estimate the model by including new up-to-date traffic to the databases.

At this moment, our group is working in obtaining better traffic databases to develop the proposals about hybrid NIDS' and their assessment in a more effective way. On the other hand, we are also working on extending the proposals to HIDS systems. All these actions will positively contribute to the IDS technologies, thus improving current information and communication infrastructures.

**Acknowledgments.** This work has been partially supported by the Spanish Government through MEC (Project TSI2005-08145-C02-02, FEDER funds 70%).

# References

1. Bologna S. & Setola R.: The need to improve local self-awareness in CIP/CIIP. In *Proceedings of the First International Workshop on Critical Infrastructure Protection* (IWCIP), 2005.
2. Lopez J., Montenegro J.A., Roman R.: Service-Oriented Security Architecture for CII based on Sensor Networks. In *Proceedings of the Second International Workshop on Security, Privacy and Trust in Pervasive and Ubiquitous Computing* (SecPerU), 2006.
3. CERT coordination Center statistics, (2006). http://www.cert.org/stats/cert_stats.html
4. Anderson, JP. Computer security threat monitoring and surveillance. *Technical report - Fort Washington*. (1980)
5. Axelsson, S. Intrusion Detection Systems: A Survey and Taxonomy. *Technical Report 99-15, Depart. of Computer Engineering, Chalmers University*, march (2000)
6. Kabiri P., Ghorbani A. "Research on Intrusion detection and response: A survey". International Journal on Network Security. Vol. 1 N°2, pp84-102. (2005)
7. Porras, A., and Valdes, A. Live traffic analysis of tcp/ip gateways. Proc. *ISOC Symp.on Network and Distributed Systems Security (NDSS) San Diego, CA. Internet society*. (1998)
8. Estevez-tapiador, J.M. *Detección de intrusiones en redes basadas en anomalías mediante técnicas de modelado de protocolos*. PhD Thesis University of Granada. (2004)
9. McHugh, J. The 1998 Lincoln Laboratory IDS Evaluation. A critique. *In RAID 2000*, LNCS 1907, pp 145-161. (2000)
10. Athanasiades, N., Abler, R., Levine, J., Owen, H., and Riley, G. 2003. Intrusion detection testing and benchmarking methodologies. In *proceedings 1st IEEE International Workshop on Information Assurance (IWIA)*, pp. 63-72. IEEE Computer society Press. (2003)
11. Pukenza, N., Zhang, K., Chung, M., Mukherjee, B., and Olsson, R. A methodology for testing intrusion detection systems. *IEEE Software. 14(5):43-51.* (1997)
12. Lippmann, R., Haines, J., Fried, D., Korba, J., and Das, K. Analysis and results of the 1999 DARPA off-Line Intrusion Detection Evaluation. In *Computer Networks*34(4) 579-595. (2000)
13. Mahoney M. & Chan P.K. An analysis of the 1999 DARPA/Lincoln Laboratory evaluation Data for Network Anomaly Detection. In *Florida Tech. tech report* CS-2003-02. (2003)

14. Rossey, L., Rabek, J., Cunnigham, R., Fried, R., Lippmann, R., and Zissmann, R. Lariat: Lincoln adaptable real-time information assurance test-bed. In *International Sypnotium on Recent Advances in Intrusion Detection (RAID)* (2001)

15. Antonatos, S., Anagnostakis, K., and Markatos, E. Generating Realistic Workloads for Network Intrusion Detection Systems. In Proceedings *of the 4th International Workshop on Software Performance (WOSP).* (2004)

16. Danzing, P., Mogul, J., Paxson, V., and Schwartz, M. The internet traffic archive. http://ita.ee.lbl.gov/html/traces.html

17. Davison, B.D. Web Caching Resources. (1999). http://www.web-caching.com/

18. Fan, J., Xu, J., Ammar, M. H., and Moon, S. B. Prefix-preserving IP address anonymization: measurement-based security evaluation and a new cryptography-based scheme. *Comput. Networks* 46, 2 (2004), 253-272.

19. Duda, R., and Hart, P: Pattern Classification and Scene Analysis. John Wiley and Sons, 1973

20. Mahoney M. & Chan P. Learning Rules for anomaly Detection of Hostile Network Traffic. *Proceedings of the 3rd IEEE ICDM* (2003)

21. Roesch, M. Snort–Lightweight Intrusion Detection for Networks. *Proc. USENIX Lisa* (1999)

# High-Speed Intrusion Detection in Support of Critical Infrastructure Protection

Salvatore D'Antonio[1], Francesco Oliviero[2], and Roberto Setola[3]

[1] Lab. ITeM - Consorzio Interuniversitario Nazionale per l'Informatica - CINI
[2] Dipartimento di Informatica e Sistemistica - University of Napoli Federico II
[3] Complex Systems & Security Lab - University CAMPUS Bio-Medico of Roma

**Abstract.** Telecommunication network plays a fundamental role in the management of critical infrastructures since it is largely used to transmit control information among the different elements composing the architecture of a critical system. The health of a networked system strictly depends on the security mechanisms that are implemented in order to assure the correct operation of the communication network. For this reason, the adoption of an effective network security strategy is seen as an important and necessary task of a global methodology for critical infrastructure protection. In this paper we present 2 contributions. First, we present a distributed architecture that aims to secure the communication network upon which the critical infrastructure relies. This architecture is composed of an intrusion detection system (IDS) which is built on top of a customizable flow monitor. Second, we propose an innovative method to extrapolate real-time information about user behavior from network traffic. This method consists in monitoring traffic flows at different levels of granularity in order to discover ongoing attacks.

**Keywords:** critical infrastructure protection (CIP), critical information infrastructure protection (CIIP), intrusion detection, flow monitoring, security management, SCADA.

## 1 Introduction

Many daily operations currently rely on services provided through systems generally indicated as critical infrastructures [1] [2] [3], such as electric grid, oil and natural gas production, transportation and distribution, water supply networks. An emerging common feature of these infrastructures is their reliance on the widespread use of distributed information, communication and control systems, both to provide more efficient and innovative services, and to meet novel user requirements and expectations. Indeed, the operation and management of these infrastructures depend more and more on the existence and correctness of the communication network.

In order to manage, control and supervise such complex, highly non-linear infrastructures, targeted control systems, called SCADA (Supervisory Control And Data Acquisition), are currently used. A SCADA system is generally composed of a master station, where system intelligence is concentrated, and a large

J. Lopez (Ed.): CRITIS 2006, LNCS 4347, pp. 222–234, 2006.

number of RTUs (Remote Terminal Units), which are geographically distributed. RTUs are equipped with both sensors capable to gather information about the status of the infrastructure and actuators. Data gathered by RTUs are transmitted to the master station, where data analysis and integration are performed both to get a global view of the infrastructure status and to define appropriate commands to be sent to actuators. RTUs communicate with the master station by sending and receiving it short control messages.

Digital information gained more and more importance for infrastructure operation, as a result, what we might call a "cyber component" of each critical infrastructure grew, thus, giving rise to the need to integrate and make interoperable the different elements that compose information systems. These cyber components are connected in complex ways and represent the information infrastructure on which the critical system relies. The increasing success of information and communication technologies, together with the progressive disuse of dedicated communication networks are bringing a new way of controlling and managing critical infrastructures, which are currently organized as strictly connected, albeit different, elements of a single system rather than as autonomous entities to be appropriately integrated.

Control systems for critical infrastructures are rapidly moving from dedicated and proprietary solutions towards IP-based integrated frameworks made of off-the-shelf products. Unfortunately, this trend brings with it security issues since in the new scenario SCADA systems are exposed to cyber-related threats.

While physical security of critical infrastructure components (including the control system) as well as protection from direct cyber attacks (e.g., hacking) have been already investigated [4] [5], little attention has been devoted to analyzing vulnerabilities resulting from the use of commercial communication networks. As stated in [6] terrorists might attack the communication network through physical or cyber actions in order to undermine the capability of controlling the critical system [7]. Therefore, new kinds of events undermine the health of networked critical infrastructures: (i) cyber-attacks, including specific actions aiming to disrupt communication services as well as effects of wide spectrum attacks to the computer equipment devoted to control the lifeline system, and (ii) failures in the information exchange due to problems regarding the communication network which connects the control system to the remote units. Delayed or errored information can bring to situations where incorrect actions are undertaken.

The remainder of the paper is structured as follows. In section 2 we present an integrated framework capable of protecting the network by following an intrusion detection strategy based on traffic flow monitoring. Section 3 illustrates the use of data mining techniques for the definition of classification criteria. In section 4 an innovative approach for real-time traffic analysis is illustrated. It is shown how data coming from a flexible flow monitoring system can be effectively analyzed to identify ongoing attacks. Related work is presented in section 5. Finally, section 6 provides some concluding remarks, together with information concerning our future work in this field.

## 2    A Component-Based Framework for Intrusion Detection

The most common security tools are firewalls. However, such tools, albeit easy to configure and use, are not enough to globally protect a system from malicious activities [8]. Basing one's own site's security on the deployment of these instruments relies on the idea that intrusion prevention will suffice in efficiently assuring data availability, confidentiality and integrity. Interestingly enough intrusions will sooner or later happen, despite the security policy a network administrator deploys. Based on this assumption, researchers started to develop instruments capable of detecting successful intrusions and, in some cases, trace the path leading to the attack source. This is a more pessimistic, though much more realistic, way to look at the problem of network security.

Intrusion detection is the art of detecting inappropriate, incorrect or anomalous activity within a system, be it a single host or a whole network. Generally, an Intrusion Detection System analyzes a data source and, after preprocessing the input, lets a detection engine decide, based on a set of classification criteria, whether the analyzed input instance is normal or anomalous, given a suitable behavior model. In this section we propose an Intrusion Detection System capable of extracting from network traffic the "user behavior", which will serve as input to a detection engine. The extraction process is carried out through a careful analysis of the network traffic. Obviously, this process is more complicated in a real-time scenario, where the user behavior computation has to be done as quickly as possible in order to reduce the packets loss. Once the user behavior has been determined, it is employed to define the set of classification criteria used by the detection engine to identify anomalous activities.

Starting from these considerations, it is possible to identify two main challenges in IDS development:

- the real-time extraction of the user behavior from the network traffic;
- the definition of a set of user behavior model to be used in the detection process.

We propose a distributed architecture that aims to address these issues. The overall architecture is composed of two parts. The first is the data mining process, which is in charge of extracting behavioral models from pre-elaborated network traffic, and consists of a database of labeled traffic patterns and a data mining algorithm. The second is the real-time intrusion detection system which analyzes and classifies network traffic based on the models inferred (Fig. 1). The proposed real-time IDS architecture consists, in turn, of three components: a *sniffer*, a *processor*, and a *classifier*. The sniffer is the lowest component of the architecture. This module, which is directly connected to the network infrastructure, captures packets passing on the wire. The sniffer also decodes the raw packets and translates them in human-readable data. The processor elaborates the packet captured by the sniffer in order to extract the set of features. The main issue of the feature computation process concerns the need to keep up-to-date information about the current connection, as well as other active sessions. A

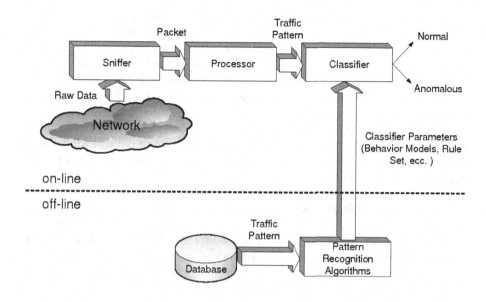

**Fig. 1.** The reference network security framework

representation of the current network status has to be stored in order to identify statistical relationships among active network connections. The classifier is the core of the architecture. This component analyzes the current connection features and classifies them. Based on the misuse detection approach, the classification process uses a set of rules extracted by exploiting data mining algorithms.

The off-line data mining task is executed on a data set in order to extract a number of rules, which will be used by a real-time classification process. Finally, this pre-computed network data will be compared to real-time network traffic to discover ongoing attacks. The data mining technique and the method for real-time traffic analysis will be described in next two sections, respectively.

## 3    Definition of Classification Criteria Based on Data Mining Techniques

Our intrusion detection system can be classified as rule-based, i.e. the classification model is coded by means of a set of rules. Each rule is divided in two logical sections: the *rule header*, and the *rule option*. The rule header is a classification filter which contains information about the rule's action, i.e. what to do when the packet matches the rule, protocol, source and destination IP, source and destination port. Instead, the rule option section provides alert message, and information about patterns to search within the payload or no payload-data, like statistical parameters, to check. Unfortunately, the definition of a rule for every attack is not an efficient solution. On one hand, this approach is not able to detect novel attack patterns, which is mandatory in a critical network system; on the other hand, the definition of new attacks negatively effects both the computation load and the average time required to analyze every single packet. In order to solve these problems data mining techniques can be adopted.

Data mining is part of a more complex KDD (Knowledge Discovery in Databases) process consisting of data analysis and discovery algorithms applied to a database in order to extract high level information — the patterns or the models — able to describe a data subset. The models can be applied to unknown data values in order to predict the right class which they belong to. As we stated in the previous section, data mining processes operate on a set of data which has been organized in a suitable fashion (e.g. all the data is identified by a label which explicitly specifies the category they belong to).

Among the numerous data mining algorithms, we have adopted the *classification* method. This process maps items from a data set into one of several pre-defined categories. The algorithm generally produces a set of classifiers in the form of either a decision tree or a set of rules. In an intrusion detection scenario, it is possible to apply a classification algorithm to a set of audit data which has been properly labeled either *normal* or *attack*, in order to instruct a set of classifiers on how to distinguish a malicious behavior from a normal one. The traffic data item can be represented in a vectorial space. The classifiers partition this space in a normal region and an attack region, based either on the decision tree or on the rules set.

In order to implement an efficient classifier, it is important to define a suitable set of parameters, which have to be extracted from the network traffic stored in the database and represent the summarization of the user behavior. The greater the capability of the set of features to discriminate among different categories, the better the classifier. There are three levels at which feature sets may be defined:

- The set of features may be defined by the single packet captured from the network; although this set is easy to compute, it is not able to detect all the potential attack types.
- A set of features may be defined by the entire session, from which the packet belongs to; this definition is linked to the fact that some intrusions may be realized by means of a sequence of packets belonging to either the same connection or different connections.
- The set of features may be defined by a statistical analysis of the relationships between the current session and other sessions; this is needed to capture intrusions that affect the correlation among different sessions.

The better the capability of the features set to summarize temporal and statistical relationships between different sessions, the greater the computational load associated with the on-line traffic analysis.

In our IDS solution pattern recognition, algorithms are implemented to extract classification criteria from a data-base of pre-elaborated connection features. Details about such algorithm are given in [9].

# 4  An Innovative Approach for Real-Time Traffic Analysis

As stated in the previous section, in order to improve the classification process it is mandatory for an IDS to extract from network traffic a set of parameters describing statistical relationships between different sessions. To accomplish such task, a flow monitor component is required. Usually monitoring techniques classify packets by grouping them into *flows*. In general, a traffic flow is referred to as "a set of packets passing at a network point during a time interval and having common properties". This definition is general and flexible and allows even a single packet, or a few packets to be considered as a flow. A traffic pattern extraction process can take advantage of the possibility of defining a flow in flexible way. This process sets the level of granularity related to the flow definition with respect to its requirements.

A user behavior can be described by a set of flow *metrics*. These connection features are measured by analyzing the properties of the observed packets. According to these assumptions, we propose a monitoring system framework, called DiFMon (Distributed Flow Monitoring) [10], which is the IDS component responsible for packet capturing and flow information exporting. This system captures packets from the network, associates them to a flow by enabling a customizable flow definition, and updates data records containing flow-related metrics. Measured data are, then, collected to make them available to the behavior classification process. The DiFMon architecture is composed of the following components:

1. *meter*, captures the packets from a network interface, or equivalently from a trace file, assigns each of them a flow identification number, the so-called *flow id*, and passes them to the next component, i.e. the flow cache;
2. *flow cache*, stores and updates data records devoted to the metrics related to the flows observed. The main issue concerning this task is represented by both the high number of flows and the short packet inter-arrival times on high speed links. This implies that the time interval spent to search for the record associated with a captured packet is often longer than the packet inter-arrival time. For this reason, we adopted a distributed approach by introducing multiple flow-caches responsible for managing flow records. The flow cache is also in charge of exporting flow information to a further component, i.e. the collector.
3. *collector*, gathers measured data from the flow caches and makes them available to applications.

Traffic flows which are of interest to an IDS can be classified in two main categories: fine-grain flows and coarse grain flows. Fine-grain flows refer to traffic generated by a single user or a small set of users. Monitoring this fine-grain flow aims to detect specific attacks. On the other hand, coarse-grain flows transport information describing network context and, then, are analyzed with the aim to identify largely distributed attacks, such as a Distributed Denial of Service (DDoS). This classification drives the metric definition process in the sense that depending on the attacks to identify the IDS requires monitoring systems to measure specific metrics on a certain class of flows. We represent the vector of fine-grain metrics $\overline{M}_f$, and the vector of coarse-grain metrics $\overline{M}_c$. For each flow the vector $\overline{M}_f$ or the vector $\overline{M}_c$ is provided according to the flow granularity.

Starting from these vectors, the intrusion detection system extracts the "context", i.e. a synthetic view of the overall network.

Therefore, the development of an intrusion detection system requires the implementation of a *context extraction algorithm* whose inputs are vectors $\overline{M}_f$ and $\overline{M}_c$ and whose output is vector $\overline{M}_w$ (Fig. 2).

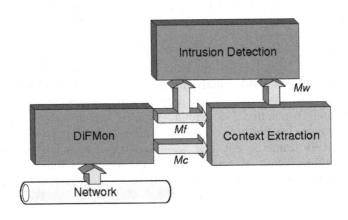

**Fig. 2.** The intrusion detection model

$\overline{M}_w$ and $\overline{M}_f$ are inputs to an intrusion detection algorithm that checks whether the analyzed flow is an attack or not. In order to give a better idea of the proposed approach we provide an example of $\overline{M}_f$, $\overline{M}_c$ and $\overline{M}_w$ in a particular attack scenario.

Let us suppose we are interested in detecting denial of service attacks against a certain server. We define two kinds of flows: a fine-grain bidirectional flow, which is identified by the 4-ple (source IP address, source port, destination IP address, destination port), and a coarse-grain flow which is identified by the fact that the destination IP address of the flow packets is the server's one. The metrics $\overline{M}_f$, computed on fine-grain flows, are the number of bytes and the byte rate. On the other side, vector $\overline{M}_c$ is computed on coarse-grain flows and contains the number of bytes and the number of packets. With reference to our example, a possible context detection algorithm performs the following tasks: it can determine whether the server bandwidth utilization is anomalous and compute the percentages of received bytes as well as of flows per server port number. This information is reported in $\overline{M}_w$.

Detecting anomalous bandwidth utilization requires the computation of daily statistics. As the usage of a server can vary over the 24 hours of a day, the algorithm produces historical data and compares it with data contained in $\overline{M}_c$ to detect anomalies in the server bandwidth utilization. Vector $\overline{M}_w$ indicates whether the server bandwidth utilization is anomalous and specifies the distribution of the port utilization in terms of flows and bytes. It also describes the overall context and drives the intrusion detection algorithm to identify malicious flows. Indeed, the intrusion detection algorithm analyzes the context vector and decides whether every single fine-grain flow has to be checked to detect specific attacks. For instance, the intrusion detection algorithm might perform a deeper analysis by measuring the byte rate related to the single fine-grain flows. If multiple fine-grain flows having the server's address as destination are characterized by a small value of byte rate, then such situation might be hiding an attack; therefore, in such case the IDS should trigger an immediate counteraction on the network.

## 5  Related Work

In this section we present related work on intrusion detection systems, on monitoring techniques, as well as, on the integration between intrusion detection methodologies and flow monitoring systems.

### 5.1  Intrusion Detection

Intrusion Detection Systems can be grouped into two main categories: *Network-based Intrusion Detection Systems*(N-IDS), and *Host-based Intrusion Detection Systems* (H-IDS). The classification depends on the information sources analyzed to detect an intrusive activity. N-IDSs analyze packets captured directly from the network. NetSTAT [11] is usually classified as a network-based system. In this work the authors introduce a new network-based intrusion detection approach where network attacks are modeled as state transition diagrams.

On the other hand, H-IDSs focus on a single host's activity: the system protects the host by directly analyzing either audit trails or system logs produced by the host's operating system. NIDES [12] and DERBI [13] belong to this category. In particular, NIDES monitors the computer users to detect unauthorized application execution, by examining audit trail information using a non-parametric statistical component as well as a rule-based component. DERBI, instead, is designed to analyze a computer's file system after an intrusion happens, to detect information useful in determining whether there was an attack and what happened. The authors suggest to use DERBI in conjunction with a traditional real-time IDS.

Depending on the detection technique employed, Intrusion Detection Systems can be classified as belonging to two main groups: *anomaly detection* and *misuse detection*, also known as *signature detection* [14]. Both this techniques depend on the existence of a reliable characterization of what is *normal* and what is not, in a particular networking scenario. More precisely, anomaly detection techniques base their evaluations on a model of what is normal, and classify as anomalous all the events that fall outside such a model. Indeed, if an anomalous behavior is recognized, this does not necessarily imply that an attack activity has occurred:

only few anomalies can actually be classified as attempts to compromise the security of the system. Thus, a relatively serious problem exists with anomaly detection techniques which generate a great amount of false alarms. On the other hand, the main advantage of anomaly detection is its intrinsic ability to discover novel attack types.

In [15] [16], two examples of anomaly detection systems are presented. In particular, in [15] the authors propose a methodology to detect and classify network anomalies by means of analysis of traffic feature distributions. They adopt *entropy* as a metric to capture the degree of dispersal or concentration of the computed distributions. NETAD [16] detects anomalies based on analysis of packet structure; in particular, the systems flags suspicious packets based on unusual byte values in network packets.

The most known open-source signature-based intrusion detection systems are SNORT [17] and BRO [18]. These systems allow the user to define a customized set of rules in order to codify specific types of attacks. P-BEST [19] is a signature-based intrusion detection system able to detect computer and network misuse by means of a rule translator, a library of run-time routines, and a set of garbage collection routines.

Recently, many research groups have focused on the definition of systems able to automatically build a set of models to be used both in anomaly and misuse detection. Data mining techniques are frequently used to audit data in order to compute specific behavior models (MADAM ID [20], ADAM [21]).

## 5.2 Monitoring

There exists a extensive literature on flow monitoring. We present some recently proposed architectures designed according to a distributed approach.

A monitoring architecture has been proposed by the IETF working group, called IPFIX (IP Flow Information eXport) [22]. This group originated in 2003. They goal is to define an architecture, as well as protocols, to let different monitoring applications interoperate. This architecture consists of two modules: the *IPFIX device* and the *collector*.

The IPFIX device captures packets and measures the flow of data. It is comprised of three components:

1. the *metering process*, captures packets from an observation point and produces the flow records, i.e. the data structures containing flow statistics;
2. the *flow recording process*, stores all the flow records sent by one or more metering processes.
3. the *exporting process* sends all the measured data to the collector.

The collector is the module which collects all the information sent by the exporting processes, stores the data, and sends it to the applications.

In [23] the authors propose a distributed framework for IP flow measurement, which is composed of the following entities:

1. a *distribution device* which forwards packets to multiple capturing devices;
2. a *capturing device* which identifies packets that correspond to flow definitions and computes statistics. Statistics are periodically sent to a manager device which returns flow definition updates;
3. a *manager device* which stores data received from multiple capturing devices, obtains flow definitions from user interfaces and sends it to the capturing devices.

In [24], the authors present a monitoring system for distributed network analysis in high-speed networks. The architecture employs standard protocols such as those proposed by IPFIX, PSAMP (Packet SAMPling) and NSIS (Next Steps In Signaling) working groups.

We remark that none of the above architectures allow defining metrics in a flexible way. They all rely on a rather static definition of the parameters to be measured. The architecture we presented in the paper, on the contrary, has been designed at the outset with the aim of enabling customized definitions of both metrics and traffic flows.

### 5.3   Monitoring and Intrusion Detection

Next we present some approaches that aim to ensure network security by exploiting traffic monitoring information.

In [25] and [26], the authors describe how to correlate netflow system and network views for intrusion detection. Their approach is human-driven, since they propose to use visualization tools in order to obtain useful information for security purposes. This approach demonstrates how data collected by flow monitoring systems can be used in the context of intrusion detection.

In [27] and [28], data coming from both network monitoring and system logs are correlated in order to detect potential attacks. The authors prove that using data from more sources increases IDS performance. However, system logs are not always available, as in the case of servers owned by Internet providers.

With respect to such approaches, our IDS solution presents some innovative elements concerning the possibility of detecting intrusive activities on the basis of flow-related information. As illustrated in section 4, the monitoring system supporting the detection engine is able to collect real-time information on flows through a flexible definition of co-related metrics. This aspect is of paramount importance since the IDS surely benefits from the availability of measurement data which has been collected with the aim of extracting traffic features useful to detect specific malicious behaviours. Furthermore, the definition of the flows to be monitored is customizable according to the requirements imposed by the Intrusion Detection System. Such capabilities allow gathering information on traffic passing into the monitored network at different levels of granularity and, then, make the analysis of network status more effective.

## 6   Conclusions

The use of communication networks to transport information between remote systems devoted to control critical infrastructures impose the definition of a new network security approach. In order to adopt appropriate solutions for the protection of the networked systems, a clear identification of the interdependencies between such systems and the underlying network has to be done.

The identification of these relationships, which allows for the prevention of dangerous cascade effects, implies the classification of both the transmitted information and the protocols used by the networked control systems.

To effectively detect malicious activities and intrusions, we propose a security approach that relies on an innovative method that extrapolates information about users' behavior from network traffic. This information can only be retrieved by carefully analyzing network traffic patterns, which are highly dependent on the flow of packets through the network. As a results, monitoring system should be capable of keeping track of traffic flows at a level of granularity which is dynamically configurable according to specific security requirements.

The combined use of fine-grain and course-grain data provided by the flow monitoring system improves the capability of the security framework to discover potential attacks within network traffic.

As a future work, we will first refine the integration between the monitoring system and intrusion detection system. By defining appropriate standard interfaces between this components, we aim to achieve let the monitoring system become general enough to be easily exploitable by any upper layer module needing customized information of users behavior and context. Finally, in order to make the proposed architecture effectively deployable, it is necessary to assess the scalability of the integrated framework we design and implement.

# References

1. Dunn, M., Wigert, I., *An Inventory and Analysis of Protection Policies in Fourteen Countries*, International CIIP (Critical Information Infrastructure Protection) Handbook 2004, edited by A. Wenger and J. Metzger, ETH Swiss Federal Institute fo Technology Zurich, 2004.
2. U.S. Government, *The National Strategy for The Physical Protection of Critical Infrastructures and Key Assets,*. Washington, USA: The White House, Feb. 2003.
3. E.U. Commission, *Green Paper on a European Programme for Critical Infrastructure Protection COM(2005)576*, Brussels, 2005.
4. Byres, E., Lowe, J., *The Myths and Facts behind Cyber Security Risks for Industrial Control Systems*, British Columbia Institute of Technology
5. Lavalle, L., Balducelli, C., Vicoli, G., *Anomaly Detection Approach to Safeguard Critical Infrastructures: A Knowledge Engineering Process on a SCADA Case Study*, in Proceedings of Complex Network and Infrastructure Protection (CNIP'06), March 2006.
6. Communication from the Commission to the Council and the European Parliament *Critical Infrastructure Protection in the fight against terrorism COM (704)2004*, Brussels, October 2004.
7. Shea, D. A., *Critical Infrastructure: Control Systems and the Terrorist Threat*, in Report for Congress RL31534. The Library of Congress, Febraury 2003

8. Davis, P., *Abuse and Misuse of Firewalls in SCADA and Control Systems Environments*, in Proceedings of Complex Network and Infrastructure Protection (CNIP'06), March 2006.
9. Esposito, M., Mazzariello, C., Oliviero, F., Romano, S.P., Sansone, C., *Evaluating Pattern Recognition Techniques in Intrusion Detection Systems*, in Proceedings of 5th Workshop on Pattern Recognition in Information Systems (PRIS '05), May 2005.
10. D'Antonio, S., Mazzariello, C., Oliviero, F., Salvi, D., *A distributed multi-purpose IP flow monitor*, in Proceedings of 3rd International Workshop on Internet Performance, Simulation, Monitoring and Measurement (IPS-MoMe '05), March 2005.
11. Vigna, G., Kemmerer, R., *Netstat: a network based intrusion detection system*, Journal of Computer Security, 7(1), 1999.
12. Anderson, D., *Detecting usual program behavior using the statistical component of the next-generation intrusion detection expert system (nides)*, Technical report, Computer Science Laboratory, 1995.
13. Tyson, M., *Derbi: Diagnosys explanation and recovery from computer break-ins*, Technical report, SRI International, 2000.
14. Rebecca Gurley Bace, *Intrusion Detection*, Macmillan Technical Publishing, January 2000.
15. Lakhina, A., Crovella, M., Diot, C., *Mining anomalies using traffic feature distributions*, in Proceedings of ACM SIGCOMM '05, August 2005.
16. Matthew Vincent Mahoney, *Network traffic anomaly detection based on packet bytes*, in Proceedings of ACM SAC 03, 2003.
17. Baker, A. R., Caswell, B., Poor, M., *Snort 2.1 Intrusion Detection - Second Edition*, Syngress, 2004.
18. Vern Paxson and Brian Terney, *Bro reference manual*, 2004
19. Lindqvist, U., Porras, P., A., *Detecting computer and network misuse through the production-based expert system toolset (p-best)*, in Proceedings of the 1999 IEEE Symposium on Security and Privacy, pages 146-161, Oakland, California, May 1999.
20. Wenke Lee, W., Stolfo, S. J., *A framework for constructing features and models for intrusion detection systems*, ACM Transactions on Information and System Security (TISSEC), 3(4):227261, November 2000.
21. Barbara, D., Couto, J., Jajodia, S., Popyack, L., Wu, N., *Adam: Detecting intrusion by data mining*, in Proceedings of the Workshop on Information Assurance and Security, 2001.
22. Sadasivan, G., Brownlee, N., Claise, B., Quittek, J., *Ipfix working group internet draft, architecture model for ip flow information export*, Internet draft, IETF, January 2005.
23. Kitatsuji, Y., Yamazaki, K., *A distributed real-time tool for ip-flow measurement*, in Proceedings of the 2004 International Symposium on Applications and the Internet, 2004.
24. Falko Dressler, F.,Carle, G., *History - high speed network monitoring and analysis*, in Proceedings of 24th IEEE Conference on Computer Communications (IEEE INFOCOM 2005), March 2005.
25. Abad, C., Li Y., Lakkaraju, K., Yin, X., Yurcik, W., *Correlation between netflow system and network views for intrusion detection*, in Proceedings of Workshop on Link Analysis, Counter-terrorism, and Privacy held in conjunction with SDM 2004.

26. Yin, X., Yurcik, W., Treaster, M., Li, Y., Lakkaraju, K., *Visflowconnect: netflow visualizations of link relationships for security situational awareness*, in Proceedings of the 2004 ACM Workshop on Visualization and Data Mining for Computer Security, pages 26-34, ACM Press, 2004.
27. Abad, C., Taylor, J., Sengul, C., Yurcik, W., Zhou, Y., Rowe, K., *Log correlation for intrusion detection: A proof of concept*, in Proceedings of the 19th Annual Computer Security Applications Conference (ACSAC), 2003.
28. Li, Z., Taylor, J., Partridge, E., Zhou, Y., Yurcik, W., Abad, C., Barlow, J., Rosendale, J., *Uclog: A unified, correlated logging architecture for intrusion detection*, in Proceedings of the 12th International Conference on Telecommunication Systems, Modeling and Analysis (ICTSM), 2004.

# Rational Choice of Security Measures Via Multi-parameter Attack Trees

Ahto Buldas[1,2,3,*], Peeter Laud[1,2], Jaan Priisalu[4],
Märt Saarepera[5], and Jan Willemson[1,2,**]

[1] Cybernetica, Akadeemia tee 21, Tallinn, Estonia
[2] University of Tartu, Liivi 2, Tartu, Estonia
{ahto.buldas,peeter_l,jan}@ut.ee
[3] Tallinn University of Technology, Raja 15, Tallinn, Estonia
[4] Hansapank, Liivalaia 8, Tallinn, Estonia
jaan.priisalu@hansa.ee
[5] Independent researcher
marts@neoteny.com

**Abstract.** We present a simple risk-analysis based method for studying the security of institutions against rational (gain-oriented) attacks. Our method uses a certain refined form of attack-trees that are used to estimate the cost and the success probability of attacks. We use elementary game theory to decide whether the system under protection is a realistic target for gain-oriented attackers. Attacks are considered unlikely if their cost is not worth their benefits for the attackers. We also show how to decide whether the investments into security are economically justified. We outline the new method and show how it can be used in practice by going through a realistic example.

## 1 Introduction

Rapid growth of society's dependence on computers and the Internet has drawn attention to the vulnerability of this technical infrastructure. Increasing numbers of IT security incidents all over the World have emphasized the importance of risk analysis methods capable of deciding whether an organization (e.g. a company) is sufficiently protected against attacks. The protection mechanisms are often costly, or at least, not for free. Managers of an organization would like the investments into security to be reasonable and worth their price. The security experts should, more and more often, explain to their managers what benefits exactly the organization is getting for the money that is invested into security [1,2].

In contrast to the cryptographic techniques, the IT risk management techniques are still in an embryonic stage. This is one of the reasons of an increasing gap between theory and practice of information security [3]. Occasional stochastic risks (natural disasters, general criminal activity) can be evaluated rather easily, since there is enough statistical data concerning both the frequency (probability) and losses associated with such threats. Targeted gain-oriented attacks are much harder to model because their

* Supported by Estonian Science Foundation grant #5870.
** Supported by Estonian Science Foundation grant #6096.

J. Lopez (Ed.): CRITIS 2006, LNCS 4347, pp. 235–248, 2006.
© Springer-Verlag Berlin Heidelberg 2006

occurrence does not usually follow any reasonable statistical patterns and they tend to be rather victim-specific, which makes it difficult to find suitable risk metrics for attacks [1].

In the risk management field, risk is mostly defined as an expected loss, which is caused by *threats* – events that are considered bad (namely because they cause losses). Hence, the risk caused by threat $\mathcal{T}$ can be computed by $\mathsf{Risk}[\mathcal{T}] = \mathsf{Pr}[\mathcal{T}] \cdot \mathsf{Loss}[\mathcal{T}]$, where $\mathsf{Pr}[\mathcal{T}]$ denotes the probability of $\mathcal{T}$ and $\mathsf{Loss}[\mathcal{T}]$ denotes the associated loss. Hence, to estimate the security risk of a company we have to find all possible threats $\mathcal{T}$, to estimate the corresponding losses $\mathsf{Loss}[\mathcal{T}]$ and the probabilities $\mathsf{Pr}[\mathcal{T}]$, and finally to sum everything up

$$\mathsf{Risk} = \sum_{\mathcal{T}} \mathsf{Pr}[\mathcal{T}] \cdot \mathsf{Loss}[\mathcal{T}] \ . \tag{1}$$

Once we are able to do so, the security management is a trivial task: (A) compute the risk by (1), (B) if the risk seems to be too high, introduce some measures and compute the risk again, (C) if the cost of the measures is lower than the difference of risks, then decide that the measures are worth their price. Otherwise, the measures are unreasonable because it would be more beneficial not to take any measures.

Unfortunately, such an approach is hard to adopt in practice. Even if we are able to estimate the losses associated with the threats, their probabilities are often very hard to judge. This is especially true for targeted attacks that for a given setting may occur only once. It is also the case that companies are rather reluctant to share information concerning their vulnerabilities and the previous security incidents. For some typical attacks there exist rough expert estimates [4]. However, such estimates can generally be given for elementary vulnerabilities, but not easily to the primary (loss causing) threats. For instance, in [4] we see estimates for the events "Attempted Unauthorized System Access by Outsider", "Abuse of Access Privileges by Other Authorized User", etc., but not for "Loss in Drop of Company's Shares due to Bad Publicity".

Thus, we need a methodology to deduce probabilities of complex attacks from the parameters of simple vulnerabilities. Note that it is insufficient to consider only the occurrence probabilities of the vulnerabilities, since the attacker may consider more parameters when deciding whether to attack or not (e.g. the probability of getting caught and the associated penalties).

One of the methods used in practical security analysis is the *threat tree* method, which has been used in several security-oriented tasks like fault assessment of critical systems [5] or software vulnerability analysis [6,7], and was adapted to information security by Bruce Schneier [8,9]. In order to apply this method, only the rational attackers are taken into account. As the latter ones attack only when the attack is profitable, their behavior can be modeled by estimating the cost of attacks. Threat trees help us when reasoning about the decision-making process of the attackers and they work by splitting complex attacks into simpler and easier to analyze sub-attacks. Hence they are suitable for computing costs and success probabilities of attacks and are useful tools for practical security management.

Even though the threat trees (also called attack trees to emphasize the attack modeling domain) can provide valuable insight to the system's security, their applications have been rather simplistic so far. Most of the reported studies only consider one specific parameter for the nodes like cost or feasibility of the attack, skill level required, etc. [8,7,10]. Opel [11] considers also multi-parameter attack trees, but the actual tree computations in his model still use only one parameter at a time.

However, it is the belief of the authors of the current paper that the actual decision-making process of attackers is more complicated and that the interactions between different parameters play an important role. For example, if the success probability and possible monetary gain are considered as parameters, their product (i.e. the expected gain) also has a meaning and can be taken into account when making decisions about attacks.

The main contribution of this paper is to study how threat trees behave and how tree computations must be done when several interdependent attack parameters are considered. In this paper, we will concentrate on the attacker's gain, the probability of success, the probability of getting caught and the possible penalties as the parameters, but the method we will develop is able to handle a much larger variety of multi-parameter sets. As an application of the attack tree computations, we will also demonstrate how to make rational decisions concerning the security measures.

The paper is organized as follows. In Section 2, we discuss the rational attackers paradigm and define attack trees. Section 3 states the main principles of attack analysis. Section 4 presents the threat tree method built on this analysis. In Section 5, we discuss the evaluation of security measures and draw some conclusions in Section 6. Throughout the paper an illustrative example of a software-producing Company is discussed which helps the reader to get familiar with the terms and the methods stated.

## 2  Rational Attackers Paradigm and Attack Trees

Starting from this section we will assume the role of an attacker and try to model his decision-making process. Since in this paper we are interested in gain-oriented attacks, we will assume that *attackers behave in a rational way*. In particular, we assume that rational attackers

(1)  do not attack if the attack-game is *unprofitable* and
(2)  choose *the most profitable* ways of attacking, i.e. those with the highest outcome (see subsection 3.1).

This assumption is called *rational attacker's paradigm*. Based on this paradigm we can model the attacker's decision-making process. First, he needs to get an overview of all his measures (bribing victim's employees, gaining physical access, gaining network access, etc.). Second, he will combine his measures to come up with possible plans of attack, and third, he will evaluate all possible plans to find whether any of them is profitable, and if so, which one maximizes the profit. We will use attack trees to clarify such a process.

An attack tree is a compact graphical representation of all possible attack-plans. It is the outcome of a *gradual refinement procedure* that gives more and more detailed descriptions of the attacks until the *atomic attacks* are reached, the parameters (e.g. the cost) of which can be estimated without further refinements.

Each node of the attack tree represents an attack or a certain (probabilistic) condition whereas the root node represents the primary threat that we will try to analyze. The non-leaf nodes of the graph are AND nodes and OR nodes:

- The child nodes of an OR node represent a list of conditions (sub-attacks) each of which is sufficient for the attack (or threat) being successful.
- The child nodes of AND node represent a list of conditions (sub-attacks) each of which is necessary for the attack being successful. The leaves of the tree represent atomic attacks.

**Definition 1.** *A successful attack is a subtree $T'$ such that: (1) $T'$ contains the root node; (2) for any AND-node $v \in T'$, all child nodes of $v$ belong to $T'$; (3) for any OR-node $v \in T'$, at least one child node of $v$ belongs to $T'$.*

In order to illustrate the process of building an attack tree and also the future concepts presented later on, we will use an example of a software-producing Company that tries to protect its intellectual property from the competitors. The main setting is stated in Example 1.[1] The corresponding attack tree is depicted in Figure 1.

---

A software-producing Company considers as the main threat the situation where a competitor steals the code of the Company during the developing phase, completes it to a product and gets "first to the market" advance. The result is a lost market share, which may cost a great deal. We call this threat a *forestalling release*.

There are two events necessary for a forestalling release: (A) The code is stolen by a competitor, **and** (B) The code is used in competitive products. In a simplified model, we consider three ways how the code can be stolen (Figure 1): (A1) via bribing a programmer, (A2) via network attack, **or** (A3) via physical (ordinary) robbery.

For a successful bribery attack (Figure 1), the attacker should: (A1.1) successfully bribe a programmer of the Company, **and** (A1.2) the bribed programmer should obtain the valuable code from the Company.

For a successful bribery attack (Figure 1), the attacker should: (A2.1) employ a hacker, (A2.2) the hacker should exploit a bug in the computer system, **and** (A2.3) there must be an exploitable bug in the computer system.

For a successful physical robbery (Figure 1), the attacker should: (A3.1) employ a robber, **and** (A3.2) the robber should successfully break into the Company and obtain the code.

A rational adversary should determine which of the three attacks is the most profitable and then perform this attack.

---

**Example 1.** The main example

## 3   Main Principles of the Attack Analysis Method

This far, the threat-tree methods have mostly been used to determine the success probability and the cost of attacks [8,7,10]. These parameters are indeed important for the risk analysis but certainly not sufficient. The decision ("to attack" vs "not to attack") made by an attacker depends also on the *attacker's risks*, i.e. on the probability that the attack will lead to a prosecution or penalty, as well as on the monetary losses that correspond to the prosecution or penalty.

---

[1] The example covered throughout the paper is a simplified version of a real analysis performed by the authors of the paper in a real company. Due to confidentiality agreements, the identity of the company will not be presented here and all the numeric data is changed.

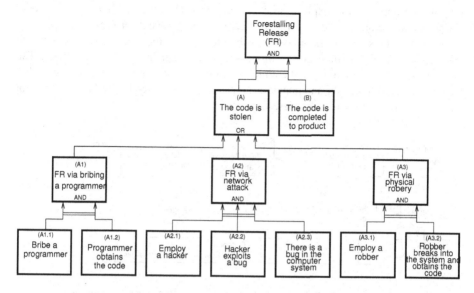

**Fig. 1.** A sample attack tree for a software developing company

Before describing our attack analysis method in detail (in Section 4), we outline the main starting points and principles, which the method is based on. In Subsection 3.1, we introduce a game-theoretic paradigm — the basis of the decision-making mechanism that we assume is used by rational attackers.

## 3.1   Attack as a Game

We view attack as a game played by the attacker. Rational attackers decide to play the attack-game if this is profitable for them. In order to decide about the profitability, the following parameters of the game will be taken into account:

- Gains – gains of the attacker, in case the attack succeeds
- Costs – cost of the attack
- $p$ – success probability of the attack
- $q$ – probability of getting caught (in case the attack was successful)
- Penalties – expected penalties in case the attacker is caught (assuming that the attack was successful)
- $q_-$ – probability of getting caught (in case the attack was not successful)
- Penalties$_-$ – expected penalties in case the attacker is caught (assuming that the attack was not successful)

In our model, each attack begins with a *preparation* phase during which the attacker prepares the necessary resources for performing the attack (e.g. bribes some internal people from the Company, buys some attack time from a bot-net, etc.). After that, the attacker tries to break into the system. With probability $p$ the attack is successful and the attacker obtains the Gains. In real life, it is possible that if later caught, the attacker may not be able to fully exploit the expected gains. However, for the sake of model simplicity we do not consider such a case here and will leave it for future research.

After the attack, it is possible (with probability $q$) that the attacker will be detected and get caught. We assume that in this case, the attacker has to pay Penalties.[2] The attacker may also get caught if the attack was unsuccessful, however, both the probability $q_-$ of getting caught and penalties he has to pay (denoted by Penalties$_-$) are not necessarily equal to $q$ and Penalties, respectively.[3]

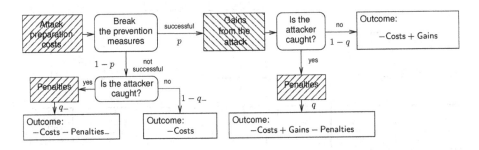

**Fig. 2.** Diagram (event tree) of the "attack game" from the attacker's point of view

Figure 2 presents our model of attack in the form of an event-tree. The oval boxes represent (probabilistic) conditions or events, the dashed boxes denote the gains and losses of the adversary. The arrows represent the change of the state during the attack and they are labeled with the probabilities that the particular branch is chosen during the attack. The leaves of the tree represent the final outcome of the attacker. For example, if the attack is successful (with probability $p$) and the attacker is caught (with probability $q$), then the final outcome of the attacker will be $-$Costs + Gains $-$ Penalties and the probability of this particular branch is $p \cdot q$.

The overall *value of the game* (or expected outcome) for the attacker is

$$\begin{aligned} \text{Outcome} &= (1-p) \cdot [q_- \cdot (-\text{Costs} - \text{Penalties}_-) + (1-q_-) \cdot (-\text{Costs})] + \\ &\quad + p \cdot [q \cdot (-\text{Costs} + \text{Gains} - \text{Penalties}) + (1-q) \cdot (-\text{Costs} + \text{Gains})] = \\ &= -\text{Costs} + p \cdot (\text{Gains} - q \cdot \text{Penalties}) - (1-p) \cdot q_- \cdot \text{Penalties}_- . \end{aligned}$$

---

[2] In practice it may happen that the probability of some penalties being enforced is rather low. In this case, we consider here the expected mean value of Penalties and Penalties$_-$.

[3] Note that the parameters Gains, Costs, Penalties and Penalties$_-$ are measured in monetary units. This approach differs from e.g. the one taken by Liu, Zang and Yu [12] who classify the risk evaluation criteria as cost and noncost constraints. However, the quantitaive nature of the methodology developed in the current paper presumes comparability of different attacker motives, and since for rational attackers most of the incentives are expressed in monetary units already, it natural to try to fit other attack targets (causing fear, achieving recognition in hacker community, etc.) into that scale, too. The authors note that since threats and attacks are more and more becoming trade articles (see also Schechter [13]), every attack will eventually have its true price. There are attack scenarios not fitting well into our model, most notably terrorism. However, according to CERT report from 2004 [14], only 1% of therats against information systems can be linked to terrorist motives.

Let the gains of the attacker be Gains $= \$150,000$, the success probability of the attack be $p = 0.1$ and the cost be Costs $= \$14,000$. If the attack is successful, then the probability of getting caught is $q = 0.01$ and the penalties are Penalty $= \$200,000$. If the attack is not successful, then the corresponding probability and the penalty are $q_- = 0.1$ and Penalty$_- = \$10,000$, respectively.

To decide, whether the attack is successful, we first compute the average penalties: $\pi = q \cdot$ Penalty $= 0.01 \cdot 200,000 = \$2000$, and $\pi_- = q_- \cdot$ Penalties$_- = 0.1 \cdot 10,000 = \$1000$. Second, we compute the expected outcome by using (2):

Outcome $= -$Costs$+p\cdot($Gains$-\pi)-(1-p)\cdot\pi_- = -14,000+0.1(150,000-2000)-0.9\cdot1000 = -\$100$,

which means that the attack is not profitable to the attacker.

**Example 2.** Parameters of the attack

We denote the average penalty of an attacker in case the attack was successful by $\pi$ and the average penalty in case the attack was not successful by $\pi_-$, i.e. $\pi = q \cdot$ Penalties and $\pi_- = q_- \cdot$ Penalties$_-$. Thus we have

$$\text{Outcome} = -\text{Costs} + p \cdot (\text{Gains} - \pi) - (1 - p) \cdot \pi_- . \qquad (2)$$

The attack is unlikely if Outcome $< 0$.

These concepts are illustrated in Example 2.

## 4    The Method

In this section, we describe the threat-tree based security evaluation method, which consists of two phases: (1) identifying the primary threats (ultimate goals for attackers) and (2) breaking complex attacks into simpler ones and computing the threat tree in order to determine the most profitable attack and to decide whether the attacker's outcome is positive. Note that there are alternative ways of describing the attacks, for example one may use the *attack simulation method* [15] in which all possible attack paths are generated first and only after that the most likely attacks are analyzed.

### 4.1    Primary Threats

The security analysis of a system begins with identifying the *primary threats* – events that directly cause losses. For example, *"software bugs in firewall"* is not a primary threat, whereas *"lost market share because of stolen IP"* is a primary threat because of direct (monetary) losses.

**Definition 2.** *A system is said to be* practically secure against rational attacks *if every primary threat is unlikely, i.e. non-profitable for attackers.*

Example 3 shows two examples of primary threats a Company may consider.

For a software-developing Company, the primary threats can be

- *Forestalling release* – a competitor, by using a stolen code or architecture, launches a similar product to the market before the Company does it. This causes a lost market share.
- *Competitive release* – a competitor, by using a stolen code or architecture, launches a similar service/product soon after the Company does it.

**Example 3.** Primary threats for a Company

### 4.2   Tree Computations

If the set $\mathfrak{T}$ of primary threats is fixed, the second step of the analysis is to construct an *attack tree* for each primary threat $T \in \mathfrak{T}$. This is done by a gradual refinement procedure where each primary or intermediate threat (or attack) is split into simpler sub-attacks until one reaches the level of atomic threats where it no more makes sense to split them any further. We distinguish between two kinds of splits: AND-split (where all the sub-attacks must be completer in order to carry out a higher-level attack) and OR-split (where only one sub-attack is sufficient).

As a result of the process, we want to be able to compare the game values of different attack scenarios. Thus, we must specify how to determine the necessary parameters throughout the computations. From equation (2) we see that the required parameters are Costs, $p$, Gains, $\pi$, and $\pi_-$. Almost all of them make sense for all nodes in the tree, with the notable exception of Gains. It is very hard to say which percentage of the desired result is obtained, if only some sub-attack is completed. Still, in order to perform the computations in intermediate nodes, we need some intermediate value of Gains as well. In this paper we will assume that this value is constant throughout the tree and that it is equal to the Gains obtained by the attacker if he is able to complete a primary threat attack.

For the leaf nodes (atomic attacks), the rest of the parameter values $(\text{Costs}, p, \pi, \pi_-)$ are deduced by the experts from the assumptions about the real environment. For non-leaf nodes, this quadruple is computed based on the corresponding parameters of the child nodes. In addition to the parameters, the Outcome value is computed for all nodes by applying (2). The parameters of non-leaf nodes (in binary case) are computed as follows:

- For an OR-node with child nodes with parameters $(\text{Costs}_i, p_i, \pi_i, \pi_{i-})$ $(i = 1, 2)$ the parameters $(\text{Costs}, p, \pi, \pi_-)$ are computed as:

$$(\text{Costs}, p, \pi, \pi_-) = \begin{cases} (\text{Costs}_1, p_1, \pi_1, \pi_{1-}), & \text{if Outcome}_1 > \text{Outcome}_2 \\ (\text{Costs}_2, p_2, \pi_2, \pi_{2-}), & \text{if Outcome}_1 \le \text{Outcome}_2 \end{cases},$$

where $\text{Outcome}_i = -\text{Costs}_i + p_i \cdot \text{Gains} - p_i \cdot \pi_i - (1 - p_i) \cdot \pi_{i-}$ $(i = 1, 2)$.
- For a AND-node with child nodes with parameters $(\text{Costs}_i, p_i, \pi_i, \pi_{i-})$ $(i = 1, 2)$ the parameters $(\text{Costs}, p, \pi, \pi_-)$ are computed as follows:

$$\text{Costs} = \text{Costs}_1 + \text{Costs}_2, \quad p = p_1 \cdot p_2, \quad \pi = \pi_1 + \pi_2,$$

$$\pi_- = \frac{p_1(1 - p_2)(\pi_1 + \pi_{2-}) + (1 - p_1)p_2(\pi_{1-} + \pi_2) + (1 - p_1)(1 - p_2)(\pi_{1-} + \pi_{2-})}{1 - p_1 p_2}.$$

The formula for $\pi_-$ represents the average penalty of an attacker, assuming that at least one of the two child-attacks was not successful. For example, if the first attack was successful and the second one unsuccessful (which is an event with probability $p_1(1-p_2)$), then the average penalty of the attacker is $\pi_1 + \pi_{2-}$. Note that the formulae above have obvious generalizations for non-binary trees.

## 4.3 Example

We illustrate the computations by using the simplified threat three depicted in Figure 1. We assume that the profit obtained by the attacker by launching a Forestalling Release (i.e. the value of the Gains parameter) is $\$6,000,000$. The Company estimates the parameters of atomic threats as follows:

*Stolen code is used in products.* We assume that the cost of creating a product from a stolen code is about $\$10^6$. The success probability of the product creation process is estimated to $0.9$. If the product creation is successful, then with probability $\frac{1}{6}$ the use of stolen code is detected and proved in court. The penalties in this case would be about $\$6,000,000$, thus $\pi = \frac{1}{6} \cdot \$6,000,000 = \$10^6$. If the project is not successful, then of course no damage is done to the Company and the attack will not be detected (at least with high probability), hence we take $\pi_- = 0$.

*Bribe a programmer.* We assume that about $\frac{1}{10}$ of the people can be bribed for 1 Million dollars. Hence, for the bribery, we take Costs $= 10^6$ and $p = 0.1$. Briberies can be made anonymous by using a chain of middle-men. Hence, we assume that the probability of getting caught is quite low – about $0.001$ – but it would still be reasonable to assume that in case the attacker (i.e. the competitor) is caught, the penalties are quite high – about $10^6$. This includes the direct penalties and the loss of trust. We also assume that the probability of getting caught and the penalties for bribery do not depend on whether the bribery was successful. Hence, $\pi = \pi_- = 10^3$.

The results are summarized in Table 1.

Table 1. Computing the threat three of Figure 1

| | Description of threat | Type | Costs | p | $\pi$ | $\pi_-$ | Outcome |
|---|---|---|---|---|---|---|---|
| | Forestalling release | AND | $1,101,000$ | $0.405$ | $1,110,000$ | $941,933$ | $+319,000$ |
| B | Stolen code is used in products | | $10^6$ | $0.9$ | $1 \cdot 10^6$ | $0$ | |
| A | Steal the code | OR | $101,000$ | $0.45$ | $110,000$ | $110,000$ | |
| A1 | Get code by bribing a programmer | AND | $1,000,000$ | $0.09$ | $101,000$ | $101,000$ | $-561,000$ |
| | A1.1 Bribe a programmer | | $10^6$ | $0.1$ | $10^3$ | $10^3$ | |
| | A1.2 Programmer obtains the code | | $0$ | $0.9$ | $10^5$ | $10^5$ | |
| A2 | Get code via network attack | AND | $11,000$ | $0.0027$ | $1,001$ | $911$ | $+4,289$ |
| | A2.1 Employ a hacker | | $10^4$ | $0.9$ | $10^3$ | $10^2$ | |
| | A2.2 Hacker exploits a bug | | $10^3$ | $0.5$ | $1$ | $1$ | |
| | A2.1 There is a bug to exploit | | $0$ | $0.006$ | $0$ | $0$ | |
| A3 | Get code via physical robbery | AND | $101,000$ | $0.45$ | $110,000$ | $110,000$ | $+2,489,000$ |
| | A3.1 Employ a robber | | $10^5$ | $0.9$ | $10^4$ | $10^4$ | |
| | A3.2 Robber breaks into the system and obtains the code | | $10^3$ | $0.5$ | $10^5$ | $10^5$ | |

*Programmer obtains the code.* We assume that the internal security measures in the Company against stealing the code are not very efficient, so that about $\frac{1}{10}$ of the stealing attempts are detected. We believe that the real situation is much worse in most of the companies. If the programmer gets caught then the losses concern the loss of trust, i.e. it would be very difficult for the programmer to find job after such an incident. We estimate the losses of the programmer to be about $10^6$.

The parameters of other atomic attacks (A2.1–A3.2) should also be estimated (in a similar way) but we omit the reasoning about them in this paper. Note also that none of these numbers are results of rigorous (social) studies, but rather depend on the estimates given by the security expert. However, often giving estimates as bounds with the precision of order of magnitude is quite enough. For example, in order to apply the OR-rule from Subsection 4.2, we only need to know which child node has the largest Outcome and just having some reasonable bounds is usually sufficient to take such decisions.

The results of the computations are presented in Table 1. First, we compute the sub-attacks A1, A2, and A3 (using the AND-node rule given in Subsection 4.2). We see that A3 is the attack with the highest Outcome and hence, by using the OR-node rule, we get the parameters for sub-attack A. Finally, by applying the AND-rule to A and B, we obtain the parameters of the "Forestalling release" attack. It turns out that

- the average outcome of the attacker is positive: Outcome = $319,000,
- the most profitable attack is a physical robbery.

The Company concludes that the system is insufficiently protected and measures must be taken against physical robbery. In the next section, we discuss how to decide about security measures in a rational way.

## 5   Security Measures

Rational choice of security measures is of the same importance as the estimation of risks. In this section, we recall the main types of measures and then introduce a simple metrics for economic justification of the measures. We also continue with our example in order to illustrate how the metrics works.

### 5.1   Types of Measures

To protect the system against attacks, various *security measures* can be taken. There are three main types of security measures:

- *Prevention measures* the purpose of which is to *reduce the success probability $p$ of attacks* and to *increase the cost* of attacks. Physical access control mechanisms, suitable choice of information-transfer protocols, as well as properly stated home rules in the company are prevention measures.
- *Detection measures* the purpose of which is to *detect* the attack as fast as possible, and to *increase the probability $q$ of getting caught*. Regular observation of competitors' business activities (e.g. in order to detect unfair use of stolen intellectual property), secure log mechanisms, patent protection of technical and business ideas (it helps to detect and prove unfair use of stolen information) – all these are detection measures, at least in the context of this work.

- *Recovery measures* the purpose of which is to *re-establish the normal function-ality* of the system after an attack. Regular backups, insurance, etc. are recovery measures.

## 5.2  Rational Choice of Measures

The main practical questions about the security (expected to be answered during the security analysis) are the following:

- Are the current security measures *sufficient* to make the attacks non-profitable to attackers?
- Are the security measures *economically justified* (*necessary*), i.e. is their cost worth the risk they reduce? Security measures are never for free. It is hence reasonable to ask whether the additional level of security they offer is worth their price.

Let $M$ denote the set of measures used in the Company and $\mathfrak{T}$ denote the set of primary threats. For each primary threat $T \in \mathfrak{T}$, let $\mathsf{Loss}[T]$ denote the losses associated with $T$ as in Section 1 (see Example 4).

---

A software-developing Company may estimate the losses as follows: $\mathsf{Loss}[\text{"Forestalling release"}] = \$6,000,000$, $\mathsf{Loss}[\text{"Competitive release"}] = \$2,000,000$.

---

**Example 4.** Losses of the Company

Let $\mathsf{Outcome}[T]$ denote the outcome of the corresponding attack game for the at-tacker estimated by using attack trees. We define *total loss* – the largest potential loss caused by primary threats – as follows:

$$\mathsf{Loss}[\mathfrak{T}] = \max\{\mathsf{Loss}[T]: \; T \in \mathfrak{T}, \text{ and } \mathsf{Outcome}[T] > 0\} \; .$$

In case the set of likely threats (those with $\mathsf{Outcome} > 0$) is empty, we set $\mathsf{Loss}[\mathfrak{T}] = 0$.

Let $\mathsf{Outcome}[T \mid M]$ denote the outcome of the attack game assuming that a set $M$ of measures is taken in the system. The *conditional (total) loss* $\mathsf{Loss}[\mathfrak{T} \mid M]$ is defined as follows:

$$\mathsf{Loss}[\mathfrak{T} \mid M] = \max\{\mathsf{Loss}[T]: \; T \in \mathfrak{T}, \text{ and } \mathsf{Outcome}[T \mid M] > 0\} \; .$$

If for all primary threats $T$, we have $\mathsf{Outcome}[T \mid M] \leq 0$, then no attack is profitable for the attacker, and we take $\mathsf{Loss}[\mathfrak{T} \mid M] = 0$.

**Definition 3.** *A set $M$ of measures is* sufficient (against rational attacks) *if* $\mathsf{Loss}[\mathfrak{T} \mid M] = 0$. *A set $M$ of measures is* adequate (worth its cost) *if* $\mathsf{Loss}[\mathfrak{T}] - \mathsf{Loss}[\mathfrak{T} \mid M] > \mathsf{Cost}[M]$.

Note that every adequate measure should make at least one primary attack unlikely. It is not sufficient for the adequacy that the average outcome of the attacker is diminished.

**Table 2.** Computing the threat three for the system protected with $\mathcal{M}_X$

| | Description of threat | Type | Costs | $p$ | $\pi$ | $\pi_-$ | Outcome |
|---|---|---|---|---|---|---|---|
| | Forestalling release | AND | 1,101,000 | 0.2025 | 1,110,000 | 984,608 | −896,000 |
| B | Stolen code is used in products | | $10^6$ | 0.9 | $1 \cdot 10^6$ | 0 | |
| A | Steal the code | OR | 101,000 | 0.225 | 110,000 | 110,000 | |
| A1 | Get code by bribing a programmer | AND | 1,000,000 | 0.09 | 101,000 | 101,000 | −561,000 |
| A2 | Get code via network attack | AND | 11,000 | 0.0027 | 1,001 | 911 | +4,289 |
| A3 | Get code via physical robbery | AND | 101,000 | 0.225 | 110,000 | 110,000 | +1,139,000 |
| | A3.1 Employ a robber | | $10^5$ | 0.9 | $10^4$ | $10^4$ | |
| | A3.2 Robber breaks into the system and obtains the code | | $10^3$ | 0.25 | $10^5$ | $10^5$ | |

**Definition 4.** *A set $\mathcal{M}$ of measures is (locally) optimal if and only if it is sufficient, adequate, and* $\mathsf{Loss}[\mathfrak{T} \mid \mathcal{N}] > 0$ *for every proper subset* $\mathcal{N} \subset \mathcal{M}$, *i.e. no proper subset of $\mathcal{M}$ is sufficient.*

For a sufficient and adequate set $\mathcal{M}$ of measures we also have $\mathsf{Loss}[\mathfrak{T}] > \mathsf{Cost}[\mathcal{M}]$, leading us to a well-known conclusion that price of the defense measures should not exceed the value of the assets protected.

## 5.3 Example

We continue with the software-developing Company example. The conclusion of the risk analysis was that some additional physical protection mechanisms must be introduced in order to protect the Company against physical robbery. Say we have two offers to the Company from security companies with the following parameters:

- Company $X$ offers a protection package $\mathcal{M}_X$ with price $\mathsf{Cost}[\mathcal{M}_X] = \$2,000,000$. The package is oriented to physical protection and reduces the probability that a robber breaks into the system from 0.5 to 0.25.
- Company $Y$ offers a protection package $\mathcal{M}_Y$ with price $\mathsf{Cost}[\mathcal{M}_Y] = \$1,000,000$. The package is oriented to detection measures and increases twice the detection probabilities $q$ and $q_-$, which means that also the average penalties $\pi$ and $\pi_-$ are increased twice.

Which package to choose? If both packages are adequate (i.e. make the "Forestalling release" threat unlikely), then it is reasonable to choose $\mathcal{M}_Y$ because of lower price. If one of the packages turns out to be inadequate, then this package cannot be chosen, regardless of the price. Hence, it remains to determine whether the packages are adequate. We start from $\mathcal{M}_X$. The computations are shown in Table 2.

We see that $\mathcal{M}_X$ is sufficient as it makes the attack unlikely. It is also adequate since its cost was $\$2,000,000$, but the prevented loss was $\$6,000,000$.

Now we do the same with the package $\mathcal{M}_Y$. The results are presented in Table 3.

As we can see, $\mathcal{M}_Y$ is not even sufficient and the attack is still likely. Hence, it is reasonable to buy the package $\mathcal{M}_X$, in spite of its higher price.

**Table 3.** Computing the threat three for the system protected with $\mathcal{M}_Y$

| | Description of threat | Type | Costs | $p$ | $\pi$ | $\pi_-$ | Outcome |
|---|---|---|---|---|---|---|---|
| | Forestalling release | AND | 1,101,000 | 0.405 | 1,210,000 | 1,041,933 | +219,000 |
| B | Stolen code is used in products | | $10^6$ | 0.9 | $1 \cdot 10^6$ | 0 | |
| A | Steal the code | OR | 101,000 | 0.45 | 210,000 | 210,000 | |
| A1 | Get code by bribing a programmer | AND | 1,000,000 | 0.09 | 101,000 | 101,000 | −561,000 |
| A2 | Get code via network attack | AND | 11,000 | 0.0027 | 1,001 | 911 | +4,289 |
| A3 | Get code via physical robbery | AND | 101,000 | 0.45 | 210,000 | 210,000 | +2,389,000 |
| A3.1 | Employ a robber | | $10^5$ | 0.9 | $10^4$ | $10^4$ | |
| A3.2 | Robber breaks into the system and obtains the code | | $10^3$ | 0.5 | $2 \cdot 10^5$ | $2 \cdot 10^5$ | |

# 6 Conclusions and Further Work

We have used the presented simple risk-analysis framework several times in practice and have found it to be very suitable. The main benefits of the framework are that (1) it provides a systematic approach to the whole security analysis task and avoids a risk-analyst from getting lost in unimportant (technical) details, (2) it is easy to implement in a computer, (3) the main principles of the method are easily understandable to the people who make financial decisions and hence it can be used to justify investments into security.

It may seem that the method uses many unknown parameters like "the sum of money needed for bribing an employee" etc. At the same time, *these parameters are essential in any other risk analysis method* that is claimed to be adequate. Our method (and the threat-tree method in general) helps to determine systematically the (social) parameters we need to know for practical security estimation, and this is, in turn, an advantage of the method.

There are still several things to be improved in the method:

- Gains is a global parameter in the whole threat-tree and is used to make decisions in all OR-nodes. This makes the computations "greedy", i.e. the complexity is linear in the number of nodes. The "local" decisions made separately in OR-nodes not necessarily give the successful attack with the highest outcome. In order to get the global maximum, we have to examine all combinations of decisions in all OR-nodes. For example, if the tree contains $m$ binary OR-nodes, the whole tree has to be computed $2^m$ times. It is not yet known how much effect this would give in practical threat trees. Further, it is possible to extend the model considering different amounts of Gains depending on whether the attack was successful or not.
- We assumed that all atomic attacks (or at least all children of AND-nodes) are independent of each other. This may not be the case. It seems that in practical security analysis we can build the tree so that possible dependencies do not have an effect. However, it is not excluded that in some cases we cannot avoid the dependencies. This needs some further research.

Risk analysis methods have not yet been discussed extensively in academic papers. In our opinion, one of the reasons has been that many such methods were (and are) business secrets of risk analysis companies. Considering the latest trends that computer criminals co-operate (and compete!) intensively, it seems to be the right time to start intense academic cooperation on the general risk analysis issues.

# References

1. Daniel Geer, Kevin Soo Hoo, and Andrew Jaquith. Information security: Why the future belongs to the quants. *IEEE Security and Privacy*, 1(4):24–32, 2003.
2. Wes Sonnenreich, Jason Albanese, and Bruce Stout. Return On Security Investment (ROSI) – A practical quantitative model. *Journal of Research and Practice in Information Technology*, 38(1):55–66, February 2006.
3. Yvo Desmedt. Potential impacts of a growing gap between theory and practice in information security. In *Information Security and Privacy: 10th Australasian Conference, ACISP 2005*, LNCS 3524, pages 532–536. Springer, 2005.
4. James W. Meritt. A method for quantitative risk analysis. In *Proceedings of the 22nd National Information Systems Security Conference*, 1999.
5. W.E. Vesely, F.F. Goldberg, N.H. Roberts, and D.F. Haasl. *Fault Tree Handbook*. US Government Printing Office, January 1981. Systems and Reliability Research, Office of Nuclear Regulatory Research, U.S. Nuclear Regulatory Commission.
6. John Viega and Gary McGraw. *Building Secure Software: How to Avoid Security Problems the Right Way*. Addison Wesley Professional, 2001.
7. Andrew P. Moore, Robert J. Ellison, and Richard C. Linger. Attack modeling for information security and survivability. Technical Report CMU/SEI-2001-TN-001, Software Engineering Institute, 2001.
8. Bruce Schneier. Attack trees: Modeling security threats. *Dr. Dobb's Journal*, 24(12):21–29, December 1999.
9. Bruce Schneier. *Secrets & Lies. Digital Security in a Networked World*. John Wiley & Sons, 2000.
10. Sjouke Mauw and Martijn Oostdijk. Foundations of attack trees. In Dongho Won and Seungjoo Kim, editors, *International Conference on Information Security and Cryptology – ICISC 2005*, LNCS 3935, pages 186–198. Springer, December 2005. In print.
11. Alexander Opel. Design and implementation of a support tool for attack trees. Technical report, Otto-von-Guericke University, March 2005. Internship Thesis.
12. Peng Liu, Wanyu Zang, and Meng Yu. Incentive-Based Modeling and Inference of Attacker Intent, Objectives and Strategies. *ACM Transactions on Information and Systems Security*, 8(1):78 –118, 2005.
13. Stuart E. Schechter. *Computer Security Strength & Risk: A Quantitative Approach*. PhD thesis, Harvard University, 2004.
14. 2004 E-CrimeWatch Survey. Summary of Findings. Conducted by CSO magazine in cooperation with the U.S. Secret Service & CERT Coordination Center. Available at http://www.cert.org/archive/pdf/2004eCrimeWatchSummary.pdf, 2004.
15. Gidi Cohen. The role of attack simulation in automating security risk management. *Information Systems Control Journal*, 1:51–54, 2005.

# Multidomain Virtual Security Negotiation over the Session Initiation Protocol (SIP)

Daniel J. Martínez-Manzano, Gabriel López, and Antonio F. Gómez-Skarmeta

Department of Information and Communications Engineering
University of Murcia, Spain
{dani,gabilm,skarmeta}@dif.um.es

**Abstract.** When organizations need to exchange critical information they need to rely on dependable and resilient channels, which define a trusted overlay network over the underlying IP infrastructure. Today, secure information sharing in these scenarios has become a main concern for domain administrators. To solve this problem, current research initiatives are focused on the establishment of (usually static) trust relationships and security services among such organizations. This paper analyzes the usage of the standard Session Initiation Protocol (SIP) for performing a multidomain virtual negotiation, in order to dynamically protect the exchange of critical data from the security risks of the public networks. As an example of this proposal, a prototype is presented in the context of secure overlay networks. This prototype shows also the integration of the virtual negotiation process with a Policy Based Network Management infrastructure (PBNM), in order to provide the security policies required by each organization.

**Keywords:** Secure Information Sharing, Overlay, Virtual Negotiation, SIP.

## 1 Introduction

When two or more organizations need to share critical information over their communication networks, either protected information among companies or simple end user data, they need to rely on trusted channels able to offer properties such as confidentiality, integrity, information assurance, etc. These secure channels between organizations define a secure overlay network upon the physical communication infrastructure.

The concept of overlay network is associated with the definition of resilient and secure logical communication infrastructures deployed over an underlying physical network. Overlays are used to solve management and scalability problems in nowadays common services such as peer-to-peer [12] or multicast [16] networks, or even to deal with problems of dependability and resilience in communication networks [1]. Needless to say, security is a key issue in those scenarios. Several research works have been carried out to add security mechanisms to these infrastructures. For example, we can find works about how to protect routing protocols in peer-to-peer networks [3] or how to protect overlays from DDoS (Distributed

J. Lopez (Ed.): CRITIS 2006, LNCS 4347, pp. 249–261, 2006.
© Springer-Verlag Berlin Heidelberg 2006

Denial of Service) attacks [10]. Other proposals try to define a generic security framework to protect any kind of high level services running in the overlay, such as [17].

However, the security requirements imposed by those solutions are often static, usually through the definition of either preconfigured secure tunnels between nodes, or access control mechanisms for reaching the infrastructure. The establishment of such a secure overlay network has to be maintained by each domain which is a part of it, which normally requires defining:

- The security requirements for protecting internal communications and services, that is, required levels of confidentiality, integrity, authentication, etc.
- How end users and internal devices will deal with these security requirements.
- How these security requirements will be mapped to specific security technologies.
- How those security requirements will be agreed among other organizations to provide interdomain secure communications.

This work does not try to answer all of the above questions, and it focuses on the last one. That is, we propose a virtual negotiation process able to allow organizations to agree on security requirements and technologies to be applied along the path between them. The starting point is a scenario where several domains want to communicate securely making use of preestablished security requirements, for example, by means of an off-line Service Level Agreement (SLA). Each security domain has its own mechanism to allow end users or systems to specify security levels such as *low*, *medium* or *high*, and has its own method to translate those levels into security parameters (for example, a *medium* security level could mean strong authentication but weak encryption).

This paper proposes a way to define a dynamic secure overlay network among such organizations by means of a negotiation protocol. The Session Initiation Protocol (SIP) will be used for this, allowing domains to agree on a common set of security requirements and technologies, which respects the internal policies of them all.

This paper is structured as follows: section 2 briefly describes the SIP protocol as the base protocol used in the virtual negotiation, and then section 3 presents the proposed design for it. Detailed implementation is described in section 4, including how the proposed protocol has been integrated with a Policy Based Network Management (PBNM) infrastructure. Section 5 presents some related work and finally section 6 gives some conclusions.

## 2   The SIP Protocol

SIP (Session Initiation Protocol, [6]) is an application-layer signaling protocol for creating, modifying, and terminating data sessions of whatever kind. SIP allows the participants to agree on session parameters, a feature which can be useful for conveying on compatible requirements resulting from the intersection of each peer's own requirements plus any other constraints that could be imposed administratively. SIP can also make use of entities called proxy servers, for handling tasks such as user authentication and authorization, call routing and dynamic user location via registry functionality. Besides, it follows a text-based, HTTP-like transaction model, which makes it human-readable.

There are several interesting features about SIP which may attract our attention when considering it as a secure negotiation protocol: SIP is a standard protocol, so a negotiation framework built around it is more easily taken advantage of by third-party software; it requires less message exchanges than other competing protocols such as H.323 [7]; signaling in SIP is supported by textual headers and it is extensible enough to fit our purposes; it allows routing call establishment dialogs through several domains; and it can be easily secured, either by running it over a secure transport such as TLS or by using S/MIME.

Once the SIP protocol and its advantages have been described, next section will introduce how our architecture has been designed.

# 3  Design of a Virtual Security Negotiation Based on SIP

## 3.1  Overview

In order to establish secure overlay networks across different domains, two kinds of negotiation need to take place: first, the involved domains need to agree a common set of security requirements, expressed with specific parameters which must be consistently understood by all of them; second, a lower level negotiation is needed for agreeing on the security technology (e.g. IPsec, SSL, etc.) that will be used between each pair of adjacent domains. This overall process, shown in Figure 1, is what we will be calling the *virtual security negotiation*. Once it finishes, the third exchange (any kind of traffic over any protocol, such as application data) may begin, conveniently secured.

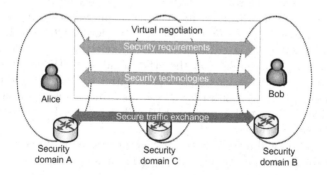

**Fig. 1.** Virtual security negotiation

The motivation of this twofold negotiation is as follows: first, domains must agree on some kind of security level which is perceived as *secure enough* by all of them, according to the sensitivity of the data they want to exchange. Second, they must ensure that they share some lower level security technology that allows them to actually implement the secure channels between them (for example, an IPsec-only domain requires that its peer domain also supports IPsec).

The security requirements should be specified in any way that is consistently understood by all involved domains, and have also to be agreed by means of an SLA among the involved organizations. We propose to use a set of numeric values for the three security parameters confidentiality, integrity and access control, both for the minimum required levels and the maximum desired ones[1]. These parameters can be easily associated to low level security technologies properties; for example, confidentiality and integrity could be associated to different IPsec, SSL or WEP security properties, and access control could be associated to MAC address filtering, login/password, WEP key, etc. Other security parameters such as availability could also be added to the negotiation process.

It is out of the scope of the virtual security negotiation process itself how the domains obtain these security requirements and the security technologies available for implementing them, as well as how the user level notation for security (for example, *high*, *medium* and *low*) will be translated into security requirements. In section 4, we present a testbed scenario where the negotiation process has been integrated with a Policy Based Network Management (PBNM) infrastructure [19], which is then used for providing this kind of information.

The properties described in the previous section make SIP a well suited protocol for performing a multidomain negotiation. In order to do this, two kinds of SIP entities must be used: user agents and proxies. User agents will be the entities demanding the establishment of a session between them, whereas proxies will route SIP calls across domains, and handle the negotiation. Custom headers will be defined for SIP messages, so that user agents and proxies can process them to carry out the security negotiation.

The proposed architecture locates these SIP entities as follows. On the one hand, one SIP user agent is placed at each end-user application or terminal which is expected to require the initiation of a virtually negotiated session. The source SIP user agent will state its security requirements using a high level description (such as *high*, *medium* or *low* security level), whereas the other one will have the possibilities of either accepting or rejecting the offering (counteroffers may also be admissible). On the other hand, one SIP proxy is placed at each negotiation-compliant domain, for both routing the SIP call and performing domain-to-domain negotiation tasks. These tasks may cause a proxy along the path to decide whether to forward the SIP call or to cancel it, according to the negotiation result at the current hop.

The next section will introduce the custom processing required at each of the SIP entities for performing the desired negotiation steps.

### 3.2   Per-hop Processing

The virtual negotiation is designed as a set of per-hop processing stages, which are carried out on both the SIP user agents and proxies. For example, per-hop

---

[1] While it may seem useless to provide an upper bound for security, this is included in case it becomes meaningful for a specific domain or security technology.

processing for a successful negotiation between Alice and Bob in the simple two-domain scenario shown in Figure 1 could be:

1. Alice sends an INVITE message carrying her security requirements to her domain SIP proxy, P1. There are several mechanisms for locating this proxy server [13].
2. P1 forwards the INVITE to P2 (Bob's domain proxy).
3. P2 forwards the INVITE to Bob.
4. When Bob receives the INVITE, he gathers together his own security requirements, Alice's requirements, and any other restrictions that may apply (for example, any policies that may exist within the security domain). Using this information, he updates the virtual security requirements in the INVITE message, and places it in an outgoing OK response which is sent to P2. (How the requirements information is merged and updated will depend on what exact representation is chosen for it.) The response sent to P2 also carries the security technologies that Bob may use for implementing the security requirements, as well as the basic parameters for them, such as specific protocols, key lengths, etc.
5. P2 learns from the OK message which security requirements it must enforce towards Bob. It then retrieves its own security requirements, merges them with the information on the OK message, and updates it. It also must choose one of Bob's proposed security technologies, and inform the next hop (P1) about its own set of security technologies, so that it can also choose one later. This information is added to the OK response, which is then forwarded to P1.
6. P1 performs towards P2 the same steps than P2 performed towards Bob, including choosing one of the security technologies offered by P2. The OK is finally forwarded to Alice, carrying P1's available security requirements and technologies.
7. After receiving the OK, Alice checks that everything is correct (i.e., her request can be enforced) and chooses one technology from those offered by P1. She then sends an ACK response back to P1, carrying the chosen security technology, which she sets up then (e.g., sets up an IPsec connection endpoint towards P1).
8. When P1 gets the ACK, it learns about the technology chosen by Alice. P1 then puts its own choice in the ACK response, forwards it to P2 and then sets up both security technologies: the one chosen by Alice for communicating with P1 and the one chosen by P1 for communicating with P2.
9. P2 performs towards P1 and Bob the same steps that P1 performed toward Alice and P2, including the instantiation of both the security technology chosen by P1 for communicating with P2 and the one chosen by P2 for communicating with Bob. The ACK, carrying P2's choice for Bob, is finally forwarded to Bob.
10. Lastly, Bob gets the ACK and sets up the security technology chosen by P2. This is the final step; all four nodes are now set up to communicate securely, while respecting the virtual security requirements.

Should any of the domains fail to support the required security, the session establishment must be shut down to allow a renegotiation. This can be done by sending canceling response messages from the proxy which detects the domain's inability to provide the required security. In order to prevent attacks from malicious users, the SIP messages exchanged between domains should be protected by using a ciphered and authenticated transport such as TLS. Finally, it is important to note that the use of a policy system implies that the enforcement of the selected security technologies will include any required routing information for the specific device.

# 4   Implementation

This section describes how the proposed architecture has been implemented. As already mentioned, the negotiation is based on per-hop processing of some pieces of information exchanged by both SIP user agents and proxies. This can be accomplished by adding custom headers to the SIP messages [14]. Table 1 describes the custom headers defined for implementing our architecture.

As a proof of concept, we now present how the design described here was implemented in a real testbed for validation. First the integration with a PBNM for policy provision will be presented, and then we will describe the implemented testbed.

## 4.1   Integration with a PBNM Infrastructure

Throughout the description of the virtual negotiation architecture, we have mentioned at several points that policy information may be needed by some network nodes. For example, end users need to know what security requirements they are allowed to get within their current security domain. In order to add policy based management support to our negotiation architecture, we have integrated it with a real implementation of a PBNM, which is described at [11]. This implementation leverages technologies like COPS [5], XML [20] and XSLT [8] to obtain a high level policy based management system, capable of modeling policies as collections of hierarchical XML rules, which can be distributed via a standard protocol and translated into configuration rules through the usage of XSLT style sheets.

The management architecture comprises five elements. The network administrator uses an interface named Policy Management Tool (PMT) to edit the relevant policies. These policies are then distributed to special policy servers, called Policy Decision Points (PDP's). The PDP's process these policies, along with other data such as network state information, and take policy decisions regarding which policies should be enforced, and how and when this will happen. These policies are sent to appropriate Policy Enforcement Points (PEP's), which reside on, or are communicated to the managed devices and are responsible for installing and enforcing the policies on them. The communication between PDP's and PEP's is the standard Common Open Policy Service (COPS, [5]). The

**Table 1.** SIP headers used in the negotiation process

| Header | Description |
|--------|-------------|
| *X-MinSecurity* | Specifies the minimum security requirements admissible for the current session, via a set of numeric values confidentiality, integrity, access control. |
| *X-MaxSecurity* | Specifies the maximum security requirements that are desired, via a set of numeric values confidentiality, integrity, access control. As already mentioned, this is provided in case it becomes meaningful for particular domains or technologies. |
| *X-Via* | Similar to standard SIP Via header, but carries both the address of the proxy and that of the domain router. Example: header "X-Via: *192.168.1.2*;router=*192.168.1.1*" states that the SIP request has been processed by a proxy at 192.168.1.2, which belongs to a domain whose border router is 192.168.1.1. |
| *X-Tunnel* | Used for setting the tunnel endpoints, once non-compliant domains have been detected. Example: header "X-Tunnel: *192.168.1.1*;to=*192.168.2.1*" would be added by a SIP proxy which detects the need for setting up a tunnel from routers 192.168.1.1 and 192.168.2.1, in order to bypass non-compliant domains. |
| *X-TechList* | Used for letting know the next hop about the security technologies that the current node has available for implementing the current security requirements. Technologies appearing here also carry the configuration parameters they need for meeting the requirements. Example: the header "X-TechList: *SSL, IPsec-3DES*" could mean that the previous node can implement the negotiated requirements by using either SSL or IPsec with 3DES encryption. This header can be represented in a similar way to the proposed in [2]. |
| *X-SelectedTech* | Used for letting know the next hop about which security technology is selected, from the set of technologies previously offered in an *X-TechList* header. This header can be represented in a similar way to the proposed in [2]. |

XML policies can be automatically translated into device/technology-dependent configuration files through the usage of XSLT style sheets.

### 4.2   The Implemented Testbed

A sample testbed was built for demonstrating our architecture for SIP-based virtual security negotiation. This testbed also featured a PBNM for supplying the policies of each domain, both the policies regarding parameters translation (from *high, medium* and *low* to numeric values) and those regarding the allowed security technologies for implementing each subset of parameters. The testbed comprised two security domains, each with a SIP proxy (P1 and P2) and a SIP user agent (Alice and Bob). All SIP entities also integrated a policy client (PEP) for communicating with their local policy server (PDP). Lastly, the policy servers used specific XML databases as their policy repositories. Figure 2 illustrates this testbed.

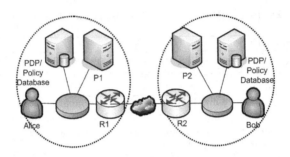

**Fig. 2.** The implemented testbed

The policy databases hosted XML policies for translating abstract security levels into sets of security parameters, as well as policies for supplying the technologies allowed within each domain for implementing these sets. For example, inside Alice's domain, policies stated that the *medium* security level had to be translated into the parameter set { *confidentiality=7, integrity=7, accessControl=4* }.

The SIP nodes use their local policy clients for requesting policy information to the domain PDP, whenever they need this kind of information. The virtual security negotiation was performed as described in this paper, just adding the requests to the PBNM at the moments in which its intervention is required.

### 4.3   Operation Example

This section describes the operation of the implemented testbed. The behavior of the SIP entities at several different stages has been analyzed during the global virtual negotiation process, as well as the usage of the custom headers. It must be noted that the processing described here is only the "custom" part; the standard SIP processing, although not detailed here, was also carried out after having performed each of these custom steps. This includes the processing of any unmentioned SIP messages.

**Processing at the SIP User Agents.** Basically, the source peer needs to specify its security requirements and initiate the session, whereas the destination peer needs to check the requested security requirements against its own, and accept or reject the offering. Both may need to intersect their own requirements with the ones which they are allowed to get within the domain they lie into, whether this means to raise the minimum level or to lower the maximum one. Regarding security technologies, the negotiation is performed by using the *X-TechList* and *X-SelectedTech* headers. Once a specific set of security requirements has been agreed (and validated via the PBNM), the current SIP node needs to learn about which security technologies are available and allowed for implementing them within the current domain. This information is also retrieved from the PBNM, and then placed in an *X-TechList* header which serves as an offering.

The next node which receives the SIP message is expected to pick one of the technologies offered in the *X-TechList* header, to remove this header from the message, and to make its own offering to the following node, by creating a new *X-TechList* header and adding it to the message before forwarding it.

This happens on the way from Bob to Alice (assuming it was Alice who made the call), when processing the OK response to the request. When the ACK travels back from Alice to Bob, each node is expected to notify the next one about the previously chosen technology. This is accomplished by using the *X-SelectedTech* header.

Now we will describe the operations carried out by SIP user agents in a more detailed way. Throughout the following stepwise description, to "cancel the call" means to shut down the SIP session establishment (by sending the appropriate CANCEL/BYE/4xx/etc. messages) and to stop the message processing. The complete step list for the SIP user agents is:

*When Alice wishes to establish a session*

– Choose the desired security level (*high*, *medium* or *low*) via the user agent's GUI.
– Use the PBNM (the PEP module in the user agent, and the domain PDP) to translate the security level to security requirements.
– Specify the virtual security requirements via the *X-MinSecurity* and *X-MaxSecurity* headers. Check these requirements against the domain policies.
– Create a SIP INVITE request for Bob, and add the created headers to it.
– Send then the request to the domain SIP proxy, P1.

*When Bob processes the INVITE request from P2*

– Check the received security requirements against both the domain policies and Bob's own requirements. If an empty intersection is found, cancel the call. Otherwise, create an OK response and update the *X-MinSecurity* and *X-MaxSecurity* headers with the merged parameters.
– Add an *X-TechList* header with the list of technologies that Bob can use for implementing the merged parameters.
– Send the OK response to the domain SIP proxy, P2.

*When Alice processes the OK response from P1*

– Obtain from the domain policies the list of available technologies for implementing the set of parameters carried in the message. Then, get the technologies available at the previous hop (P1) from the *X-TechList* header. If a non-empty intersection exists between both lists, pick up a technology from that intersection and proceed with the next step. Otherwise, cancel the call.
– Send an ACK confirmation message to P1, holding the selected security technology in an *X-SelectedTech* header.
– Instantiate the selected security technology.

*When Bob processes the ACK response from P2:* Get the agreed security technology from the *X-SelectedTech* header and instantiate it.

*When either Alice or Bob process any error final response (SIP codes 4xx, 5xx or 6xx), a CANCEL or BYE request:* Rollback any security configuration done previously.

This completes the custom processing at the SIP user agents. The domain proxies follow a slightly different set of actions, which is described next.

**Processing at the SIP Proxies.** The processing at the proxies is somewhat more complex than at user agents. The main tasks of the proxy at each domain are: to ensure that the agreed security requirements can be provided; to negotiate the technology used to implement them; and to detect non-compliant domains for bypassing them.

The first of these tasks can be performed by using the *X-MinSecurity* and *X-MaxSecurity* headers to signal the required security requirements, and checking them at each step. The requirements signaled within the SIP request can be modified by the proxy, if the current security domain makes it necessary. For example, if the minimum security level that is acceptable is higher at one of the traversed domains than as specified in the end user's requirements, then the minimum values in the *X-MinSecurity* header must be updated to reflect the higher values. In case one of the traversed domains cannot provide the minimum level of security that the end user is requesting, then the SIP call must be terminated. This is done at SIP level, by sending an appropriate response to the caller and an appropriate request to the callee that let them know that the call has been unauthorized to progress because of not acceptable parameters, and thus allowing both parties to try a renegotiation.

The second task is carried out by using the *X-TechList* and *X-SelectedTech* headers, just like in the case of the SIP user agents.

The third task, that is, the detection of non-compliant domains, is carried out by using the *X-Via* and *X-Tunnel* headers. Each proxy at a compliant domain needs to know whether the call has traversed any non-compliant domains, and then it must take some action to allow a tunnel (such as an IPsec tunnel) to be established for bypassing them. To detect the non-compliant domains, each proxy gets from the standard SIP *Via* header the address of the last SIP proxy visited. Then, it gets from the custom *X-Via* header the address of the last one which was negotiation-compliant. If both proxies are not the same, then at least one non-compliant domain has been traversed, and a tunnel must be set up between the router of the last compliant domain (taken also from the *X-Via* header) and the router of the current domain. These endpoints are recorded in an *X-Tunnel* header which is created and appended to the SIP request, for later processing.

To summarize, the proxy behavior at each stage is described here, from P1's point of view. P2 would perform an analogous process:

*When processing the INVITE request from Alice*

– Check if any non-compliant nodes have been traversed, by comparing the contents of the *Via* and *X-Via* headers. If such is this case, create an appropriate *X-Tunnel* header and add it to the original request: "X-Tunnel: *this*

*domain router*;to=*last compliant router seen*". This case is not met in this call, anyway.
- Add own *X-Via* header, including proxy and router addresses: "X-Via: *P1*; router=*R1*"
- Forward the request to P2.

*When processing the OK response from P2*

- Get the technologies available at the previous hop (P2) from the *X-TechList* header and then remove it from the message. Let *prevTechList* be this list of technologies.
- Merge the security requirements carried in the message with the domain policies and P1's own capabilities. If requirements are not compatible, cancel the call; otherwise, update the *X-MinSecurity* and *X-MaxSecurity* headers accordingly. Then, obtain from the domain policies the list of available technologies for implementing the resulting set of parameters, and place it in a new *X-TechList* header. Let *ownTechList* be this list.
- If the intersection of *prevTechList* and *ownTechList* is empty, cancel the call. Otherwise, pick up a technology from it, store it internally (this includes its needed configuration parameters such as key lengths) and proceed with the next step. Let *chosenTech* be the chosen technology.
- If the response carries any *X-Tunnel* header meaning that this node should be the endpoint of a tunnel, set up the tunnel interface.
- Forward the response to Alice.

*When processing the ACK response from Alice*

- Get the security technology chosen by Alice from the *X-SelectedTech* header and remove this header. Let *prevTech* be this technology.
- Retrieve the previously stored security technology (*chosenTech*), and put it in a new *X-SelectedTech* header.
- Forward the ACK to P2, carrying the new *X-SelectedTech* header.
- Instantiate both the *chosenTech* and *prevTech* technologies.

*When processing any error final response (SIP codes 4xx, 5xx or 6xx), a CANCEL request or a BYE request*

- Rollback any configuration done previously at the domain router.
- Forward the response to the appropriate node.

# 5   Related Work

There are a wide number of security protocols which define how to negotiate security preferences or parameters before establishing protected communications. Some examples are SSL/TLS [4] or IKE [9]. In order to provide a higher level approach, several proposals have been designed using SIP. For example, in [2], SIP is used by user agents to agree on security technologies with the SIP entity at the next hop. This proposal supports only the agreement between the user agent and the next hop, whether it is a proxy or another user agent. It is based only on the technology point of view of the negotiation process, and does not take into account security requirements imposed by the peers.

A Content Negotiation Framework for SIP is described in [15]. It provides a more general approach allowing SIP peers to indicate capabilities and characteristics through the negotiation. Although it could be used to describe security technologies in a similar way as described in this work, it lacks a more complete per-hop processing able to define a secure overlay across heterogeneous domains. Another similar approach, based on the establishment of caller preferences is described in [14].

From another point of view, the establishment of secure overlay networks has also been treated in other proposals; perhaps, X-Bone [18] is the most important. This proposal allows the establishment of overlay networks in a dynamic way by means of secure IPsec tunnels between network elements. X-Bone allows the establishment of those secure channels when the information is exchanged between two peers, but it does not allow negotiating any kind of security requirements or technologies.

## 6    Conclusions

This work presents a way to define security overlay networks in a dynamic way, taking into account the security requirements inside each security domain, and with complete independence of low level security technologies. We have presented how SIP can be extended to transport the security requirements and technologies imposed by organizations in order to implement a virtual security negotiation and how the standard SIP entities have to deal with those requirements. It is important to note that no new entities are added or defined in this proposal and no standard SIP headers have been modified.

The work also introduces a way to represent security requirements, based on different security parameters such as integrity, authentication or access control, and proposes a way to represent minimum and maximum values as well as the necessary headers to transport the definition of security technologies. In order to show a valid scenario, we also have presented a real testbed which implements the exposed work.

As a statement of direction, we are working on the integration with bootstrapping mechanisms and high level applications that could require protected exchange of information, such as multimedia videoconferencing, peer-to-peer applications, etc. Another interesting way to extend this work is to enrich the semantics of the custom headers, in order to detect end-to-end support of shared security technologies and instantiate them that way, thus reducing the amount of configuration at the domains.

**Acknowledgments.** This work has been funded by the DESEREC EU IST Project (IST-2004-026600), within the EC Sixth Framework Programme (FP6).

# References

1. D. G. Andersen, H. Balakrishnan, M. F. Kaashoek, and R. Morris. *Resilient Overlay Networks*, 2001. In proceedings of the18th Symposium on Operating Systems Principles.
2. J. Arkko, V. Torvinen, A. Niemi, and T. Haukka. *Security Mechanism Agreement for the Session Initiation Protocol (SIP)*, January 2003. IETF RFC 3329.
3. M. Castro, P. Druschel, A. Ganesh, A. Rowstron, and D. S. Wallach. *Security for structured peer-to-peer overlay networks*, December 2002. In proceedings of the 5th symposium on Operating Systems Design and Implementation OSDI02.
4. T. Dierks and C. Allen. *The TLS protocol version 1.0*, January 1999. IETF RFC 2246.
5. D. Durham et al. *The COPS (Common Open Policy Service) protocol*, January 2000. IETF RFC 2748.
6. J. Rosenberg et al. *SIP: Session Initiation Protocol*, June 2002. IETF RFC 3261.
7. ITU-T. *ITU-T Recommendation H.323. Packet-based multimedia communications systems*, July 2003.
8. M. Kay. *XSL Transformations (XSLT) Version 2.0*, November 2005. W3C Recommendation. World Wide Web Consortium (W3C).
9. S. Kent and R. Atkinson. *Security Architecture for the Internet Protocol*, November 1998. IETF RFC 2401.
10. A. Keromystis, V. Misra, and D. Rubenstein. *SOS: Secure Overlay Services*, August 2002. In proceedings of ACM SIGCOMM.
11. University of Murcia. Spain. *UMU Policy Based Network Management (UMU-PBNM)*, June 2006. http://pbnm.dif.um.es.
12. S. Ratnasamy, P. Francis, M. Handley, R. Karp, and S. Schenker. *A scalable content-addressable network*, 2001. In proceedings of the 2001 conference on applications, technologies, architectures and protocols for computer communications.
13. J. Rosenberg and H. Schulzrinne. *Session Initiation Protocol (SIP): Locating SIP servers*, June 2002. IETF RFC 3263.
14. J. Rosenberg, H. Schulzrinne, and P. Kyzivat. *Caller Preferences for the Session Initiation Protocol (SIP)*, August 2004. IETF RFC 3841.
15. J. Rosenberg, H. Shulzrinne, and P. Kyzivat. *Indicating User Agent Capabilities in the Session Initiation Protocol (SIP)*, August 2004. IETF RFC 3840.
16. S. Shi. *Design of Overlay Networks for Internet Multicast*, August 2002. PhD Thesis.
17. J. Touch and S. Hotz. *The X-Bone*, November 1998. Third Global Internet Mini-Conference at Globecom '98.
18. J. Touch, Y. Wang, V. Pingali, L. Eggert, and R. Zhou. *A Global X-Bone for Network Experiments*, March 2005. Finn.Proc. IEEE Tridentcom 2005.
19. D. C. Verma. Simplyfing network administrator using policy-based management. *IEEE Network*, 20-6(16), 2002.
20. F. Yergau, T. Bray, J. Paoli, C. M. Sperberg-McQueen, and E. Maler. *Extensible Markup Language (XML) 1.0 (Third Edition)*, February 2004. W3C Recommendation. World Wide Web Consortium (W3C).

# Vulnerabilities and Possible Attacks Against the GPRS Backbone Network

Christos Xenakis and Lazaros Merakos

Security Group, Communication Networks Laboratory
Department of Informatics & Telecommunications, University of Athens
15784 Athens, Greece
{xenakis,merakos}@di.uoa.gr
http://www.cnl.di.uoa.gr/

**Abstract.** This paper presents the security weaknesses and the possible attacks, which threaten the GPRS backbone network and the data that either reside at the network or are transferred through it. These attacks may be performed by malicious third parties, mobile users, network operators or network operator personnel, which exploit the weaknesses of the employed technology and the security measures applied to the GPRS backbone. The possible attacks against the GPRS backbone may result in the compromise of end-users security, the users over billing, the disclosure or alteration of critical information, the services unavailability, the network breakdown, etc. The analyzed attacks and their consequences increase the risks associated with the usage of GPRS, and, thus, influence its deployment that realizes the concept of the mobile Internet.

## 1 Introduction

The General Packet Radio Services (GPRS) [1] is a service that provides packet radio access for Global System for Mobile Communications (GSM) users. The GPRS network architecture, which constitutes a migration step toward third-generation (3G) communication systems, consists of an overlay network onto the GSM network. In the wireless part, the GPRS technology reserves radio resources only when there is data to be sent, thus, ensuring the optimized utilization of radio resources. The fixed part of the network employs the IP technology and is connected to the public Internet. Taking advantage of these features, GPRS enables the provision of a variety of packet-oriented multimedia applications and services to mobile users, realizing the concept of the mobile Internet.

For the successful implementation of the new emerging applications and services over GPRS, security is considered as a vital factor. In order to meet security objectives, GPRS uses a specific security architecture, which aims at protecting the network against unauthorized access and the privacy of users. This architecture is based on the security measures applied in GSM, since the GPRS system is built on the GSM infrastructure. However, GPRS is more exposed to intruders compared to GSM [2][3]

J. Lopez (Ed.): CRITIS 2006, LNCS 4347, pp. 262–272, 2006.
© Springer-Verlag Berlin Heidelberg 2006

because it uses the IP technology, which presents known vulnerabilities. Similarly to IP networks, intruders to the GPRS system may attempt to breach the confidentiality, integrity, availability or otherwise attempt to abuse the system in order to compromise services, defraud users or any part of it.

This paper presents the security weaknesses and the possible attacks, which threaten the GPRS backbone network and the data that either reside at the network or are transferred through it. These attacks may be performed by malicious third parties, mobile users, network operators or network operator personnel, which exploit the weaknesses of the employed technology and the security measures applied to the GPRS backbone. The possible attacks against the GPRS backbone may result in the compromise of end-users security, the users over billing, the disclosure or alteration of critical information, the services unavailability, the network breakdown, etc. The analyzed attacks and their consequences increase the risks associated with the usage of GPRS, and, thus, influence its deployment that realizes the concept of the mobile Internet.

The rest of this article is organized as follows. Section 2 briefly describes the GPRS technology and the security measures applied to the GPRS backbone network. Section 3 presents the weaknesses of the security measures applied to the GPRS backbone. Section 4 analyzes the possible attacks that threaten the GPRS backbone and the data that either reside at the network or are transferred through it. Finally, section 5 contains the conclusions.

## 2 GPRS Technology

### 2.1 Network Architecture

The network architecture of GPRS [1] is presented in Fig.1. A GPRS user owns a Mobile Station (MS) that provides access to the wireless network. From the network side, the Base Station Subsystem (BSS) is a network part that is responsible for the control of the radio path. BSS consists of two types of nodes: the Base Station Controller (BSC) and the Base Transceiver Station (BTS). BTS is responsible for the radio coverage of a given geographical area, while BSC maintains radio connections towards MSs and terrestrial connections towards the fixed part of the network (core network).

The GPRS Core Network (CN) uses the network elements of GSM such as the Home Location Register (HLR), the Visitor Location Register (VLR), the Authentication Centre (AuC) and the Equipment Identity Register (EIR). HLR is a database used for the management of permanent data of mobile users. VLR is a database of the service area visited by an MS and contains all the related information required for the MS service handling. AuC maintains security information related to subscribers' identity, while EIR maintains information related to mobile equipments identity. Finally, the Mobile Service Switching Centre (MSC) is a network element responsible for circuit-switched services (e.g., voice call) [1].

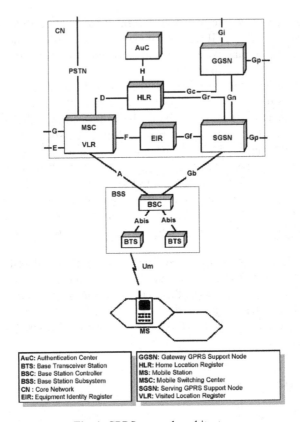

**Fig. 1.** GPRS network architecture

As presented previously, GPRS reuses the majority of the GSM network infrastructure. However, in order to build a packet-oriented mobile network some new network elements (nodes) are required, which handle packet-based traffic. The new class of nodes, called GPRS support nodes (GSN), is responsible for the delivery and routing of data packets between a MS and an external packet data network (PDN). More specifically, a Serving GSN (SGSN) is responsible for the delivery of data packets from, and to, a MS within its service area. Its tasks include packet routing and transfer, mobility management, logical link management, and authentication and charging functions. A Gateway GSN (GGSN) acts as an interface between the GPRS backbone and an external PDN. It converts the GPRS packets coming from the SGSN into the appropriate packet data protocol (PDP) format (e.g., IP), and forwards them to the corresponding PDN. Similar is the functionality of GGSN in the opposite direction.

Signaling exchange in the GPRS backbone is mainly based on the Signaling System 7 (SS7) technology [5], which does not support any security measure for the GPRS deployment. Similarly, the GPRS Tunneling Protocol (GTP) [4] that is employed for communication between GSNs does not support security. Thus, user data and signaling information in the GPRS backbone network are conveyed in clear-text exposing them to various security threats. In addition, inter-network communications (between different operators) are based on the public Internet, which enables IP spoofing to any malicious third party who gets access to it. In the sequel, the security measures applied to the GPRS backbone network are presented.

## 2.2 Security Measures for the GPRS Backbone

The responsibility for security protection of the GPRS backbone as well as inter-network communications belongs to mobile operators. An operator utilizes private IP addressing and Network Address Translation (NAT) [6] to restrict unauthorized access to the GPRS backbone. He may also apply firewalls at the borders of the GPRS backbone network in order to protect it from unauthorized penetrations. Firewalls protect the network by enforcing security policies (e.g., user traffic addressed to a network element is discard). Using security policies the GPRS operator may ensure that only traffic initiated from the MS and not from the Internet should pass through a firewall. This is done for two reasons: (a) to restrict traffic in order to protect the MS and the network elements from external attacks; and (b) to protect the MS from receiving un-requested traffic. Un-requested traffic may be unwanted for mobile subscribers since they pay for the traffic received as well. The GPRS operator may also want to disallow some bandwidth demanding protocols preventing a group of subscribers to consume so much bandwidth that other subscribers are noticeably affected. In addition, application level firewalls prevent direct access through the use of proxies for services, which analyze application commands, perform authentication and keep logs.

Since firewalls do not provide privacy and confidentiality, the Virtual Private Network (VPN) technology [7] has to complement them to protect data in transit. A VPN is used for the authentication and the authorization of user access to corporate resources, the establishment of secure tunnels between the communicating parties, and the encapsulation and protection of the data transmitted by the network. In the majority of GPRS implementations, pre-configured, static VPNs can be employed to protect data transfer between GPRS network elements (e.g., an SGSN and a GGSN that belong to the same backbone), between different GPRS backbone networks that belong to different mobile operators, or between a GPRS backbone and a remote corporate private network. The border gateway, which resides at the border of the GPRS backbone, is a network element that provides firewall capabilities and also maintains static, pre-configured VPNs to specific peers.

## 3 Security Weaknesses of the GPRS Backbone

Although GPRS have been designed with security in mind, it presents some essential security weaknesses, which may lead to the realization of security attacks that threaten network operation and data transfer through it. In the following, the security weaknesses of GPRS that are related to the GPRS backbone network for both signaling and data plane are presented and analyzed.

## 3.1  Signaling Plane

As mentioned previously, the SS7 technology, used for signaling exchange in GPRS, does not support security protection. Specifically, it does not support any security measure that provides node and message authentication, data confidentiality and message integrity. Until recently, this was not perceived to be a problem, since SS7 networks belonged to a small number of large institutions (telecom operator). However, the rapid deployment of mobile systems and the liberalization of the telecommunication market have dramatically increased the number of operators (for both fixed and mobile networks) that are interconnected through the SS7 technology. This fact provokes a significant threat to the GPRS network security, since it increases the probability of an adversary to get access to the network or a legitimate operator to act maliciously.

The lack of security measures in the SS7 technology, used in GPRS, results also in the unprotected exchange of signaling messages between a VLR and a VLR/HLR, or a VLR and other fixed network nodes. Although these messages may include critical information for the mobile subscribers and the networks operation like ciphering keys, authentication data (e.g., authentication triplets), user subscription data (e.g., International Mobile Subscriber Identity - IMSI), user billing data, network billing data, etc., they are conveyed in a clear-text within the serving network, as well as between the home network and the serving network. For example, the VLR of a serving network may use the IMSI to request authentication data for a single user from its home network, and the latter forwards them to the requesting VLR without any security measure. Thus, the exchanges of signalling messages, which are based on SS7, may disclose sensitive data of mobile subscribers and networks, since they are conveyed over insecure network connections without security precautions.

## 3.2  Data Plane

Similarly to the signaling plane, the data plane of the GPRS backbone presents significant security weaknesses, since the introduction of IP technology in the GPRS core shifts towards open and easily accessible network architectures (i.e., lack of authentication, confidentiality and integrity security measures). More specifically, the data encryption mechanism employed in GPRS does not extend far enough towards the core network, resulting also in a clear-text transmission of user data in it. Thus, a malicious, which gets access to the network, may either obtain access to sensitive data traffic or provide unauthorized/incorrect information to mobile users and network components. As presented previously, the security protection of users data in the fixed segment of the GPRS network mainly relies on two independent and complementary technologies, which are not undertaken by GPRS, but from the network operators. These technologies include firewalls that enforce security policies to the GPRS backbone network that belongs to an operator, and pre-configured VPNs that protect specific network connections.

However, firewalls were originally conceived to address security issues for fixed networks, and, thus, are not seamlessly applicable in mobile networks. They attempt to protect the clear-text transmitted data in the GPRS backbone from external attacks, but they are inadequate against attacks that originate from malicious mobile subscribers, as well as from network operator personnel or any other third party that gets access to the GPRS core network. Another vital issue regarding the deployment of firewalls in GPRS has to do with the consequences of mobility. The mobility of a user may imply roaming between networks and operators, which possibly results in the changing of the user address. This fact in conjunction with the static configuration of firewalls may potentially lead to discontinuity of service connectivity for the mobile user. Moreover, in some cases the security value of firewalls is considered limited as they allow direct connection to ports without distinguishing services.

Similarly to firewalls, the VPN technology, in many cases, fails to provide the necessary flexibility required by typical mobile users. Currently, VPNs for a significant number of GPRS subscribers are established in a static manner between the border gateway of a GPRS network and a remote security gateway of a corporate private network. This fact allows the realization of VPNs only between a security gateway of a large organization and a mobile operator, when a considerable amount of traffic requires protection. Thus, this scheme can provide VPN services neither to individual mobile users that may require on demand VPN establishment, nor to enterprise users that may roam internationally. In addition, static VPNs have to be reconfigured every time the VPN topology or VPN parameters change.

# 4   Attacks on the GPRS Backbone Network

Based on the previous analysis, it can be perceived that the GPRS technology presents some essential security weaknesses. This fact may lead to the realization of attacks that threaten the GPRS network and the data that either reside at the network or are transferred through it. In the following, the possible attacks that target the backbone network of a GPRS operator (see Fig. 2), the interface between network operators (Gp interface) and the interface to the public Interne (Gi interface) are presented and analyzed.

## 4.1   Attacks on the Backbone of a GPRS Operator

The backbone network of a GPRS operator, which connects the fixed nodes of the GPRS architecture, is threatened by malicious actions. These actions refer to both IP and SS7 technologies that are employed to convey user data and signaling information in this part of the network. In the following, the security attacks against the backbone network of a GPRS operator, classified by the transmission technology used (IP and SS7), are presented and analyzed.

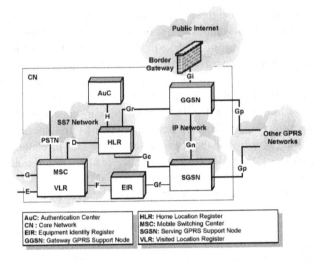

**Fig. 2.** GPRS backbone network

### 4.1.1  Attacks on the IP Technology (Gn Interface)

The IP technology is used to connect the SGSN and the GGSN of the same network operator (Gn interface) (see Fig.2). This connection may be built on the top of an already existing IP network, which is not dedicated to the GPRS traffic. Therefore, traffic that originates from outside of the GPRS network shares the GPRS backbone links with the GPRS traffic. The latter is conveyed in clear-text in the GPRS backbone since the GTP protocol, which is employed for both signaling and user data, does not support any security measure. The above situation might cause performance problems to the GPRS backbone (i.e., network overload) and expose the GPRS traffic to security threats (e.g., denial of service attacks, IP spoofing, compromise of confidentiality and privacy etc.) that the public Internet encounters. Therefore, the Gn Interface is vulnerable to attacks that can potentially lead to network downtime, loss of service, revenue loss and disgruntle customers. In the following, the most prominent security attacks that may be carried out against this part of the GPRS backbone network are presented.

Since the IP network that is used as a basis for the GPRS backbone is not dedicated to it, a malicious third party may masquerade as a legitimate part of the GPRS network by spoofing the address of a GPRS network component (e.g., GGSN or SGSN). Once the malicious party establishes himself as a legitimate network element, he is able to perform various actions that are detrimental to the mobile subscribers and the network operator. By executing commands that normally a legitimate network component does, the attack remains undetected until its results are noticeable. One of these attacks is related to the GTP protocol, and more specifically to the exploitation of the GTP commands like PDP context create, PDP context delete, PDP context update, etc. [4]. The attacker, who has access to the GPRS backbone network, is able to get information regarding the GTP tunneling by simply monitoring the GTP traffic, which is unencrypted. Without encryption, data carried by the GTP protocol can either be read or manipulated. Possessing the appropriate information, the attacker may create and forward to the GGSN of the network PDP context create, delete and update commands. These commands overload the GGSN under attack and change the servicing contexts of the mobile users that are currently served by the network, resulting in denial of service.

In addition to malicious third parties that get access to the GPRS backbone network, the mobile users (legitimate or not) may represent a threat to it. Since the MSs are behind the firewall, which is located between the GGSN and the public Internet, they may get access to the network elements of the GPRS backbone (i.e., SGSN, GGSN, DNS servers, O&M workstations, etc.). Having access to these elements, a malicious MS may perform various attacks such as denial of service, IP spoofing, compromise of confidentiality and privacy, etc. In addition, once the malicious MS gets access to the GPRS network, it may send massive amounts of data to unsuspecting users. Since the GPRS is a usage-based service, the mobile users under attack are over billed for content that they did not request for. Such an attack would be even more harmful than spam is for email, as it becomes much more than an annoyance.

Finally, a malicious MS in cooperation with a malicious server, which is located outside of the GPRS network, may also perform an over billing attack to a legitimate mobile subscriber. The malicious MS may hijack the IP address of the legitimate MS, and invokes a download from the malicious server. Once the downloading begins, the malicious MS exits the session. The legitimate MS (MS under attack) receives and gets charged for traffic that never requests for. The malicious parties could also execute this attack by sending broadcasts of unsolicited data to legitimate mobile subscribers. The result is still the same: the subscribers are billed for data that they did not solicited and might not have wanted.

### 4.1.2  Attacks on the SS7 Technology

If an attacker gets access to the GPRS backbone, he may also gain access to the signaling part of the network, and consequently to the network components that are connected through it, such as the AuC, the HLR, the VLR, etc. Having access to the signaling part of the network, the attacker is able to listen to critical information for the mobile subscribers and the network operation such as the permanent identities of mobile users (IMSI), temporary identities (Temporary Mobile Subscriber Identity – TMSI, and Temporary Logical Link Identity - TLLI), location information, authentication triplets, charging and billing data, etc [1]. This is feasible because the signaling network (SS7), used in GPRS, does not support security measures. Except for listening to the critical information exchanged, the attacker may either perform denial of service attacks to the GPRS signaling components or try to retrieve the sensitive information that they hold. For example, the AuC contains authentication information of the subscribed home users. A similar attack to that performed to retrieve the unique subscriber key, Ki, from a SIM-card can also be carried out to retrieve the Ki from the AuC. The AuC has to answer to a request made by a GPRS network component and returns valid authentication triples to be used in the authentication procedure of the involved MS. Thus, exploiting the absence of authentication and integrity protection mechanisms in SS7, a malicious party may masquerade as a network element and retrieve critical information that should be kept confidential.

## 4.2  Attacks on the Interface Between Network Operators (Gp Interface)

The Gp Interface (see Fig. 2), which provides connectivity between GPRS networks that belong to different operators, is also vulnerable to malicious actions. This interface supports users roaming and conveys: (a) GTP traffic between a local network and the home network of a roaming user; (b) roaming information between a GPRS network and a GPRS Routing Exchange (GRX) operator, which provides roaming services to cooperating networks; and (c) Domain Name Server (DNS) information. The security threats to the Gp interface mainly concern with the availability of resources and services, the authentication and authorization of users and actions, and the integrity and confidentiality of the data transferred. A vital security issue of the Gp interface is the lack of security measures in the GTP protocol. In the following, the most important security attacks that target the Gp interface are presented and analyzed.

Trust and reliability between the cooperating GPRS network operators influence the level of security that each operator supports. A malicious operator has the ability to generate a sufficient amount of traffic (either IP or GTP) directed at the border gateway, the SGSN or the GGSN of an operator under attack. In this way, the GPRS nodes are flooded with useless and unwanted traffic that consumes the majority of processing and communication resources. This may result in preventing subscribers from being able to roam, to be attached to the GPRS network, to forward data to external networks (i.e., Internet), etc. In addition, the attacker (the malicious operator) might perform attacks that target the GTP protocol, such as deleting or updating PDP contexts. These actions remove or modify the GTP tunnels between the SGSN and the GGSN (of an operator under attack) that are used for user data transfer, and, thus, denying users service.

Since the GTP protocol provides no authentication for SGSNs and GGSNs, a malicious operator or an attacker with access to the Gp Interface may create a bogus SGSN. Using information regarding users subscription, which can be captured from the GTP traffic (GTP messages are conveyed unencrypted), the bogus SGSN may create GTP tunnels between itself and a legitimate GGSN. After the establishment of such tunnels, the network, where the legitimate GGSN belongs to, provides unauthorized Internet access to the attacker and, possibly, access to cooperating networks. In addition, the bogus SGSN may send Update PDP context request messages [1] to a legitimate SGSN, which is handling the GTP sessions of a mobile subscriber. In this way, the bogus SGSN takes the responsibility for handling the GTP sessions of the user. Thus, the attacker may intercept the user data exchanged by the sessions, compromising end-user security.

## 4.3  Attacks on the Interface to the Public Internet (Gi Interface)

The network of a GPRS operator is not only threatened by attacks that originate from inside of it and the networks of cooperating operators, but also from outside of them. The Gi interface (see Fig. 2) connects the GPRS network to the public Internet and service providers that provide services to mobile subscribers. Since the applications of mobile subscribers can be whatever is carried by the Internet technology, the Gi interface may carry any type of traffic. This fact exposes the GPRS network elements and the mobile subscribers to a variety of threats that the public Internet encounters, such as viruses, worms, Trojan horses, denial of service attacks, and other malicious network traffic.

Similarly to the Gp interface, denial of service attacks represent the largest threat to the Gi interface. Attackers may be able to flood the links that connect the GPRS network to external packet data networks with useless traffic, thereby, prohibiting legitimate traffic to pass. The flood traffic might target to the MSs or the network elements causing availability problems to the followed network paths and the involved components.

Apart from harm to the network availability, the GPRS data are conveyed unprotected over the public Internet enabling anyone to read and/or manipulate them, and, thus, compromising user data confidentiality and integrity. In addition, an adversary may exploit the unprotected user related information causing huge bills to the GPRS users. This is feasible because the GPRS billing system is based on the amount of traffic transmitted and received. The over billing attack can be achieved by sending large emails from a malicious external network to the MSs, or by creating viruses that are transferred to the MSs. A virus may have the property to send dummy packets from the infected MS to a malicious server, without any notice to the user.

## 5  Conclusions

This paper has presented the security weaknesses and the possible attacks, which threaten the backbone network of a GPRS operator and the data that either reside at the network or are transferred through it. The identified weaknesses can be exploited by malicious third parties, mobile users, network operators or network operator personnel, which target both IP and SS7 technologies that are employed to convey user data and signaling information in the GPRS backbone network. The results of possible attacks might be the monitoring of MS usage, the downloading of unwanted files, the realization of unwanted session calls, the availability of resources and services, the authentication and authorization of users and actions, and the integrity and confidentiality of the data transferred. The analyzed attacks and their consequences increase the risks associated with the usage of GPRS, and, thus, influence its deployment that realizes the concept of the mobile Internet. In order to defeat these risks and the inabilities of the GPRS technology, research activities on the identified security issues should be triggered and specific security measures should be designed and applied.

## References

[1] 3GPP TS 03.6 (V7.9.0), "GPRS Service Description, Stage 2", Sept. 2002.
[2] P. Pagliusi, "A Contemporary Foreword on GSM Security", Proc. Infrastructure Security International Conference (InfraSec 2002), LNCS 2437, Springer-Verlag, 2002, pp 129-144.
[3] C. Mitchell, "The security of the GSM air Interface protocol", Technical Report, Royal Holloway University of London, Aug. 2001, http://www.ma.rhul.ac.uk/techreports/

[4] 3GPP TS 09.60 (V7.10.0), "GPRS Tunneling Protocol (GTP) across the Gn and Gp Interface", Dec. 2002.

[5] 3GPP TS 09.02 (v7.15.0) "Mobile Application Part (MAP) specification", March 2004.

[6] P. Srisuresh, M. Holdrege, "IP Network Address Translator (NAT) Terminology and Considerations", RFC 2663, Aug. 1999.

[7] B. Gleeson, A. Lin, J. Heinanen, G. Armitage, A. Malis, "A Framework for IP Based Virtual Private Networks", RFC 2764, Feb. 2000.

[8] C. Xenakis and L. Merakos, "Security in third Generation Mobile Networks", Computer Communications, Vol. 27, No. 7, May 2004, pp. 638-650.

# A Framework for Secure and Verifiable Logging in Public Communication Networks

Vassilios Stathopoulos[1,*], Panayiotis Kotzanikolaou[1,*], and Emmanouil Magkos[2]

[1] Authority for the Assurance of Communications Security and Privacy (ADAE)
3 Ierou Lochou str., 15124 Maroussi, Greece
{v.stathopoulos,p.kotzanikolaou}@adae.gr
[2] Ionian University, Department of Informatics,
Palaia Anaktora, 49100, Corfu, Greece
emagos@ionio.gr

**Abstract.** In this paper we are focusing on secure logging for public network providers. We review existing security threat models against system logging and we extend these to a new threat model especially suited in the environment of telecommunication network providers. We also propose a framework for secure logging in public communication networks as well as realistic implementations designs, which are more resilient to the identified security threats. A key role to the proposed framework is given to an independent Regulatory Authority, which is responsible to verify the integrity of the log files.

## 1 Introduction

Public network providers, (fixed, mobile telephony and Internet Providers) consider privacy in communication as a valuable asset. Indeed, attacks against the confidentiality of communications and the privacy of their customers may lead to severe consequences of commercial and legal nature. In many countries Regulatory Authorities ($RAs$) are responsible to regulate and audit the security level of public network providers, in order to preserve communications security and privacy for the citizens.

Although a lot of security measures are in place in telecommunication networks and well defined standards exist there are still security holes. Threats such as external intrusion, communication interception, unauthorized access to private data (*e.g.* CDR files) and abuse of privileges by insiders must be considered. Existing vulnerabilities such as overestimation of security measures, non conformance with security measures and lack of dependable and secure logging and auditing mechanisms increase the security risks. Since it is not always possible to prevent security breaches, it is required to have in place adequate detective security measures.

---

\* Research supported by the Hellenic Authority for the Assurance of Communications Security and Privacy (ADAE) – http://www.adae.gr

J. Lopez (Ed.): CRITIS 2006, LNCS 4347, pp. 273–284, 2006.

System logging is the most important detective security measure. Log files are maintained in almost every system and they are usually examined during security audits, either external or internal. Indeed, during regular security audits, log files may be examined and correlated, in order to assure that the intended technical measures are in place and that the security policies and procedures are implemented. During non-scheduled security audits, *e.g.* as a response to a security incident, log files are analyzed in order to discover the cause of the incident, such as lack of security measures, non conformance with security procedures, system miss-configuration etc.

In this paper we are focusing on secure logging for public network providers. We review existing security threat models against system logging and we extend these to a new threat model especially suited in the environment of telecommunication network providers. We also propose a framework for secure logging in public communication networks as well as realistic implementations designs, which are more resilient to the identified security threats. A key role to the proposed framework is given to an independent Regulatory Authority. Each provider is responsible to send integrity proofs of its log files to the Regulatory Authority, which in turn is responsible to to remotely store the integrity proofs and verify the integrity of the log files.

Our paper is motivated from the recently announced interception case in a mobile telecommunications provider in Greece (see for example [1]). As the Greek authorities and the provider itself revealed, part of the core network of the provider was compromised by some unknown trojan-like program. According to published information, the malicious software infected the core network. Then, it activated the Lawful Interception (LI) component in the infected elements, which is by default installed in inactive mode, and made possible the call interception of several subscribers.[1] The malicious program turned off several logging procedures in order not to alarm about its presence or the fact that the LI component had been activated. The underestimation of several security threats and vulnerabilities regarding logging procedures and mechanisms, did not allow the immediate detection of the incident.

The rest of this paper is organized as follows. In Section 2 we review the related work in secure logging. In Section 3 we describe our threat model for secure logging in telecommunication networks in comparison with existing threat models. In Section 4 we describe the proposed framework for secure logging which deals with the identified threats. Finally, Section 5 concludes this paper.

## 2    Related Work

In *real logging systems*, the security of logging and auditing procedures is usually relied on the assumption that the host's Operating System is not corrupted. Secure systems aim at improving the robustness of the logging system itself without relying on the security features of the underlying system. The *Syslog-sign*

---

[1] The announced list of the victims included among others the Prime Minister, Ministers and Ex-Ministers.

IETF draft [2] describes a logging system with message source authentication and message integrity, built above *Syslog*, a cross-platform standard for remote logging on a central repository. In the ReVirt system [3] the OS is moved to a virtual machine and the integrity of the logging system is protected against external attacks with OS-level privileges.

Cryptographic research in secure logging systems aims at building logs that are irrevocably *tamper-evident*. In a scheme presented by Bellare and Yee [4], the MAC key that authenticates the logs entries is sequentially computed using an one-way cryptographic function, in order to achieve the *forward integrity* (FI) property, *i.e.* if an adversary compromises the current MAC key, she cannot modify old entries without being detected.

Schneier and Kelsey [5] propose a secure logging scheme that detects any attempts to delete or modify log entries on a host that has been compromised. Log entries are linked using a technique called *hash chaining* [6], where each entry contains a cryptographic digest of the previous entry. Moreover, each entry is encrypted and authenticated using an "epoch" secret that is updated using an one-way cryptographic function. The initial secret is shared with an external trusted party $T$ who is able to independently verify the integrity of the logged data. The scheme of [5] satisfies the FI property and it allows the selective disclosure of the encrypted log data, using permission masks as an authorization list.

In recent works [7,8,9,10], the scheme of [5] has been extended to provide for keyword searching on the encrypted data using public key based cryptographic techniques [8], to enable tamper-evident remote logging in resource-poor devices [9], or to detect software tampering in DRM systems [7]. In [10] the *LogCrypt* system implements the scheme of [5] and extends it to support public-key signatures for accountability and public verifiability of the submitted logs, while it also discusses secure aggregation of multiple logs in a distributed logging system. Secure aggregation of multiple logs for forensic computing was also addressed in a recent scheme that uses distributed *Merkle Trees* [11] for the collection of the log files.

## 3   Threat Models

In the general case, the logs are generated by one or more log *Generators* (devices, systems, software e.t.c.) and are sent to the *Log Server* through a relay mechanism. Existing threat models include:

*Trusted Generators and Marginally Trusted Log Server.* In this model (*e.g.* [5]) the logs are generated and relayed to the Log Server within a trusted environment. However, although the log server is protected, it cannot be guaranteed that it will not be compromised. Consequently, in this threat model the security attacks which are mainly considered are disclosure and modification attacks against the stored logs.

*Distributed Log Generators and Marginally Trusted Log Server.* In this case (*e.g.*[9]) the log generators and the log servers are in a fully distributed environment. The log servers are considered, as in the previous case, marginally trusted. In addition to the previous model, attacks during the transmission of log data are considered. Since the logs are generated in a distributed environment, the log messages are not assumed by default to originate from the claimed device. Hence, attacks against the transmission of log entries are also examined such as: impersonation attacks against log generators, and impersonation and disclosure attacks against log messages during transmission.

### 3.1    Our Threat Model for Public Network Providers

Existing threat models do not consider *insider attacks* and *collusion attacks* between log generators and log servers. Our threat model integrates and extends existing threat models in order to protect log files from attacks which have been identified within the environment of public network providers. For example, a possible threat may be that the log generators deliberately send modified log messages, or that the stored logs are deliberately modified after their storage to the log server with the active participation of the log server administrator.

Our threat model assumes that all entities involved in the logging process are *semi-trusted*, including the generator(s) of log entries, the log server(s) that stores the log files and the communication channel. Consequently, in addition to the threats described in the previous models, we also consider the following threats:

- Modification attacks on the stored logs from compromised log servers.
- Modification attacks from compromised log generators.
- Modification attacks from colluding log generators and log servers.

## 4    A Framework for Secure Logging in Public Networks

We consider a semi-trusted environment for the provider as described in Section 3.1. Thus, the security framework must protect logging systems from both external and internal attacks. We assume the existence of a trusted Regulatory Authority $RA$ which is responsible to assure that the Providers take all reasonable measures to preserve communications' security and privacy. In regular audits or after a security incident, the $RA$ may examine the log files of the provider, in order to determine the cause of the incident.

Provided that log files are important evidence, a security framework is required that will guarantee the availability and the integrity of logging operations and log files. Such a framework consists of the following phases:

### 4.1    Phase 1: Define the Network and Operational Events

Before any security measures are taken, it is important to explicitly define what is important to be logged. This decision involves both the Provider and the $RA$. From the Provider's side, an effective logging supports system maintenance,

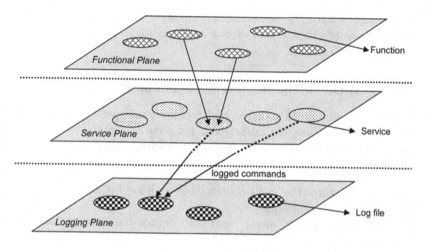

**Fig. 1.** An abstract representation of a Log Reference Model

troubleshooting and internal security audits. From the *RA*'s side, logging information helps in investigating the cause of a security incident and as evidence in a court of law.

In order to determine the events that must be logged within a Provider, a *Log Reference Model* is defined – see Fig. 1. This model is an abstract representation linking *Functions i.e.* general categories of network and operational events, to the corresponding *Log Files* that monitor these Functions, through the *Services* which implement the Functions. This model analyzes the logging needs from three different views, called *Planes*. These planes are:

- **Functional Plane.** It models the network and operational events within a network, without taking into consideration implementation details, architectural or topology constraints and design requirements. Suggestively and not limitedly in a provider's environment the following categories of Functions should be logged: (1) *Security Functions* (*e.g.* system access control, password management, user management, Lawful Interception, Data Retention). (2) *Service Management Functions* (*e.g.* monitoring, troubleshooting, management services) and (3) *Network Management Functions* (*e.g.* network configuration, network connectivity, routing).
- **Service Plane.** It describes all specific services which are executed within the network or IT nodes. It discriminates system from application services, while it takes into consideration the OS platform, communication protocols and interconnections and hardware. Examples of services of this plane are the snmp service, the dsl service, the password management service, the AAA service, the radius service etc.
- **Logging Plane.** It describes specific commands and events of each used service, which can be grouped into separated log files. For example, the command "show user" (captured for displaying user names) will be logged

in a log file named "password management". This log file will correspond to the password management service, which implements part of the security management functions.

## 4.2   Phase 2: Define the Requirements of Log Files

After the list of Functions to be logged has been interpreted to Services and consequently to Log Files, the operational and security requirements of each log file must be determined. In particular, requirements in this category define for each log file:

1. Log File Structure (the fields contained in each log file),
2. Required generation frequency,
3. Storage requirements (form, local and/or remote storage and storage duration).

Organizing logging and log files requirements, depends on the agreement among the Providers and the Regulatory Authority. This constitutes an administrative procedure without requiring any extra equipment at the providers' premises. Hence the cost is minimized.

## 4.3   Phase 3: Security Measures Against External Attacks

In order to secure the log files from external and common internal threats all the functions which have been identified in the previous phases must be securely logged. This can be achieved by using the secure logging scheme of Schneier and Kesley [5] (see Fig. 2). We briefly describe this approach.

Each log server is supplied with an initial symmetric key $A_0$. The log file consists of consequent log entries $L_1, ..., L_n$. The key $A_0$ is updated for each new log entry, through a cryptographic one-way hash function $hash$, i.e. $A_i = hash(A_{i-1})$. Each log data entry $L_i$ contains the log data $D_i$, which is encrypted and integrity protected. In order to encrypt the log data, a key $K_i$ is derived from $A_i$, by hashing the concatenation of the key $A_i$ with the permission mask $W_i$ of the data entry $D_i$. Thus, $K_i = hash(W_i, A_i)$ and the encryption is $E_{K_i}(D_i)$. For integrity protection of the log entries, a hash-chain is used. Each log entry $L_i$ contains the hash value $Y_i = hash(Y_{i-1}, E_{K_i}(D_i), W_i)$, (for $Y_0$ a padding value is used), as well as the Message Authentication Code $Z_i = MAC_{A_i}(Y_i)$. Thus, each time only one $MAC$ and one hash value is stored, which contains all the previously hashed results. This preserves forward integrity from outsiders, since if the key $A_i$ is not compromised, the attacker cannot modify the log entries undetected.

## 4.4   Phase 4: Security Measures Against Internal Attacks

Although after each log entry $L_i$ is stored in the log file and $A_i$ has been updated to $A_{i+1}$, the previous key $A_i$ is deleted, it is possible for a compromised log server to modify the log file. Suppose that the system is compromised at the time $t_i$, with or without the active participation of the log server administrator. This means that the current key, say $A_i$, is revealed to the adversary and also that the adversary has access to the log files from the time $t_i$ and after. The adversary does not change the log entries at that time. Then, at time $t_j$, $j > i$, the adversary modifies the log entries $i, i + 1, ..., j$. By using the key $A_i$ that the adversary possesses, the keys $A_{i+1}, ..., A_j$ are reconstructed and the original log entries are replaced by the manipulated log entries. This attack cannot be traced, even if the logging mechanism simply replaces the $MAC$s with digital signatures (as in [9]), since if the symmetric key is compromised, then all the keying material will have been compromised, including signature keys.

To deal with these attacks, we enhance the secure logging system described above with digital signatures and a trusted $RA$. In addition with the security measures described in the previous section, the following security measures are combined:

- Limited interaction of the provider with the trusted $RA$.
- Digital signatures of log files in predefined time periods.
- Digital signatures of log files in random time intervals.
- Remote storage of digital signatures in the $RA$.

The proposed extension is shown in Fig. 2. We assume that a secure communication interface is always available between the Provider and the $RA$. Moreover, in addition with the symmetric keys used to protect the log entries, each log server is assigned with two independent public/secret key pairs, $PK_1/SK_1$, $PK_2/SK_2$ and the corresponding digital certificates $Cert_1$, $Cert_2$. The digital certificates are issued by a trusted certification authority, so that all the parties can verify the validity of the signatures generated with the keys $SK_1$, $SK_2$. The key management functions such as generation, certification, revocation and updating of the signature keys may be supported by one or more independent certification authorities, which are trusted by the $RA$ and the Providers.

**Manual signing of the log files.** In order to retain integrity proofs for the provider's log files, the $RA$ periodically receives digital signatures of each log file. The $RA$ has defined a signature period $T$ for each log file[2]. The predefined signatures are generated as follows:

The Log Server administrator manually takes a copy of the log file instance and signs it in an isolated (off-line) environment. The signature is generated with the key $SK_1$. Note that $SK_1$ is not installed in the Log Server so that a successful attack in the Log Server will not affect the security of the key $SK_1$. Then, each signature $sig_1, sig_2, ...$ is send to the $RA$ through a well-defined interface (marked as A in Fig. 2). The whole procedure is periodically repeated at the end of each period $T$.

---

[2] This can be performed in the second phase where the requirements of each log file are set.

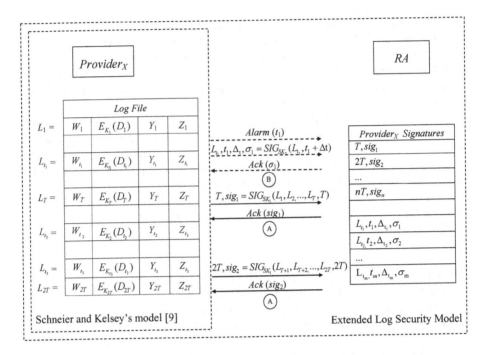

**Fig. 2.** Extending the secure log system

On receiving a signature, the $RA$ acknowledges it and stores it in a secure storage space for future audits. These signatures can be later verified by the $RA$ by accessing the certificate $Cert_1$ and the actual log file at the provider's premises. Since the $RA$ holds the signatures of the log file instances, any malicious modification of these instances *after* the corresponding signatures have been sent to the $RA$ can be detected, even if the symmetric keys $A_0, A_1, \ldots$ at the Provider's side have been compromised.

Since the predefined signing procedure is off-line and requires human intervention, it cannot be performed in short time periods. On the other hand, a very long time period $T$ reduces the integrity protection of the protected log files. According to the security needs, it is recommended that $T$ is between one day to one week. In order to reduce the operational overhead involved with the manual signing and the key management procedures, these can be integrated with ordinary manual operations of the administrators. Well-defined signing and key management procedures may reduce the additional operational costs to an acceptable level.

**Automated signing of critical log events.** As described above, the manual signing of the log files may detect any modification of a log file instance *after* the signature has been send to the $RA$. However, it does not protect from modification attacks, which have taken place *before* the signature has been generated.

In order to protect from modification attacks within signing periods, the *critical* log events are automatically signed and send to the $RA$. The automated signatures are generated as follows:

The *RA* defines a list of critical events, *i.e.* log events which should be immediately stored in the *RA*'s side. A critical log event concerns actions which might be part of a malicious attack. Examples of critical events may include system restart, service mode modification (start, stop), modification of users and user privileges, modification of the log file and modification of the criticality level of a command.

Each critical event generates an *alarm*. A distributed *Alarm Service* is responsible to recognize the alarms and open a session with the *RA*. The alarm service has access to the signature key $SK_2$. It reads the critical log entry along with a number of the following log entries for a limited period $\Delta_t$, signs them with the key $SK_2$ and sends the corresponding signatures $\sigma_1, \sigma_2, \ldots$ to the *RA* (marked as B in Fig. 2). At the end of the session, the *RA* acknowledges the receipt of the signature and stores the log event signature for future audits.

For additional security the *RA* can also request at random time intervals, signatures of the running log entries of the log file. A random request is processed as an alarm and may be performed several times within a period $T$, so that the *RA* has integrity evidence within a logging period.

Note that the alarm and the random request procedure is executed transparently from the Log Server administrator. Since the alarm service will sign any critical log event, it will be feasible for the *RA* to trace possible modification of log entries. Moreover, the use of random requests will increase the uncertainty of an attacker since the time of a random request will not be known to an attacker, even if the attacker is an internal user with advanced access privileges.

The automated signing procedure requires the development of dedicated software, such as a distributed execution environment for critical log event management and signing mechanisms. Before the implementation of this procedure a detailed cost analysis is required.

## 4.5   Phase 5: Implementation Design

The above requirements need to be incorporated within an implementation environment. Figure 3 proposes a generic implementation design.

The implementation of security measures against external attacks requires the establishment of a synergy protocol between the *RA* and the Provider. Hence, from the Provider's side a *Mediation Device* is required with two interfaces; one for the communication with the *RA* and a second one for the communication with the internal entities. In the *RA*'s side a *Switching Device* manages the corresponding interfaces.

The Mediation Device sends configuration commands to various *Physical Entities* (PE) (*e.g.* Remote Log Servers, Local Log Servers), receives captured information, collects this information and delivers this to the *RA*. The Mediation Device manages the automated signing procedure through the *Alarm Manager*. The *Alarm Agents* operating within the Provider's physical entities are programmed to inform the Alarm Manager for the critical log events. The Alarm Manager has access to the key $SK_2$ and executes the automated signing procedure. It also forwards to the $RA$ the off-line signatures of the log file instances, generated in an isolated Secure Signature Device, which stores the key $SK_1$. Finally, it receives the random requests for automated signing from a *Signature Request Manager* (SRM) and processes them as an alarm. Remote or local logging can be properly parameterized.

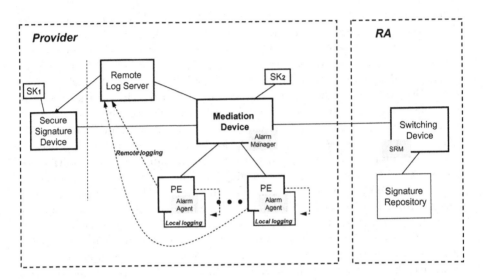

**Fig. 3.** An generic implementation design of logging management procedures

## 4.6   Phase 6: Log Verification Procedure

In case of a security audit or after a security incident, the $RA$ will compare the log files that are stored in its environment, with the log files stored in the environment of the provider.

First, the $RA$ will verify the validity of the signatures generated with the key $SK_1$. Recall that in the previous phase, the log administrator uses this key off-line in order to periodically sign the instances of the log file. The verification requires access to the public key $PK_1$, derived from $Cert_1$ and to the log file itself, stored into the Log Server. If some signature is not verified, then the $RA$ has evidence that the log file stored in the Provider's side has been modified.

If all the deterministic signatures of the log file are verified, then the $RA$ will verify the randomly generated signatures. Again, this requires access to the certificate $Cert_2$ and to the specific log entries of the log file. If all these signatures are verified, then the $RA$ accepts the validity of the log file. In case one or more signatures are not valid, then the $RA$ has strong indication that some of the log entries have been modified, before the entire log file was signed by the administrator. This also provides valuable information about the time of the intrusion to the log server.

# 5  Security Analysis

The use of the secure logging scheme of [5], protects the confidentiality and the integrity of the log files from external and common internal threats. Indeed, an attacker cannot read the log files or modify them without being detected, provided that the key $A_0$ or the keys derived from it, are not revealed.

The use of manual off-line signatures, protects the log files from modifications by external or even internal attackers, *after* the file has been signed and the signatures have been sent to the $RA$. Indeed, if a malicious or compromised log server administrator attempts to modify the log files by using the symmetric key $A_0$, after the file has been signed for the current period, the modified log file will not match with the corresponding signature, which is remotely stored within the $RA$. Recall that the manual signing procedure is performed off-line and thus even if the log server has been compromised by an intruder, it will not be possible to generate a valid signature for the compromised log file. Moreover, the use of manual signatures of the log files also provide non-repudiation for the Provider, since in case of a security incident, the Provider will not be able to repudiate a signature of the log file.

In addition, the automated signing of the critical log events and the remote storage of these signatures, minimizes the available time-frame for an intruder to manipulate the log events, before their storage to the log file and the manual signing of the log file. Indeed, even if all the systems of the Provider have been compromised, including the physical entities (switches, routers etc), the Mediation Device, the local log files and the log servers, it will be extremely hard to prevent all the alarm agents from generating and sending an alarm to the $RA$.

Even if an internal attacker could be able to intercept the automated signatures and attempt to modify their values before they are sent to the $RA$, it would require that the Alarm Manager and all the Alarm Agents in all possible affected systems have been properly compromised. Even if the attacker controls the majority of the Provider's systems, he cannot be assured that his attack will not be logged. Note that the Alarm Manager and the Alarm Agents are software entities that have been approved by the $RA$ (for example by using singed code). Any possible attempt to update their code, or modify them will also cause a critical event and the generation of an automated signed event towards the $RA$.

# 6  Conclusions

Existing secure logging systems mainly protect the log files from external attacks. In public communication networks however, the security requirements of log files must also consider internal attacks such as compromised log generators, compromised log servers or combinations of both. In this paper we consider an extended threat model for logging systems and we define a generic framework for secure logging for public network providers. Through the proposed framework the logging requirements of each provider are defined, as well as the required security measures and procedures for the protection of the log files. A trusted

Regulator Authority *RA* has a central role in this framework, in the definition of the logging requirements as well as in the integrity verification of the maintained log files. In addition with known security measures for secure logging, we propose the use of digital signatures in two different ways, as well as the remote storage of the signatures in the environment of the *RA*. Although modification attacks against log files cannot always be prevented, it is possible to detect such attacks with well defined mechanisms and procedures.

# References

1. Schneier, B.: Schneier on security: Phone tapping in Greece. web page, http://www.schneier.com/blog/archives/2006/02/phone_tapping_i.html (2006)
2. Kelsey, J., J.Callas: Ssyslog-sign protocol. DRAFT, Network Working Group (2002)
3. Dunlap, G.W., King, S.T., Cinar, S., Basrai, M., Chen, P.M.: Revirt: Enabling intrusion analysis through virtual-machine logging and replay. In: In Proc. 2002 Symp. Operating Sys. Design and Implementation. (2002)
4. Bellare, M., Yee, B.: Forward integrity for secure audit logs. Technical report, Computer Science and Engineering Department, University of California at San Diego (1997)
5. Schneier, B., Kelsey, J.: Cryptographic support for secure logs on untrusted machines. In: Proceedings of the 7th USENIX Security Symposium, USENIX Press (1998) 53–62
6. Haber, S., Stornetta, W.: How to time-stamp a digital document. In Menezes, A., Vanstone, S.A., eds.: Proc. of CRYPTO'90. Volume 537 of Lecture Notes in Computer Science., Springer-Verlag (1990) 437–455
7. Chong, C.N., Peng, Z., Hartel, P.H.: Secure audit logging with tamperresistant hardware. Tech. Rep., Universiteit Twente, Enschede, The Netherlands (2002)
8. Waters, B., Balfanz, D., Durfee, G., Smetters, D.: Building an encrypted and searchable audit log. In: The 11th Annual Network and Distributed System Security Symposium. (2004)
9. Accorsi, R.: On the relationship of privacy and secure remote logging in dynamic systems. In: Security and Privacy in Dynamic Environments. Volume 201., Springer-Verlag (2006) 329–338
10. Holt, J.: Logcrypt: Forward security and public verification for secure audit logs. In: Proc. of Australasian Information Security Workshop. (2006)
11. Kawaguchi, N., Obata, N., Ueda, S., Azuma, Y., Shigeno, H., Okada, K.: Efficient log authentication for forensic computing. In: In Proc Of IEEE 6th Information Assurance Workshop, IEEE (2005) 215–223

# Author Index

# Lecture Notes in Computer Science

For information about Vols. 1–4254

please contact your bookseller or Springer

Vol. 4293: A. Gelbukh, C.A. Reyes-Garcia (Eds.), MICAI 2006: Advances in Artificial Intelligence. XXVIII, 1232 pages. 2006. (Sublibrary LNAI).

Vol. 4292: G. Bebis, R. Boyle, B. Parvin, D. Koracin, P. Remagnino, A. Nefian, G. Meenakshisundaram, V. Pascucci, J. Zara, J. Molineros, H. Theisel, T. Malzbender (Eds.), Advances in Visual Computing, Part II. XXXII, 906 pages. 2006.

Vol. 4291: G. Bebis, R. Boyle, B. Parvin, D. Koracin, P. Remagnino, A. Nefian, G. Meenakshisundaram, V. Pascucci, J. Zara, J. Molineros, H. Theisel, T. Malzbender (Eds.), Advances in Visual Computing, Part I. XXXI, 916 pages. 2006.

Vol. 4290: M. van Steen, M. Henning (Eds.), Middleware 2006. XIII, 425 pages. 2006.

Vol. 4289: M. Ackermann, B. Berendt, M. Grobelnik, A. Hotho, D. Mladenič, G. Semeraro, M. Spiliopoulou, G. Stumme, V. Svatek, M. van Someren (Eds.), Semantics, Web and Mining. X, 197 pages. 2006. (Sublibrary LNAI).

Vol. 4288: T. Asano (Ed.), Algorithms and Computation. XX, 766 pages. 2006.

Vol. 4287: C. Mao, T. Yokomori (Eds.), DNA Computing. XII, 440 pages. 2006.

Vol. 4286: P. Spirakis, M. Mavronicolas, S. Kontogiannis (Eds.), Internet and Network Economics. XI, 401 pages. 2006.

Vol. 4285: Y. Matsumoto, R. Sproat, K.-F. Wong, M. Zhang (Eds.), Computer Processing of Oriental Languages. XVII, 544 pages. 2006. (Sublibrary LNAI).

Vol. 4284: X. Lai, K. Chen (Eds.), Advances in Cryptology – ASIACRYPT 2006. XIV, 468 pages. 2006.

Vol. 4283: Y.Q. Shi, B. Jeon (Eds.), Digital Watermarking. XII, 474 pages. 2006.

Vol. 4282: Z. Pan, A. Cheok, M. Haller, R.W.H. Lau, H. Saito, R. Liang (Eds.), Advances in Artificial Reality and Tele-Existence. XXIII, 1347 pages. 2006.

Vol. 4281: K. Barkaoui, A. Cavalcanti, A. Cerone (Eds.), Theoretical Aspects of Computing - ICTAC 2006. XV, 371 pages. 2006.

Vol. 4280: A.K. Datta, M. Gradinariu (Eds.), Stabilization, Safety, and Security of Distributed Systems. XVII, 590 pages. 2006.

Vol. 4279: N. Kobayashi (Ed.), Programming Languages and Systems. XI, 423 pages. 2006.

Vol. 4278: R. Meersman, Z. Tari, P. Herrero (Eds.), On the Move to Meaningful Internet Systems 2006: OTM 2006 Workshops, Part II. XLV, 1004 pages. 2006.

Vol. 4277: R. Meersman, Z. Tari, P. Herrero (Eds.), On the Move to Meaningful Internet Systems 2006: OTM 2006 Workshops, Part I. XLV, 1009 pages. 2006.

Vol. 4276: R. Meersman, Z. Tari (Eds.), On the Move to Meaningful Internet Systems 2006: CoopIS, DOA, GADA, and ODBASE, Part II. XXXII, 752 pages. 2006.

Vol. 4275: R. Meersman, Z. Tari (Eds.), On the Move to Meaningful Internet Systems 2006: CoopIS, DOA, GADA, and ODBASE, Part I. XXXI, 1115 pages. 2006.

Vol. 4274: Q. Huo, B. Ma, E.-S. Chng, H. Li (Eds.), Chinese Spoken Language Processing. XXIV, 805 pages. 2006. (Sublibrary LNAI).

Vol. 4273: I. Cruz, S. Decker, D. Allemang, C. Preist, D. Schwabe, P. Mika, M. Uschold, L. Aroyo (Eds.), The Semantic Web - ISWC 2006. XXIV, 1001 pages. 2006.

Vol. 4272: P. Havinga, M. Lijding, N. Meratnia, M. Wegdam (Eds.), Smart Sensing and Context. XI, 267 pages. 2006.

Vol. 4271: F.V. Fomin (Ed.), Graph-Theoretic Concepts in Computer Science. XIII, 358 pages. 2006.

Vol. 4270: H. Zha, Z. Pan, H. Thwaites, A.C. Addison, M. Forte (Eds.), Interactive Technologies and Sociotechnical Systems. XVI, 547 pages. 2006.

Vol. 4269: R. State, S. van der Meer, D. O'Sullivan, T. Pfeifer (Eds.), Large Scale Management of Distributed Systems. XIII, 282 pages. 2006.

Vol. 4268: G. Parr, D. Malone, M. Ó Foghlú (Eds.), Autonomic Principles of IP Operations and Management. XIII, 237 pages. 2006.

Vol. 4267: A. Helmy, B. Jennings, L. Murphy, T. Pfeifer (Eds.), Autonomic Management of Mobile Multimedia Services. XIII, 257 pages. 2006.

Vol. 4266: H. Yoshiura, K. Sakurai, K. Rannenberg, Y. Murayama, S. Kawamura (Eds.), Advances in Information and Computer Security. XIII, 438 pages. 2006.

Vol. 4265: L. Todorovski, N. Lavrač, K.P. Jantke (Eds.), Discovery Science. XIV, 384 pages. 2006. (Sublibrary LNAI).

Vol. 4264: J.L. Balcázar, P.M. Long, F. Stephan (Eds.), Algorithmic Learning Theory. XIII, 393 pages. 2006. (Sublibrary LNAI).

Vol. 4263: A. Levi, E. Savaş, H. Yenigün, S. Balcısoy, Y. Saygın (Eds.), Computer and Information Sciences – ISCIS 2006. XXIII, 1084 pages. 2006.

Vol. 4262: K. Havelund, M. Núñez, G. Roşu, B. Wolff (Eds.), Formal Approaches to Software Testing and Runtime Verification. VIII, 255 pages. 2006.

Vol. 4261: Y. Zhuang, S. Yang, Y. Rui, Q. He (Eds.), Advances in Multimedia Information Processing - PCM 2006. XXII, 1040 pages. 2006.

Vol. 4260: Z. Liu, J. He (Eds.), Formal Methods and Software Engineering. XII, 778 pages. 2006.

Vol. 4259: S. Greco, Y. Hata, S. Hirano, M. Inuiguchi, S. Miyamoto, H.S. Nguyen, R. Słowiński (Eds.), Rough Sets and Current Trends in Computing. XXII, 951 pages. 2006. (Sublibrary LNAI).

Vol. 4258: G. Danezis, P. Golle (Eds.), Privacy Enhancing Technologies. VIII, 431 pages. 2006.

Vol. 4257: I. Richardson, P. Runeson, R. Messnarz (Eds.), Software Process Improvement. XI, 219 pages. 2006.

Vol. 4256: L. Feng, G. Wang, C. Zeng, R. Huang (Eds.), Web Information Systems – WISE 2006 Workshops. XIV, 320 pages. 2006.

Vol. 4255: K. Aberer, Z. Peng, E.A. Rundensteiner, Y. Zhang, X. Li (Eds.), Web Information Systems – WISE 2006. XIV, 563 pages. 2006.